For Bill and Sarah June

For Roxie and Bekka—
the first of my dogs to be with me through two editions of this text.

Guidance of Young Children

Fifth Edition

Marian Marion
University of Wisconsin–Stout

Merrill,
an imprint of Prentice Hall
Upper Saddle River, New Jersey 07458

Library of Congress Cataloging-in-Publication Data

Marion, Marian
    Guidance of young children / Marian Marion. — 5th ed.
       p.   cm.
    Includes bibliographical references and indexes.
    ISBN 0-13-901166-8 (alk. paper)
    1. Child psychology.   2. Child rearing.   I. Title.
HQ772.M255   1999
649'.1—dc21   98-19194
                                      CIP

Cover photo: ©Barbara Stitzer/Photo Edit
Editor: Ann C. Davis
Production Editor: Julie Peters
Production Manager: Laura Messerly
Cover Design Coordinator: Diane C. Lorenzo
Text Designer: Custom Editorial Productions, Inc.
Cover Designer: Dan Eckel
Photo Coordinator: Sandy Lenahan
Director of Marketing: Kevin Flanagan
Marketing Manager: Suzanne Stanton
Advertising/Marketing Coordinator: Krista Groshong

This book was set in New Baskerville by Custom Editorial Productions, Inc. and was printed and bound by R.R. Donnelley & Sons Company. The cover was printed by Phoenix Color Corp.

© 1999 by Prentice Hall, Inc.
Upper Saddle River, NJ 07458

Photo credits: pp. 4, 233 by Scott Cunningham/Merrill; pp. 9, 12, 85, 140, 146, 172, 206 by Barbara Schwartz/Merrill; pp. 15, 62, 68, 84, 100, 160, 168, 182, 188, 189, 202, 228, 234, 238, 264, 267, 275, 295 by Anne Vega/Merrill; pp. 40, 284 by Tom Watson/Merrill; p. 52 by Kevin Fitzsimons/Merrill; p. 61 by James Marshall/The Stock Market; pp. 74, 256 by Todd Yarrington/Merrill; p. 136 by Robert Brenner/Photo Edit; p. 191 by Lloyd Lemmerman/Merrill; p. 211 by Monkmeyer Press/Monkmeyer/Shackman; p. 214 by Dan Floss/Merrill

Printed in the United States of America

10 9 8 7 6 5 4

ISBN: 0-13-901166-8

Prentice-Hall International (UK) Limited, *London*
Prentice-Hall of Australia Pty. Limited, *Sydney*
Prentice-Hall of Canada, Inc., *Toronto*
Prentice-Hall Hispanoamericana, S. A., *Mexico*
Prentice-Hall of India Private Limited, *New Delhi*
Prentice-Hall of Japan, Inc., *Tokyo*
Pearson Education Asia Pte. Ltd., *Singapore*
Editora Prentice-Hall do Brasil, Ltda., *Rio de Janeiro*

Preface

Welcome to the fifth edition of *Guidance of Young Children*. The first edition of *Guidance of Young Children* was published in 1981, the second edition in 1987, the third in 1991, and the fourth in 1995. My purpose in writing the fifth edition is exactly the same as it was with earlier editions—to give you a book grounded in solid theory and research, a book that will help you understand the process of child guidance. I have designed this textbook so that it continues to reflect my beliefs about children and child guidance.

I believe we have choices about how we think about and behave with children. John Steinbeck said in *East of Eden* that the beauty of being human is our ability to make choices. What we choose to think about children, how we act with them, and the discipline strategies we use *do* matter. The strategies we use affect children on a daily basis; they also have a long-term impact on children—helping them become self-responsible, competent, independent, cooperative people who like themselves and who have a strong core of values.

I believe that our style of guiding children has an effect on several parts of their personality and on their approach to life—for example, their moral compass and their level of self-esteem, how they manage anger and aggression, how they manage stress, their willingness to cooperate with others, whether they can take another person's perspective, and their social skills.

I believe that all effective child guidance is based on solid knowledge of child and family development. Without this knowledge, we might have unrealistic expectations of children. Having this knowledge gives us a firm foundation on which to build child-guidance skills.

I believe that a child's behavior is influenced by the several systems in which the child exists—family, peer group, school, community, and culture. Different children have quite different histories, and we should not expect all children to think or behave in exactly the same way. Some children in your classes, for example, will have had very good models of anger management, but others will have had irresponsible models and will themselves have poor anger management skills.

I believe that there is no one right way to deal with any issue, but that there are many good ways. This is not a cookbook in which you will find nice, neat answers. I will not give you a set of *tricks* to use with children. You will, however, find numerous exercises and questions that should help you understand the basic concepts of child guidance. My hope is that you will enjoy using these concepts to make decisions about child guidance.

I believe we should each develop a personal approach to guiding children and that this approach is best built on theoretical eclecticism. In this text, you will study the decision-making model of child guidance, a model that evolves from understanding various theoretical approaches to child guidance. It is wise to understand the positive strategies that come to us from each theory and not to discount any theory, because you may well use strategies from any of these approaches to help children. I believe that all the theories deserve our respect, and I have tried to treat each one fairly in this book.

I believe that some things hurt children and should never be used, such as shaking, hitting, and other forms of physically hurtful interaction; hostile humor; embarrassment; ridicule; sarcasm; judging; manipulation; mind games; hurtful punishment; ignoring; terrorizing; isolating; and boundary violations. These personality-numbing horrors are abusive and have no place in our lives with children. We do our job of teaching and protecting children most effectively when we make active, conscious decisions about positive strategies and when we refuse to use strategies that are degrading or hurtful.

SPECIAL FEATURES OF *GUIDANCE OF YOUNG CHILDREN*

I am, first of all, a teacher, and it was my goal to write a *student-friendly* book that encourages you to be actively involved in your learning. Therefore, I've retained certain features from other editions that have worked, and I have added specific features designed to help you learn this material even more effectively. Here are some of these features:

- *Objectives* for each chapter.
- A *chapter overview* that outlines the chapter.
- A *chapter summary* to help you reflect on what you've learned rather than just listing the main points. The objectives, chapter overview, and chapter summary are learning devices called *advance organizers* that should help you get an overall picture of the chapter content before you begin studying it.
- *Case studies* at the beginning of every chapter. Case studies focus on children within the early childhood age range and were designed to illustrate the major points in each chapter.
- *Case study analyses* in every chapter. These studies require your active participation in immediately applying newly acquired knowledge to the chapter's case study.

- *Parent Talk* boxes in each chapter will help you use the chapter's information with parents of the children you teach.
- The "Apply Your Knowledge" section at the end of each chapter will help you to apply the information you've learned to real situations.
- Expanded use of *Examples* throughout the text describing children from birth through age eight.
- An *appendix* that summarizes the major positive discipline strategies in outline form.
- Liberal use of *italics* to highlight definitions and other important terms.
- A *writing style* that is conversational, yet informative.

STRUCTURE OF THE FIFTH EDITION

This edition is organized by chapters within three parts. The first part emphasizes child development as the foundation for developmentally appropriate child guidance, different caregiving styles, specific positive discipline strategies, and managing the physical environment effectively.

The second part targets five topics of current interest to early childhood educators. The chapter on anger management, for example, will give you information on how anger develops and offer suggestions that may help you teach children (and yourself) how to manage this strong emotion responsibly. The chapter on stress management now includes tips on helping children manage specific and common early childhood stressors.

The third part presents specific information on various child-guidance theories and on the positive strategies that come from each one. You will have lots of opportunities to solve specific problems using these strategies and to discover how useful theory is in real-life situations with real children. In the final chapter you will also learn about and practice using the decision-making model of child guidance as a way to bring closure to this book—but certainly not to your study of child guidance.

ACKNOWLEDGMENTS

I teach in a department of child development and family studies. The early childhood program at University of Wisconsin–Stout is firmly grounded in these two disciplines and the colleagues in my very large department nurture my understanding of children, families, early childhood practices, and child guidance.

The students in my child guidance classes have asked questions that have made me think about specific issues. For example, time-out has been a subject of debate in my classes for several years now, and I credit my students with asking the questions that helped me deal with some of the issues swirling around this most overused of discipline strategies.

A special note of thanks to the child guidance classes of 1995, 1996, and 1997 for field-testing the case study analyses and "Apply Your Knowledge" sections of each chapter. My students do an excellent job with the decision-making model of child guidance, and I believe their developing skills will carry over into their teaching.

Several colleagues from around the country who have used the other editions and have reviewed material for the fifth edition are: Richard P. Ambrose, Kent State University; Susan H. Christian, Patrick Henry Community College; Elaine Goldsmith, Texas Woman's University; Kathy Hamblin, Aims Community College; and M. Francine Stuckey, Eastern New Mexico University. Their comments were especially helpful as I refined the book's content and structure, and I am grateful for their suggestions about reorganizing the text, incorporating additional research, and adding material to the chapter on stress management.

Robin Muza also teaches the child guidance course at University of Wisconsin–Stout. I value her comments about specific topics in the text and suggestions on how to teach specific sections.

Marian Marion

Contents

Chapter 2: Guiding with Positive Discipline and an Authori*tative* Caregiving Style   40

PART TWO: SPECIAL TOPICS IN CHILD GUIDANCE   133

Chapter 5: Guiding Children in Times of Stress   136

Chapter 6: Guiding Children Toward a Healthy Sense of Self and Self-Esteem   160

Chapter 7: Guiding Young Children's Understanding and Management of Anger 182

Chapter 8: Understanding and Guiding Aggressive Children 202

Chapter 9: Prosocial Behavior: Guiding Its Development   228

Part 1

Developmentally Appropriate Child Guidance: Essential Elements

Part One of this textbook will help you understand the essential elements in developmentally appropriate child guidance. You will study these four essential elements:

- A child's developmental level
- An adult's authori*tative* (not authoritarian) caregiving style
- An adult's use of *positive* discipline strategies
- Good classroom management of space, curriculum, activities, and materials

There are four chapters in this part of the book, each focusing on one of the four essential elements.

Chapter 1. Understanding Child Development: The Foundation for Developmentally Appropriate Child Guidance. You are much more likely to build developmentally appropriate child guidance skills when you understand how children develop. You will have more realistic expectations about children with a good knowledge base and you will be able to make informed decisions about child-guidance issues. Chapter 1 describes different areas of child development, such as memory and perception, and applies that information to guiding young children.

Chapter 2. Guiding with Positive Discipline and an Authori*tative* Caregiving Style. You will be much more successful in dealing with normal day-to-day discipline encounters if you adopt an authori*tative* style (not authoritarian or permissive). This chapter describes the authoritative style as positive, supportive, and developmentally appropriate. You will also read about discipline encounters, discipline strategies, and the basic processes that we adults use to influence but not determine a child's behavior.

1

Chapter 3. Positive Discipline Strategies: Direct Guidance. Setting good limits, redirecting behavior, changing something about a situation. Your confidence in dealing with day-to-day issues will grow as you learn and use these other *positive discipline strategies*. After reading this chapter, you will know exactly how to use a great many positive, specific, and practical discipline strategies.

Chapter 4. Developmentally Appropriate Practices and Early Childhood Classroom Management. This chapter discusses how to use *indirect guidance* by designing and managing the physical environment effectively. You can minimize or even prevent problems by setting up

Chapter 1

Understanding Child Development: The Foundation For Developmentally Appropriate Child Guidance

After reading and studying this chapter, you will be able to:

❖ Explain the meaning of "developmentally appropriate child guidance."

❖ Summarize the positive cognitive accomplishments of the first three Piagetian stages and explain how a child's level of cognitive development will affect your guidance strategies.

❖ Trace the development of social perspective-taking and explain why perspective-taking skills are important.

❖ Describe a young child's memory capacity, memory skills, and perceptual problems, and list and describe specific guidance strategies for helping children remember things and for dealing with preschool perceptual limitations.

❖ Define "temperament" and describe different temperament styles. Explain how temperament style may affect a child's development and interactions.

❖ Describe how young children view the behavior of others, friendship, and conflict relations.

◆ Trace the development of self-control and give examples of self-control in children.

◆ Analyze case studies on developmentally appropriate child guidance.

Case Studies: Child Guidance Based on Child Development

Mr. Kennedy's Infant Room

Mr. Kennedy planned some "memory" games for 6-month-old Kevin. Kevin smiled when his teacher showed him his favorite stuffed bear, which had been lost for about two weeks. Then Mr. Kennedy turned Kevin away so he couldn't see it. When Kevin turned his head to look for the bear, the teacher praised his effort and helped him retrieve the toy. On another day, Mr. Kennedy showed Kevin a plastic block and then slowly covered it with a cloth. Kevin grabbed the cover and pulled it off. Mr. Kennedy encouraged his effort by saying, "Oh, Kevin, you found the toy!"

Seventeen-month-old Ben waddled out the door as the aide opened it, and then he started down the corridor. Mr. Kennedy called, "Ben, stop!" Ben turned and looked at his teacher, who had stooped and held out his arms. "Come on, Ben." Ben walked toward Mr. Kennedy who said, "You came when I called you, Ben."

Mr. Soto's Preschool Classroom—Selected Observations

Monday: "I'm making clouds," said Sylvia, smoothing white finger paint onto the clear plastic tray and swirling puffy cloud shapes into the paint with her knuckles. "So are we," called Tim and Janet, as they rolled chunks of white dough into "cloud" shapes.

Tuesday: Mr. Soto's group of 4- and 5-year-olds dictated a story about their walk to look at clouds. Tim, Janet, and Sylvia bent white pipe cleaners into cloud shapes and Mr. Soto suspended the clouds from the ceiling.

Wednesday: Throughout the morning several children at the sand table poured sand from one unbreakable container into others.

Thursday: Tim ran into the classroom and zoomed right into the crowded block area. Mr. Soto called Tim aside and said, "Tim, please look at the sign. It says '4.' Now, count the children. There are four children here already. Let's find something else for you to do until you can play with the blocks."

Mr. Anderson's Third-Grade Classroom

Rick and Jackson were working on a social studies project together—making a model of a farm with the unit blocks. After they built the road leading to the farm, the boys put a large building off to the right. Rick said that it was the equipment shed, but Jackson wanted it to be the garage for the farm's trucks and cars. Mr. Anderson heard the discussion escalate into an argument, with Rick getting a tractor to place in the shed and Jackson insisting that he wanted to put the trucks and cars in the enclosure. Mr. Anderson was approaching the boys when Jackson angrily grabbed the tractor and threw it on the floor and punched Rick on the arm. Rick retaliated by hitting Jackson.

"Whoa, there! No hitting. You both know the rules. I want each of you to sit here next to me and take some slow breaths." Rick started to explain. "We'll talk in a minute,

(continued)

Rick. For now, just take slow breaths." (Both boys sat and did deep-breathing.) "Good. Now, let's talk about what happened, OK?" Both boys nodded.

"It sure looks like we have a problem here. You were working together on the farm and finished the road. What happened next?"

Rick, "I want the building to be the tractor shed!"

Jackson, "But, I want it to be the garage for cars and trucks!"

"You each want the shed to be something different," said the teacher, "so let's figure out how to solve this problem. One big building and two different ideas. What do you think you could do?"

Jackson, "But, it's not really big enough for all the trucks, cars, and tractors" (he demonstrates by trying to put all the vehicles in the building). "Maybe," said Rick, "we could build one of those 'lean-to' buildings that we learned about on the shed. Then we'd have a lot more room."

"H-m-m. Do you mean that you could add more space and then use it for all of the cars, trucks, and tractors?" asked Mr. Anderson. "Yeah," said both children. Mr. Anderson asked if they had the material for building the lean-to and then had them agree on a time to get started on their work. Then he said to them, "I like the way you thought this out. Let's try your idea and then see if it's working for both of you. We'll talk after you finish the lean-to."

THE CONCEPT OF DEVELOPMENTALLY APPROPRIATE CHILD GUIDANCE

Teachers like Misters Kennedy, Soto, and Anderson who use *developmentally appropriate child guidance:*

1. *Understand child and family development, the most important element in the foundation for developmentally appropriate child guidance.* Each teacher has taken formal coursework in child and in family development. Each has realistic expectations of children of different ages in terms of motor, physical, cognitive, social, and emotional development. They understand family development and the impact that a child's family may have on a young child's development.

2. *Understand that their guidance must be both age appropriate and individually appropriate.* These teachers use age-appropriate guidance; their strategies are appropriate for the general age group that they teach. And they use individually appropriate strategies when they choose a strategy appropriate for a specific child, regardless of the child's age, as Mr. Soto did with Tim.

3. *Understand that adults and children influence each other in any interaction.* Researchers started to think about this concept in the late 1960s (Bell, 1968; Bell & Harper, 1977). We know now that children are not blank slates but active members in every interaction with other children or with adults.

4. *Understand the responsibilities of adult role in the guidance system.* The teachers realize that children have an important part in any interaction, but they know that adults always have a greater responsibility (Maccoby & Martin, 1983). Mr. Kennedy realizes, for example, that a very young infant will gaze or smile at him, but that it is his responsibility to tune in appropriately to the infant's

efforts. Mr. Soto knows that his 4- and 5-year-olds will offer to help with cleanup, but it is his responsibility to recognize and encourage their effort and cooperation. Mr. Anderson knows that his third-graders can solve conflict peacefully but that it is his responsibility to teach specific steps in resolving conflicts and then to encourage their efforts.

PIAGET: COGNITIVE DEVELOPMENT

Adults who use developmentally appropriate guidance understand that there is a strong link between a child's cognitive and social development. You, too, will be most effective with children when you keep in mind how a specific child thinks, whether he can understand what you say, whether he can take somebody else's perspective, and whether he can even remember what is said. This section focuses on cognitive development during very early childhood (infancy and toddlerhood) and early childhood in Piaget's framework (Piaget, 1952, 1965, 1968, 1976a, 1976b, 1983).

Sensorimotor Stage

Piaget called the first stage of cognitive development (birth to approximately 24 months) the *sensorimotor stage* because infants are equipped with sensory actions (looking, listening, touching) and motor actions (grasping, head turning, hitting, etc.). They use sensorimotor actions or schemes to acquire information about and impose order on their world. Infants do not think or reflect on problems as older children or adults do.

Piaget divided the sensorimotor stage into six substages to describe an infant's blossoming cognitive skills. An infant spends most of his first few months of life practicing those sensory and motor (sensorimotor) schemes, but by 24 months he will be starting to use symbols. Progress through the six substages occurs partly because of an infant's ability to imitate, which is evident quite early in life and improves as the infant gets older. Infants also acquire knowledge about object permanence as they progress through the sensorimotor stage.

Human infants are competent, active, information-processing creatures. A baby's perceptual skills are good enough, even at birth, to allow him to explore and discover his world, but perceptual skills change in several ways as infants grow older (Gibson & Spelke, 1983). Young infants seem to prefer some patterns over others and are able to perceive depth and color in their surroundings. The visual and nervous systems undergo continual development during a child's first year, making more sophisticated perception possible.

An infant's sensorimotor and perceptual skills affects learning and remembering. Infants do not process information as well in their first few months because their motor skills and neurological systems are somewhat immature. Sensory, perceptual, and attentional skills develop rapidly from birth to 12 months. From about 6 months to a year, infants use all of their skills to acquire and retain a knowledge base.

Profound cognitive changes occur between 12 and 24 months. We see the result of all of these changes when they converge in the development of *symbolic thought*. By age 2, a child does several things to show us that he is able to use symbols: he pictures things in his mind, imitates things he saw earlier (such *deferred imitation* is actually seen by 9 or 10 months), and understands and uses language.

Preoperational Stage

Children from 2 to 5 years old are usually in the second of Piaget's stages of cognitive development, the preoperational stage. The early childhood years are a time of positive intellectual accomplishment, but preoperational thinkers also have some major limitations on their ability to think. This section focuses on the major positive features and describes some of the cognitive limitations of preoperational thinking. These cognitive abilities and limitations influence the child's interactions with adults and the child's capacity for self-control.

Major cognitive ability: 2- to 5-year-old children can represent their experiences

Children from 2 to 5 years old can use symbols to represent (stand for) their experiences (Piaget, 1952, 1976b, 1983). In early childhood classrooms there are many examples of how 2- to 5-year-olds are able to represent their experience. They show us that they can represent their experience through deferred imitation, with language, and through the use of art media.

Deferred imitation. Young children learn from models. They observe an event, form and hold a visual image of the event, and then often "defer" or put off imitating the action until some later date. Each of the children in the following examples has observed models and is only now imitating them for the first time.

Manage your classroom so that children work and talk with each other. They begin to understand that others have a point of view through social interaction.

Examples: Jenessa slapped her doll on the face and said, "There. That'll teach you not to sass me!"

Joseph smeared shaving cream on his face and then scraped it off with his finger.

Sarah softly sang "Hush, little baby," as she cradled her doll in her arms.

Language. One of the major ways that children have to tell us about their experience is to talk about it (Flavell, 1977). The major cognitive accomplishment of this stage is that children can use a symbol to stand for something else, and words are the symbols through which they represent their experiences.

Example: Jackie used words to tell Mr. Soto that he and his family had adopted a cat and a dog from the Humane Society.

Use of art media. Children also record their experiences through art media such as painting, drawing, or play dough. They use chalk, paint, play dough, markers, pencils and other media to create an artistic expression that symbolizes, represents, or stands for an experience that they have had. Mr. Soto's 4- and 5-year-olds (case study chapter opener) represented their "cloud" experience with finger paint, pipe cleaners, and white play dough.

Implications for guidance

Expect children to represent—to tell you about—their experiences. Realize that children will tell you about their experiences in a variety of ways. You will see evidence of a child's experience in her behavior; for example, one child might hit another person and another will help others. In either case you will have seen *deferred imitation.* Responsible adults believe that they influence, but do not determine, children's behavior by modeling positive behavior, no matter what that child's other models have been. Even children who experience negative discipline at home can observe and learn a different, more positive way of behaving from us.

Limitations of preoperational thinking

A 4-year-old's cognitive skills seem so much more advanced than the skills of an 18-month-old because the older child can represent experiences. But our 4-year-old preoperational thinker still has a limited ability to think logically. Here is a list of some of the major limitations.

Preoperational thinkers tend to:

- be somewhat egocentric.
- judge things by how they look.
- focus on the before-and-after and ignore *how* things change (transformations).
- have trouble reversing a process.

Let's first examine each of these limitations and then turn to the implications for how we guide children during this phase because of the limitations.

Preoperational thinkers tend to be somewhat egocentric. Listen to a preschool child for a short time and you will smile at some of the things he says and the charm with which he says them. You may also be slightly puzzled, as I was in the following conversation with my 5½-year-old niece.

> Marian (adult): "Lisa, tell me how to get to the ice cream store."
> Lisa: "You go to the corner and then turn."
> Marian: "Which corner?"
> Lisa: "You know, the one with the trees."

At the time of our conversation, Lisa was somewhat egocentric and not very good at perspective-taking. She did not give me all the necessary information, largely because she did not understand exactly what I needed to know. She, as do others in the preoperational stage, probably also thought I had the same information she did.

Egocentric thinkers center on themselves and what they want, but this is *not* the same thing as being selfish. A selfish person understands somebody else's perspective and chooses to ignore it, but an egocentric thinker cannot take the other person's perspective; there is a blurring of their own viewpoint with the perspective of the other person (Piaget, 1968). A preoperational thinker such as Lisa believes that everyone thinks the same way she does.

For a number of years, researchers have noted that, under certain conditions, children may be somewhat less egocentric than originally thought (Black, 1981; Gelman & Baillargeon, 1983; Newcombe & Huttenlocher, 1992). Nevertheless, children are not skillful in dealing with different viewpoints or confrontations and need your guidance to learn and practice these skills.

Implications for guidance

Social interaction is one of the best ways to decrease egocentricity and increase understanding of another person's point of view (Piaget, 1968, 1976b). Manage your early childhood classroom, whether you teach infants or primary school aged children, so that children have plenty of chances to play with other children—for example, blocks, dramatic play, water or sensory table, playground—in order to expose them to challenging ideas from others. Rely on positive discipline strategies to help children acknowledge and deal with different ideas.

Preoperational thinkers have difficulty with perspective-taking. Perspective-taking is a cognitive developmental skill that takes several years to develop and is first evident at the end of early childhood from age 6 or 7 on (Dixon & Soto, 1990; Newman, 1986). Selman (1976) described an orderly series of "levels" in perspective-taking (ages are approximate):

- *Level 0: Egocentric Perspective* (3 to 6 years old). Major characteristic: the child usually does not distinguish between his own and someone else's perspective.
- *Level 1: Social-Informational Role-Taking* (6 to 8 years old). Major characteristic: the child still believes that another person shares his perspective, but for a different reason. The child's guiding rule is "same situation equals same viewpoint"; that is, because the other person is in the same situation as the child himself, he believes that the other person will respond to the situation just as he would. (*Note:* This book is about children up to 8 years of age. We can expect children we teach to be inexperienced in the art of perspective-taking.)
- *Level 2: Self-Reflective Role-Taking* (8 to 10 years old). Major characteristic: the child is now able to see himself as another person might and is aware that two persons can have different perspectives.

Deferred imitation: These children are observing an adult feeding a doll and will very likely imitate him later.

- *Level 3: Mutual Role-Taking* (10 to 12 years old). Major characteristic: children are now aware of the recursive nature of different perspectives (e.g., "Mom thinks that I think that she wants me to . . .").

Special Focus: Q & A: Why Are Social Perspective-Taking Skills Important?

Question: What is social perspective-taking?

Answer: It is the ability to control one's viewpoint when making judgments of others (Higgins, 1981).

Question: Why is social perspective-taking an important skill for all people?

Answer: These skills form the foundation of effective social interaction (Chalmers & Townsend, 1990; Selman, 1980). Good perspective-taking skills enable us to anticipate what others might be thinking, and this makes our interactions more predictable (Dixon & Soto, 1990). We can actually see ourselves as others see us if we can take their perspective. If, for example, one of the reactions that you arouse in others is that they seem to like you, then you will begin to use this information as you *define* your self. You can use this information in deciding that the self you see is well liked.

continues on the next page

Question: Do people with poor perspective-taking skills have any specific problems?

Answer: Yes. They systematically misread societal expectations. They misinterpret the actions and intentions of others. They act in ways judged to be callous and disrespectful of the rights of others (Chalmers & Townsend, 1990). Parents with these tendencies use harsh discipline (Marion, 1995); adults who cannot take a child's perspective are "at risk" for child abuse (Milner, Robertson, & Rogers, 1990).

Question: What does the research tell us about children who have good social perspective-taking skills?

Answer: Children who are good at perspective-taking are better at persuading others and are better able to regulate aggressive impulses (Jones, 1985). Older children with good perspective-taking skills tend to be more generous, helpful, and cooperative.

- *Level 4: Society or In-Depth Perspective* (adolescence and adulthood). Major characteristics: a person at this level of perspective-taking believes that perspectives among individuals form a network, and has conceptualized society's viewpoints on legal or moral matters.

Preoperational thinkers focus on the before and after, ignoring how things change. Preoperational thinkers ignore the process through which something changes, the transformation. As shown in Figure 1–1, a preoperational thinker focuses first on water in the two short glasses (the "before" state). Then he focuses on water in one short glass and one tall glass (the "after" state). He tends to ignore the pouring of the water from the short glass to the tall glass (the transformation) (Figure 1–2). An older child, adolescent, or adult, aware of the pouring, would explain things by saying, "All you did was pour water from one container to another."

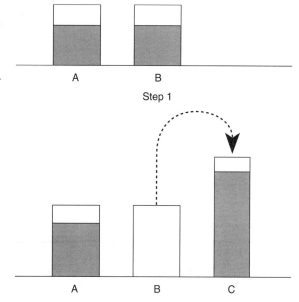

Figure 1–1. *Step 1:* Child agrees that each container holds an equivalent volume of water. *Step 2:* Child watches adult pour liquid from container B into container C. A preoperational thinker will say that container C contains more than container A. His reason: he will say that it *looks* like more.

Figure 1–2. The *pouring* of the liquid is the *transformation*.

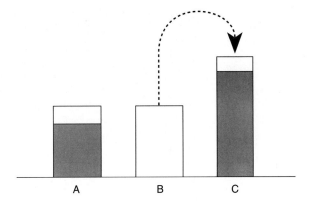

A B C

This cognitive limitation affects how young children operate in their social world, as the following example shows.

Example: Three-year-old Jeff watched as his older brother, Erik, transformed himself into a Halloween monster. Jeff cried and ran to Dad when he saw the finished product, and Dad made the mistake of trying to explain the transformation: "Oh, Jeff, that's just Erik." Jeff was *not* convinced, having focused on plain old Erik (the "before" state) and then on the monster (the "after" state). In spite of having intently observed the whole makeup and costume process, Jeff seems to have ignored it completely.

Implications for guidance

Do not waste your time trying to explain a transformation to a child. A child tends to pay attention to the "before and after" and simply does not attend to transformations, even though he observes a transformation (e.g., pouring of the water or putting on of makeup). Instead, give children lots of chances to do "transformations."

Examples: Jeff's dad encouraged Jeff to put on some of the makeup to create his own disguise, thus having Jeff actually perform a transformation.

Mr. Soto's curriculum includes daily opportunities to transform things, such as pouring things from one container to another (water table, sand table, outdoor sandpit) or changing the shape of things (squishing play dough from a large ball to a flat pancake, rolling the pancake into a sausagelike shape).

Preoperational thinkers tend to judge things by how they look. In the classic Piagetian conservation problem, when presented with two containers, one short and one tall, which contain the same amount of water (Figure 1–1, Step 2), preoperational thinkers say that the tall container has more water in it "because it looks like it has more." They are often deceived by appearances because they tend to judge something by how it appears on the surface.

Implications for guidance

Remember that children focus on appearances and that they only have a limited ability to take another person's perspective. Rely on this knowledge when you make guidance decisions—for example, when you have to deal with a child's own hurtful

Provide lots of opportunities for children to perform transformations like pouring water or sand from one container to another.

behavior. Avoid using negative, hurtful (and ineffective) discipline that simply mirrors the young child's behavior.

Example: When 27-month-old Jack pinched another child, his baby-sitter grabbed and pinched him, hissing, "Now you know how it feels when you pinch other people." (Do not use this negative strategy.)

To a child Jack's age, deceived by appearances, it looks as if this adult wants to hurt him. His attention will be on the intense stimulus—the painful squeezing of his skin, and he will not understand what the adult says. The baby-sitter's hurtful strategy grew out of her *mis*understanding of a toddler's ability to take someone else's perspective.

Jack's dad took a different approach. He said, "Oh, no, Jack! Ouch! Pinching hurts Sara. Use words to tell her to move. No pinching." Dad's discipline was positive. He was firm but kind in making it clear that pinching was not allowed. He understands his egocentric son's need for information along with limit setting: "Use words to tell her to move."

Preoperational thinkers have difficulty reversing a process. Preoperational thinkers focus on one thing at a time, either the "before" or the "after" in any action. An older child can think about a couple of things at once and is not deceived by how things look. You, as an adult, realize that you could quickly show that the volume of

Figure 1–3. Preoperational thinkers have difficulty reversing their thought. They will *not* say that you could prove that the two containers hold an equivalent volume by simply pouring the contents of container C back into container B.

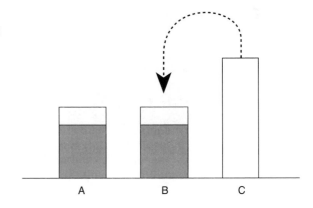

liquid in the tall glass is equivalent to that in the short glass by simply pouring the contents of the tall glass back into the short glass (Figure 1–3)—reversing the process—but young children would not think so logically.

Concrete Operational Stage

Children in this stage of cognitive development are usually between the ages of about 6 and 11 and in primary or elementary school. The cognitive skills of the concrete operational child are qualitatively different from those of the preoperational thinker.

A primary (first, second, or third grade) or elementary school child (fourth, fifth, or sixth grade) is even better able than the preoperational thinker to distinguish reality from appearances. Concrete operational thinkers are not deceived by the appearance of apparent changes as easily as preoperational thinkers are. Concrete operational thinkers are better able than preoperational thinkers to attend consistently to both relevant dimensions (height and width) in the standard conservation task. A concrete operational thinker uses this information about dimensions to arrive at an understanding of conservation.

One of the changes in cognition during this period is that the concrete operational child can now pay attention to how things change or the transformations, even in standard conservation tasks. Thus, they show evidence of the further development of skills that emerged during the preschool years. Concrete operational thinkers still have some cognitive milestones to accomplish, however, and these milestones are reached in the next stage of cognitive development.

Implications for guidance

Rely on positive discipline as you guide late early childhood children. They are fairly sophisticated in their ability to comprehend your modeling, direct instruction, and coaching; your statements of what you expect from them; and your attempts to help them understand why they should or should not do things.

PERCEPTION

Perception During Early Childhood

Infancy is a time of remarkable perceptual development, as you know from your study of child development, and children continue to develop perceptual skills as they get older. A 2-year-old has many perceptual skills and, by age 5, has skills that are even better than when he was a toddler. However, young children still have problems with directing their attention and these problems fall into four areas.

Young children have poor searching and scanning skills

Young children can search for something, but they are not systematic in their search. Their search is not as accurate or efficient as an older child's, and some children do not seem to realize that they should stop searching at some point.

Example: Robert watched Mr. Soto write Robert's name on a name tag. Robert easily recognized his when the teacher showed Robert his name tag along with three others. The next day, however, Robert's name tag was on the chart with 22 others. Robert looked for a long time, but became frustrated when he could not find his name tag.

Young children have difficulty "tuning out" irrelevant information

Another perceptual problem is caused by a preschooler's inability to completely control her attention. Young children have difficulty tuning out (ignoring) meaningless information or stimulation. Their attention is more likely to be captured by stimuli that are intense or novel.

Example: A new student teacher was frustrated when he read a story to a small group of his 3-year-olds. A squealing sound from the parking lot and the squeaking from wheels on the lunch cart easily distracted them. Older children might also have noticed the noise, but would have been better able to "get back" to listening to the story (provided the story was developmentally appropriate and interesting).

Young children have difficulty focusing on more than one aspect of a problem

This was evident in the section on limitations of preoperational thinking. Figure 1–1 shows that preoperational thinkers focus on either the height or the width of the liquid in the glasses, but they cannot focus on both at the same time. This inability makes it difficult for young children to focus on their own viewpoint and on somebody else's viewpoint in daily classroom interactions.

Example: Two of Mr. Soto's 4-year-olds were playing at the sand table, constructing a tunnel. Then they had an argument about which way the tunnel should turn. Each child was focused on his own idea and could not seem to also deal with the other child's idea.

Young children's impulsivity might affect perception

Children who are reflective work slowly enough to be accurate. Impulsive children tend to work too quickly, thereby missing important information and making unnecessary mistakes. Tim, in the case study at the beginning of this chapter, is an example. Younger children tend to be more impulsive, and this creates an additional perceptual problem for them.

How Perception Changes as Children Get Older

More mature reasoning skills, more efficient memory, more mature language abilities, abstract concepts, and more experiences to draw on are some of the things that go along with changing perceptual abilities as children get older. Here are some of the ways in which perception changes during the early childhood period.

Selective attention becomes refined

Even infants select—and seem to prefer—certain patterns (Fantz, 1966). A 2-year-old has the ability to attend selectively to stimuli, but this ability improves during childhood as he eventually learns to ignore distracting stimuli. Older children are much better than are younger children at *selecting* the things to which they prefer to attend or which they ignore.

Children spend more time "on task" as they get older

Older children tend to stay with a task for a longer period of time than younger children do. The length of time a child spends on an activity, whatever a child's age, depends in part on how attractive the activity is to the child and whether a child chooses to pay attention to an activity in the first place.

Example: Mr. Soto set out small plastic tubs filled with wet sand on a table. Robert walked around the room that day and looked in each center. When he saw the wet sand and things for making impressions in the sand, he sat down at that table and then stayed there for 30 minutes, working industriously at smoothing sand, making impressions, then smoothing sand again.

Children are better able to redirect their attention as they get older

Older children can more easily redirect their attention than can younger children. When a task has a number of parts, the older child has an advantage because she is able to shift her focus from one aspect to another quickly. She is better able to say, for example, "OK, I'm done with that part. I can start on the next part and then I can finish with the third part. Whoops! I forgot something in part one."

Example: Almost all of Mr. Anderson's third-graders worked with a specialist of some kind during the week. This meant that the children's classwork was interrupted so that they could leave the classroom to go with the specialist. Mr. Anderson has made anecdotal records of which children could or could not quickly get back to their work when they returned to the classroom. Most, but not all, of his 8-year-olds can indeed shift gears and redirect their attention to classroom work when they return.

Implications for guidance

What does this information about perception and attention mean for you as a teacher? Do you just say, "Well, children have short attention spans," and leave it at that? Hopefully, your answer is "No, there some specific things that I as a teacher can do to guide children effectively with this knowledge about perception and attention during childhood." Here are some practical and specific suggestions for developmentally appropriate practice based on your knowledge of perception during early childhood.

Screen for sensory impairments. Children with sensory impairments are challenged in how they function in their environments. This can pose problems for the adult–child relationship. For example, a child who has a mild hearing problem might appear to be ignoring rules about cleaning up after a work period but just does not hear the directions for cleanup.

Manage the environment well by minimizing intense intruding stimuli. The idea that children have a short attention span seems to be taken as a given when adults talk about young children. The phrase is like a mantra, and lots of students and teachers say it without really thinking through specific situations. We do know that young children tend to be easily distracted by sudden or intense stimuli, but you can help children concentrate on activities and learn self-control by minimizing intruding intense stimuli.

Teach children to scan systematically. Mr. Soto noticed Robert's frustration and inability to pick out his name tag when all the name tags were hanging on the chart, so he decided to teach Robert some scanning skills because Robert's search was so haphazard and unsystematic.

Example: "Robert, look at only one row—this one. Now, touch each name tag as you look at it. Your name begins with R. Look for the first letter. Look for R." He encouraged Robert to ignore names beginning with other letters.

Encourage impulsive children to slow their reaction time. Impulsive children work very quickly and are frequently less accurate in their responses. They search even less efficiently than age-mates. They often get themselves in trouble, both academically and socially, because they are so impulsive. Suppose, for example, that your children are doing a counting activity and an impulsive child hurries through the counting and misses things to be counted. Consider helping this child by helping him slow down and touch each of the things to be counted.

MEMORY

Definitions

Memory is the basic cognitive process by which we store information and then later retrieve it. There are several terms that you will need to know in order to understand information on how children develop memory.

Long-term memory is a place to store the information that we perceive and then make an effort to learn. We collect such information and then store it as a permanent record. Most of us can call up information from our long-term memory because we often have stored the memory as a strong sensory image of places and events, sometimes from years or even decades ago. We can store pleasant memories. For instance, I remember one sunny afternoon in my grandfather's garden whenever I smell basil because he crushed some of the fragrant herb that day and let me sniff it. Unpleasant or scary events are also stored. For example, people who were in Oklahoma City on April 19, 1995, will probably never forget the sounds of the explosion as the federal building was blown up.

Short-term memory is "working" memory, and we use it to temporarily store new information or well-known information to which we need access. A child's space for short-term memory increases with age, allowing him to work with and process more information and for longer periods of time (Case, 1992).

Example: Jessie is in Mr. Anderson's third-grade class and is working on a classification activity that the teacher developed—classifying fruits as citrus or noncitrus. Mr. Anderson defined a citrus fruit and then Jessie had to take his memory of names of different fruits out of long-term memory and place them in his short-term memory while he worked on the activity.

Recognition memory is the realization that we have seen or experienced some information that we now encounter (Perlmutter & Myers, 1979; Shaffer, 1996). Ask a child, for example, to look at the items in Figure 1–4 and then let the child study them for 2 minutes. Later, ask the child to select the items from a larger set of items and he probably will recognize nearly all of the original objects (Brown, 1975). Recognition tasks are easier than the next type, recall.

Recall memory is used when you are required to retrieve or call up some information. There are different types of recall memory, and these are important when we look at the memory capacity of infants and young children. *"Cued" recall memory* is a memory that has to be prompted by some sort of cue or reminder.

Example: Mr. Soto's class had used the obstacle course during the morning activity period; during group time he wanted the children to remember the steps in the

Figure 1–4. Show these pictures to a young child and let him look at them for a few minutes. Then mix them in with a larger number of pictures. The child will probably *recognize* all the items in the figure. Later, ask the child to *recall* as many of the 12 pictures as possible. He will remember some but not all, because pure recall memory is not very good in early childhood.

course. He used hand motions as cues. He said, "First you went *over* the block [he made one of his hands go "over" the other], then you stepped *into* the middle of the tire [he made a circle with one arm and put the other arm into the circle], *under* the bar [one hand under the other], and *around* the table [one hand circled the other]."

"Pure" recall memory is a memory that does not require any cue or reminder to prompt the memory. A child actively retrieves information from memory with no cues involved, as Jessie did with names of fruits in the classification activity.

The Development of Memory in Childhood

Birth through 3 years

Babies are well equipped even at birth to recognize familiar objects. Infants become bored with—habituated to—a stimulus, for example, a toy that is put in front of them several times, and this boredom indicates that they remember or *recognize* the object. But, between 5 and 12 months of age, babies are able to recognize an object after seeing it only a few times, meaning that their recognition memory has improved. They also seem to be able to remember the object for several weeks (Fagan, 1984).

Recall memory is also evident in infants, but it also improves during a baby's first year. At first, infants rely on *cued recall memory* because they seem to need to be reminded about a familiar event or experience. Here is an example. Researchers taught 2- to 3-month-old infants to kick a mobile and reminded the babies 18 days later about the mobile by moving it while the babies looked on. The infants recalled having kicked the mobile (Rovee-Collier, 1987). Note, however, that the researchers had to remind the babies, so the recall was actually passive. Infants begin to actively recall things from memory during the last several months of their first year.

Older infants and toddlers, approximately 12 months to 36 months, show improved recall memory (Howe & Courage, 1993; Perlmutter, 1986). After about age 2 children can recall exciting events that happened quite some time before and occasionally even tell about the memory in the form of a story. By the time a child is 3 years old he might be able to recall something that happened to him 1 or 2 years ago.

Ages 4 to 12

Suppose that you student teach in a preschool and then in a third-grade classroom. One of the things that you will quickly notice is that your third-graders are much better at pure recall memory than were your 4-year-olds. Show Figure 1–4 to your preschoolers and you will notice that they will recognize almost all of the items but wil not be able to simply recall more than three or four of the items. Your third-graders should be able to recall about eight of the items (Baker-Ward et al., 1993).

How Can We Explain the Changes in Memory?

Shaffer (1996) points to four reasons for the dramatic improvement in memory from ages 3 to 12:

1. *There are changes in basic capacities.* Older children can process information faster and can manipulate information better than younger children because they have more "working" memory (short-term memory) space in

their brains. This means that your third-graders can keep more information in their mind and can perform mental operations much more rapidly than can a younger child.

2. *There are changes in the strategies used for remembering things.* Older children will have learned a greater number and more effective methods for getting information into their long-term memory and then for retrieving it later. There are a number of different memory strategies, all of which are more efficiently used by older children. For example, 12-year-olds use the strategy called **rehearsal**, that is, they will rehearse something over and over until they remember it. Preschool children generally do not use this strategy, and primary-grade children use it but not very effectively—they have to be prompted to rehearse things to be remembered. Older elementary school children are able to rehearse lists or other things to be remembered very effectively (Flavell, Miller, & Miller, 1993; Ornstein, Medlin, Stone, & Naus, 1985).

    Older children also use another memory strategy called **organization** more effectively than do younger children. Figure 1–4 can be organized into four groups—vehicles, animals, food, and things for drawing. Researchers have shown us that young children do not organize groups of items in order to make recalling the items easier. Older children do make these logical groupings and are therefore much better at recalling such lists (Hasselhorn, 1992).

3. *There are changes in knowledge about memory.* As an adult, you understand how and why memory strategies work and are therefore more efficient in memory tasks. This overall understanding of memory is called **metamemory**. Children who are at least 10 years old seem to understand memory strategies, whereas younger children do not (Schneider & Pressley, 1989). It also seems that older children who understand *why* a memory strategy is useful are much more likely to use such strategies in their everyday life and in their schoolwork (Brown & Campione, 1990).

4. *There are changes in knowledge about the world.* Younger children simply have been on this earth for a shorter time than older children and have not had the opportunity to acquire the wealth of knowledge that an older child has. Older children have learned more and are therefore more familiar with a greater amount of knowledge, which makes remembering things much easier (Schneider & Bjorklund, 1992).

Special Focus: Teachers Can Set the Stage for Memory Development

Teachers in elementary schools do not spend much time teaching children specific memory strategies. But Moely et al. (1992) found that when they do, their students then use such strategies and do much better on tests of recall memory. Similarly, preschool teachers have lots of opportunities every day to focus on memory development. Here are some practical strategies for you to try.

(continued on next page)

1. *Encourage children to use memory strategies.* Preschool children remember better when they use memory strategies, but they tend to use them only when prompted by adults. Verbal rehearsal (e.g., repeating the names of the bones in the leg until you memorize them) is one memory strategy. Mr. Soto (chapter opener case study) encouraged the children to use verbal rehearsal when they sang a "name song" at the beginning of the year to learn each child's name.

   Mr. Anderson (chapter opener case study) gave his third-graders lots of opportunities to organize things to be remembered. For example, they remembered the zoo animals by categorizing them into logical groups.

2. *Teach children "why" memory strategies are so useful.* Teaching strategies is good but it is not enough. Tell children why a memory strategy is useful and tell them when to use each strategy. Mr. Anderson told his 8-year-olds that putting a whole list of things into smaller categories would help them remember the list.

3. *Use familiar pictures, sounds, and objects.* Mr. Soto used slides of the children's trip to the zoo to help them retrieve information from their long-term memory. Mr. Anderson, after a visit to the zoo, played a tape of sounds made by the new animals that the children had seen.

4. *Plan activities and lessons with fewer steps.* Mr. Soto arranged an obstacle course with only four parts so that the children could easily remember it: *over* the rope, *through* the tire, *up* the ladder, and *down* the slide.

5. *Present only a few bits of new information.* Mr. Soto introduced the names of six birds in one lesson and discovered that the children could not handle this much new information, but they easily remembered the names of the birds when he focused on only three.

6. *Think of different and creative ways to repeat things.* Mr. Soto showed the pictures of the three birds at several group times and repeated their names with the children. Remembering that a square is a rectangle with four equal sides was easier when he repeated the information in creative ways over several days using transparencies, styrofoam models, a construction paper mural, and square cookie cutters.

7. *Actively involve children with things to be remembered.* Active involvement enhances memory. The preschool children in Mr. Soto's class learned about squares by forming one themselves at group time with four children on each side of the square. During Fire Safety week, Mr. Anderson helped the third-grade class remember the emergency fire escape route by having them walk it a number of times and then by drawing the route on pieces of paper.

8. *Label things and experiences.* Labeling things helps children remember them. Before the trip to the zoo, Mr. Anderson showed pictures of animals he thought might be unfamiliar and named them for the children. At the zoo, he repeated the names and the class wrote the names on a chart when they returned to school.

TEMPERAMENT

Definition

The children you teach will have different personalities; those of you who work with infants will quickly notice that even infants have different personalities. Where do the differences start? One of the starting points for personality differences is *temperament*—the predictable, characteristic way that any person—infant, child, or adult—responds to events. A person's temperament is one of the major building blocks of his personality and refers to how he expresses emotion. It is a person's behavioral "style" (Kagan et al., 1988; Thomas, Chess, & Birch, 1970). Researchers who have examined temperament usually look at several different things (Buss & Plomin, 1984; Goldsmith et al., 1987) including:

- *Activity level* (whether activity level is fast-paced, slow-paced, vigorous, not so vigorous)
- *Irritability level* (how negative events affect a child, e.g., how upset does he get?)
- *Soothability* (whether and how easily a child can be soothed)
- *Levels of fearfulness*
- *Sociability* (whether a child is receptive to social stimulation)

Three Basic Temperamental Styles

Some of the earliest research on temperament found that the infants seemed to fall into one of three general or broad categories of temperamental style. The temperamental qualities listed above tend to group together to form an overall style for each infant. This longitudinal research (Thomas et al., 1970; Thomas & Chess, 1977, 1986) gave us information on the following three basic temperamental styles. The effects of temperament on a child's development comes from Buss and Plomin (1984) and Sostek and Anders (1977).

Easy temperament

Children with easy temperaments have predominantly positive moods, adapt easily, and have a positive approach to new situations. They express emotions in a mild way and have predictable and regular eating and sleeping patterns.

    Example: Sasha, 8 months old, has an easy temperament. She spends very little time crying and spends a great deal of time watching, listening to, and playing with things and people. This allows her to take in information and she has more time to accommodate to that information and to learn than does a baby who cries a lot.

Slow-to-warm-up temperament

Like the easy babies, the slow-to-warm-up child's responses of happiness or anger are not very intense; that is, they have very mild expressions of emotion. Slow-to-warm-up children tend to be cautious and somewhat moody. They are slow to adapt to change and withdraw from or are passively resistant to new objects and people. Their reluctance to try new things might well result in their being ignored by others.

Difficult temperament

Children with difficult temperaments tend to have predominantly negative dispositions and have highly intense expression of emotion; that is, when they are happy they express their happiness intensely, when they are angry or upset they express these emotions intensely. Children with difficult temperaments are quite slow to adapt to change or even dig in their heels and resist change. They withdraw from new stimuli and have irregular bodily functions.

Implications for guidance

Think about your own temperament "style." Then, tune in to the temperamental differences of children in your care. Acknowledge that you may well be puzzled or even irritated by the behavioral styles of some children when they differ from your own, and occasionally even if a child's style matches your own. Finally, learn and consciously use the positive guidance strategies described in this text. Along with your sense of humor, patience, sensitivity, and goodwill, they will help you deal with different temperaments so that you can help children to thrive.

Parent Talk. Creating a "Good Fit" Between Temperament and Child Guidance

Clayton is now 7 years old, but his mother has had concerns about his temperament ever since he was born. Clayton spent a lot of time crying when he was an infant and his mother noticed that he tensed up a lot, seemed to be highly distractible, and was unable to pay attention to things. Mom was concerned that he would have trouble learning things if he did not pay attention. Her worries were legitimate because some, but certainly not all, children with difficult temperaments are more irritable and aggressive and are more likely to have trouble adjusting to school (Brody, Stoneman, & Burke, 1987).

Parents whose babies have a difficult temperament are likely to be concerned about whether the baby will always be so difficult or whether they can help him change his difficult temperament. A parent's style in dealing with a child was a major factor in whether a baby with a difficult temperament still had a difficult temperament when he was older (Thomas & Chess, 1986). Clayton's mother got some advice from an infant specialist when Clayton was just a baby, advice that has helped Clayton become less grumpy and more adaptive. Here is that advice:

- **You *can* change a baby's early temperamental pattern.** Parents need to understand this concept. They need to know that their baby's temperament is not set for life, but the parent bears the respon-

sibility for making it possible for the temperament to change.

- **Create a "good fit" between infant temperament and caregiving style.** This is another concept that parents need to understand. Clayton's mother was told that she could create a "good fit" between her style and Clayton's temperament by focusing on a couple of things.

1. *Remember that your baby is not being irritable or crying or resisting your bids for attention to spite you.*
2. *Remain calm.* This will be difficult at times, and it is a good idea to have somebody to turn to to talk to about your baby's temperament.
3. *Allow your baby to respond to new foods, people, and other situations at his own pace.* Do not force him to try new things.
4. *Resist the urge to be demanding and to punish.* Babies and young children whose parents are demanding and forceful or punitive are much more likely to be difficult as they get older and are more likely to have behavior problems. Clayton's mother learned how to be firm but not forceful by attending early childhood family education support groups.
5. *Document the slow but steady changes in your baby's temperament!* Clayton's mother

continues on the next page

kept a diary so that she could see the outcome of her patient and sensitive
approach. She kept track of how she felt
and strategies she used as she and her hus-
band dealt with Clayton's difficult tempera-

ment. She also made a video of Clayton
finally trying new foods after resisting them
for a long time and of him playing with children in a play group for the first time.

SOCIAL COGNITION

Piaget showed us that a child gradually constructs increasingly more complex ideas
about the physical world as he grows older. At the same time, a child also constructs
increasingly more complex ideas about his social world (Shantz, 1983). Thus, a
child uses his *cognitive* abilities to make sense of and understand ideas about many
aspects of social life, just as he uses cognitive abilities to understand aspects of his
physical world.

Researchers use the term ***social cognition*** to refer to how children think about
the behavior, motives, feelings, or intentions of others (Shaffer, 1996). For instance,
how will the children you teach describe how other people behave? Will they understand the difference between another person's accidental behavior and intentional
behavior? How will they view friendship? How will they think about resolving conflict? Your knowledge about these developmental issues will give you a firm foundation for making developmentally appropriate child-guidance decisions.

This section focuses on ***social cognition*** in the early childhood period. All of a
child's developments in perception, attention, memory, and verbal expression
seem to converge, enabling him to more accurately describe how others behave
and feel, to tell the difference between accidental and intentional behavior, to
make and maintain friendships, and to resolve conflicts. All of these developing
abilities will affect how you guide infants, toddlers, preschool, kindergarten, and
primary school-age children.

How Children Describe Other People and Their Behavior

Teachers spend a lot of time thinking about children's social development and are justifiably concerned about helping children interact with others in friendly and amicable
ways. We adults also want children to be able to deal with conflicts in a nonaggressive
way. Our social interactions are more likely to be friendly if we perceive others accurately and if we can predict what they might be feeling (Shaffer, 1996).

You will be able to guide children more effectively if you understand that their
interactions are often affected by how they understand the behavior of other
people. Researchers have given us a lot of information about what children of different ages pay attention to in others, what they remember, and how they describe
other people and their behavior.

Younger Than 7 or 8 Years

During early childhood, children tend to use concrete terms to describe another
person, such as "My mommy is pretty. She smells good. She likes dogs." They do not

often describe more abstract qualities, such as trustworthiness or honesty. Occasionally, a young child will describe someone by using what seems to be a more abstract term, such as "He's *mean!*" Here, though, the child usually is describing something the other has recently done, such as yelling at the child for running onto the lawn, rather than identifying a major psychological characteristic (Rholes, Jones, & Wade, 1988).

Show a video to young children and ask them to describe what they saw. Again, they will concentrate on describing concrete, observable actions: "She opened the gate and the kitten got out." They might describe obvious emotional reactions, ". . . and the girl cried." But young children will not try to interpret feelings (Flapan, 1968).

After Age 8

Children at this age use fewer concrete terms and begin using broader, more psychological terms terms to describe other people (Barenboim, 1981). First-, second-, or third-graders, for example, might describe their friends by *comparing* their behaviors in some way: "Carl *draws better* than anybody in our class," or "Cecil *spells better* than most of the class." Children usually use fewer and fewer such behavioral comparisons as they get older. When our first-, second-, and third-graders are in the fifth grade—10 years old—and describe Carl and Cecil, they are likely to use broader psychological constructs in their description (Shaffer, 1996), "Carl is very *artistic*" and "Cecil is one of the *smartest* people in class."

Eight- to 10-year-olds are also much better able to describe another person's behavior. Show a video to this group and you will hear interpretations of some of the feelings and intentions of other people, but only in familiar situations. For example, "She cried when the kitten got out of the yard. She's probably feeling sad and afraid that her kitten will get hurt."

Implications for guidance

Avoid the urge, when a child has hurt somebody, to ask, "How do you think he feels?" Expect young children *not* to understand how somebody else feels. Instead of just asking about how the other person feels, be helpful. Use age-appropriate child guidance and give this age group information about how other people usually feel in different situations.

Examples: Teacher to 3-year-old: "Oh, Sarah! The gerbil is hiding. I think you scared him when you banged on his house."

Teacher to kindergarten class: "The cook seemed irritated when she had a hot meal all ready for us and we weren't ready to eat."

Expect older children to begin to take other people's perspective and to begin to understand that factors *inside* another person have a lot to do with the person's behavior. Expect older children to begin to understand feelings and to begin to interpret feelings. Remember, though, that some children have had poor role models and might not be very good at recognizing feelings. Use individually appropriate child guidance with these children by teaching them about emotions or by reminding older children about how somebody might be feeling. Remind children about limits on behavior that hurts others.

> **Example:** Teacher to 8-year-old: "Terri is crying. She's upset because you called her that name. You know that one of the classroom rules is that we do not hurt others by name-calling."

How Children Understand Intentional/Accidental Behavior

Children are better able to control themselves when then can look at another's behavior and decide whether the person intended to act that way or whether the behavior was accidental. Children can distinguish between accidental and intentional behavior as their cognitive skills develop and if the adults in their lives help them understand what others intended to do. Four-year-olds tend not to differentiate between intentional and accidental behavior, but by 5½ years many children can make the distinction, and at 9 they are even more accurate (King, 1971).

Implications for guidance

Do not expect the youngest children to know the difference between accidental and intentional behavior. Use age-appropriate guidance strategies with this group by explaining what an accident is. Expect older children to understand the difference if they have learned the difference. If they do understand the difference, *remind* them of the difference between accidental and intentional behavior. If an older child has not learned the difference, use an individually appropriate strategy to teach him what it is.

> **Examples:** "Mary didn't mean to run into you, Chuck. It was an 'accident'" (Chuck was 4 years old).
>
> Mr. Anderson to one of his third-graders: "Sometimes, Tom, people aren't very careful, and I think Sam ran into you by accident. He really wasn't looking at where he was going. He didn't mean to hurt you."

How Children View Friendship

You have already read about how important it is to be able to take another person's perspective. Perspective-taking ability changes as a child gets older and affects how children view friendship. At first, young children are rather self-centered or egocentric about who their friends are because a friend is viewed as somebody who simply plays with the child (Hartup, 1992) or who can help a child. In late childhood and early adolescence, children view friends as people who understand each other and who provide emotional support (Furman & Buhrmester, 1992).

Friendship becomes important during the early childhood years for three reasons (Damon, 1983). First, children have a blossoming sense of moral obligation, a willingness to share or to take turns. Even though the roots of sharing or turn-taking were evident earlier, they now occur with regularity. Second, children now begin to view peers as friends as well as momentary playmates. Social interactions are seen for the first time as part of a system of relationships that goes beyond the present moment. Third, a wide range of social interactional possibilities opens because of a young child's developing symbolic awareness.

Social skills needed for effective interaction

Peer relationships are necessary for a child's healthy development (Bullock, 1997). Teachers can help children develop the skills that they need to have pleasant and rewarding peer relationships. First, though, we should know about the competencies that a child has to have before he can have such rewarding relationships. Asher, Renshaw, and Hymel (1982) reviewed the research on the competencies, or social skills, needed for effective interaction with peers. They focused on a child's ability to initiate interaction with peers, the ability to maintain a relationship, and the ability to deal with conflict.

Popular and unpopular children initiate contact with peers differently. When asked how a new child could get acquainted with others in the class, unpopular kindergarten children suggested that an adult help the child get to know the others. The popular children, however, demonstrated superior social skills when they volunteered to play with the new child themselves (Asher & Renshaw, 1981; Asher et al., 1982). Corsaro (1979) observed how preschool children attempt to become a part of a group activity with peers they know. Children who approached the group, watched the ongoing activity, and then engaged in the same behavior without disrupting the group were likely to be admitted to the group.

Implications for guidance

Teach specific social skills to children who are aggressive or unpopular and who are therefore rejected by their peers (Bullock, 1991, 1997). Renee, for example, had been having a lot of trouble with the other children because she barged in on play groups and tried to take over the play. She did not seem to know a better way to join a group. Mr. Soto decided to teach her this social skill. He followed the practical, step-by-step strategies of modeling, direct instruction and coaching, and feedback and reinforcement recommended by Asher et al. (1982).

Modeling. Mr. Soto did a puppet play about a child who successfully joined a group playing in the housekeeping corner by asking if she could play and then by sitting at the table while "dinner" was served. This was an excellent example of modeling and was likely to be successful with Renee because the model was similar to her and because the teacher focused attention on what the model was doing and why she joined the group in that specific way.

Direct instruction and coaching. After watching the puppet play, Mr. Soto gave specific direct instructions to Renee on how to join a group. "OK, Renee. You want to play at the water table, and there are two children there already. Go over to the table and pick a spot where you won't be in somebody's way, and then use a toy that nobody else seems to be using. Remember our water table rules? That's right. No splashing and no grabbing!" Renee then practiced by joining the group at the water table.

The teacher modeled a behavior and then gave direct instruction, or coaching, which involves telling a child how to perform a social skill. Direct instruction, or coaching, is an effective tool for helping children gain acceptance by peers (Bullock, 1997; Zahavi & Asher, 1978).

Encouragement/Positive reinforcement. Mr. Soto nodded encouragingly at Renee when she took her place at an unoccupied side of the water table and played with an unclaimed toy. After observing for about 3 minutes, he walked over to the table and said to the entire group, "Each one of you is playing at your own spot and only with your own water toys, and the water is staying in the table."

Renee will probably continue to use her new and positive social skill because her teacher encouraged her verbally and nonverbally.

A child who has initiated contact with peers must be able to maintain the relationship. Children who are cooperative and friendly when interacting with peers are generally successful in maintaining relationships. Children who are unfriendly, make fun of, or interfere with other children have great difficulty maintaining relationships and are often rejected by other children (Asher et al., 1982).

Resolving Conflict

The ability to resolve conflict peaceably is an important social skill that rests on a child's ability to take another person's perspective and whether a child has been taught how to do conflict resolution. Resolving conflicts is an important part of social cognition. By age 5, children realize that they can defend their rights (e.g., not allow somebody to take a toy with which they are playing), but their skill in resolving conflict varies considerably.

Successful conflict resolution requires that a child be able to think of more than one thing at a time, to think about alternative ways of solving problems, to understand how the other person might view the problem, to know how another person is likely to respond to different solutions, and to understand how their actions will affect another person. These steps involve focusing on a conflict as a problem to be solved and not as an argument. Steps in conflict resolution are to:

- *Identify and define the conflict.* Avoid accusing the other person. Approach it like this, "We have a problem . . ."
- *Invite children to participate in solving the problem.*
- *Work together to generate possible solutions.* Accept a variety of solutions and do not evaluate solutions during this brainstorming phase.
- *Examine each idea for how well it might work.* Decide which one to try. Thank the children for coming up with ideas.
- *Help children with plans to implement the solution.* Young children will not know how to put the plan into action unless you teach them how to get started.
- *Follow up to evaluate how well the solution worked.* If the solution worked, thank the children for their help in cooperating to solve the problem. If the solution did not work, ask the children to try to figure out why and to fine-tune the solution or to try another solution.

SELF-CONTROL

What Is Self-Control?

Self-control is voluntary, internal regulation of behavior. First, children actually construct their concept of self as their cognitive system develops. Second, they observe and then evaluate the self, deciding whether they like the self that they see (these two facets are described more fully in Chapter 6). Third, the self must learn to regulate its own behavior (Harter, 1983). Self-control is a major issue in *metacognition,* one's knowledge and control of the cognitive domain (Brown, Bransford, Ferrara, & Campione, 1983).

Self-control, or self-regulation, may well be one of the most significant changes during a child's preschool years. Self-regulatory functions are an integral part of the learning process, are important mechanisms in a child's growth and development, and are an essential part of preserving social and moral order (Brown et al., 1983; Harter, 1983; Shaffer, 1996).

How Children Demonstrate Self-Control

Children demonstrate self-control when they:

- *Control impulses, wait, and suspend action.* Children show self-control when they step back, examine a situation, and then decide how to act. They resist reacting impulsively.

Example: Things went smoothly in the block corner until Kyle joined the group and took a block from Joel's structure. Joel's usual reaction has been an aggressive one, such as slugging or screaming at the other child. But Mr. Soto has been teaching him to be self-controlled and verbally assertive. So he "used words" like his teacher suggested: "Kyle, I was using that block. Give it back!"

- *Tolerate frustration.* A child demonstrates self-control when she can refrain from doing something that is either forbidden or inappropriate to the situation.

Example: While on a Christmas shopping trip, Joel was attracted to a huge tree with hundreds of glass ornaments. He stood and looked, raised his hand to touch one, and then withdrew his hand, showing self-control.

- *Postpone immediate gratification.* Adults demonstrate self-control when they carry through with some important task and only then engage in some gratifying (pleasurable) activity, for example, studying before meeting a friend for coffee. Please try to remember how difficult it is for you, an adult, to delay gratification, especially when dealing with people far younger than you.

Use modeling, direct instruction, and all the other methods of influence to teach delay of gratification. Even older children need our guidance to figure out when it is important to put off until later something that they want right now.

Example: Michael, 6 years old, popped several chocolate chips into his mouth as he and his brother helped Dad make chocolate chip cookies. Dad said, "Hey, Mike. Remember the ad on TV where that man sings 'Please don't eat all the morsels—or your cookies will look like this' [a chipless chocolate chip cookie]? Put the chips into the mix, not your mouth." Mike said, "Oh, OK!" and sang the jingle a few times as he added chips to the batter.

- *Initiate a plan and carry it out over a period of time.* Rick and Jackson, two boys in the chapter opener third-grade example, planned how to build a model of a farm, drew the plans, and then set about building their model. It took them several days to complete their project.

How Does Self-Control Evolve?

Self-control evolves "from the outside to the inside," slowly and haltingly.

Self-control evolves "from the outside to the inside"

Responsible adults actually perform most of an infant's or toddler's ego functions (e.g., remembering things for the infant, reminding a toddler to hold the kitten gently), thereby regulating the young child's behavior for her. In this case, the very young child's actions are heavily controlled by an external agent, the adult. But responsible adults also understand child development and realize that a child can and should take on more responsibility for controlling herself as she grows older and acquires different cognitive skills. They expect children to begin to internalize control taught by the adult. Responsible adults communicate this expectation when they gradually transfer executive control to children (Brown et al., 1983; Flavell, 1977). The adult might, for example, expect a child to try solving a problem with the adult observing and offering advice or help only when necessary.

Pulkkinen (1982) noted that child-rearing practices affect a child's level of self-control. She found that parents of adolescents with strong self-control used positive guidance strategies. These parents used strategies that helped adolescents understand why control was necessary and did it in such a way that the parents did not seem to be on a "power trip." Parents of adolescents with weak self-control used selfish, negative guidance strategies. They tried to use raw power and thought it unnecessary to explain their adult actions.

Self-control develops slowly

Children are not born with self-control, but begin to develop it around age 2. It takes several more years before this emerging ability develops fully. Children are better able to control themselves as they get older, for a number of reasons. First, their cognitive, perceptual, and linguistic systems have developed, allowing them to understand things from a different perspective and giving them access to better skills for dealing with impulses. Control of the self also implies that a child realizes that a self exists; this knowledge develops during late infancy and early childhood.

Self-control evolves haltingly

Preschool children often astonish adults with remarkable self-control, but demonstrate considerable lack of control at other times. Joel controlled himself in the block corner, but on the same day he shoved someone out of the way in his rush to the sliding board. Young children have to practice self-control, just as musicians have to practice their skills. It is reasonable to expect some measure of self-control in young children, but it is usually a mistake to expect perfect control.

Stages in the Development of Self-Control

Birth to approximately 12 months

Kopp (1981) believes that young infants are not capable of self-control. The reflex movements of the first several months of life give way to voluntary motor acts such as reaching and grasping, but, she notes, infants do not consciously control the movements.

Between age 1 and age 2

Children begin to be able to start, stop, change, or maintain motor acts or emotional signals. They also demonstrate an emerging awareness of the demands made on them by caregivers. Communication skills become more sophisticated, enabling a child to understand another person's instructions and modeling. Caregivers usually discover that children this age are ready to follow an adult's lead.

At approximately 24 months: Transition to self-control

Children are now able to recall what someone has said or done, and they are also able to engage in representational thinking. These new abilities help them make the transition to beginning self-control. At this stage, however, children have only a limited ability to control themselves, that is, to wait for their turn or to delay gratification.

At about 3 years: Self-control emerges

Children are now able to use certain strategies that help them delay gratification, and this sets the stage for better self-control. Kopp (1981) did research with groups of 18-, 24-, and 36-month-old children to find out how they differ in their use of strategies to better tolerate delay. Raisins were hidden under a cup, and the child being tested was told not to eat them. The older children did things spontaneously to distract themselves, such as singing, talking, sitting on their hands, or looking away. Younger children could be instructed to use delaying strategies, but they did not use them automatically (Meichenbaum & Goodman, 1971).

Middle childhood to late adolescence

Pulkkinen (1982) carried out a longitudinal study of 8-year-olds in which individual differences in behavior were again examined when the children were 14 and 20 years old. The individual tendencies noted in the children at age 8 in how they coped with impulses seemed to endure through adolescence.

Case Study Analysis: Child Guidance Based on Child Development

The three teachers in the chapter opening case studies rely on child development knowledge to make good child-guidance decisions. Analyze the case studies by answering the following questions.

Mr. Kennedy's Infant Room

1. Explain why the "memory" games that Mr. Kennedy planned for 6-month-old Kevin were *age-appropriate.*
2. Decide which stage in the development of self-control 17-month-old Ben is in. Explain why Mr. Kennedy's guidance with Ben was age-appropriate.

Mr. Soto's Preschool Classroom

1. Explain how Mr. Soto demonstrated his understanding of child development.

(continued)

a. Why were the activities that Mr. Soto planned for Monday and Tuesday—dictation of a story, white play dough, finger paint, and "pipe cleaner clouds"—an age-appropriate way to help the children recall and tell about their experiences?

b. Some people would scoff at the idea of pouring sand from one container to another as "mere play." Explain to such a person why Mr. Soto set up sand play and how it shows that he understands a preschool child's cognitive limitations. Be sure to explain which specific cognitive limitation sand and water pouring focuses on.

c. How did Mr. Soto's actions with Tim show us that this teacher also seems to understand that developmentally appropriate guidance is *individually appropriate*?

Mr. Anderson's Third-Grade Classroom

1. Explain why Mr. Anderson's approach to Rick and Jackson's conflict was so effective.

REFLECTING ON KEY CONCEPTS

1. What does it mean when early childhood professionals say that **developmentally appropriate** child guidance is both age-appropriate and individually appropriate? What sort of a knowledge base does an adult who uses developmentally appropriate child guidance have to have and what does that person tend to believe about his role in interacting with children?

2. Suppose that you are assigned to student teach in a preschool classroom with 4-year-old children. Summarize the cognitive accomplishments of this age group and then explain what you would expect in terms of their cognitive limitations. Do the same thing with a group of 7- or 8-year-olds. Explain why your guidance strategies will be most effective when they are based on the cognitive accomplishments of a child's current level of development and when they also take into account the cognitive limitations of a particular stage or level of development.

3. Now suppose that you are the master teacher and are talking with a new student teacher. He said, "I have worked in child-care centers for 3 years now and have noticed that preschool children have short attention spans." What could you tell this new teacher about children's perception that would help him acquire a more accurate understanding of this issue?

4. Explain why developmentally appropriate guidance strategies are based on the somewhat limited memory capacity and skills of young children. There are several things that adults can do to set the stage for memory development.

5. You are the principal of a school for children from birth through third grade and you decide to do a group-based early childhood family education meeting. Your goal is to help parents understand the concept of children's temperament. Outline what your session would deal with in terms of what **temperament** is, the three temperamental styles, and how parents can help their children who have difficult temperaments to change their temperaments.

6. What is **social cognition** and how is this skill affected by and similar to a child's level of cognitive development? How would you explain to a

parent of a child in your preschool class how that child now describes other people and their behavior that will change over the next 4 to 5 years?

7. Name several ways in which a child can demonstrate *self-control*. Explain what it means to say that adults who use developmentally appropriate child guidance teach children how to control themselves and gradually transfer executive control to the child.

APPLY YOUR KNOWLEDGE

1. Planning Activities for Memory Development. Mr. Soto's preschool class used a large recipe sheet with pictures when they made a heart-shaped cake for Valentine's Day. The children learned about the ingredients and the process for making their cake. Mr. Soto then used the recipe sheet in group time as an activity to enhance **cued recall** memory of the cake making.

   Now it is 3 weeks later and the teacher wants to work on **pure recall memory** with the children. He has decided to do more baking, but this time will make cupcakes. He will use the same cake ingredients and the same process for mixing, but will use cupcake pans instead of the heart-shaped pan. Please reread the section on recall memory in the chapter. Then write what he should say to the "bakers" from the start of the new baking project to the end. Remember to focus on pure recall memory.

2. Transferring Control to Children. As you look at parents and teachers you will quickly notice that adults expect different things of children at different ages and this is true for self-control. Apply your knowledge about how children develop self-control by observing how adults seem to behave in terms of expectations for children's self-control for children of three different ages.

Infants: Observe an adult–infant interaction. Look for evidence that the adult actually performs the infant's ego functions—that is, that the adult does not expect the infant to control himself (e.g., does not expect the infant to remember things, to manage his emotions, or to do things for himself). Describe specific things an adult does *for* the infant (rocks him to sleep, calms him down, burps her, wipes his mouth, changes his diaper).

Toddlers, younger preschoolers, and older preschoolers: Now look for evidence that the adult is *beginning* to expect these children to show some measure of self-control. Gather several examples that indicate that this adult is indeed *transferring control* to children. For example, does the teacher expect the children to remember to wash their hands after using the bathroom or does the teacher expect the children to begin to manage feelings by saying, "Use words to say that you are upset"?

Kindergarten and primary school children. What evidence do you find in a classroom for 5- to 8-year-olds that teachers really do expect older early childhood children to be better able to control themselves?

References

Asher, S. R., & Renshaw, P. D. (1981). Children without friends: Social knowledge and social skill training. In S. R. Asher & J. M. Cottman (Eds.), *The development of children's friendships*. New York: Cambridge University Press.

Asher, S. R., Renshaw, P., & Hymel, S. (1982). Peer relations and the development of social skills. In S. Soto and C. Cooper (Eds.), *The young child: Reviews of research* (Vol. 3). Washington, DC: NAEYC.

Baker-Ward, L., Gordon, B.N., Ornstein, P.A., Larus, D.M., & Clubb, P.A. (1993). Young children's long-term retention of a pediatric examination. *Child Development, 64*, 1519–1533.

Barenboim, C. (1981). The development of person perception in childhood and adolescence: From behavioral comparisons to psychological constructs to psychological comparisons. *Child Development, 52*, 129–144.

Bell, R. Q. (1968). A reinterpretation of the direction of effect in studies of socialization. *Psychological Review, 75*, 81–95.

Bell, R. Q., & Harper, L. V. (Eds.) (1977). *Child effects on adults*. Hillsdale, NJ: Erlbaum.

Black, J. K. (1981). Are young children really egocentric? *Young Children, 36*, 51–55.

Brody, G. H., Stoneman, Z., & Burke, M. (1987). Child temperaments, maternal differential behavior, and sibling relationships. *Developmental Psychology, 23*, 354–362.

Brown, A. L., Bransford, J. D., Ferrara, R. A., & Campione, J. C. (1983). Learning, remembering and understanding. In P. Mussen (Ed.), *Handbook of child psychology* (Vol. 3). New York: Wiley.

Brown, A.L., & Campione, J. C. (1990). Communities of learning and thinking, or a context by any other name. In D. Kuhn (Ed.), *Developmental perspectives on teaching learning and thinking skills*. Basel: Karger.

Bullock, J. (1991). Supporting the development of socially rejected children. *Early Child Development and Care, 66*, 15–23.

Bullock, J. (1997). Children without friends: Who are they and how can teachers help? *Annual Editions/Child Growth and Development*. Guilford, CT: Duskin/McGraw-Hill, 121–125 (reprinted from *Childhood Education*, Winter 1992, 92–96).

Buss, A. H., & Plomin, R. A. (1984). *Temperament: Early developing personality traits*. Hillsdale, NJ: Erlbaum.

Case, R. (1992). *The mind's staircase: Exploring the conceptual underpinnings of children's thought and knowledge*. Hillsdale, NJ: Erlbaum.

Chalmers, J. B., & Townsend, M. A. (1990). The effects of training in social perspective-taking on socially maladjusted girls. *Child Development, 61*, 178–190.

Corsaro, W. A. (1979). "We're friends, right?" Children's use of access rituals in a nursery school. *Language in Society, 8*, 315–336.

Damon, W. (1983). *Social and personality development*. New York: W. W. Norton.

Dixon, J. A., & Soto, C. F. (1990). The development of perspective-taking: Understanding differences in information and weighting. *Child Development, 61*, 1502–1513.

Fagan, J. F. (1984). Infant memory: History, current trends, and relations to cognitive psychology. In M. Moscovitch (Ed.), *Infant memory: Its relation to normal and pathological memory in humans and other animals.* New York: Plenum.

Fantz, R. L. (1966). Pattern discrimination and selective attention as determinants of perceptual development from birth. In A. H. Kidd & J. L. Rivoire (Eds.), *Perceptual development in children.* New York: International Universities Press.

Flapan, D. (1968). *Children's understanding of social interaction.* New York: Teacher's College Press.

Flavell, J. H. (1977). *Cognitive development.* Englewood Cliffs, NJ: Prentice-Hall.

Flavell, J. H., Miller, P. H., & Miller, S. A. (1993). *Cognitive development* (3rd ed.). Englewood Cliffs, NJ: Prentice-Hall.

Furman, W., & Buhrmester, D. (1992). Age and sex differences in perceptions of networks of personal relationships. *Child Development, 63,* 103–115.

Gelman, R., & Baillargeon, R. (1983). A review of some Piagetian concepts. In P. Mussen (Ed.), *Handbook of child psychology* (Vol. 3). New York: Wiley.

Gibson, E. J., & Spelke, E. S. (1983). The development of perception. In P. Mussen (Ed.), *Handbook of child psychology* (Vol. 3). New York: Wiley.

Goldsmith, H., Buss, A., Plomin, R., Rothbart, M., Thomas, A., Chess, S., Hinde, R., & McCall, R. (1987). Roundtable: What is temperament? Four approaches. *Child Development, 58,* 505–529.

Harter, S. (1983). Developmental perspectives on the self-system. In P. Mussen (Ed.), *Handbook of child psychology* (Vol. 4). New York: Wiley.

Hartup, W. W. (1992). Friendships and their developmental significance. In H. McGurk (Ed.), *Childhood social development: Contemporary perspectives.* Hove, England: Erlbaum.

Hasselhorn, M. (1992). Task dependency and the role of category typicality and metamemory in the development of an organizational strategy. *Child Development, 63,* 202–214.

Higgins, E. T. (1981). Role taking and social judgment: Alternative developmental perspectives and processes. In J. H. Flavell & L. Ross (Eds.), *Social cognitive development.* Cambridge, MA: Harvard University Press.

Howe, M. L., & Courage, M. L. (1993). On resolving the enigma of infantile amnesia. *Psychological Bulletin, 113,* 305–326.

Jones, D. C. (1985). Persuasive appeals and responses to appeals among friends and acquaintances. *Child Development, 56,* 757–763.

Kagan, J., Reznick, J., Snidman, N., Gibbons, J., & Johnson, M. D. (1988). Childhood derivatives of inhibition and lack of inhibition to the familiar. *Child Development, 59,* 1580–1589.

King, M. (1971). The development of some intention concepts in young children. *Child Development, 42,* 1145–1152.

Kopp, C. B. (1981). "The antecedents of self-regulation: A developmental perspective." Unpublished manuscript, University of California, Los Angeles.

Maccoby, E., & Martin, J. A. (1983). Socialization in the context of the family: Parent-child interaction. In P. Mussen (Ed.), *Handbook of child psychology* (Vol. 4). New York: Wiley.

Marion, M. (1995). *Guidance of young children* (4th ed.). Columbus, OH: Merrill/Prentice-Hall.

Meichenbaum, G., & Goodman, J. (1971). Training impulsive children to talk to themselves: A means of developing self-control. *Journal of Abnormal Psychology, 77,* 115–126.

Milner, J. S., Robertson, K. R., & Rogers, D. L. (1990). Childhood history of abuse and adult child abuse potential. *Journal of Family Violence, 5*(1), 15–34.

Moely, B. E., Hart, S. S., Leal, L., Santulli, K. A., Rao, N., Johnson, T., & Hamilton, L. B. (1992). The teacher's role in facilitating memory and study strategy development in the elementary school classroom. *Child Development, 63,* 653–672.

Newcombe, N., & Huttenlocher, J. (1992). Children's early ability to solve perspective- taking problems. *Developmental Psychology, 28*(4), 635–643.

Newman, D. (1986). The role of mutual knowledge in the development of perspective-taking. *Developmental Review, 6,* 122–145.

Ornstein, P. A., Medlin, R. G., Stone, B. P., & Naus, M. J. (1985). Retrieving for rehearsal: An analysis of active rehearsal in children's memory. *Developmental Psychology, 21,* 633–641.

Perlmutter, M. (1986). A life-span view of memory. In P. B. Baltes, D. L. Featherman, & R. M. Lerner (Eds.), *Life-span development and behavior* (Vol. 7). Hillsdale, NJ: Erlbaum.

Perlmutter, M., & Myers, N. A. (1979). Development of recall in 2- to 4-year-old children. *Developmental Psychology, 15,* 73–83.

Piaget, J. (1952). *The origins of intelligence in children.* New York: W. W. Norton.

Piaget, J. (1965). *The moral judgment of the child* (M. Gabain, Trans.). New York: Free Press.

Piaget, J. (1968). *Six psychological studies.* New York: Random House.

Piaget, J. (1976a). *The grasp of consciousness: Action and concept in the young child.* Cambridge, MA: Harvard University Press.

Piaget, J. (1976b). The stages of intellectual development of the child. In N. Endler, L. Boulter, & H. Osser (Eds.), *Contemporary issues in developmental psychology* (2nd ed.). New York: Holt, Rinehart, & Winston.

Piaget, J. (1983). Piaget's theory. In P. Mussen (Ed.), *Handbook of child psychology* (Vol. 1). New York: Wiley.

Pulkkinen, L. (1982). Self-control and continuity from childhood to late adolescence. In P. Bates and O. Brim (Eds.), *Life-span development and behavior* (Vol. 4). New York: Academic Press.

Rholes, W. S., Jones, M., & Wade, C. (1988). Children's understanding of personal disposition and its relationship to behavior. *Journal of Experimental Child Psychology, 45,* 1–17.

Rovee-Collier, C. K. (1987). Learning and memory. In J. D. Osofsky (Ed.), *Handbook of infant development* (2nd ed.). New York: Wiley.

Schneider, W., & Bjorklund, D. F. (1992). Expertise, aptitude, and strategic remembering. *Child Development, 63,* 461–471.

Schneider, W., & Pressley, M. (1989). *Memory development between 2 and 20.* New York: Springer-Verlag.

Selman, R. L. (1976). Social-cognitive understanding. In T. Lickona (Ed.), *Moral development and behavior.* New York: Holt, Rinehart, & Winston.

Selman, R. L. (1980). *The growth of interpersonal understanding: Developmental and clinical analysis.* New York: Academic Press.

Shaffer, D. R. (1996). *Developmental psychology* (4th ed.). Pacific Grove, CA: Brooks/Cole.

Shantz, C. U. (1983). Social cognition. In P. Mussen (Ed.), *Handbook of child psychology* (Vol. 3). New York: Wiley.

Sostek, A., & Anders, T. (1977). Relationships among the Brazelton neonatal scale, Bayley infant scales, and early temperament. *Child Development, 48,* 320–323.

Thomas, A., & Chess, S. (1977). *Temperament and development.* New York: Brunner/Mazel.

Thomas, A., & Chess, S. (1986). The New York longitudinal study: From infancy to early adult life. In R. Plomin & J. Dunn (Eds.), *The study of temperament: Changes, continuities, and challenges.* Hillsdale, NJ: Erlbaum.

Thomas, A., Chess, S., & Birch, H. (1970). The origin of personality. *Scientific American, 223,* 102–109.

Zahavi, S., & Asher, S. R. (1978). The effect of verbal instructions on preschool children's aggressive behavior. *Journal of School Psychology, 16,* 146–153.

Chapter 2

Guiding with Positive Discipline and an Authori*tative* Caregiving Style

After reading and studying this chapter, you will be able to:

- ✿ Summarize information on the concept of discipline.
- ✿ Name and describe the two major dimensions of caregiving.
- ✿ Name, describe, and explain the three styles of caregiving.
- ✿ Explain the major similarities and differences between the two types of permissiveness.
- ✿ Explain how each caregiving style tends to affect children's development.
- ✿ Name and explain basic processes through which adults influence children.
- ✿ Analyze case studies and determine how each case illustrates a specific caregiving style.

Discipline: A word derived from the Latin *disciplina,*
teaching, learning, from *discipulus,* pupil.
(Merriam Webster's Dictionary)

Case Studies: Styles of Caregiving

Matthew

Matthew parked his bike in the driveway. His mother called out to him, "Put the bike away, Matt." Matthew heard, but ignored her as he walked away. "Matthew, did you hear me? Put that bike away this instant. I mean it. No Dairy Queen for you tonight if you don't put that bike away." Matthew shuffled on and Mom continued, "Matthew, get back here. I want that bike put away." Finally, Mom just turned back to the house. "That boy never listens to me." Matt pays little attention to his mother's limits. He also knows that she hardly ever follows up on her threats. That night, for example, Mom took Matthew to the Dairy Queen, seeming to have forgotten the bike incident.

Joel

At 18 months old, Joel, when visiting a friend with his mother, banged on the friend's television screen and pushed at the door screen. His mom said nothing until the friend expressed concern for her property. Then she said, "Joel, do you think you should be doing that?" To the friend she said, "You know, I want Joel to know that the 'world is his oyster,' and I don't think I should order him around." When he was 4 years old Joel stayed up until 11:30 when his family had company. To the friend who inquired about his bedtime, Joel's mom replied, "Oh, I let Joel make decisions on his own." Joel fell asleep in the book corner at his child care center the next day. At 6 years Joel smacked another child on the face at school, and Mom said to the teacher, "Boys will be boys!" He pushed his way ahead of others at a zoo exhibition and Mom ignored others when she said, "Go ahead. Can you see? Move up closer."

Jim

Dad barks orders and expects his children to obey immediately, despite anything else they might be doing. Jim has watched as Dad used a belt on an older brother. To a neighbor who looked disapprovingly on a slapping incident, Dad said, "Got a problem? Butt out. These are my kids. They're not hurt."

During toilet training, 2½-year-old Jim was spanked when he had an accident. When Jim was 4 years old, Dad grabbed one of his arms and yanked him to make Jim move along at the store, saying, "I'm sick of you holding us up all the time." At preschool Jim had trouble with other children because he hit them when he was angry. The children started to leave him out of activities. Now that he is 8, he has a dog that he wants to train. When she does not sit on command, Jim tightens Ginger's choke chain until she howls in pain. Jim and his brothers avoid Dad as much as they can. And Ginger avoids Jim, too.

Krista

Krista's mother is a home care provider for Krista, 18 months old, and her friend's two children, Robert, 24 months, and Steven, 9 months. Steven's mother asked Krista's mom what to do when Steven bites her during feeding. "Quickly tell him NO and pull his mouth off your breast. Don't make a joke of it, either, or he'll think you're playing a game." Krista wanted a toy that Robert had, but she didn't seem to have the words for asking. She grew more agitated and then, even to her own surprise, she bit him! Krista's mother, also surprised, immediately took care of the bite on Robert's arm. Then, to her daughter, she said, "No, Krista. Biting is a no-no. Biting hurts Robert. If Krista needs help, come to Mommy and I will help you get a toy."

SOME QUESTIONS ABOUT DISCIPLINE

What Part Does Discipline Have in Socialization?

Socialization is a process through which children acquire their culture and the values and habits that will help them adapt to that culture. Children attain their culture's values through education, training, and imitation, with teachers and parents using a process called *scaffolding* to gradually lead a child to accept certain behaviors and values (Pratt, Kerig, Cowan, & Cowan, 1988). Discipline is only one part of the process of socialization.

What Is a Discipline Encounter?

One part of the whole process of socialization involves an interaction called a ***discipline encounter***, an interaction between an adult and child in which the adult attempts to help a child to alter her behavior in some way (e.g., to stop doing something harmful or destructive, to treat someone with respect, to take responsibility for cleaning up or putting away one's possessions). Discipline encounters occur frequently during the early childhood period, even in classrooms and homes where adults are warm and supportive. They occur as we help children understand that they have an obligation to respect the rights of others, and they occur as we help children comply with *legitimate authority* (Baumrind, 1996). Each of the adults in the following examples is faced with a discipline encounter.

Examples: Two-year-old Patrick and his friend were both pulling wagons when two of the vehicles' wheels became entangled. Patrick was clearly frustrated and ended up punching his companion.

Kindergartners Tobias and Jenesa argued over who should control the jar of paste at the collage table.

Four-year-old Callie and Levi left blocks and accessories strewn all over the block area in their classroom.

Mrs. McKinney, the teacher in the school-age child-care room, noticed that Frank and Joe were bouncing their basketball against the building's wall near a large window.

Frank's father realized that his son had not taken out the garbage, Frank's job for the month.

Some teachers, especially teachers of toddlers and young preschoolers, deal with numerous discipline encounters like these every day. Helping young children learn to be cooperative, to treat others with respect, and to accept legitimate authority is a substantial part of an early childhood professional's job. Some discipline encounters deal with everyday concerns (leaving blocks strewn about the block area) and others deal with more serious issues (e.g., a child's mean-spirited treatment of animals), but they are all discipline encounters.

Teachers and parents spend quite a bit of time managing discipline encounters and are justifiably concerned about such encounters for a couple of reasons. One reason is that adults have to help children learn to control their short-term behavior, the second reason is that adults want to influence long-term behavior even though they know that they cannot fully determine long-term behavior.

Example: Mrs. Lu, a first-grade teacher, has noticed that Ryan is fairly aggressive and faces several discipline encounters with Ryan each week over aggressive behavior. She is responsible for the safety of all the children in her class and therefore has to help Ryan control his aggression for the short term. She must stop him from hurting other children and the classroom animals, but she is also concerned about Ryan's long-term attitude and behavior. She knows he will have an increasingly difficult time getting along with other children if he continues to hurt them, so she wants to help him willingly accept a more nonaggressive way of interacting with others.

What Are Discipline Strategies?

Discipline strategies are the specific actions that adults use in managing discipline encounters, and there are a large number of specific discipline strategies. Some adults use strategies such as explaining rules, redirection, or teaching new behaviors, all of which focus on teaching rather than on punishment. They give children the type of information that they need for learning and practicing appropriate behavior (you will learn how to use specific positive discipline strategies in Chapter 3). Other adults rely on strategies that focus more on punishment than on teaching. Examples are isolation, physical punishment, or withdrawal of love. Still other adults use strategies that are simply unhelpful such as nattering and nagging.

What Influences the Discipline Strategies That Adults Use?

There are two major influences on an adult's choice of discipline strategy. One is learning, and the other is the set of rules operating in a particular system.

Learning

All adults have learned discipline strategies that they then use when facing a discipline encounter. They learn discipline strategies formally and informally. One major way of learning how to manage discipline encounters is by observing how other people, such as parents and extended family members, neighbors, teachers, television parents, adults in books, and scout and church youth leaders, manage discipline encounters. We also learn about discipline strategies by taking courses in child guidance, reading articles and books about discipline, attending parent education workshops, and talking with others about how to manage discipline encounters.

It is possible to learn a discipline strategy and then decide not to use it. For example, a teacher might have learned how to do time-out but also have decided not to use it because it does not fit her philosophy of child guidance. It is also possible to learn and then use a discipline strategy even though a person does not agree with it. For example, a teacher might use time-out and feel uncomfortable using it but might not know what else to do.

System rules

The *system rules* governing a family or a classroom also influence an adult's discipline strategies. Some systems operate with rules calling for mutual respect, rules that are overt (or out in the open), and rules that are negotiable (when possible) and flexible. Rules in such a system allow both individual and group needs to be met and encourage individual differences in system members. Adults in this type of system tend to manage discipline encounters with appropriate and positive discipline strategies. Other systems, however, operate with rules that call for controlling all behavior, being perfect, blaming others when wrong, denying feelings, and not talking openly or directly (Bredehoft, 1991). Adults in such systems manage discipline encounters with old, inappropriate, and negative discipline strategies.

Is Discipline Positive or Negative?

Discipline can be either positive or negative. The word *discipline,* in itself, has no positive or negative meaning. The actions or discipline strategies that you choose give your discipline its positive or negative quality. And some discipline strategies are neither positive nor negative but instead are simply unhelpful (Figure 2–1).

Some adults guide primarily with discipline strategies that focus on teaching.

Some adults use negative discipline strategies that focus on punishing children.

Some adults use unhelpful discipline strategies that confuse children.

Figure 2–1. Discipline strategies can be positive, negative, or unhelpful.

Examples: Mrs. McKinney managed the discipline encounter with Frank and Joe (who were bouncing the basketball on the wall near the window) by reminding them firmly but kindly to throw it only at the basketball backboard. Her action (the discipline strategy of reminding about a limit) was a positive one and her overall discipline style is a positive one.

At home, when Frank forgot to take out the garbage, Dad managed this discipline encounter by yelling at and calling his son a name. Dad's actions (the discipline strategy of yelling and name calling) were degrading and therefore negative.

There is a lot of confusion in the field of early childhood about whether discipline is positive or negative. Adults who use positive discipline strategies think of discipline as teaching, and believe in treating children with respect in any discipline encounter. Adults who primarily use negative discipline strategies tend to link the word discipline with punishment.

Some early childhood professionals do not like to even think about discipline strategies that are negative because they understand the possible harm that such negative discipline can do. However, our goal is to guide children effectively, and this requires that we acknowledge that many of them come from families that use negative, harsh discipline. Acknowledging what some of our children have experienced will help us understand their behavior and develop appropriate guidance plans for them. All children benefit from positive discipline strategies, but children who have experienced harsh discipline at home most desperately need us to use positive constructive guidance and discipline strategies.

TWO MAJOR CAREGIVING DIMENSIONS: RESPONSIVENESS AND DEMANDINGNESS

Researchers have long been interested in the characteristics that highlight differences in adults who are caregivers and how these differences affect children. For example, it has been almost 50 years since Becker (1954) analyzed several studies and classified a parent's style by looking at whether the parent was (a) hostile or warm and (b) restrictive or permissive. This text concentrates on describing the work of Diana Baumrind, who has found that two major dimensions of caregiving form the basis of an adult's caregiving style. These two dimensions are an adult's degree of *responsiveness* and *demandingness* (Baumrind, 1967, 1971, 1977, 1979, 1996; Baumrind & Black, 1967). Baumrind found that adults differ in how responsive they are to children's needs and differ in how demanding they are. Some adults are highly responsive to children, while others are not very responsive. Some adults are high in demandingness, while others make very few demands (Figure 2–2).

Responsiveness

Responsiveness is one of two major caregiving dimensions. It refers to how supportive an adult is and the degree to which she is tuned in to a child's developmental level and meets a child's needs. A study has demonstrated that parents who are unresponsive and who emotionally neglect their children set their children up for acting out types of problem behavior (Simons, Johnson, & Conger, 1994). This section

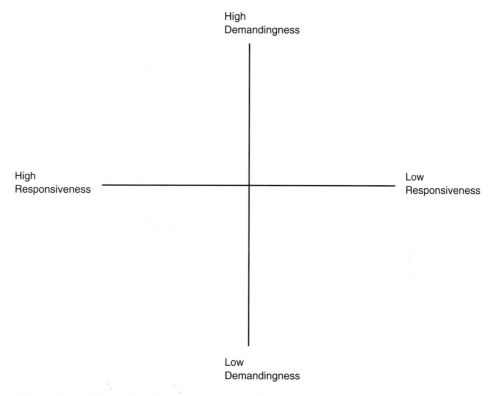

Figure 2–2. Two major dimensions—demandingness and responsiveness—form the basis of a caregiver's style.

describes several important aspects of responsiveness: warmth, the reciprocal nature of interaction, communication style, and the use of reason in discipline encounters (Baumrind, 1996).

Warmth

Adults differ in the degree of warmth that they show. ***Warmth*** refers to the emotional expression of liking or love. Some teachers and parents are highly responsive in that they show a high degree of sincere warmth, but others are low in responsiveness and do not express affection or love. This is an important dimension of responsiveness because children whose parents show a lot of negative feelings are often quite aggressive (Gursec & Lytton, 1988). These children, including attention-deficit hyperactive children, show acting-out behavior problems in school when their parents are angry, nonaccepting, and disapproving (Anderson, Hinshaw, & Simmel, 1994). Baumrind (1996) cautions that warmth should be sincere and believes that insincere expression of affection might prevent parents and teachers from appropriately managing discipline encounters when limits are necessary.

The reciprocal nature of interaction

This refers to the dance of interaction in which both a child and an adult are partners. Children depend on parents or teachers to give them what they need or want, and use an array of responses to try to get the adult to help them. But it is the adult who decides whether and how much she will let the child influence her. Highly responsive adults are tuned in to a child's developmental level and willingly comply with a child's needs whenever possible and if it is safe for the child. But adults low in responsiveness do not seem to understand child development, are not tuned in to a child's needs, and frequently refuse to meet those needs.

Communication style

Highly responsive adults communicate in an open, congruent, validating, and direct way. They deliver messages simply, kindly, firmly, and consistently. Children tend to readily accept this type of communication because it relies on persuasion, not force, to get an adult's point across. Children are socialized most effectively by adults who use this type of communication and who enforce their directives (Applegate et al., 1985; Baumrind, 1993, 1996; Dunn, Brown, & Beardsall, 1991). Their positive communication style tells us that they understand their responsibilities as people who socialize children. It also tells us they know their legitimate adult right to expect certain types of mature behavior from children, depending on the child's developmental capabilities. Their positive style tells us that they also accept children's need to see themselves as competent, as having choices, and as being worthy of respect (Bishop & Rothbaum, 1992).

Example: Vinnie and Sam scurried off to the computer, leaving their library books on the table, even though the classroom limit is that people put one thing away before they start a new activity. Mrs. Lu was responsive in this discipline encounter when she used a direct and validating style of communication, "I know that you've been waiting for your turn at the computer and I'll save your spot for you. First, though, I want you to put your library books in your cubbies."

Adults who are low in responsiveness tend to communicate in a way that children view as *coercive* (i.e., using force). They mistakenly believe that their role as parent or teacher gives them the right to exercise control by telling children that they are in charge, that adults have the power. Their communication style, then, is unresponsive in that it fails to use persuasion and relies on force. Here are the major patterns they use (Bredehoft, 1991; Satir, 1976):

- *Ordering.* These unresponsive adults deal ineffectively with discipline encounters because they order children to feel a certain way or to do something. (To Danielle who said that she did not want to wash her paint cup, the aide said, "Don't you dare tell me what you don't want to do.")
- *Blaming.* Unresponsive adults find fault and induce guilt. ("I hope you're satisfied now. You made a real mess when you spilled the paint.")
- *Distracting.* These unresponsive adults avoid issues and occasionally make completely irrelevant statements. (Four-year-old Mitchell, irritated when Sammy grabbed a gelatin wiggler from his plate, told the teacher about the incident. The teacher replied, "Tell me about your block structure, Mitch.")

- *Criticizing.* These adults are unresponsive by focusing on the negative and criticizing, even when a child does something he has been asked to do or when they think they are encouraging a child. (Ceil sat quietly through the entire group time, something her teacher has been requesting. The teacher remarked, "Well, you finally made it through the group time. It took you long enough, don't you think?")

Use of reason in discipline encounters

Highly responsive adults make their positive strategies even more effective by using a reason with the discipline strategy. A discipline encounter usually deals with one specific act, and a good strategy helps a child understand what is appropriate for that incident. But giving a reason along with the strategy paints a broader picture for the child of when that appropriate behavior would apply (Baumrind, 1996).

Example: Patrick was the 2-year-old who punched his companion when they were pulling wagons. His teacher used a positive strategy when she restated the limit, "Oh, Patrick! No hitting." She then gave him a short and simply stated reason, "Hitting hurts people."

Adults low in responsiveness tend to use negative discipline strategies and rarely use reasons to help children understand a limit. When they do give reasons, the reasons tend to be related to their power as adults.

Example: When Frank asked his father why his sister never had to empty the trash, his father said, "I don't have to explain myself to you, boy. You'll empty the trash because I told you to do it."

Demandingness

Demandingness is the second major caregiving dimension described in Baumrind's work. Demandingness refers to having and stating expectations for developmentally appropriate mature behavior from a child (developing appropriate limits), supervision and monitoring, type of discipline strategies, and willingness to confront a child. Adults differ in how demanding they are with children. Some adults are high in demandingness, but others are not.

Having and stating expectations for developmentally appropriate maturity from children (developing good guidelines and limits)

Adults differ in their demands for developmentally appropriate mature behavior from children. They differ in the ability and willingness to help children understand that there are boundaries, or limits, on behavior. Demanding and responsive adults understand the importance of proper boundaries and appropriate limits in guiding young children. They develop and clearly communicate limits that encourage developmentally appropriate mature behavior in children. Chapter 3 shows you how to develop, set, and maintain reasonable and fair limits with children.

Supervision and monitoring

One part of demandingness is whether adults monitor and supervise children's activities and behavior and whether they provide an orderly and consistent physical environment and time schedule. It takes effort and time to effectively monitor children in a classroom or at home, but close monitoring prevents or stops some inappropriate behavior in children (Baumrind, 1996; Patterson, 1986). In early childhood, students learn quickly that, when in a classroom with young children, they must be aware of the entire room or playground and what is going on. They learn that they must monitor all activities. It also takes time, effort, and skill to develop a responsive physical environment and time schedule.

Type of discipline strategies

Demanding and responsive adults use *positive discipline strategies* to encourage children to accept and express developmentally appropriate mature behavior. They use strategies that respond or sensibly match a child's behavior. For example, they demonstrate approval or disapproval for a child's behavior through the positive discipline strategies that they use. Some adults, however, make unrealistic demands and are not responsive to children. They use discipline strategies arbitrarily and in a way that does not seem to be connected to (they are *noncontingent*) a child's behavior. These inconsistent, noncontingent discipline strategies are harmful to children, leading them to think that their environment is not responsive to their behavior (Baumrind, 1996).

Willingness to confront a child

Guiding children to understand how important it is to treat others well, cooperate with others, and accept legitimate authority means that adults will have to decide whether and how to confront children with behavior that is clearly hurtful or inappropriate. One part of demandingness, then, is *confrontation,* which refers to being firm yet kind and willing to take a stand, even if doing so provokes a conflict.

Example: Mrs. Lu heard Jack say to a child in a wheelchair, "We don't want you to play with us. Get that stupid chair out of here." She quietly asked Jack to come with her so that she could talk to (confront) him. She did not accuse him but dealt with this discipline encounter by using a discipline strategy called an I-message, "I heard you say . . . to Gina. I was surprised to hear you say that because we have talked about kindness in our room and I know that you are usually very kind."

STYLES OF CAREGIVING: AUTHORI*TATIVE*, AUTHORI*TARIAN*, PERMISSIVE

Baumrind's longitudinal study is called the Family Socialization and Competence Project (FSP). The focus of this research begun in the 1960s is on the relationship between adult authority and normal children's development. Over time Baumrind has studied the effects of demandingness and responsiveness on the same children's development at three ages—preschool, school age, and adolescence. She assessed parents' specific discipline strategies, but focused most sharply on their overall levels of demandingness and responsiveness (Baumrind, 1996).

Baumrind identified and labeled several styles of parenting or caregiving based on the adult's level of demandingness and responsiveness as shown in Figure 2–3. These caregiving styles are the authori*tative*, authori*tarian*, and permissive styles. For

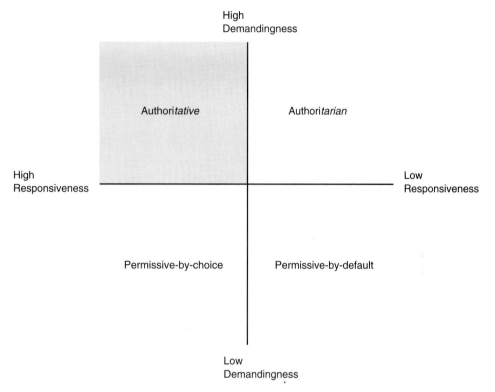

Figure 2–3.   Authoritative caregivers are high in demandingness and high in responsiveness and guide children with positive discipline.

each style you will read about an adult's level of demandingness and responsiveness and the impact of the style on children. I will emphasize, though, the positive authori*tative* style.

The Authori*tative* Style

Level of demandingness and responsiveness

Authoritative caregivers are high in both demandingness and responsiveness. In terms of demandingness, they expect developmentally appropriate mature behavior. They set and maintain reasonable, fair limits and closely supervise and monitor children's activities. They are willing to confront a child when necessary. In terms of responsiveness, authoritative adults are warm and nurturing. They understand child development, are tuned in to a child's developmental level, and tend to have realistic expectations from children of different ages.

Authoritative adults have a clear communication style. They deliver messages simply, kindly, firmly, and consistently. They use persuasion, not force, to help children understand things. They use positive, developmentally appropriate discipline strategies. The strategies, described and explained in detail in Chapter 3, focus on

Authoritative adults expect developmentally appropriate mature behavior from children and set clear and reasonable limits for them.

teaching, not on punishment. Authoritative adults believe in giving simple and clear reasons in discipline encounters.

What is the impact of authoritative caregiving and relying on positive discipline strategies?

An adult's general style of caregiving, which includes her discipline strategies, has a powerful and long-lasting effect on a child's development (Baumrind, 1993; Dekovic & Janssens, 1992). Baumrind's research has demonstrated that the authoritative pattern—making reasonable, firm demands accepted as legitimate by the child, giving directions in ways that give the child some degree of choice, and consistently using positive discipline strategies—is the pattern most likely to help children achieve competence. Children of authoritative parents tended to be socially responsible and independent when first observed in preschool. When these children were 8 and 9 years old, both boys and girls from authoritative families were still quite competent in the cognitive and social spheres (Baumrind, 1996; Baumrind & Black, 1967).

Other chapters in this text show that as consistent a use of positive discipline strategies as possible by an authoritative caregiver:

- Helps children feel safe and secure
- Encourages children to be self-responsible
- Fosters healthy self-control
- Encourages children to be empathic
- Helps to build authentic self-esteem *and* a strong core of personal values

The authoritative style and positive discipline strategies help children feel safe and secure. One of a child's most basic needs is for safety and security, and an authoritative care-giver who uses positive discipline strategies in discipline encounters helps children feel both psychologically and physically safe. The caregivers clearly communicate rules that say, "I will not hurt you and I expect you not to hurt others." Adults who use positive discipline strive to speak to children respectfully and refuse to degrade or demean chil-dren. Authoritative adults know that children control their own behavior best when they are not afraid of being hurt and when they feel safe and secure.

The authoritative style and positive discipline strategies encourage children to be self-responsible. Children learn to take responsibility for their own actions when they have good models of self-responsible behavior. Authoritative caregivers use positive discipline strategies such as I-messages which model self-responsible behavior. They accept responsibility for their actions and do not blame others for how they them-selves feel or act. They are nonjudgmental as they explain the consequences of a child's choice of safe behaviors.

The authoritative style and positive discipline strategies foster healthy self-control. Our long-range goal in guiding children is to help children achieve healthy self-control. We want them to be able to regulate their own behavior and to *want* to behave appropriately in school as well as 5, 10, or 20 years from now. Children develop the ability to regulate or control their behavior when they interact with warm and sup-portive adults who use positive discipline (Hart, DeWolf, Wozniak, & Burts, 1992). Teachers and parents who use positive discipline strategies help children learn to regulate their own behavior because they:

1. model self-control.
2. clearly communicate their expectation that children will show age-appropriate self-control.
3. give specific information on how children can control themselves.
4. recognize and encourage children who act in an age-appropriate self-controlled way.

The authoritative style and positive discipline strategies encourage children to be empathic. Piaget (1970) believed that there are certain *classical factors of development*—maturation, social interaction, and physical activity. He noted that social interaction helps children gradually become less egocentric and more empathic because contact with other chil-dren and adults exposes children to ideas different from their own. The ability to see things from somebody else's perspective—***perspective-taking***—is a cognitive develop-mental skill that begins to develop in early childhood but does not develop automati-cally (Selman, 1976). Authoritative teachers and parents who guide with positive discipline are themselves more empathic (Brems & Sohl, 1995). They model empathy and encourage children to look at things from someone else's perspective. Adults can guide children's understanding of that other viewpoint by taking the time to explain the other person's perspective.

Example: Teacher to a 5-year-old "I think that you hurt Shondell when you hit him. I can tell because he is crying." This teacher's discipline strategy will help the child understand how Shondell might feel after being hit. The teacher has actually told the child how Shondell feels and has avoided simply asking, "How do you think Shondell feels?"

The authoritative style and positive discipline strategies help to build authentic self-esteem and a strong core of personal values. Competence, confidence, and a sense of worthiness are the cornerstones of positive self-esteem. One of our goals as early childhood educators is to help children develop authentic self-esteem and develop a core of personal values that guides them to believe in the rights of others to dignified, fair treatment.

Children are motivated by a need to be competent and to have confidence in their ability to do things well, whether it is finger painting, making and keeping friends, doing math problems, or training a puppy. A positive approach to discipline helps children feel competent and confident enough to behave appropriately (Bishop & Rothbaum, 1992). It takes time and effort to use positive discipline strategies, and children who experience positive discipline view themselves as worthy of an adult's time and effort. Adults who rely on positive discipline strategies also model, expect, teach, and encourage fair, dignified treatment of other people and animals.

Example: Mrs. Lu quietly and calmly introduced the gerbils to her first graders during the morning's circle time. With the teacher's guidance, the entire group developed the *kindness rules* when dealing with the gerbils. They printed the kindness rules and posted them near the gerbil house. Mrs. Lu reminded the children about the kindness rules at other group times, and she pointed to the rule about being quiet around the gerbils when Jessie and Lee started talking too loudly near the gerbil's house.

The Author*tarian* Style

Level of demandingness and responsiveness

Authoritarian adults are high in demandingness but low in responsiveness. In terms of demandingness, they develop arbitrary limits and then state them poorly. They tend not to monitor or supervise children's activities very well. They do not confront children; when they do confront a child, they do so in a mean-spirited way.

In terms of responsiveness, authoritarian adults show a lot of negative affect, such as irritability and anger. They view their caregiving role as difficult and do not enjoy it. They tend to have a rigid interactional style with children and also report negative perceptions of children (Trickett & Susman, 1988).

Authoritarian adults tend not to understand child development and therefore tend to have unrealistic expectations of children. They find it difficult to tune in to a child's signals or needs. For example, they would very likely ignore a baby's signals or cries; when they do respond, their irritation is evident as they abruptly pick the baby up. Authoritarian caregivers usually view toddlerhood as the time of an inevitable clash of wills as the adult tries in vain to control the independence-seeking toddler. Authoritarian adults also tend to ignore needs and signals from 3- to 8-year-olds, concentrating on what they themselves want, regardless of whether it hurts or is in the best interests of their child.

Authoritarian adults order and blame when communicating with children. Their style relies on force, and they place great value on unquestioning obedience and discourage verbal give-and-take between an adult and child. They tend to suppress individuality and independence or autonomy in their children.

Authoritarian adults arbitrarily rely on negative discipline strategies and equate discipline with punishment (Trickett & Kuczynski, 1986). Adults in authoritarian systems use a combination of **negative discipline strategies** such as harsh corporal punishment, threats, lies, shame or ridicule or sarcasm, hostile humor, love with-drawal, and refusal or inability to teach a different way to behave. These negative discipline strategies reflect their need to control and blame and their inability to deal openly with issues. Authoritarian adults tend to focus on short-term control, possess fewer actual discipline skills than do authoritative adults, and are more crit-ical and less praising of children's behavior (Aragona, 1983).

This textbook devotes an entire chapter to positive discipline strategies, but I will describe the major negative discipline strategies in the next brief section. Many of the children you will teach or work with have experienced these strategies, and you will better understand their background with this knowledge base. We are justified in our concern about the negative discipline strategies used by authoritarian parents because parents who abuse children frequently are frustrated and angry after using ineffective adult discipline strategies (Herrenkohl, Herrenkohl, & Egolf, 1983).

Authoritarian adults often use harsh corporal punishment. There are many ways to hurt a child in the name of discipline, and, sadly, we have all seen examples of this hurtful strategy: slapping, hitting with hands or some other instrument, punching, biting, pinching, pushing, yanking. The common thread that ties all of these together is the use of harsh corporal punishment (physical force or coercion) to try to change behavior.

Why would an adult do something this hurtful to a child? And, once they see the effect, how can they continue to hurt a child? Researchers have identified pos-sible explanations, all of which may help us as we work to help authoritarian adults change their style. Adults who inflict physical pain either refuse to or cannot take the perspective of the child they have hurt, and they even try to defend what they think is their right to use harsh physical punishment (Bavolek, 1980). They also minimize the real harm that they inflict.

Examples: Two-year-old Judy bit her playmate on the arm. Judy's baby-sitter, frustrated and angry about Judy's biting, grabbed and bit Judy and asked, "How does *that* feel?" Later, the baby-sitter told a friend that she taught Judy not to bite other children when she showed her how much it hurt to be bitten. Judy, however, did not stop biting.

Two-year-old Sam ran out into the street. His father ran out after him, grabbed him by both arms, and started shaking him. Sam's neck and head were whipped back and forth. (Shaking causes life-threatening damage such as hematomas, reti-nal detachment, and hemorrhages to children of all ages and should *never* be used.)

Authoritarian adults use threats. Garbarino, Guttman, and Seeley (1986) cite ter-rorism as a form of psychological abuse, a form whose goal is to create a climate of fear and anxiety. Threats create fear and anxiety and are negative and hurtful because a child knows that the threat may actually be carried out.

Example: At the fish and bait store, 5-year-old Tim was fascinated by all the fishing gear. He was gazing at a display of lures when his dad, who was eager to get going, said, "You come with me right now or I'll leave you here."

Authoritarian adults are willing to lie to children. Adults with an authoritarian style do not talk openly and honestly about issues. So, instead of identifying and stating their needs or legitimate limits, some use lies, a form of manipulation, to change or control a child's behavior. However, this ends up eroding whatever trust has been established. They also model lying to others and that lying is the lazy person's way of getting out of the hard work of interacting honestly with others. Philosopher Sissela Bok (1978) notes that lying is almost never an acceptable way to interact with others, even with other liars.

Authoritarian adults often use shaming, ridicule, and sarcasm. Some authoritarian adults use shaming strategies to try to change children's behavior. These adults shame or ridicule their children, or allow a sibling to shame a younger child. A child who is shamed may think that she is fundamentally bad or unworthy. Constant shaming may prevent adapting appropriately to life and may interfere with the development of self-discipline and authentic self-esteem (Bradshaw, 1988; Bredehoft, 1991; Greenberg, 1991). Authoritarian adults who deny their own feelings have great difficulty allowing children to acknowledge feelings, especially unpleasant feelings such as anger. As a result, they shame a child's anger (Marion, 1993, 1994, 1998).

Authoritarian adults often use hostile humor. A sense of humor is a gift we have been given, a gift that helps us put things in perspective and relate to others in a funny, loving way. But there are several ways in which humor can be misused, and one of these misuses is when humor is used as a weapon, to express hostility. Adults who cloak their anger and hostility as humor demean children. Hostile teasing is aggression, not humor. Hostile aggression humiliates children and has no place in a relationship in which both adult and child have a right to respectful treatment.

Example: When Ryan had his first ice-skating lesson, he was afraid of falling down. His dad called him a sissy and made him get moving. At home that night, Dad cruelly imitated what he called "sissy-boy Ryan's" fearful approach to the ice and his wobbly start on skates. Ryan burned with embarrassment.

Some authoritarian adults withdraw love. Some adults, thinking that a child has misbehaved, show their disapproval by withdrawing their love and affection. Adults withdraw love in a variety of ways: refusing to talk or listen to, threatening to leave or abandon, or glaring at the child (Hoffman, 1970). Adults tend to withdraw love when they have trouble dealing with their own feelings and when they can't figure out how to deal with problems. They rely on an old, ineffective system rule to decide how to deal with a child's annoying behavior.

Withdrawing love has some of the same negative effects as hitting or being sarcastic. The adult does not tell the child why he is angry, and therefore does not help the child understand how his behavior caused a problem for others. Withdrawing love does not help a child develop empathy, and it diminishes interaction between adult and child.

Example: Michael, 7 years old, was a little slow in getting to his dad's car after softball practice. Dad was angry and Michael sensed it when his father refused to talk to him and stared straight ahead. As they drove, dad glanced at Michael occasionally and shook his head, but he said nothing.

Authoritarian adults forget or refuse to teach and encourage a different way to behave. These adults tend to focus on misbehavior, putting lots of energy into telling children what *not* to do, and they also tend to ignore children's efforts at doing things right. These adults follow their system's rules, and the rules do not allow the adults to think about new and more appropriate ways to deal with issues.

Example: When 5-year-old Samuel cursed, Dad would say, "Knock it off now, Samuel!" His dad never told Samuel why cursing might not be acceptable and never gave him any other ways to express his emotions.

What is the impact of authoritarian caregiving and relying on negative discipline strategies?

The authori*tarian* caregiving style sets the stage for harm to children and encourages children's noncompliance (Baumrind, 1996). Other chapters in this text show that a consistent and arbitrary use of negative discipline strategies in the absence of a warm relationship:

- fosters poor self-esteem
- results in poor self-control
- does not stop unacceptable behavior
- fosters aggression
- reinforces adults for using harsh discipline and may become child abuse

Authoritarian caregiving and negative discipline strategies foster poor self-esteem. Children who experience negative discipline tend to have negative self-esteem (Coopersmith, 1967). They do not develop the competence, confidence, or sense of worthiness on which self-esteem is built. Instead, they mirror the lack of trust that is communicated through negative discipline. Negative discipline strategies are degrading and demeaning, and children who are ridiculed, hit, or rejected tend to feel degraded by such tactics.

Authoritarian caregiving and negative discipline strategies result in poor self-control. One of the major system rules followed by authoritarian adults is to control others, so they disagree with the idea that adults should help children make the gradual transition from *external control* (control by adults) to *internal control* (self-control). Children achieve self-control when adults teach them about how their behavior affects others and when they learn more acceptable behaviors. Authoritarian adults fail to give these important lessons, and their children do not learn or practice self-control. These children show little guilt or remorse when they have hurt someone and they are not very willing to confess a misdeed if they think they can get away with it (Hoffman, 1970).

Authoritarian caregiving and negative discipline strategies do not stop unacceptable behavior. Many adults are convinced that harsh forms of discipline are the best way to stop what they perceive as misbehavior. The problem, as we have known for decades now, is that high levels of punishment can suppress behavior for only for a short time and, surprisingly, can make the undesired behavior even worse (Church, 1963; Rollins & Thomas, 1979). Undesired behavior seems to occur at a more intense level than it did before the punishment, a phenomenon called **response recovery**. After the punishment is meted out, the behavior appears to stop. But when the adult stops punishing, the behavior often recovers and is often more intense.

Authoritarian caregiving and negative discipline strategies foster aggression. Children who experience negative discipline tend to be more aggressive than children who live in more positive systems. They either aim their aggression toward the adult who hurt them (Patterson, 1982) or they recycle their anger and use the same degrading behavior with people or animals who had nothing to do with hurting the child.

Example: Dad, angry with 6-year-old Ryan for crying, said, "Cut the crying or you'll really get something to cry about." Ryan stopped crying and walked outside. His dog barked a greeting to him, but Ryan threw a rock that smashed against his dog's kennel.

Children who experience authoritarian caregiving and negative discipline strategies also tend to use aggression with their own children when they become parents. Many children imitate the discipline of their parents when they become parents (Egeland, Jacobvitz, & Papatola, 1987).

Authoritarian adults are negatively reinforced for using harsh discipline. Authoritarian adults who rely on negative discipline strategies wrongly believe that this sort of discipline works because they have been *reinforced* for using it. For example, when Jim, a toddler, kicked his high chair, his teacher slapped Jim's legs and Jim stopped kicking. The teacher was reinforced for using slapping. The sequence goes like this:

- Jim kicked his high chair (a behavior that annoyed the teacher).
- Teacher slapped Jim's legs (a negative discipline strategy).
- Jim was surprised and stopped kicking—but only for the moment.
- Teacher thought, "Hmm, that worked." (Teacher was reinforced because the negative discipline strategy of hitting seemed to work to stop an annoying behavior.)
- The next day, Jim kicked his high chair again. (Response recovery is operating. Negative discipline strategy only stopped the behavior temporarily.)
- Teacher slapped Jim again. (Remember, slapping *seemed* to work yesterday.)

The real problem here is that hitting Jim became firmly entrenched in this caregiver's repertoire of disciplinary strategies. He has begun to believe that hitting was effective (Patterson, 1982). It becomes easy for adults to rely on an ineffective discipline strategy, especially when they do not know or do not practice more effective strategies or when they rationalize their harsh behavior.

Authoritarian caregiving, in its extreme form, is child abuse. How can this happen? One reason is that we live in a society in which many people accept violent ways of resolving conflicts. Many parents reflect this idea by using violence to solve family problems, and they use physical or psychological force that results in injury as discipline (Marion, 1983). Another reason is that negative discipline *seems* to work, but adults who use it do not realize just how ineffective negative discipline strategies are. A third reason is that adults are reinforced for using negative discipline and will tend to use the same method again. Finally, an adult who relies almost exclusively on harsh negative discipline strategies soon discovers that she must increase the intensity of the punishment in order for it to be "effective." The adults have to yell more loudly or hit harder, intensifying the strategy until it becomes abusive.

The Permissive Style

Level of demandingness

Permissive adults are low in demandingness. They allow children to regulate their own behavior and to make their own decisions. They establish very few guidelines, even about when children eat, watch television, or go to bed. They make few demands for mature behavior, such as showing good manners or carrying out tasks. They avoid imposing any controls or restrictions and have a tolerant, accepting attitude toward the child's impulses, even aggressive ones.

Level of responsiveness

Permissive adults are alike because they are all low in demandingness but they differ in their degree of responsiveness. Some permissive adults are highly responsive to children, but the others are quite low in responsiveness. Thus, there are two types of permissive adults.

The first type is called *permissive-by-choice*—low in demandingness and high in responsiveness. This group is permissive because they choose to be permissive. Their view is a part of their belief system about how children should be treated, and they firmly believe that children have rights that ought not to be interfered with by adults (Sears, Maccoby, & Levin, 1957). These parents do not demand much from their children, but they tend to be warm and responsive.

The second type of permissiveness is called *permissive-by-default* (Baumrind calls this group unengaged). These adults are also low in both demandingness *and* responsiveness. This group has drifted into being permissive. They are permissive not because of a strong philosophical belief in a child's rights but because their method of discipline has been so ineffective (Patterson, 1982). They would like to be able to set and maintain limits, but have been so ineffective in getting compliance from children that they have given up trying and might even begin to see some behaviors, such as aggression, as normal. Once on the slippery slope of permissiveness, these adults could not get off and have become unresponsive and indifferent toward children—they have become permissive.

Permissive adults tend to use unhelpful discipline. They do not hurt children, but they are not very helpful, either. For example, permissive adults often fail to set appropriate limits and, even when they do set a limit, they frequently fail to maintain it.

Example: The teacher told Liz to clean up her space at the art table. When Liz left the art table without cleaning her space, the teacher just shrugged her shoulders and walked away.

We guide children effectively by giving them enough of the right type of information so that they will be able to act appropriately under different conditions. This teacher did not follow through with her legitimate limit.

Permissive-by-default adults tend to natter and nag. These adults have tried to set limits but have been very ineffective. On occasion they still try to set limits, but they tend to talk so much that their child ignores their limits.

Some permissive adults use inconsistent discipline. One way of being inconsistent is for one person to deal differently with the same situation each time it occurs. Take biting as an example. Jerod's teacher was inconsistent when she ignored his biting one day and the next day told him, "No, no, Jerod. Biting hurts." The third time he bit another child, she ignored him.

Another way of being inconsistent is for two adults to deal with a behavior differently. They might disagree about how they will deal with any number of issues. Ryan's parents, for example, inconsistently dealt with Ryan's biting when Ryan was a toddler. Dad hit him and Mom ignored the biting (both techniques are ineffective and negative [Greenberg, 1991]).

The impact of permissiveness on children

Both children and adults pay a heavy price when adults refuse to make or give up making demands for maturity or to set clear, firm standards of behavior. Children from permissive systems tend to be low in impulse control and self-reliance, dependent, and not very competent either socially or cognitively. These results held when the children were 8 and 9 years old (Baumrind, 1967, 1971).

Case Study Analysis: Styles of Caregiving

Analyze the case studies at the beginning of the chapter by answering the following questions.

1. Both Matthew's and Joel's parents are permissive.
   a. Which boy has the permissive-by-default parent? Explain specifically what led you to this conclusion.
   b. In what way are the parents of the two boys alike? In what major way do they differ?
2. Jim's father is an authoritarian caregiver. Cite at least three pieces of data that you could use to support this statement.
3. Krista's mother is an authoritative caregiver. Explain why her way of dealing with Krista's biting another child so clearly illustrates the authoritatve style.

Parent Talk. Helping Parents Feel Competent and Confident About Dealing With Discipline Encounters

Parents are justifiably concerned about discipline. Many parents are aware of the effect that they have on their children's development, and most parents want to do the best for their children. Early childhood teachers can help parents gain the competence and confidence they need to manage discipline encounters well through well-planned early childhood family education activities. Parents need three things in order to understand and manage discipline encounters effectively and to feel confident in this part of their parenting role:

- A knowledge base
- Specific skill development
- An attitude favoring authoritative caregiving

Knowledge base. Becoming a parent does not guarantee that a person will know about discipline or any other parenting issue. Early childhood teachers can help parents learn fundamental information about the nature of discipline—what it is, that it can be positive or negative, that there are different styles of caregiving, and that they influence but do not determine their child's behavior. This knowledge base is essential for dealing appropriately with discipline encounters.

Specific skill development. Parents need and can learn specific skills related to discipline, skills that will add to their competence and confidence (Patterson, 1982; Patterson & Capaldi, 1991). There are many skills that you can help parents learn formally or informally, for example, how to set limits well, how to help children accept limits, how to use redirection, how to teach a new behavior.

An attitude favoring authoritative caregiving. Think about four different parents, one from each style described in this chapter. An authoritative parent has an attitude about discipline that will allow her to learn a lot from any source on discipline. She has a positive view of her child and understands that her style and chosen strategies affect her child. She is willing to learn about discipline. The authoritarian, the permissive-by-choice, and the permissive-by-default adults, on the other hand, need a shift in attitude before they can effectively use knowledge and skills about discipline.

BASIC PROCESSES ADULTS USE TO INFLUENCE CHILDREN

Modeling, direct instruction and coaching, using reinforcement and feedback, managing the environment, stating expectations, and encouraging children to modify their attitudes and understanding are the basic processes that all adults, whether they are authoritarian, permissive, or authoritative, use to directly and indirectly influence children. In this section you will read about each of these basic processes used by adults, whatever the caregiving style, to influence children. For example, all adults use the basic process of modeling, but an authoritarian adult models behavior that is very different from the behavior modeled by an authoritative adult. The process is the same, but the content is different.

Modeling

Much human behavior is learned simply by watching someone else perform the behavior. The other person is the model, and the basic process is *modeling.* Perhaps the best-known researcher to give us information about this process is Albert Bandura. His research (1971) demonstrates that children can effectively learn a behavior just by watching it. Even though children can learn from several types of models (e.g., cartoon characters, pictures in books, and movie or video characters), Bandura's group demonstrated just how powerful adult models are in demonstrating aggression. You will read more about this work in Chapter 10, which discusses different models of child guidance.

Mr. Simmons models cooperation in everyday activities like baking.

Children learn undesirable behaviors—such as aggression or abusiveness—by observing models. An authoritarian parent or teacher who disciplines by hitting or with sarcasm actually models (demonstrates) aggressive behavior. You will also see evidence throughout this book that children just as effectively learn more desirable and positive behaviors—such as generosity, cooperation, kindness, and helpfulness—through the same basic process. An authoritative adult who uses positive discipline teaches quite a different lesson than does the authoritarian adult.

Direct Instruction and Coaching

Direct instruction, or coaching, involves intentional and explicit teaching. There are lots of examples of adults influencing children through direct instruction. Teacher education students take curriculum courses so that they can learn to give direct instruction in math, science, social studies, and language arts. Adults also instruct children in matters of physical safety, such as traffic safety, safe use of toys, and how to recognize good and bad touches. We also instruct children about the correct way to hold a baseball bat, build a campfire, or skate a figure eight.

Adults influence children through direction instruction. Sean's father and their neighbor are teaching Sean about cars.

We can also give children instruction in the social sphere: how to make and keep friends, how to take another person's perspective, how to work cooperatively with friends, and how to resolve conflicts (King & Kirschenbaum, 1992).

Using Reinforcement and Feedback

Feedback is critical to learning. It gives a child information about how he is doing and allows for making changes. Maintaining a new skill is easier with a specific type of feedback called *reinforcement. Social reinforcement* refers to smiles, positive attention, praise, or positive physical contact. *Tangible reinforcement* refers to things like toys or food. Some adults use a *generalized reinforcement,* such as points, tokens, or smiley faces on a chart, and have the child acquire points or tokens for desired behavior and then trade them for an object or event that the child finds especially desirable.

Reinforcement, then, is the basic process that all adults use. An important thing to remember, however, is that adults reinforce behaviors that fit their value system and general caregiving style. Authoritative adults do not agree with authoritarian adults about appropriate behavior for children. Consequently, adults from the two caregiving styles would naturally reinforce different behaviors in children just as they model different behaviors for children. Which caregiving style, do you think, would reinforce children for fighting and hurting others and which would reinforce cooperation and generosity?

Managing the Child's Environment

Adults manage a child's environment by providing physical materials, the setting in which the child exists, and a time schedule. Researchers have examined the effects of a child's physical or temporal environment on several areas of development. For example, a well-designed and well-managed physical environment helps children become independent and to take the initiative (Howes, 1991; King, Oberlin, & Swank, 1990). A child's physical environment affects the development of several other social behaviors such as sharing (Caplan, 1991), expressing emotions (Honig & Wittmer, 1992), and managing anger (Denham, Zoller, & Couchoud, 1994; Marion, 1997).

Stating Expectations of Desired Behaviors

Example: "Ryan," called Mrs. Lu, "wash your hands and then you can help us cut up the fruit for our snack."

Mrs. Lu makes a conscious effort to define cooperative, helpful behavior. Authoritative adults like Ryan's teacher develop good rules or limits and then communicate them clearly to children. Authoritarian adults, on the other hand, tend to set too many arbitrary limits, and permissive adults may fail to communicate expectations at all.

Encouraging Children to Modify Attitudes and Understanding

Infants, toddlers, and young children have a central nervous system that enables them to process information and make sense of the world. Children can modify their behavior when someone takes the time to present them with additional or different information in a way that is appropriate to the child's particular level of development. Focus on teaching children to understand why they should or should not do certain things. Be gently firm about the need for the children to act more appropriately, and make it clear that there is a reason for acting more appropriately.

An effective way to do this is to help a child become more empathic. The goal is to gradually help a child to understand how his actions affect others and to gradually be able to take somebody else's perspective. Like most learning, this takes place gradually over a period of years and begins in infancy. The goal here is *not* to induce excessive guilt or to shame a child. A good way to arouse empathy is to describe another's situation in an open, direct way that still validates the other person and that does not accuse him.

Examples: After Ryan washed his hands, he went to the table where the teacher was cutting up fruit. Mrs. Lu said, "What nice clean hands, Ryan! That'll keep the germs away from the fruit."

Teacher to 4-year-old Bill: "I see from the job chart that it's your day to feed the gerbils. I'll bet that they're hungry. So, get the gerbil food and I'll help you put it in their house."

Third-grade teacher to Matthew: "No, Matt. Name-calling hurts feelings. We do not call other people names in this class."

Each adult avoided sarcasm, threats, and accusations while focusing on how the other person or animal might have felt. Arousing a child's empathy—having him "walk a mile in somebody else's shoes or tracks"—is a powerful technique because it encourages the child to examine and begin to understand how her behavior might well have affected someone else.

A common thread linking different forms of antisocial behavior, including child abuse, is the perpetrator's inability to take another person's perspective (Chalmers & Townsend, 1990). Preventing abuse involves helping abusive adults learn social perspective-taking. Helping children become empathic, to take the perspective of others, then, is an important task for teachers and parents during a child's first 8 years.

REFLECTING ON KEY CONCEPTS

1. Suppose that you are designing a workshop for newly hired teacher assistants. Explain to them what a *discipline encounter* is and then explain what a *discipline strategy* is.

2. One of the workshop participants says, "Discipline! That's so negative. I don't want to discipline the children." Help this teacher's aide understand why discipline can be either positive or negative.

3. You want to explain to your workshop participants the two dimensions of caregiving. Use Figure 2–2 to help you explain to participants what demandingness and responsiveness mean.

4. Next you want to name and describe the three styles of caregiving for participants. Do this by briefly describing how demanding and how responsive a person from each style would be. Describe for the group the effect that each style seems to have on young children.

5. Finally, list the ways in which all adults influence children. Give examples of each.

APPLY YOUR KNOWLEDGE

1. You have read several examples of Mrs. Lu's authori*tative* style in this chapter. One morning, this is what she saw. Ryan, one of the children in her first-grade classroom, yelled loudly into the gerbil's house, sending the frightened animals scooting for cover. Role-play how you think that Mrs. Lu would guide Ryan in this discipline encounter, using information from the chapter on how she manages her classroom and deals with similar situations. From the several examples featuring Ryan in the chapter, what would you say is likely to be the origin of his aggressive behavior?

2. Accentuate the positive! Do a real-world observation and find examples of positive authori*tative* caregiving. You should be able to see lots of good examples by visiting a variety of places in which you can observe adults and children interacting, for example, grocery store, park, family reunion, laundromat, place of worship, school. Briefly describe the setting and record the approximate age of the child(ren). Write a description of each interaction. Report why you think that this was an example of authori*tative* caregiving.

3. You are the leader of a parent education group. A frustrated parent of a 5-year-old child asks you what she should do to get her child to put her trike away and not leave it in the driveway. Use the ***basic processes of influence*** (e.g., modeling, direct instruction, and others described in the chapter) as you offer this mother some practical and realistic suggestions for guiding her child. Be prepared to present your suggestions to your class.

References

Anderson, C. A., Hinshaw, S. P., & Simmel, C. (1994). Mother-child interactions in ADHD and comparison boys: Relationships with overt and covert externalizing behavior. *Journal of Abnormal Child Psychology, 22,* 247–265.

Applegate, J., Burke, J., Burleson, B., Delia, J., & Kline, S. (1985). Reflection-enhancing parental communication. In I. E. Sigel (Ed.), *Parental belief systems: The psychological consequences for children* (pp. 107–142). Hillsdale, NJ: Erlbaum.

Aragona, J. A. (1983). Physical child abuse: An interactional analysis (Doctoral dissertation, University of South Florida). *Dissertation Abstracts International, 44,* 125B.

Bandura, A. (1971). Analysis of modeling processes. In A. Bandura (Ed.), *Psychological modeling.* Chicago: Aldine-Asherton.

Baumrind, D. (1967). Child care practices anteceding three patterns of preschool behavior. *Genetic Psychology Monographs, 75,* 43–88.

Baumrind, D. (1971). Current patterns of parental authority. *Developmental Psychology Monograph, 4*(1, Pt. 2).

Baumrind, D. (1977, March). "Socialization determinants of personal agency." Paper presented at the meeting of the Society for Research in Child Development, New Orleans, LA.

Baumrind, D. (1979). "Sex-related socialization effects." Paper presented at the meeting of the Society for Research in Child Development, San Francisco, CA.

Baumrind, D. (1993). The average expectable environment is not good enough: A response to Scarr. *Child Development, 64,* 1299–1317.

Baumrind, D. (1996). Parenting: The discipline controversy revisited. *Family Relations, 45,* 405–414.

Baumrind, D., & Black, A. E. (1967). Socialization practices associated with dimensions of competence in preschool boys and girls. *Child Development, 38,* 291–327.

Bavolek, S. (1980). "Primary prevention of child abuse: The identification of high-risk parents." Unpublished manuscript, University of Wisconsin–Eau Claire.

Becker, W. C. (1954). Consequences of different kinds of parental discipline. In M. L. Hoffman & L. S. Hoffman (Eds.), *Review of child development research* (Vol. 1). New York: Russell Sage Foundation.

Bishop, S., & Rothbaum, F. (1992). Parents' acceptance of control needs and preschoolers' social behaviour: A longitudinal study. *Canadian Journal of Behavioural Science, 24*(2), 171–185.

Bok, S. (1978). *Lying: Moral choice public and private life.* New York: Partheon Books.

Bradshaw, J. (1988). *Healing the shame that binds you.* Deerfield Beach, FL: Health Communications.

Bredehoft, D. (1991). No more shame on you: Discipline without shame. *Family Forum,* 6–7. St. Paul, MN: Minnesota Council on Family Relations.

Brems, C., & Sohl, M. A. (1995). The role of empathy in parenting strategy choices. *Family Relations, 44,* 189–194.

Caplan, M. (1991). Conflict and its resolution in small groups of one- and two-year-olds. *Child Development, 62*(6), 1513–1524.

Chalmers, J. B., & Townsend, M. A. R. (1990). The effects of training in social perspective—taking on socially maladjusted girls. *Child Development, 61,* 178–190.

Church, R. M. (1963). The varied effects of punishment on behavior. *Psychological Review, 70,* 369–402.

Coopersmith, S. (1967). *The antecedents of self-esteem.* San Francisco: W. H. Freeman.

Dekovic, M., & Janssens, J. (1992). Parents' child-rearing style and child's sociometric status. *Developmental Psychology, 28*(5), 925–932.

Denham, S. A., Zoller, D., & Couchoud, E. A. (1994). Socialization of preschoolers' emotion understanding, *Developmental Psychology, 30*(6), 928–937.

Dunn, J., Brown, J., & Beardsall, L. (1991). Family talk about feeling states and children's later understanding of others' emotions. *Developmental Psychology, 27,* 448–455.

Egeland, B., Jacobvitz, D., & Papatola, K. (1987). Intergenerational continuity of abuse. In R. Gelles & H. Lancaster (Eds.), *Child abuse and neglect: Biosocial dimensions.* Hawthorne, NY: Aldine deGruyter.

Garbarino, J., Guttman, E., & Seeley, J. W. (1986). *The psychologically battered child.* San Francisco: Jossey-Bass.

Greenberg, P. (1991). *Character development: Encouraging self-esteem and self-discipline in infants, toddlers, & two-year-olds.* Washington, DC: NAEYC.

Gursec, J. E., & Lytton, H. (1988). *Social development: History, theory, and research.* New York: Springer-Verlag.

Hart, C., DeWolf, M., Wozniak, P., & Burts, D. (1992). Maternal and paternal disciplinary styles: Relations with preschoolers' playground behavioral orientations and peer status. *Child Development, 63,* 879–892.

Herrenkohl, R., Herrenkohl, E., & Egolf, B. P. (1983). Circumstances surrounding the occurrence of child maltreatment. *Journal of Consulting and Clinical Psychology, 51,* 424–431.

Hoffman, M. L. (1970). Moral development. In P. Mussen (Ed.), *Carmichael's manual of child psychology* (Vol. 2). New York: Wiley.

Honig, A., & Wittmer, D. (1992). *Prosocial development in children: Caring, sharing, and cooperation: A bibliographic resource guide.* New York: Garland Press.

Howes, C. (1991). Caregiving environments and their consequences for children: The experience in the United States. In E. Melhuish & P. Moss (Eds.), *Day care for young children.* New York: Routledge.

King, C., & Kirschenbaum, D. (1992). *Helping young children develop social skills.* Pacific Grove, CA: Brooks/Cole Publishing Company.

King, M., Oberlin, A., & Swank, T. (1990). Supporting the activity choices of two-year-olds. *Day Care and Early Education, 17*(2), 9–13, 67–70.

Marion, M. (1983). Child compliance: A review of the literature with implications for family life education. *Family Relations, 32,* 545–555.

Marion, M. (1993, April). Responsible anger management: The long bumpy road. *Day Care and Early Education, 21,* 4–9.

Marion, M. (1994). Encouraging the development of responsible anger management in young children. *Early Child Development and Care, 97,* 155–163.

Marion, M. (1997). Research in review: Guiding young children's understanding and management of anger. *Young Children, 52*(7), 62–27.

Patterson, G. R. (1982). *Coercive family process.* Eugene, OR: Castalia Press.

Patterson, G. (1986). Performance models for antisocial boys. *American Psychologist, 41,* 432–444.

Patterson, G., & Capaldi, D. (1991). Antisocial parents: Unskilled and vulnerable. In P. E. Cowan & M. Hetherington (Eds.), *Family transitions* (pp. 195–218). Hillsdale, NJ: Erlbaum.

Pratt, M. W., Kerig, P., Cowan, P. A., & Cowan, C. P. (1988). Mothers and fathers teaching three year olds: Authoritative parenting and adult scaffolding of young children's learning. *Developmental Psychology, 24,* 832–839.

Rollins, B. C., & Thomas, D. L. (1979). Parental support, power, and control techniques in the socialization of children. In W. R. Burr, R. Hill, F. Nye, & I. Reiss (Eds.), *Contemporary theories about the family* (Vol. 1). New York: Free Press.

Satir, V. (1976). *Making contact.* Millbrae, CA: Celestial Arts.

Sears, R. R., Maccoby, E. E., & Levin, H. (1957). *Patterns of child rearing.* Evanston, IL: Row Peterson.

Selman, R. L. (1976). Social-cognitive understanding: A guide to educational and clinical practice. In T. Lickona (Ed.), *Moral development and behavior.* New York: Holt, Rinehart, & Winston.

Simons, R. L., Johnson, C., & Conger, R. D. (1994). Harsh corporal punishment versus quality of parental involvement as an explanation of adolescent maladjustment. *Journal of Marriage and Family, 56,* 591–607.

Trickett, P., & Kuczynski, L. (1986). Children's misbehaviors and parental discipline strategies in abusive and nonabusive families. *Developmental Psychology, 22,* 115–123.

Trickett, P., & Susman, E. (1988). Parental perceptions of child-rearing practices in physically abusive and nonabusive families. *Developmental Psychology, 24*(2), 270–276.

Chapter 3

Positive Discipline Strategies: Direct Guidance

After reading and studying this chapter, you will be able to

☼ List and explain the nature of positive discipline strategies, and explain why each is a positive strategy.
☼ Demonstrate how to use specific positive discipline strategies.
☼ Summarize and explain methods for talking with parents about positive discipline strategies.
☼ Analyze a case study by determining how positive discipline strategies could be used.

"Above all, we shall not harm children. We shall not participate in practices that are disrespectful, degrading, dangerous, exploitative, intimidating, psychologically damaging, or physically harmful to children. This principle has precedence over all others in this code."
(*Code of Ethical Conduct*, 1990, NAEYC)

Case Studies: Positive Discipline Strategies

The Infants and Toddlers

In the infant/toddler room of the child-care center, 7-month-old Simone grabbed the teacher's hair. The teacher removed Simone's hand and said, "O-o-o-h! Look at the birds, Simone," as she turned toward the window. Simone brightened when she saw the birds at the feeder. Seventeen-month-old Juanita scooted across the room toward the kitchen area, and the teacher scooped her up and carried her back to a small table, singing, "Juanita, Juanita, bubbles, bubbles. Let's make some bubbles." "Bubbles, bubbles . . . ," chanted Juanita. When two 23-month-olds banged their paper cups on the table, the teacher placed her hands lightly on each small hand, saying, "Listen carefully. Tell me whether you want grape juice or orange juice. John, tell me what kind of juice you want." John piped up cheerfully, "I want grape!"

Mike

In the same child-care center, in the room for older children, 4-year-old Mike stood next to the gerbil house and tapped rhythmically on the screen lid. The teacher's aide noted, "Good sound, Mike, but I can't let you disturb the gerbils. So I want you to come with me to the music corner to choose a drum for you to play." Later that day, Mike drummed on the gerbil cage lid again, and the aide was gently persistent in her limit that he use drums and not the gerbil house. Mike got the drums and did not try to drum on the animal's house again.

Jenny

Jenny, 6 years old, and Mom went to the store to buy a backpack for Jenny. They were in a hurry, and had just enough time to pick out the backpack and still get to a doctor's appointment. Mom could afford to buy a backpack but nothing else before she was paid again, but she forgot to tell Jenny about the hurried nature of the shopping trip and was too embarrassed to say that she had so little money. At the store Jenny started the "Look-Mommy-I-want-that-WHY-can't-I-have-it" game. "Mom, can I get the lunch box, too?" "No, Jenny. No lunch box." "But Mom, I want the lunch box. It has Big Bird on it, just like my new backpack!" "Jenny, stop it. No lunch box." "Why, Mom?"

At this point, Jenny increased her whining, and her mother, covering embarrassment with anger, responded with, "Shut up, Jenny!" Jenny then seemed to lose control and started crying. Mom grabbed her wrist, yanked her around, and yelled, "Knock it off, Jenny, or you'll get what's coming to you!" (Jenny's mother typically uses corporal punishment when she is very angry.)

In the last chapter, you studied the concepts of discipline and styles of caregiving. You learned that authoritarian, permissive, and authoritative caregivers differ in how responsive and demanding they are with children. They also manage discipline encounters in different ways. Authoritative, skillful teachers and parents know how to use a large number of different positive discipline *strategies*, each strategy appropriate with a specific child at a specific time. They realize that they are most effective when they have a large repertoire of skills to meet the individual needs of the children.

Example: Mr. Cunningham repeated a limit to Meg; used an I-message with Juan; listened actively to Sean who was upset that someone had run over his toys; ignored the "Why" game two children played when it was time for cleanup; used a cue to remind Darnell to use his new behavior of washing hands; redirected behavior several times by using substitution; and taught Harry to withdraw from anger-arousing situations and then to responsibly manage angry feelings.

This teacher has achieved his high level of skill in the art and science of child guidance through learning, practicing, making mistakes, evaluating how strategies work, and learning and practicing some more. Now, when he is confronted with a discipline encounter, he automatically thinks about how to match a specific positive discipline strategy to a specific situation and child's needs. He has become increasingly more skilled in guiding children effectively (Frantz, 1993).

POSITIVE DISCIPLINE STRATEGIES

You will work with or have worked with lots of children in your career. Each child's unique genetic makeup, temperament, personality, family system, and other experiences have created an *individual*. Each child's needs call for individual solutions to the expression of those needs. Therefore, discipline strategies that an adult chooses should reflect this approach.

The major focus in this chapter is to describe a large number of specific positive discipline strategies (Figure 3–1). Baumrind (1996) says that adults differ in their tendency to use such discipline strategies like those those described in this chapter. This occurs because the strategies have to be learned and take effort to use. The value in knowing about these strategies and how to use each one effectively is that you will have more tools—a larger repertoire of positive strategies—for helping individual children meet their needs. You will be able to choose the most effective strategy in a variety of discipline encounters and will not be locked into dealing with each situation in the same way.

I have intentionally arranged the strategies in the order presented. Positive discipline strategies begin with adult behaviors: good limit-setting, clearly communicating limits, teaching more appropriate behavior; giving cues for the new behavior; giving choices; supporting children in their new behavior; changing something about a situation; and ignoring behavior when it is appropriate to do so.

Positive discipline continues when adults manage typical discipline encounters with positive, helpful strategies: redirection, active listening, I-messages, natural or logical consequences, conflict resolution, recognizing and dealing with strong emotions, and withdrawal from emotion-laden situations. The core of positive discipline strategies, however, is the last one presented in this chapter: helping children save face and preserve their dignity in discipline encounters. This is the *sine qua non*, the most important and essential element, in child guidance.

Develop Appropriate Limits

Adults influence children by stating their expectations for desired behavior and helping children understand that there are boundaries, or limits, on behavior.

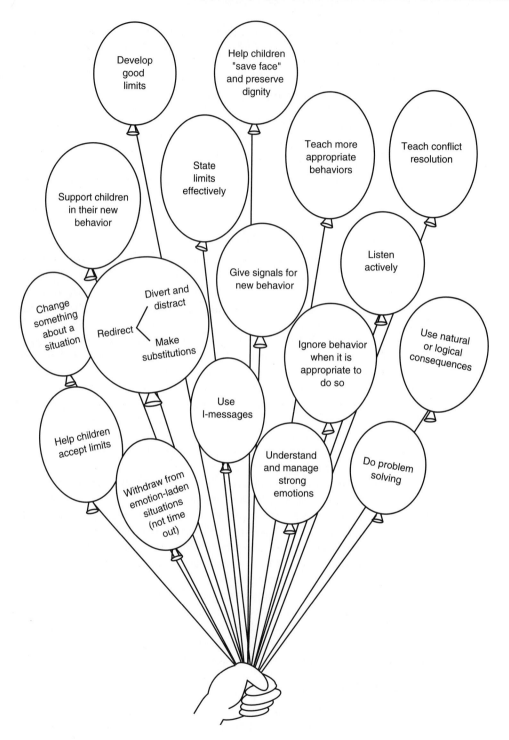

Figure 3–1.   Authoritative adults know how to use many positive discipline strategies.

Authoritative caregivers understand the importance of proper boundaries in relationships in general and appropriate limits in an adult–child relationship in particular. They figure out and clearly communicate limits that will be most helpful in encouraging children to behave appropriately. They understand what a good limit is and what appropriate limits do for children (Marion, 1992; Minuchin, 1974).

Appropriate limits focus on important things and are never arbitrary

Good limits focus on important, not trivial, things. They protect children's health and safety, encourage the development of healthy self-control, and transmit our values of dignified, fair, humane treatment of people and animals to children.

Health and safety rules. Disease spreads easily in group settings for children. Appropriate limits are designed to protect the health of both adults and children.

Examples: Thorough hand-washing, proper handling of food, washing and sterilization of toys and other equipment, use of tissues when sneezing, hand-washing after sneezing, wearing of appropriate bad-weather clothing, and proper diapering routines are all important in group settings for children.

Appropriate limits ensure safety. Think about safety on different levels. One level governs the use of toys and equipment. Typical rules might be "You can ride your trike, but crashing is not allowed," or "You can only play inside the playground's fence." Another level of safety rules deals with a child's inner feeling of safety and security. Children feel safe when they know that they will not be hurt; therefore, a safe place for children has rules that forbid hurting others.

Examples: "Yes, Joe. You *are* angry, and that's OK, but I won't let you hit Jim."

"Use words to tell him that you want your truck back. No hitting in this room. Hitting hurts."

Center director to teachers in a workshop: "In this center, we use positive discipline strategies as outlined in the policy manual. This means that we refuse to hurt children. We NEVER shake children of any age, we NEVER use corporal punishment, and we NEVER say anything that is degrading or demeaning."

Encouraging healthy self-control through limits. We help children achieve internal control and learn how to work well with others when we encourage them to make choices and help them experience safe consequences for their choices. Reasonable, fair rules help children develop self-control because they clearly communicate choices to be made and safe consequences for those choices (e.g., having a child paint only on her own paper or choosing another activity).

Good limits help children develop a firm set of values about respectful treatment of others. Responsible adults set and maintain limits prohibiting degrading or hurtful treatment of others. Examples include rules on humane treatment of animals ("Hold the kitten gently") and forbidding name-calling and making fun of others ("I think Donna feels sad because you called her 'fatso.' No name-calling in this room, Tom").

Good limits are developmentally appropriate.

NAEYC published the booklet *Developmentally Appropriate Practice* that focuses on appropriate practice in several key areas, including guidance (Bredekamp, 1986) and issued a position statement on developmentally appropriate practice (DAP) in early childhood education (Bredekamp, 1997). A part of developmentally appro-

Good limits, e.g., "Pet the rabbit gently," teach children about respectful treatment of other people and animals.

priate guidance is the area of limit setting based on a child's developmental level, that is, setting limits that are suitable for a particular child at a specific age (Toepfer, Reuter, & Maurer, 1972).

Authoritative adults are highly responsive, and a part of this is that they understand how children grow and develop. They are aware of the rapid cognitive, linguistic, motor, and social changes that set the stage for the development of self-control during the first 8 years of life. As children grow and develop, authoritative adults begin to expect different behavior from them. They are ready and willing to examine limits as children get older to make sure that the rules are valid for a child's changing developmental level. For example, an authoritative teacher might permit a 2½-year-old to climb only to the second rung on a rope ladder but allow the same child at age 4 to climb higher because she has greater motor skills and self-control.

Help Children Accept Limits

Authoritative caregivers and teachers use know-how to work on helping children willingly accept good limits. They do several things to set the stage so that children will accept legitimate boundaries on behavior. Here are some practical ways to get you started on communicating limits effectively.

Researchers demonstrated many years ago how important it is to set the stage so that children can accept a limit (Schaffer & Crook, 1980; Stayton, Hogan, & Ainsworth, 1971). Adults who effectively help children accept limits tend to believe that children are naturally compliant (Haswell, Hock, & Wenar, 1981). These authoritative adults tune in to a situation, help children focus on the task at hand, and give good cues. Here are some practical hints for helping children accept reasonable limits. These sound quite involved, but when you observe a teacher doing this you will note how smoothly and quickly the process goes.

- *Observe what the child is doing before stating a limit.* Be responsive and take into account what a child is doing because her activity is important to her. If Carlotta is putting together her favorite puzzle when the cleanup signal is first given, she will very likely try to finish her work before putting things away.
- *Give children a reasonable amount of time to complete their work before officially beginning to clean up.* Announce cleanup quietly to the whole group, to small groups, or to individuals and then allow the children a bit of time to finish up their work.
- *Decrease the distance between you and a child.* Avoid calling out limits from across the room. Decrease horizontal distance by walking toward a child. Decrease vertical distance by bending or stooping so that you can talk directly to a child (Satir, 1976).
- *Get a child's attention.* Touch Carlotta on the arm and look at her directly but in a nonthreatening way. The use of nonthreatening, nonverbal cues and appropriate physical contact[1] is essential with toddlers (Schaffer & Crook, 1980) and is highly recommended with preschoolers, especially those who have not learned to live with reasonable boundaries and limits.
- *Direct a child's visual attention to a specific object or task.* "Here's one of the puzzles that you worked on, Carlotta, at the puzzle table," you say as you show her the puzzle you are holding and then point to the puzzle table. (This is called **orientation compliance;** its purpose is to properly orient the child before stating a limit or making a request.)
- *Have the child make contact with a specific object.* Place the puzzle in her hands, "You hold the puzzle while we walk over to the puzzle table." (This is called **contact compliance;** its purpose is to help the child tune in to the task at hand before she is asked to do anything specific.)
- *Make your specific request (ask for **task compliance**).* Carlotta is much more likely to comply with your request because you have properly oriented her. It is much easier for a child to accept the cleanup limit when she is at the puzzle table holding the puzzle than when she is sitting in another area listening to a story when cleanup is announced.

STATE LIMITS EFFECTIVELY

Use a clear, direct, validating communication style. Our goal in the art and science of child guidance is to be helpful to children. Help them accept necessary limits by

---

[1]A note on appropriate physical contact: it is a source of comfort to a young child and is a part of the style of sensitive, supportive, encouraging adults. Appropriate physical contact reassures a child, is never imposed on a child, and is given in response to the *child's* needs. With recent concern about child abuse in child-care centers, it would be prudent for center personnel to be clear about the center's policy of appropriate physical contact between staff and children. This policy must also be clearly communicated to and discussed with parents (Phyffe-Perkins & Birtwell, 1989).

clearly communicating enough information so that they are able to carry out a suggestion:

- *Speak naturally, but speak slowly enough that the child hears everything you say.*
- *Use concrete words and short sentences when stating limits.* "Put your puzzle in this first slot of the puzzle rack" tells a child exactly where the finished puzzle goes and is a more effective thing to say than "Put it over there." Avoid using abstract words or phrases like "in a little while," "be a good boy," or "knock it off."
- *Tell a child exactly what to do rather than what not to do, and be as positive as possible.* It is more helpful to say, "Use this tissue to clean your nose" than "Don't pick your nose!" (Go to the Apply Your Knowledge activities at the end of the chapter for an opportunity to practice this skill.)
- *Use suggestions whenever possible.* Suggestions are statements very often phrased as a request.

Example: Jenny's mom (chapter opening case study) said, "I have an idea, Jenny. Let's write what we want to buy at the store on this piece of paper and take it with us today." Children cooperate more frequently and willingly when adults use suggestions than if they order children to do things. Suggestions are a part of the communication style of authoritative adults and suggestions rely on persuasion, not force, to gain a child's cooperation (Applegate et al., 1985; Baumrind, 1993, 1996; Lytton, 1979).

- *Use direct, self-responsible statements when you think it is necessary to use a command.* Authoritative adults occasionally have to state a very direct request but their style is highly responsive. For example, Mr. Cunningham had warned the children about cleanup on the playground, but Jacob was still zipping around on his trike. "Whoa, there!" said the teacher as he signaled Jacob to stop. "I gave the signal for cleanup and now want you to park the trike. See if you can fit it in the first space." This type of direct request is firm but still responsive because it relies on persuasion. Self-responsible adult communication elicits much more cooperation than do power-centered orders, for example, "Jacob, put that trike away right now!" Ordering others around is a part of communication based on power (Applegate et al., 1985) and seems to arouse anger and resistance, not cooperation.
- *Give choices when appropriate.* Making wise choices is a skill and must be learned and practiced. It does not happen automatically. Authoritative caregivers skillfully offer manageable choices to children.

Example: Mr. Cunningham asked Anthony, "Do you want to wear the green or yellow paint apron?"

When-then statements help children make a choice: "When you put on your paint apron, you may paint at the easel." Avoid giving a choice when the child really has no choice, for example, "Do you want to wear a paint apron?" A very likely response from a child to this question is a yes or no because this is a closed type of question.

Time and pace suggestions well

Good *timing and pacing of limits* helps children accept and comply with limits (Schaffer & Crook, 1980). You have good *timing* if you are focused and remain aware of what children are doing before stating a limit. You have good *pacing* of instructions and suggestions if you give instructions at a rate the child can easily deal with or if you ask a child to work at a speed that matches her developmental capabilities.

Here are suggestions for timing and pacing your limits properly:

- *Issue only a few suggestions at a time.* "Hang your painting. . . . Now, wash the part of the table on which you worked . . . OK . . . nice and clean. . . . Now, wash your hands and hang up your apron."
- *Avoid giving a chain of limits.* Children tend not to remember and therefore not comply with a rapid-fire series of commands.
- *Allow enough time for the child to process the information and carry out the limit.*
- *Allow enough time for the child to complete a task before issuing another suggestion.*
- *Repeat a limit if necessary, but do it effectively.* Avoid restating the limit every 5 seconds or simply stating the limit again in exactly the same way, because this tends to result in noncooperation.
- *Look for ways to restate the limit more effectively.* Suppose a child ignores your request. Frustrating? Yes, but avoid taking the child's behavior personally. Avoid getting angry; remember that your job is to help this child accept a simple limit. You will be most effective if you manage your emotions well and repeat the limit calmly and with goodwill. Try calling his name again, picking up one of the toys, matter-of-factly handing the toy to him, and then repeating the request.

Give reasons for rules and limits

Children accept limits much more readily when they understand the rationale behind them (Baumrind, 1996; Lytton & Zwirner, 1975). These practical suggestions will help you give reasons well.

- *Give short, simple, concrete reasons along with the limit.*

Example: "No hitting in our room." (The reason?) "Hitting hurts."

- *Decide when to state the reason*—either before or after stating the limit, or after a child complies with the limit.

Examples: State the rationale *before* you give the limit: "We need tables cleared of toys before we can have snack [the reason]. Put each puzzle back in the rack [the limit]." Children tend to argue less about a rule if they hear the reason first and the limit second.

State the rationale *after* you state the limit: "I want you to put the puzzles away [the limit] so that the table is clear for snack [the reason]."

State the rationale after the child complies with the limit: "The puzzle table is clear! Now we can eat snack at that table."

- *Decide whether you need to repeat the rationale* if you restate the limit. Repeating the rationale is a good idea when you want to emphasize the reason for the limit, perhaps when children are first learning a limit. Be aware, however, that some children might try to distract you from carrying through with a limit by playing the "Why" game, that is, repeatedly asking, "Why?" Ignoring their "Why?" is one of the most helpful things you can do for them. Or you can say, "I think you're having fun asking me why and I'll tell you why one more time and then the game is over" (Seefeldt, 1993).

Example: Mr. Cunningham said to his group of children before going out to the playground on the second day of school, "Tell me our safety rule about how many children are allowed on the sliding board at one time. . . . That's right . . . only one at a time so that nobody gets hurt."

Teach More Appropriate Behavior and Give Signals or Cues for Appropriate Behavior

Teach more appropriate behavior

Mr. Cunningham realized that proper hand-washing was critical in promoting wellness in early childhood settings (Niffenegger, 1997). He was concerned because most of the children in his group of 4-year-olds did not wash their hands after using the bathroom or before they ate. And his reminders after they forgot to wash their hands did not seem to be working. To achieve his goal of getting the children to willingly wash their hands, he decided to teach the more appropriate behavior—hand-washing—rather than nag about not washing hands. He focused on modeling the more appropriate behavior.

Example: Mr. Cunningham made up a puppet play showing hand-washing before lunch and after using the bathroom. He invited one of the fathers, who was a nurse, to model correct hand-washing, and small groups of children practiced hand-washing with him. Finally, the teacher taught an action song about hand-washing to the whole group.

Give cues for the appropriate behavior

Children might not remember to do things, even though they have learned how. We can remind them of the limit in a low-key way by giving them a *signal* or *cue*.

Example: At the end of group time Mr. Cunningham verbally reminded the children to wash their hands for snacktime by having them sing the action song and then sending them to the bathroom. In the next few days he drew a picture of a child washing her hands and showed it to the group. "Where can we hang our picture so that it can remind us to always wash our hands after going into the bathroom?"

Support Children in Using More Appropriate Behavior

Some new behavior is rewarding all by itself. Consider teaching new behaviors that a child will find attractive enough to want to continue without any other reward.

Example: Paul did not wipe his paint smock when he painted. Mr. Cunningham made a new job for the job chart and assigned that job to Paul for 2 days. The new job entailed being the person who ran the paint smock wash. This person was in charge of checking all the smocks to make sure they were clean, and was also responsible for the new sponge and bucket.

Consider adding external support. This strategy comes from the social learning model of child guidance and is described in greater detail in Chapter 10. Effective praise and token systems are practical and positive ways to encourage new behavior (see Hitz and Driscoll [1988] for a good discussion of praise and encouragement).

Example: Jenny's mother (chapter opening case study) learned how to use a token system to encourage Jenny to ask for things in a normal tone of voice. She devised a simple chart, and for each time Jenny asked for something in a normal tone of voice, Jenny got to use a special ink stamper on the appropriate day's spot. Her mom asked her what she would like to trade for a completed card (3 days of at least two stickers), and Jenny said she would like to rent a video at the store.

Mom also encouraged Jenny with effective praise—specific, sincere, and non-judgmental: "You used a normal voice for asking for your juice, Jenny. Thanks!"

Change Something About a Situation

Managing discipline encounters effectively usually involves asking yourself the following question: "What can I do about this situation that will help this child be safe or help her choose a different, more appropriate behavior?" For example, "Do I want to keep telling these two children to stop fighting over the blocks, or can I change something to help them accept the idea of cooperating?" There are three major ways to change a situation to prevent or stop potentially dangerous or inappropriate behavior: increase options, decrease options, and change the physical environment and time schedule if necessary.

Increase options available to the child

Authoritative adults are tuned in to a child's developmental level and closely supervise and monitor activities. They recognize when children need more options from which to choose, that children might be stuck on a nonproductive course of action and need additional information or choices. Here are three practical ways to increase options for children.

- *Introduce **new ideas** to children engaged in an activity.* Children can play cooperatively for a time and then run out of ideas to continue the play or they might have a conflict and not have the skills with which to solve the problem. Help them by offering a new idea or by walking them through the problem-solving process.

Example: Mr. Cunningham noticed that some of the children had worked cooperatively on building a train from large blocks for about 10 minutes. When he heard the arguing about who would be the conductor, he said, "Looks like you have a problem." Then he helped them decide on a rotation system so that everybody got a turn in the conductor role.

- *Introduce **new materials** into an activity.* There are a number of ways to do this. After assessing the situation and deciding that new materials would be helpful, you can quietly add the new item without comment, as Mr. Cunningham did when he brought out some new accessory toys when he realized that the children were building a farm and seemed to be ready for an expansion of the activity. You can also formally introduce the new materials to play or work sessions as needed.

Example: The day after the children argued about who would be the train conductor, they started to build the train again. Mr. Cunningham reminded them about their turn-taking system and told them about train tickets. He had prepared some simple tickets and said that there was one ticket for every child who was a passenger that morning on the train.

- *Prevent* *predictable problems.* Authoritative, responsive caregivers understand that young children have a difficult time controlling themselves or coming up with new ideas. They understand that it is their responsibility to observe the group for signs that adult intervention is necessary. One way to do this is to identify the times in your group's schedule when things could go wrong and prevent these problems whenever possible.

Example: Mr. Cunningham knew that some children awoke from nap before the others but still had to be quiet. Instead of just asking them to sit quietly, he increased their options by developing special quiet-time activities. He forestalled the problem by gathering a special group of toys and books for quiet play and then brought these materials out only after the nap. The children chose one of these activities.

Decrease options available to the child

Occasionally, the problem is not that children need new ideas or materials but that they need fewer options. Children are easily overwhelmed by too high a level of stimulation or too many choices.

- *Limit choices.* Making wise choices is a skill that develops over time. We are helpful when we teach young children how to make choices from only a few alternatives.

Example: Mr. Cunningham knew that Diane had great difficulty zeroing in on one activity, so he helped Diane focus her attention and limited her choices by asking, "I know how much you like to paint and to play with the flannelboard. Which of those two things would you like to do first today?"

- *Change activities.* Authoritative caregivers understand that a variety of things might affect children's attention or behavior. They are skillful enough and have enough confidence in their ability to vary plans or to abandon a plan if necessary.

Example: Mr. Cunningham had just gathered the entire group for the story when the roaring noise started. The earthmovers had moved onto the school grounds to start digging the swimming pool. "There goes group time," he thought. "OK, let's walk outside and stand out of the way so that we can watch for a little while. Then I'm going to tell you the story of an earthmover called 'Mike Mulligan'!"

Change the physical environment and time schedule if necessary

Guide children effectively by managing the environment well. You can easily change something about a situation by looking at how you have structured the physical environment and whether changes are necessary and asking yourself if a slight change would be helpful to children.

Example: When Mr. Cunningham was a first-year teacher he was surprised to find that the children ran, not walked, from the dramatic play area to the block area. His director observed one morning and said that the classroom had a zoom area in it—a tunnel-like space that just invited running. The teacher changed something about the situation by rearranging the room to eliminate the zoom area. The running stopped.

Example: Mrs. Winslow, a kindergarten teacher, found that her opening group time with the children was almost unpleasant because of all the talking and squirming. She asked the other kindergarten teacher to help her. Together they examined Mrs. Winslow's time schedule and discovered that the group time was too long. Mrs. Winslow adjusted the schedule and had a much shorter, much more productive and peaceful group activity.

Ignore Behavior When It Is Appropriate to Do So

Julie, 4 years old, used a wheedling, whiny voice when she wanted something. Her teacher felt irritated by the high-pitched, nasal sound, and since she wanted Julie to ask for help in a normal tone, she decided to ignore the whining and encourage Julie to speak in a normal voice.

This teacher used positive discipline strategies by teaching, cuing, and then supporting Julie's new, more appropriate behavior. She also knew that it is just as important for her to stop paying attention to certain inappropriate behaviors, such as whining. *Ignoring behavior* (also called *extinction*) involves withdrawing reinforcement for a specific behavior or no longer paying attention to the behavior. Ignoring certain behaviors weakens the inappropriate behavior because the child stops getting reinforced for it. And, because the payoff is eliminated, there is no reason for the child to continue with it.

Some behaviors should not be ignored

It is irresponsible to ignore such dangerous behaviors as running into the street, hitting other children, hurting animals, or playing with an electrical outlet.

1. *Do not ignore a child's behavior that endangers anyone, including the child.* Authoritative adults do not hesitate to forbid certain classes of behavior, including dangerous, aggressive behaviors or behaviors that degrade others. A responsible, supportive adult teaches that such harmful behaviors will not be tolerated. Adults who ignore dangerous, destructive behavior lead children to believe that the environment is unresponsive to their behavior (Baumrind, 1996). Ignoring aggressive, destructive, or ego-damaging behavior gives tacit approval to this behavior, and the aggression will usually increase, which can also lead other children to think that adults will not protect them from aggressive outbursts.

2. *Do not ignore a child who damages or destroys property or acts in a way that could damage or destroy property.* Again, ignoring such destructive behavior conveys adult approval. Instead, give children a clear, direct, nonblaming message of disapproval for destructive behavior.

Example: "No banging into the tree trunk with the wagon, Kyle. You'll damage the tree. Keep the wagon on the path."

3. *Do not ignore children when they treat someone rudely, embarrass someone, are intrusive, or cause an "undue" disturbance.* Young children do some of these things because they might not yet know a better way of behaving; some older children may act this way because they have been permitted to. With younger children our job is to state guidelines and to teach that better way, not to ignore inappropriate behavior. Older children must learn that some adults value politeness and respecting boundaries and will set limits that convey these values.

Example: Calia charged right up to the computer station and sat down just as Lee was about to take his turn. Mr. Cunningham said quietly to her, "You are really eager to work at the computer! But, it's Lee's turn right now. Let's put your name on the list."

Guidelines for ignoring behavior

Adults who use this strategy successfully and humanely use the following guidelines:

1. *Tell the child that you will ignore a specific behavior whenever it occurs.* Julie's teacher has a right to try to stop giving attention to and to decrease an irritating behavior like whining, but she also has an obligation to act self-responsibly. She should tell Julie that she will stop paying attention to her when she asks for something with a whine: "Julie, I'm not going to pay attention to you when you whine. I won't look at you, and I won't talk to you when you whine."

2. *Realize that it takes time to effectively use the ignore strategy* because adults have given lots of attention to the very behaviors they want to eliminate.

Example: Later that afternoon, Julie, in her high-pitched voice, asked her teacher for paint. Julie's teacher followed through with her plan to stop giving attention and to stop reinforcing whining. Julie was surprised, even though the teacher had explained the procedure, because previously the teacher had paid attention to Julie's whining and was giving her what she wanted.

Julie did not stop whining after being ignored only one time. Like most children whose irritating behavior is being ignored for the first time, she tried even harder to recapture the teacher's attention by whining even more insistently. Her teacher was prepared for Julie's "bigger and better" whine. She knew that she would have to carry out the procedure at least one or two more times before Julie finally realized that she would not get what she wanted by whining.

3. *Decide to thoroughly ignore the behavior.* This is difficult because the adult has decided to change her own customary behavior. In order to help herself stop paying attention to and encouraging the whining, the teacher wrote the following list of reminders:

"Don't mutter to myself under my breath."

"Don't make eye contact."

"Don't communicate with this child verbally or with gestures."

4. *Teach and encourage more acceptable behavior.* Go beyond *ignoring* a behavior to teaching children some other, more appropriate behavior. Julie's teacher realized that Julie needed to be firmly and kindly reminded of a better way to ask for what she wanted. She said, "Julie, you're whining. I'll pay attention to you when you speak in a normal voice."

Redirect Children's Behavior—Divert and Distract the Youngest Children

Diverting and *distracting* are forms of redirection in which an adult immediately does something to distract a child from the forbidden or dangerous activity and then involves the child in a different activity.

Authoritative, responsible caregivers understand that they perform most of an infant's or young toddler's ego functions. For example, they remember things for the child and keep the very young child safe because an infant's or young toddler's concept of danger is just emerging. Authoritative adults accept responsibility for stopping very young children from doing something by setting limits that discourage certain behaviors, but they do so in a way that avoids being drawn into a power struggle.

Diverting and distracting the youngest children accomplishes both of these tasks. An adult who has told a child not to do something can avoid getting drawn into a power struggle by *immediately* doing something to distract the child from the forbidden activity and steering her toward a different activity.

Example: Mary, 16 months old, walked over to the bowl of cat food, picked up a piece, and started to place it in her mouth. The baby-sitter told her, "Put the cat food back in the bowl, Mary" (a short, clear, specific limit). Then the baby-sitter picked Mary up and said, "You know, I think it's time for us to take a walk!"

Example: Take another look at the case study for the infants and toddlers (case study chapter opening). The teacher in the infant/toddler room has attempted to redirect behavior through diversion and distraction. Which behavior did she try to stop for Simone? For Juanita? For the two toddlers? Remember how she immediately did something to distract each child from the forbidden activity and steered him or her toward a different activity. Give at least two examples of how the teacher effectively used the discipline strategy called *redirection through diversion and distraction.*

Redirect Children's Behavior—Make Substitutions When Dealing with Older Children

Substitution is a form of redirection in which an adult shows a child how to perform an activity or type of activity in a more acceptable and perhaps safer way. Substitution is an excellent strategy to use when you are faced with inappropriate behavior in children who are at least in Piaget's preoperational stage, approximately age 2 to age 6. It is also a good strategy to use with older children because it acknowledges

Tony's dad used diversion and distraction when he scooped Tony up to get him away from the kitchen where pots were bubbling on the stove: "Oh Tony, look at the puppet."

the child's desire to plan and engage in a specific activity. But first the adult must accept the responsibility of developing the substitutions to demonstrate the first step in the process of problem solving.

Example: Mr. Cunningham saw Celia aim her brush at Jerry's picture. The teacher stepped in and said, "Paint on one of these pieces of paper, Celia, not on Jerry's. Which size do you want to use?" He then led Celia to the other side of the easel.

Children may test adult commitment to substitution by trying the inappropriate activity again—later in the day, the next day, or with a different person.

Example: Celia swung around from her side of the easel to try to paint on her friend's painting. The teacher said, "Paint on *your* paper, Celia." Celia eventually accepted the substitution because the teacher resisted getting drawn into a power struggle and continued to make the substitution calmly and with goodwill.

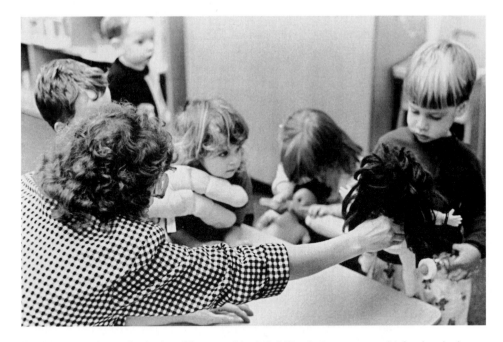

Redirect by using substitution: "You use this doll, Mike, but you may not take Jessica's doll."

Example: Mike's teacher (see chapter opening case study) used substitution effectively. When did the teacher show Mike how to perform the same activity in a more acceptable way? How did Mike test the adult's substitution? Explain how the teacher continued to use a positive discipline strategy when he responded to Mike's testing of the substitution.

Listen Actively

Active listening is a positive discipline strategy that comes from the work of Carl Rogers and which is taught in Gordon's (1978) Parent Effectiveness Training (P.E.T.) program (see Chapter 10 for a detailed description of this strategy). Active listening is the skill that responsible adults use when a child *owns a problem,* when something is troubling a child, and when the adult can best help a child by listening actively and responsively to the feelings implied in the child's words.

Active listening involves focusing on what the child says, not interrupting, not offering solutions, listening for the feelings in the words, suspending judgment, avoiding preaching, and then feeding back your perception of the feelings.

Example: Janelle was about to be vaccinated. She jumped off the examination table and scooted under it. The doctor knelt down, peered under the table, and said, "Looks like you'd rather hide than have this vaccination, right?"

"I don't like needles."

"Sounds to me like you really don't like them."

"They hurt!" More quietly, "They hurt my arm."

"They sure do hurt for a little while, don't they?"

An authorit*arian* caregiver would have dealt with Janelle's behavior quite differently. Such a caregiver would very likely have perceived her jumping off the table and hiding as misbehavior and would have punished her in some way. In many cases children communicate their deepest fears or try to tell us through their behavior that something is wrong in their world. We will discover what is wrong only if we take the time to listen actively. And we discover through active listening that a child can change her own behavior with our assistance.

Deliver I-Messages

An *I-message* is a positive discipline strategy used by an adult when a child has done something that interferes in some way with that adult's needs. The essential element is the adult's acknowledgment that the adult owns his own feelings of irritation, annoyance, sadness, anger, or fear. He does not accuse the child of causing these feelings, but does take responsibility for communicating these feelings to the child in a respectful, nonaccusatory way. The goal is to give the child the opportunity to change his behavior out of respect for the adult's needs.

Effective I-messages have three parts

Mr. Cunningham is a mentor for a first-year teacher at the center. The teacher had a discipline encounter with Matthew who immediately left a center when the signal for cleanup was given, leaving whatever he had been working on to somebody else (usually the new teacher) to put away. Mr. Cunningham helped her understand that she "owned" the problem, that she was annoyed, and that she should let Matthew know in a nonaccusatory way. He asked her to consider using an I-message.

1. *I-messages give data about the child's behavior but avoid accusing a child:* "Matthew, when I give the signal for cleanup, I have seen you leave the block area and go to another center every day this week. . . ."
2. *I-messages tell the child how his behavior tangibly affects the adult:* ". . . and that has meant that I have had to put away the things that you are working with. . . ."
3. *I-messages tell the child how the adult feels:* " . . . and I feel a little irritated because I don't have enough time to get ready to read our story."

Use Natural and Logical Consequences

A well-delivered I-message implies that an adult accepts responsibility for her own feelings. But, after infancy, children also have some responsibility for their behavior (Maccoby & Martin, 1983), and some adults use the *consequences* strategy to let a child know what her part is in a problem and how she can change things.

Natural and logical consequences support children in accepting responsibility for their own behavior. Consequences encourage children to choose appropriate behavior because they know what the consequences of their behavior will be before they choose the behavior. Advocates of using consequences believe that this strategy helps children learn from the natural or social order of events (Dinkmeyer & McKay, 1988). The discipline strategy of using consequences comes from the work of the Adlerians (see Chapter 10); this skill is taught in the parenting course known as Systematic Training for Effective Parenting (STEP).

Natural consequences

Examples: Susan refused to eat lunch. The natural consequence of choosing not to eat lunch was hunger well before afternoon snacktime.

Tom took off his mittens when making snowballs. The natural consequence was cold hands.

Notice that each result (consequence) followed the child's behavior inevitably (naturally), without an adult's intervention. There are some natural consequences that responsible adults would *never* allow to occur if they could prevent them, because such consequences bring great bodily harm to children, such as getting hit by a car while playing near or in a busy street; getting burned after touching a barbecue grill, iron, or stove; or getting shocked by electricity while playing with electrical outlets. They would, instead, substitute safe logical consequences.

Logical consequences

Logical consequences are safe consequences that would not have occurred naturally and are designed by an adult. The natural consequence of running into a busy street is getting hit by a vehicle, but a logical consequence is to choose to play inside the house. Logical consequences are most effective when

- *the adult has delivered an I-message* so that the child is aware of the exact nature of the issue.
- *the consequence is "logically" related to the unsafe or inappropriate behavior.* You will have used punishment, and not consequences, if the consequence is unrelated to the behavior.

Example: Tim's dad had to move Tim's bicycle and toys from the driveway before he could park his car. He used logical consequences when he stated an I-message and then said, "Tim, I can't park the car with all the toys lying around. So I'll put them in the shed if you decide not to pick them up tomorrow." (He would have used punishment if he had said, "You either pick up those toys or there will be no baseball game for you on Saturday!")

- *the consequence is one the adult can really accept and that the child would likely view as fair even though he might be unhappy about it at first.* Tim's dad could accept putting the toys in the shed for a short time but would probably not have been able to accept running over the toys with the car or giving the toys away. Tim would probably view Dad's actions as fair. (*Note:* Some authoritarian adults could accept giving away the toys or running over them, but this a mean-spirited, negative strategy often used by parents who psychologically abuse their children.)

- *the consequence is well timed.* All discipline strategies are more effective when they are timed well. Adults guide children most effectively when they accept a child's choice and then allow the consequence to occur as soon as possible after the child chooses.

Steps in using logical consequences

The following steps for using logical consequences are based on Dinkmeyer and McKay (1988).

1. *Respectfully restate expectations and tell the child how to change things.* Give the child a safe choice. This is a critical part of using consequences. Remind the child of the limits and give specific suggestions about how to change things. Offer alternatives. You design the safe consequences. Adults usually are feeling irritated when they have to apply logical consequences, and it is easy to turn irritation into sarcasm. So state the choices in a way that conveys your respect along with your message. You will be more effective if your tone of voice is friendly, firm, and nonthreatening.

Example: "We're in the gym to play a game, Penny. I expect you to listen for directions and for safety rules. You can listen to the directions and safety rules and play with us, or you can see how the game is played while you sit on the sidelines. You choose."

2. *Allow the child to make a choice.* You can accept either choice because you have designed these choices to be safe and they do not degrade the child.
3. *Tell the child that you accept her choice* by allowing safe consequences to occur. Take action.

(Penny continues to be disruptive.) "OK, you've decided to wait for us on the sidelines and see how to play the game. You can try again the next time we have gym."

(Penny settles down and joins the group.) "I see that you've decided to play the game with the class. We sure like to have you playing."

There is some disagreement about the consequences strategy. For instance, Alfie Kohn (1996) describes it as a pseudo- or false-choices strategy. Kohn believes that consequences are just a lighter form of punishment. How do you feel about this?

Teach Conflict Resolution and Problem-Solving

Conflict between two people or within a group is almost inevitable. Relationships do not have to be severed because of conflict, but can actually become stronger if people learn to resolve conflict through good problem-solving. Responsible, authoritative caregivers adopt this perspective and accept the challenge of supporting young children in learning how to recognize and manage conflict creatively rather than merely punishing behavior that frequently accompanies conflict between children (e.g., conflict over possessions) (King & Kirschenbaum, 1992; Marion, 1993, 1994, 1997; Smith, 1982).

You will study Gordon's method (1978) of conflict resolution called the *no-lose* method in Chapter 10. This method involves teaching children five steps in resolving a conflict, from identifying and defining the conflict to following up and evaluating how well the solution worked. This is a direct method of positive discipline because it focuses on teaching skills in problem-solving.

Parent Talk. "But, What About Spanking?"

One of your tasks as a teacher is to clearly communicate the school's or center's policies, including discipline policies and strategies, to parents. You will have to think through this issue and then be able to articulate the center's policy without insulting parents who, according to Socolar (1995), believe in spanking. Your goal is to establish rapport and then maintain a good relationship with parents so that you can work effectively with each family and child. There are a number of steps that you can take to explain the school's policies about positive discipline strategies to parents.

Write it down! Let parents know from the outset what the center's child-guidance policies are. Use the NAEYC Code of Ethical Conduct (NAEYC, 1990) as a base and write your own center or school policies from that. Incorporate your guidance policies in a policy manual written just for parents. Then it will be clear to parents that the school has a guidance policy, that it is based on a professional group's guidelines, and that it is positive in nature.

Focus on teaching. Are you going to do home visits? Then, as a small part of your visit, plan on talking with each parent about a few of the specific positive discipline strategies that you use. Does your school have a newsletter? Write a brief article explaining a specific discipline strategy. Does your school have a parent's bulletin board? Use this space to display information about a specific strategy. Are you having a group parent meeting? Then, explain the guidance policy along with all the other policies and highlight one or two positive discipline strategies.

For example, explain how you set limits and then how you restate them if a child does not seem to listen the first time. Lots of parents react almost with a reflex action with spanking when their child does not obey immediately. Or explain how you use redirection. You are a teacher and you can best help parents through teaching.

Do a needs assessment. Effective teachers work as a partner with parents. Make a list of the many positive discipline strategies that your school will use and ask parents to check off the ones that they would like to know more about. Work with parents by giving them information on the strategies that they have identified as an area of need. Do this through your early childhood family education program, which includes one-on-one interaction with parents as well as more formal methods like group meetings.

Listen with respect, avoid being judgmental, and avoid arguing. Some parents will ask questions about the school's policies that simply call for clarification of a specific policy. A few parents will challenge a policy. Some might even want to engage you in a protracted debate about controversial discipline strategies like spanking that are often perceived as negative. In all cases you will best help parents by remaining calm and professional. Do not argue with a parent.

Suppose a father says, "I was spanked when I was a kid and it never hurt me!" You can neutralize such a statement and avoid arguing by *not* taking his statement as an attack and by saying respectfully, "Yes, lots of people were spanked and believe in spanking. Our school does not want to force ideas on anybody. But we do want parents to know that we guide children with positive discipline strategies."

Understand and Manage Strong Emotions

Harry is 4 years old and is often rejected by the other children, largely because he has such a difficult time dealing with anger. He strikes out at other children if they take something from him or if they frustrate him in some way. Mr. Cunningham, his teacher, sought help from his director and a child development consultant in developing a guidance plan that would help Harry. The teacher's immediate concern—that Harry got so angry that he hit somebody—was to protect the other children and to stop Harry's aggression. His long-term goal was to help Harry deal effectively with the issues that triggered his angry outbursts.

They developed a discipline plan that included several of the strategies described in this chapter. In addition, they thought Harry needed special help in recognizing and dealing effectively with the strong emotion of anger (Marion, 1993, 1994, 1997). (See Chapter 7 for specific guidelines on dealing with anger.)

Withdraw from Situations (*Not* Time-out)

Withdrawing from situations when necessary is a skill that a person can use throughout her lifetime, and teaching the skill of withdrawing is a positive discipline strategy. The main purpose of this strategy is to teach children how to take themselves out of situations when they lose control, are extremely angry, or endanger their own or someone else's safety. It gives children time to get their autonomic nervous system under control (Hole, 1981).

A secondary purpose in teaching withdrawal from certain situations is for adults to recognize that developmentally appropriate guidance/discipline involves attention to the special needs of specific children. Mr. Cunningham recognized that Harry's level of self-control was not very good when he was angry, as is true for lots of adults as well (Goleman, 1995). He felt uncomfortable with merely putting Harry in time-out, understanding that a punishment such as time-out would not teach Harry anything about himself or about anger management. So he decided to help Harry by gradually transferring management of his emotion of anger to him by teaching him how to withdraw from anger-arousing situations, which is exactly what he learned to do himself in an anger management workshop.

Guidelines for withdrawing/cooling off

1. *Encourage the child to focus on the times when the strong emotion is aroused.* In Harry's case, they focused on Harry's hitting, which followed his anger episodes.
2. *Give the child information about when and why he should withdraw.* Demonstrate respect for a child. Mr. Cunningham had a dual obligation: first, to prevent Harry from threatening or hurting other children and, second, an equally great responsibility to Harry—to act self-responsibly.

Example: Mr. Cunningham said, "You sure get angry. Angry enough that you hit the other children. I can't let you hurt them, and I want you to figure out when you are getting angry. I'll help you figure out those times. The teacher will thus actually perform the *ego function* of monitoring an emotion. "When you feel like you're getting angry, I want you to put up your imaginary STOP sign and to play the getaway game instead of hitting somebody."

3. *Demonstrate, explain, and make sure a child understands the process.* Mr. Cunningham gave Harry direction on how to withdraw, to take himself out of an anger-arousing situation.

Example: "Let's figure out what to do. You told me that you feel the motor in your chest when you are mad. [Harry had described the physical sensation of anger arousal as an R-R-R-R feeling.] When that motor starts, you put up your STOP sign. Let's practice putting up our STOP signs!" (They practiced.)

"Now, let's figure out where you'd like to go to get away from what made you mad." Harry decided that he would get away and watch the fish swim in the tank.

"You can tell me that the motor is starting up and that you would like to go watch the fish."

"Or, I will tell you that I think your anger motor is starting up and that it is time to STOP and go watch the fish."

"Then you'll go to the fish tank" (both walk to the tank).

Mr. Cunningham decided to also sit with him because he believed that Harry would benefit from learning how to relax. He taught him how to do deep-breathing exercises as a way to relax, regain control, and diffuse some of the energy of his anger.

4. *Follow through.* Help the child identify the target behavior when it occurs.

Example: "Hey, you! Give that to me!" was all the teacher heard before he saw Harry's arm swing up in preparation for a hit. He went quickly to him, catching his arm. He stooped and talked quietly to Harry: "Harry, your anger motor is going. Put up your STOP sign and take a deep breath and then go over to the fish tank. Let's do that right now." An adult is much more respectful if he reminds a child about the procedure, especially the first time it is used. And it is quite important you present this option respectfully and calmly.

5. *Help the child withdraw every time that behavior he has identified appears.* You will be most helpful if you use strategies consistently (Baumrind, 1996). Inconsistent discipline is not helpful and often makes behavior like Harry's hitting even worse. This is a difficult skill to learn and then to use, so you can expect to have to help some children for quite some time. They will not be able to withdraw on their own even after they have learned the strategy. There were times, for example, that Mr. Cunningham had to stoop and look in Harry's anger-struck face and say quietly, "Put up the STOP sign, Harry." Harry was so upset that he needed his teacher's help even though he had practiced withdrawing.

6. *Teach the child to withdraw as soon as possible after the target behavior occurs.*

7. *Teach and encourage more appropriate behavior when the child returns to an activity* after the withdrawal/cooling off. This is crucial. In addition to teaching stress management with breathing exercises, Mr. Cunningham also taught Harry the skill of verbalizing his frustration and telling someone what he wants (Marion, 1993, 1994, 1997).

Whatever happened with Harry? Progress was slow but steady, and hitting episodes and anger outbursts decreased gradually. After several weeks of encouraging Harry to get away when he felt anger, Mr. Cunningham observed him as he played in the block area, a place where he had previously had lots of unfriendly, angry interactions. He watched him look surprised and annoyed when John took one of his blocks. He gave a silent cheer when Harry stopped for a few seconds, scrunched up his mouth, closed his eyes, mouthed the word STOP, and then said, "That's *my* block, John. You can use it later. I have it now!" He did not need to physically remove himself to regain control. He had made an important transition—thinking about what to do instead of reacting to anger (Goleman, 1995).

Save Face and Preserve Dignity

Our ultimate responsibility is to help children save face and preserve their sense of dignity, no matter what positive strategy we use. Authoritarian adults degrade children by using negative discipline strategies. Some continue to humiliate the child by telling others about what the child did in front of the child, by saying, "I told you so" or "Now, let this be a lesson to you," to the child.

Use your perspective-taking skills. Put yourself in a child's place and think about how it would feel to have an adult telling you that you have to calm down or that you've done something wrong. How would you want this adult to treat you after the telling is over? With dignity.

This means that once you are done with the positive discipline strategy you let the episode go, let it become history, and allow the child to get on with things. No speeches or reasoning are necessary. This is especially important when a child has become enraged and has lost control and you have helped him regain control.

CHOOSING AN EFFECTIVE POSITIVE DISCIPLINE STRATEGY

This chapter described many positive discipline strategies. When a person is confronted with such a large number of possibilities, there is a tendency to feel overwhelmed. Avoid this feeling by looking at things differently. Adopt an optimistic perspective by keeping three things in mind. First, you are not expected to be an expert in using positive discipline strategies after reading this chapter. Expertise evolves over time. You should be able, at this point in the book, to describe each strategy and realize why it would be an effective thing to do in some cases. That is called a knowledge base, the beginning of expertise.

Second, you will have a chance at the end of this chapter to build your professional self-esteem by doing some skill development in the Application of Knowledge section. I will "walk you through" using several positive discipline strategies. Then, as you work with children in classrooms, you will practice using these strategies and you will become more skillful over time.

Third, you will learn in this book specifically how to make decisions about which strategy to use in specific discipline encounters. You will be able to do this because you have learned and practiced the strategies. Chapter 11 in this text describes the Decision-Making Model of Child Guidance and shows you in a step-by-step fashion how to make wise decisions about which strategy to use.

Case Study Analysis: Positive Solutions for Jenny's Mother

Jenny's mother (chapter opening case study) was embarrassed and angry and used a negative discipline strategy. Boost her confidence as a parent by helping her learn that there are a lot of other more positive ways to deal with the same discipline encounter and then teach the skills that will enable her to use the positive strategies. Show her how to use the positive discipline skills called for in each of the following.

Help Jenny's Mom Learn to Set Limits

1. Show Jenny's mom how to set a limit on what they would be buying at the store before going to the store. (Be specific and follow the guidelines for limit-setting.)
2. People forget things! Suppose that Jenny's mom simply forgot to state a limit. Then, in the store, Jenny started whining. Tell Mom how she could state the limit in a direct, nonaggressive way by saying . . .

Help Jenny's Mom Teach and Cue More Appropriate Behavior

1. Show Jenny's mother how to teach Jenny a new behavior that is different from whining, such as asking for things in a normal, conversational tone of voice. Consider showing her how to model and give direct instruction.
2. Show Mom how to use cuing when they are in the store, if reminding Jenny is necessary. Explain why it is best to cue her daughter in a matter-of-fact, low-key way in a public place. Be prepared to role-play what this would look like.

Help Jenny's Mother Ignore Behavior

This time, help Jenny's mom ignore certain behaviors. Suppose that Mom *had* set limits before going into the store and that she had restated the limit when Jenny said she wanted a lunch box.

1. Explain why it would be appropriate to ignore Jenny's whining and arguments once appropriate limits had been clearly stated. Tell Jenny's mom specifically how to effectively use the ignore strategy in this case. List the essential things that you would tell her to do, or not to do.
2. How do you think she might feel when Jenny reacts with a bigger and better whine? Give her some hints on how to cope with the feeling and with other adults in the store who say that she "should do something to that kid to stop her squealing!"

Help Jenny's Mother Use an I-Message

Mom needs to know that even the most positive strategies do not always "work." She needs to know what to do when this happens so that she does not start using negative strategies out of frustration again. Suppose that Jenny's whining made them miss their clinic appointment and Mom has to reschedule. Show Jenny's mother how to use an I-message by writing exactly what you think she should say in each section. This skill is easy to learn but difficult to carry out, because a person is usually expressing some sort of unpleasant emotion like irritation, anger, or frustration.

1. Name the exact behavior that caused her problem.
2. Say how the behavior tangibly affected her (not how she felt, but the actual effect on her time, energy, plans).

(continued)

3. Then Jenny's mom has to actually say how she feels, because Jenny's whining has tangibly affected her. (Remember, the goal is not to induce guilt but simply to say how she feels. Jenny did not cause the feeling.) Mom owns that feeling and says, "I feel _____ because now I _____."

Help Jenny's Mom use Logical Consequences

Show Jenny's mother how to use logical consequences to support Jenny in making choices about her behavior and in her developing sense of self-responsibility.

1. What were Jenny's mother's expectations about Jenny's behavior while shopping?
2. Jenny's mom should restate this expectation/limit by saying this to give Jenny a choice.
3. Show Jenny's mom what to say that shows her acceptance of Jenny's choice.
   a. What would she say if Jenny had continued whining?
   b. What would she say if Jenny had stopped whining?

Help Jenny's Mother Preserve Jenny's Dignity

1. Children whose goals are blocked experience a great deal of frustration and even anger. They might even lose control. Explain to Mom why it might be best just to withdraw with Jenny to a spot (e.g., the bathroom of the store) and help Jenny regain control. Show Mom how to do this by holding Jenny's hands, encouraging her to breathe deeply, washing her face with a cool cloth, and saying little besides "It'll be OK."
2. Help Mom take Jenny's perspective again when they are ready to leave the bathroom. Explain how the other customers will be curious and that she can prevent any further embarrassment for Jenny. I believe that Mom would be most effective if she said the following to Jenny before leaving the bathroom. (Remember: no speeches, no preaching, no reminding of limits now. Remind her later. This is the time to let Jenny know that this episode is *over*).
3. I believe that, under the circumstances, Jenny should have a choice about whether to continue shopping this day, even if they think they should buy the backpack. I would ask her what she wanted to do by saying . . .

REFLECTING ON KEY CONCEPTS

1. What do you see as the main focus of a positive, as opposed to a negative, discipline strategy, that is, what is the major difference between the two?
2. Authoritative adults are skillful in using a cluster of positive discipline strategies. Explain to someone who has not read this chapter why it is so important for teachers and parents to understand and know how to use a large number of positive discipline strategies.
3. Some parents will have questions about a school's policies on positive discipline strategies and some parents will challenge the policies. Describe at least three practical and time-efficient ways in which teachers can help parents understand the child-guidance policies of the school, policies including the use of positive discipline strategies.

APPLY YOUR KNOWLEDGE

1. *Problems and Solutions: Each adult in the following vignettes is facing a discipline encounter (the problem).* Help this adult deal effectively with the discipline encounter by offering advice on how to use the specific positive discipline strategy mentioned (the solution). Refer to information in this chapter when writing your solution.

   The Problem: Cami walked over to the piano and started to bang on the keys. Her teacher called out, "Stop banging on the piano!"

   My Solution: I think that this teacher would be helpful and effective by telling Cami what to do instead of what not to do. The teacher can be positive, polite, and firm as she says, ". . . ."

   The Problem: Ed and Jim rode their trikes at breakneck speed and their teacher said, "Stop driving so fast!"

   My Solution: This teacher would be more helpful and effective by telling the boys what to do rather than what not to do. I would advise that she say, ". . . ."

   The Problem: Tim's parents had been sitting in the booth at Burger Palace for 15 minutes. They had finished eating and were talking to each other. Three-year-old Tim wiggled off the bench, ran around, and then crawled under the table. His dad scooped him up and told him, "Now, you sit here and be quiet." Five minutes passed, and Tim, who had missed his morning nap, started screaming in frustration. His dad grabbed Tim's arm to try to quiet him, but Tim continued screaming.

   My Solution: I would change this situation by. . . . (Note: Tim must be supervised constantly, so sending him to the restaurant's playspace is not an option unless the parent goes with him.) Start your solution by stating whether you would increase options, decrease options, or change the physical environment and then go on to explain exactly how you would proceed.

   The Problem: Dad was frustrated when 10-month-old Richard kept crawling right to the uncovered electrical outlets. He said "No, no," every time his son approached the outlet.

   My Solution: I suggest that Dad change this situation by. . . .

   The Problem: John, 4 years old, has been working for 20 minutes in the sandpile constructing a "canal" for water (he has no water yet) when you glance over and notice that he is tossing sand into the air.

   My Solution: In addition to stating a safety rule, I would change this situation by. . . .

   The Problem: Sylvia finger painted on the window because, she says, she likes how the sun shines on the colors.

   My Solution: I would use the following substitution: (Note: The substitution must be appropriate and safe for the child and acceptable to you.)

   The Problem: Jake pulled a chair over to the shelf holding the record player and twisted all the knobs, trying to see how they worked.

My Solution: I would use this substitution:

The Problem: Pat wiped his nose on his sleeve.

My Solution: I would use this substitution:

2. *Spotlight on Positive Discipline Strategies.* You will be gratified when you get a sense of how well many adults use the positive discipline strategies described in this chapter. Get started by looking for examples of such strategies. Observe adults and children together in several different settings. Write brief descriptions of the adult–child interactions. After recording several examples, pick out and identify the positive discipline strategies. If you do see a negative discipline strategy used, resist the urge to make judgments, blame, or criticize. Instead, think about how the adult could just as easily have used a positive discipline strategy—if they had had the knowledge, skills, and attitude.

3. *To Ignore or Not to Ignore—That Is the Question.* The director of a large child-care center located in a manufacturing plant was preparing for the workshop on discipline for new aides at the center. He developed the following handout to go along with a discussion of behaviors that should or should not be ignored. He planned to have each group member circle their responses and offer their reasons. Based on the information about ignoring behavior in this chapter, what are the correct responses?

Should I Ignore This Behavior?

Look over this list and decide which of the behaviors you, as a teacher, should not ignore. Which could you safely ignore? Give reasons for your choices. Think about the types of behaviors that should *not* be ignored.

1. One child tells another child, "You're ugly!" Ignore?
   Yes No Reason:
2. A 3-year-old girl scribbles all over her drawing. Ignore?
   Yes No Reason:
3. Another child scribbles all over another child's collage. Ignore?
   Yes No Reason:
4. One of the children in your group forcefully splashes water from the water table onto the floor. Ignore?
   Yes No Reason:
5. Jan pulled Raphael's hair. Ignore?
   Yes No Reason:
6. "I don't want to clean up. Why do I have to clean up?" a 4-year-old asked argumentatively to the aide. Ignore?
   Yes No Reason:

References

Applegate, J., Burke, J., Burleson, B., Delia, J., & Kline, S. (1985). Reflection-enhancing parental communication. In I. E. Sigel (Ed.), *Parental belief systems: The psychological consequences for children* (pp. 107–142). Hillsdale, NJ: Erlbaum.

Baumrind, D. (1993). The average expectable environment is not good enough: A response to Scarr. *Child Development, 64,* 1299–1317.

Baumrind, D. (1996). Parenting: The discipline controversy revisited. *Family Relations, 45,* 405–414.

Bredekamp, S. (Ed.) (1986). *Developmentally appropriate practice.* Washington, DC: NAEYC.

Bredekamp, S. (1997). Position statement on developmentally appropriate practice in early childhood education. *Young Children, 52,* 34–41.

Dinkmeyer, G., & McKay, G. (1988). *S.T.E.P.: Parents handbook,* Circle Pines, MN: American Guidance Service.

Goleman, D. (1995). *Emotional intelligence.* New York: Bantam Books.

Gordon, T. (1978). *P.E.T. in action.* Toronto: Bantam.

Haswell, K., Hock, E., & Wenar, C. (1981). Oppositional behavior of preschool children: Theory and intervention. *Family Relations, 30,* 440–446.

Hitz, R., & Driscoll, A. (1988). Praise or encouragement? *Young Children, 43*(5), 6–13.

Hole, J. (1981). *Human anatomy and physiology.* Dubuque, IA: W. C. Brown.

Kohn, A. (1996). *Beyond discipline.* Alexandria, VA: Association for Supervision and Curriculum Development.

King, C. A., & Kirschenbaum, D.S. (1992). *Helping young children develop social skills.* Pacific Grove, CA: Brooks/Cole Publishing Company.

Lytton, H. (1979). Disciplinary encounters between young boys and their mothers and fathers: Is there a contingency system? *Developmental Psychology, 15,* 256–258.

Lytton, H., & Zwirner, W. (1975). Compliance and its controlling stimuli observed in a natural setting. *Developmental Psychology, 11,* 769–779.

Maccoby, E. E., & Martin, J. A. (1983). Socialization in the context of the family: Parent-child interaction. In P. Mussen (Ed.), *Handbook of child psychology* (Vol. 4). New York: Wiley.

Marion, M. (1992). Keynote address at the annual conference of the Oregon Association for the Education of Young Children, Portland, OR, October.

Marion, M. (1993). Responsible anger management: The long bumpy road. *Day Care and Early Education.* April 4–9.

Marion, M. (1994). Encouraging the development of responsible anger management in young children. *Early Child Development and Care, 97,* 155–163.

Marion, M. (1997). Research in review: Guiding children's understanding and management of anger. *Young Children, 52*(7), 62–67.

Minuchin, S. (1974). *Families and family therapy.* Cambridge, MA: Harvard University Press.

Niffenegger, J. P. (1997). Proper handwashing promotes wellness in child care. *Journal of Pediatric Health Care, 11*(1), 26–31.

Phyffe-Perkins, E., & Birtwell, N. (1989). "Comprehensive child abuse prevention: Working with staff, parents, and children." Presentation at the Annual Conference of the NAEYC, Atlanta, November.

Satir, V. (1976). *Making contact.* Millbrae, CA: Celestial Arts.

Schaffer, H. R., & Crook, C. K. (1980). Child compliance and maternal control techniques. *Developmental Psychology, 16,* 54–61.

Seefeldt, C. (1993). Parenting. Article in *St. Paul Pioneer Press.* Sunday, May 23.

Smith, C. (1982). *Promoting the social development of young children.* Palo Alto, CA: Mayfield.

Socolar, R. (1995). Spanking children is in even though it's out. *The New York Times,* Jan 15 V144, Sec. 1, p. 26 (col 1).

Stayton, D. J., Hogan, R., & Ainsworth, M. D. S. (1971). Infant obedience and maternal behavior: The origins of socialization reconsidered. *Child Development, 42,* 1057–1069.

Toepfer, D., Reuter, J., & Maurer, C. (1972). Design and evaluation of an obedience training program for mothers of preschool children. *Journal of Consulting and Clinical Psychology, 32*(2), 194–198.

Chapter 4

Developmentally Appropriate Practices and Early Childhood Classroom Management

After reading and studying this chapter, you will be able to

- Identify principles of designing DAP early childhood classrooms.
- Summarize effects of developmentally appropriate and inappropriate classrooms.
- List and describe well-designed and managed activity areas for early childhood classrooms for children 3 to 8 years old.
- Briefly describe curriculum, activities, and materials in a DAP early childhood classroom.
- Summarize research findings on the impact of the physical environment on cognitive development of infants and toddlers.

- ✹ Explain how these findings can help teachers of infants and toddlers make decisions about designing the physical environment.
- ✹ List activity areas appropriate for infants and toddlers and explain how these areas meet the developmental needs of infants and toddlers.

"The children in your care experience the environment indirectly through interactions with you and directly through their own experience with the physical setting."
(Colbert, 1997, page 22)

Case Studies: Classrooms Based on Developmentally Appropriate Practice

Miss Hume's Preschool Classroom

Miss Hume is one of the preschool teachers in a university child development lab. When her 19 4-year-olds come to school, they find a classroom organized into activity areas. The preschool teachers work together to develop a curriuclum that is based on principles of developmentally appropriate practice (DAP), and the activities in small-group learning centers reflect the DAP approach. On arrival each day, children find areas ready for work/play, and Miss Hume encourages each child to choose an area. On Monday these were the activities that the children worked on in different areas:

Reading/language arts area: There were four new library books on the rack. One of the books was about mixing colors, one of the current topics of interest to her class. She put out the flannelboard with figures for retelling a story she had told the previous week and set out the tape recorder and headset, along with a set of pictures illustrating a story on the table.

Science/math area: Math is a "hot topic" in this class! The parents have helped the teachers develop many homemade math materials (these homemade items are packaged, labeled, and stored for easy retrieval). Today, some of the children will work on the concept of larger/smaller "sets" on the table. She placed a "seriation" game on the table again because three of the children have showed interest in this particular concept. Three other math-related games were neatly placed on shelves in the math area.

The children seem especially interested in the butterflies fluttering around outside. So, Miss Hume added butterfly-related materials to the science table. She placed a butterfly display and a magnifying glass on the science table along with a new book about butterflies.

Dramatic play area: Children found a "backyard" complete with a small picnic table, umbrella, toy lawn mower set on a green carpet, and hand gardening tools along with artificial plants. Miss Hume planned to leave the new area up for several days.

Block area: To follow up a visit to the bus barn of the bus station, the teacher set out large pictures of buses, a real bus driver's hat, and a steering wheel set in a large wooden block in the block corner.

Art area: "Squish-squash, closely watch . . ." Miss Hume arranged four chairs around a small table and placed one lump of smooth, white play dough in front of each chair. The children had made white dough on Friday, and today's focus was to add one drop of red food coloring to each lump of white dough and to encourage squishing, squashing,

(continued)

predicting, observing, and describing color changes. The study and pleasure of observing color changes continued at the finger-painting table where blue and yellow paint was available. (The play dough and finger painting are both art and science activities in this integrated curriculum.) And, as always, there were lots of other art materials neatly arranged in see-through plastic tubs on the art shelf.

Manipulative toy area: The school invests a little each year in small, manipulative toys and a good storage system, so Miss Hume has access to lots of these items. On Monday she placed three old, frequently used, but well-cared-for puzzles on the table and set two tubs of small, interlocking blocks on the floor. The children could also choose from seven or eight other manipulative toys stored neatly on low, open shelves.

Mr. Pelander's and Miss Starr's Third-Grade Classrooms

Mr. Pelander and Miss Starr teach third grade in the Charles Wright Academy in Tacoma, Washington. The third-grade classrooms are set up in much the same way and the two teachers work together on developing the curriculum and activities for the children. Mr. Pelander (Pelander, 1997) has written about his transition from a conventional to a more DAP primary classroom, noting that one of the biggest changes was to have the courage to encourage children to make choices and be in control of their learning. For example, he used to list work to be done on the board and each child completed the work in sequential order.

Now he and Miss Starr provide a menu of activities that children can do in any order that they want. Assignments from the menus are due in seven or eight periods rather than in one period. Children may choose where they sit when working—at their table, on the floor, at a study carrel, or in the library. Here is a sample menu for morning work for a week (Pelander, 1998):

English:
> Journal/letter editing
> Job cards
> Daily oral language
> Word search
> Spelling
> Compose sentences

Reading:
> Comprehension cards (two)
> Reading skill cards
> Critical-thinking cards

Handwriting:
> Five of each lowercase letter (get the coach's signature:_____)

Math:
> Division paper (choose either half page or full page)
> Holey cards: Multiplication
> Fraction cards: Write them here: _____, _____, _____, _____, _____
> Math safari: Multiplication

Social Studies:
> Geo Safari
> States puzzles

(continued)

Choose a "differently abled" book. Read at least four pages and explain what you learned from the book. Explain why what you learned is important. Use complete sentences. This may be done with a partner.

Science:
Hypothesis/stop watches (done in pairs; please check boards)

Computer:
Math
Oregon trail
(Check Post-it notes on management chart)

Writing:
Copy your first writing of the year with your nondominant hand. With your dominant hand, tell about your experience.

Many children spend a good part of their early childhood years in some sort of group setting for young children—preschool, kindergarten, and primary grades. Many early childhood professionals in these classrooms base practice on principles of DAP. They understand the value of designing the physical environment, curriculum, and materials of any early childhood setting with DAP principles in mind.

This chapter will help you understand what a DAP classroom is like, what it looks like, how it was designed, the type of activities in it, and how a DAP classroom affects children's behavior. Most important, the chapter will describe and explain a set of principles that you can apply when designing any early childhood classroom, whatever the age of the children who will use that space.

The chapter first describes a set of principles for creating DAP classroom spaces. Then we will look at how those principles may be applied when you manage classrooms for infants and toddlers, preschoolers and kindergarten children, and for children in the primary grades (first, second, and third grade).

CLASSROOM SPACES BASED ON DAP

At first glance, classrooms for infants, toddlers, preschool, kindergarten, and primary children might seem to have very little in common. A classroom/caregiving space and curriculum for infants would certainly be different from a classroom and curriculum for second-grade children. And a preschool classroom would differ from a classroom for all other age groups in the early childhood years.

Our goal as early childhood educators is to create a developmentally appropriate learning environment for children, regardless of their age. All DAP early childhood classrooms share certain characteristics. There is a common thread that ties all DAP classrooms together whether the room is for infants or for second- and third-graders. That thread is a set of principles that was used to design the space and to plan the curriculum and the activities.

Principles of Designing DAP Early Childhood Classrooms

Developmentally appropriate early childhood classrooms are based on the following principles, which emphasize developmental needs of children; provide options; encourage choice, movement, and interaction; and emphasize positive guidance and concrete experiences.

- Developmental needs. Base the design of the physical environment on the developmental needs of the children using the space and acknowledge and accommodate individual differences among children.
- Developmentally appropriate curriculum. Plan a developmentally appropriate curriculum based on the needs, interests, and abilities of the children. Integrate the curriculum across traditional domains (math, science, social studies, language arts, music, art) through meaningful and relevant child hands-on activities (Hart, Burts, & Charlesworth, 1997; Krogh, 1995).
- Learning environment. Plan and develop a learning environment so that it is full of concrete experiences (Hart, 1993; Hart et al., 1997; Kostelnik, 1992). There are, for example, more stories, music, and center activities in DAP classrooms and more worksheets, waiting, and transitions in developmentally *in*appropriate practice (DIP) classrooms (Burts, Hart, Charlesworth, Fleege, Mosley, & Thomasson, 1992).
- Options. Provide options for children. Do not expect all children to be doing the same thing at the same time (Hart et al., 1997).
- Choice. Allow and encourage children to make choices from among the options.
- Active involvement. Encourage children to be actively involved with materials, peers, and adults.
- Movement. Arrange space to make it easy for children to move among equipment and materials. Allow and encourage children to move about the room (Caples, 1996; Marion, 1995; Pelander, 1997).
- Child guidance. Use developmentally appropriate child-guidance and positive discipline strategies (Marion, 1995).

The Effects of DAP Classrooms

Both researchers and practitioners have been interested for quite some time in the effect of a DAP classroom on children's development and behavior (Charlesworth, Hart, Burts, & DeWolf, 1993; David & Weinstein, 1987; Kritchevsky & Prescott, 1977). A classroom based on principles of DAP helps children become independent, learn to make sound choices and decisions, and to take the initiative (Howes, 1991; Jones & Prescott, NAEYC film #806; King, Oberlin, & Swank, 1990). Several studies suggest that children who attend more developmentally appropriate programs have better academic achievement (Marcon, 1993) and fewer behavioral problems (Marcon, 1994).

The physical design of the environment and equipment influences children's play and social interaction. Gandini (1993) described the schools in Reggio Emilia, Italy, and said that the layout of physical space in these schools encourages positive encounters, communication, and relationships, all of which are elements of a DAP classroom. The physical arrangement of specific activity areas influences children's play. For example, certain arrangements of play spaces specifically influences the level of sophistication of dramatic play (Petrakos & Howe, 1996).

On the other hand, a DIP classroom or program can contribute to poor academic achievement and behavioral problems (Marcon, 1994; Marion, 1995). Some of these discipline problems are very likely linked to stress that comes from being in a DIP classroom. A group of researchers has studied and continues to study the effects of inappropriate and more appropriate classrooms on stress in young children. They have found that there are higher levels of stress behavior in DIP versus DAP preschool and kindergarten classrooms (Burts et al., 1992).

In summary, all DAP classrooms are based on a common set of principles, and DAP classrooms have a positive effect on a child's development. Classrooms that are more developmentally appropriate result in far less overall stress than developmentally *in*appropriate classrooms.

Let's turn now to some of the specifics of designing DAP classrooms for the different phases of the early childhood period. We will look first at classrooms for preschool, kindergarten, and primary-grade (grades 1–3) children.

SETTING UP THE PHYSICAL ENVIRONMENT: DAP CLASSROOMS FOR PRESCHOOL, KINDERGARTEN, AND THE PRIMARY GRADES

Children more easily develop self-control, independence, competence, and prosocial behavior in well-organized classrooms (Stallings, 1975). Figure 4–1a is a floor plan of Miss Hume's preschool classroom and Figure 4–1b is the floor plan of Mr. Pelander's third-grade classroom (chapter opening case study teachers). One of Mr. Pelander's third-graders, Warren Kim, drew the floor plan. These are obviously classrooms for children at different points in the early childhood period but there are striking similarities.

Each teacher has designed the room following the principles of DAP. Each classroom's design is based on the developmental level of the children using the space. The space and schedule in each room encourage children to move and to control their environment. Both teachers look to the children's needs, interests, and abilities when designing the curriculum, so the learning environment emphasizes concrete experiences. Children in these well-designed, safe physical environments interact with the objects and people in that environment. The children choose activities from the array of DAP activities available. Children in each classroom are free to move about the room, and both teachers set reasonable, fair limits on movement to protect the children's safety.

Let's turn now to some practical things to consider when setting up or designing the physical environment in early childhood classrooms—organize the classroom into activity areas, develop enough activity areas, arrange activity areas logically, and create attractive and sensory-rich areas.

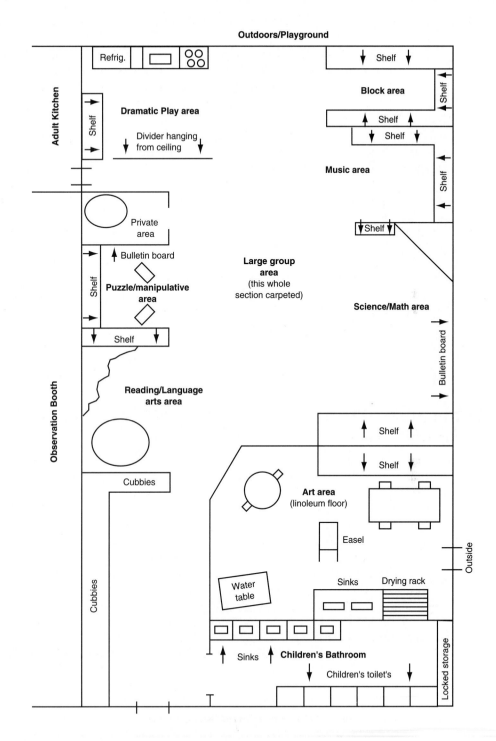

Figure 4–1a   Floor plan of Miss Hume's preschool classroom.

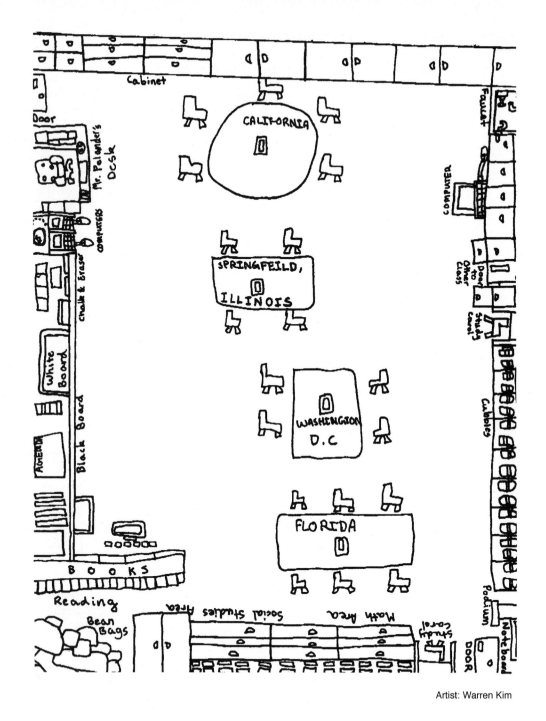

Artist: Warren Kim

Figure 4–1b Floor plan of Mr. Pelander's third-grade classroom.

Organize the Classroom into Activity Areas

One of the things that you will notice almost immediately about DAP classrooms is that they are organized into areas or zones of activity. This arrangement embodies the principles of DAP stated in the first part of this chapter. In spite of this common thread, teachers in DAP classrooms develop and arrange activity areas that support the overall curriculum goals that have evolved for the children in that classroom.

There are several different types of classroom activity areas. Some of the areas are small, some large; some have seating, others do not; specific materials are stored in some areas but other areas have no materials stored there. DAP classrooms tend to develop several learning centers (individual or small-group), a large-group area, and some sort of a private area. This section describes each type of classroom activity area and explains why each area is important in a DAP early childhood classroom.

Learning center: Small-group

Definition. A **small-group learning center** is a permanent or semipermanent space large enough for five or six children. Well-designed small-group learning centers serve a specific function reflecting the age of the children in that class as well as the school's curriculum goals. Examples of well-defined small-group areas include the following: math and science, computer center, a "manipulative" area (puzzles and other small-muscle equipment), reading and language arts, dramatic play, block center, and a creative arts area (Figure 4–2 shows two examples).

Figure 4–2a   Small-group learning centers in the preschool classroom. (Source: Adapted from Alward, K. R. [1973]. *Arranging the Classroom for Children.* San Francisco: Far West Laboratory for Educational Research and Development. Reprinted with permission.)

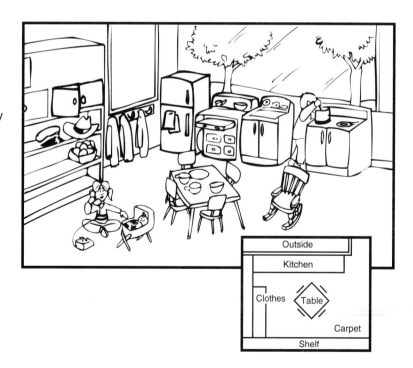

Figure 4–2b Puzzle and manipulative area (small-group learning center). (Source: Adapted from Alward, K. R. [1973]. *Arranging the Classroom for Children*. San Francisco: Far West Laboratory for Educational Research and Development. Reprinted with permission.)

Teachers in DAP classrooms create the types of centers that meet the needs of the children in that class. Therefore, not all classrooms will have the same small-group learning centers.

Seating arrangement. The seating arrangement varies with the purpose of each center, making this type of center quite flexible. Some centers call for a table and chairs, as in the preschool's manipulative toy area and the kindergarten's listening center. Some small-group learning centers do not require a table and chairs, such the kindergarten's block area or the third grade's reading area. You may also decide to arrange a center so that children can work either at a table or on the floor, as in the preschool's manipulative center. Clearly communicate a center's special function by separating it well from other areas in the room.

Some primary-grade teachers who have taught in more traditional classrooms are gradually moving toward a more developmentally appropriate approach. This entails allowing children to choose the order of the activities that they will do in a work period and then giving children more choices in where they work. Pelander (1997) said that during work periods children in his third-grade classroom have the choice of sitting at one of the tables, on the floor, or at a study carrel.

Materials for the center. The clear purpose of a learning center suggests that it would be wise to store materials related to the activity in the area. Avoid storing materials that are *not* related to the area's function in that area. Guide children indirectly by storing materials you want children to have access to within their reach, but store materials you do not want children to have access to out of their reach, for example, in closed cabinets or on higher shelves, as the preschool teacher has done in the dramatic play area (Figure 4–2a) and as Mr. Pelander has done in all of his third-grade centers.

Learning centers for small groups change over time. Small-group learning centers in DAP classrooms change as the needs, interests, and abilities of the children change over time. Teachers in more developmentally appropriate classrooms add materials needed for new activities, rearrange the seating of a center as needed, and remove materials no longer needed.

Example: At the beginning of the school year, Miss Hume set up the dramatic play area as you see it in Figure 4–2a. The children used the center a lot for a while but then Miss Hume noticed less and less play in that area in spite of placing different items of interest in the kitchen area.

Miss Hume concentrated on changing the area to rekindle interest in dramatic play. She recruited parent volunteers to develop prop boxes (Myhre, 1993) and collected some great dress-up clothes. The "office," the "backyard" (see case study), the "gardening" center, and the "fix-it shop" were all hits. Boys and girls working in the fix-it shop wore special "inspector" shirts and checked books and puzzles for needed repairs, inspected trikes for squeaks that needed oiling, examined dolls for necessary bathing and clothes-washing, and inspected animal housing for necessary cleaning and repair. They listed needed repairs in a notebook. Then they carried out these tasks under a parent's supervision.

Learning center: Individual

Some early childhood teachers include learning/work centers for individuals when designing their classroom. Mr. Pelander, the third-grade teacher, put in individual study areas and computer desks for individuals (Figure 4–1b). Figure 4–3 shows several examples for creating individual learning or work centers. This is a fairly flexible area because the same comments about seating arrangements and materials for the small-group learning area also apply to individual learning centers.

Large-group area

Definition. **Large-group area:** a space large enough to accommodate most or all the children for large-group activities (Alward, 1973) or several children during a work period. This space should be large, open, and flexible to accommodate group activities such as music, language arts, creative dramatics, stories, nutrition education, dance, and others that a teacher thinks would be appropriate to do as a group.

Seating arrangement. This depends entirely on the activity that takes place in the area. Some preschool teachers have a permanent large-group area in their room (Figure 4–4). Some teachers move a table or two to make room for a large-group activity. The third-grade classroom teacher does a large-group activity in several ways. At

Figure 4–3 Individual learning centers. There are lots of easy and inexpensive ways to create individual centers. (Source: Adapted from Alward, K. R. [1973]. *Arranging the Classroom for Children.* San Francisco: Far West Laboratory for Educational Research and Development. Reprinted by permission.)

times all the children sit at their group tables and at other times the class pushes aside a few tables and they sit in chairs or on the floor for a group activity.

Materials for the center. The large-group area serves many purposes. Therefore, specific materials are not stored in the large-group area but are brought there by the teacher. Miss Hume, the preschool teacher, has brought items for an obstacle course to the large-group area (Figure 4–4).

Figure 4–4   Large-group area in a preschool classroom. An obstacle course has been set up in this area for the day. (Source: Adapted from Alward, K. R. [1973]. *Arranging the Classroom for Children*. San Francisco: Far West Laboratory for Educational Research and Development. Reprinted by permission.)

Many teachers store items there that help them manage the large-group area well, such as individual pieces of carpeting that can be arranged in seating patterns and indicate to children where they are to sit before group begins. Some teachers keep the daily calendar there, or the puppet who introduces the activity for the day.

Private space

Definition. A **private space** is a small, semienclosed space with room for only one or two children, visually isolated from other children but easily supervised by adults (Bowers, 1990, Marion, 1995). There are no chairs or tables or special materials in the private area. Figure 4–5 shows the private space for our preschool classroom. A private space for a kindergarten or a primary-grade classroom would follow the same principles when developing them.

Reason for having a private space. Healthy systems acknowledge the right to privacy and the right to choose or limit contact with others. Teachers in DAP classrooms pay attention to the needs of both the whole group of children and of individuals.

Like adults, children need breaks from large groups, but we must make a special effort to teach children how to take these breaks and to pace their interactions. Well-designed private spaces can help us teach children to focus on learning when they can and should be alone without being disturbed (Bredekamp, 1987). Children

Figure 4–5   Private area in the preschool classroom. No special materials are stored here. There is room for one child. The private area is a place for quiet relaxation.

who are allowed to pace their interactions and control the degree of contact with others tend to be more independent and cooperative than children who are not permitted such control (Stallings, 1975). The NAEYC sells a book by Jean Vergeront called *Places and Spaces of Preschool and Primary (Indoors)*. Use this book if you want sketches and patterns for make-them-yourself "soft spaces and small spaces." (Order #310, ISBN: 0-935989-07-2)

Classroom management of the private space. Manage this part of your classroom well by clearly defining how everyone—teachers and children—may use the private space. Make sure that every adult who works in your room knows that the private space is a place of refuge and relaxation and should never be used as a time-out/punishment area (time-out or punishment areas have no place in DAP classrooms). Make sure each child knows that she can retreat to this spot to be alone and will not be disturbed. Teach children the strategies for politely telling another person that they do not wish to be disturbed when in the private area. Set limits prohibiting group play in the private area.

Develop Enough Activity Areas

The principles of designing DAP early childhood classrooms call for children to have choices, to move about the classroom, and to be active with materials, other children, and adults. Teachers who put this principle into action design a classroom with enough activity areas so that children do indeed have choices, are actively involved, and can easily move from one activity to another.

Consider the number and age of the children in the classroom when deciding how many of each type of area to include in the room. Provide one-third more spaces than there are children, so children can change activities without having to wait.

Example: A kindergarten classroom for 20 5-year-olds would need 27 work spaces (20 + ⅓ of 20 = 27) or one-third more spaces than children. This means that any child who completes a project in one area can move on to another activity, because there are always more work spaces in the classroom than there are children. These 27 spaces might consist of one small, private spaces, five small-group areas, and a large-group area.

Example: Mr. Pelander's third-grade class has 18 children. Their classroom (Figure 4–1b) has six learning centers based on the needs of his children—a reading, social studies, math, art, science, and writing center. In addition, there are three computers, an individual study carrel, and room for large-group activities.

Table 4–1 shows how many of each type of space would be useful, depending on the number and age of the children. It is possible to create a classroom that is too "busy," so it is wise to avoid filling your classroom with so many activity areas that children are overstimulated, frustrated, and unable to move around easily.

Table 4–1

Number of Activity Areas Needed Based on Ages and Numbers of Children in Class				
Area	Ages of Children	Number of Children in Class		
		Up to 9	10–14	15–24
Private area	3–4	1	1	1
	5–6	1	1	1 or 2
	7–9	1	1	1 or 2
Small-group area	3–4	1	3	4 or 5
	5–6	2	3	4 or 5
	7–9	2	3	5
Large-group area	3–4	1	1	1
	5–6	1	1	1
	7–9	1	1	1

Adapted from Alward (1973).

Arrange Activity Areas Logically

Another important step in designing a DAP physical environment is to logically arrange activity areas. Do this by thinking about the type of work or play in each center, by separating centers from each other, and by regulating the flow of traffic in the classroom.

Type of play in each center

Our goal as early childhood professionals is to design a classroom environment that is both stimulating and peaceful. Developmentally appropriate practices classrooms are characterized by quiet, purposeful, enthusiastic, and even vigorous interaction; they *are not* excessively noisy. Recent research shows that a DAP classroom is a far less stressful place than is an inappropriate classroom with excessive noise and seemingly unconnected or purposeless activity (Burts et al., 1992). Young children's cognitive development is enhanced when their physical environment is relatively quiet (Wachs and Gruen, 1982).

"Quiet" learning centers. Some learning/play centers lend themselves to relatively quiet, less vigorous work or play. Children tend to sit or stand and work quietly on projects or activities in these centers even if they work with several other children. This does *not* mean that children are silent in these centers. On the contrary, children in DAP classrooms talk quite a bit as they work together on math or if they work together at the computer or on puzzles. The overall tone of these quiet centers is simply more subdued. The "quiet centers" typically include:

- Private space
- Language arts centers (reading, writing, listening)
- Science
- Math
- Puzzles and other small-table toys
- Computer center

"Less quiet" learning centers. Other learning/play centers lend themselves to somewhat noisier, more vigorous work or play. You will quickly notice that children move around a lot more in certain centers because the nature of the work or play encourages a lot of movement. And as they move around, children engaged in these centers tend to talk to each other. Activity in these centers is less subdued than in the quieter centers. This movement and talk is what makes certain centers into "less quiet learning centers," which typically include:

- Dramatic play
- Blocks
- Physical education
- Music
- Arts
- Water or sand table
- Large-group area

Logically arrange areas so that quieter areas are placed near other quiet areas and so that they are well separated from areas encouraging more active play.

Example: Miss Hume, the preschool teacher, appropriately placed the dramatic play area near the block area (Figure 4–1a) because both are high-activity areas, and dramatic play can flow so easily from one to the other. She wisely placed the language arts center close to the puzzles/manipulative toy center, with both of these centers well separated from the noisier areas. She also developed and clearly stated limits on noise level. Children in her class work and play together without disrupting other people, and she emphasizes everyone's right to a quiet place in which to work. The children are learning that one of their basic classroom values is respect for the rights of others.

Create physical boundaries for areas

In Chapter 3 you learned about setting appropriate limits. This section carries forward with limit-setting but in a slightly different way. You will learn why it is necessary and how to create good physical boundaries for activity areas.

Creating proper boundaries for activity areas is not trivial. It is both an age and individually appropriate thing to do. Creating good boundaries between areas is age appropriate because all children need to know how to function in the physical environment, and good boundaries give them good cues. Creating good boundaries is individually appropriate because some children especially need help understanding limits and boundaries.

Creating good boundaries may well be one of the most appropriate things you do for children from chaotic, disorganized homes. People in *un*healthy systems tend to violate the psychological and physical boundaries of others. One of the clearest marks of a healthy system, however, including a developmentally appropriate classroom, is the idea of clear and distinct boundaries. These boundaries include psychological boundaries (e.g., no hitting, name-calling) and the physical boundaries within the classroom itself.

On a practical level, this information tells us to very clearly define and properly separate classroom areas from each other. Children tend to be more cooperative and far less disruptive when they understand where one area ends and the next begins (Olds, 1977). Clear physical boundaries, along with well-organized materials, also help children know where each piece of equipment belongs and encourage them to put things in their proper areas.

The "inset pictures" in Figure 4–2a and b show how each area looks from an overhead view. You can see in these insets how each area of the classroom has been separated from the rest of the classroom. Figures 4–3 and 4–6 show close-ups of ideas for practical and efficient boundaries.

Define good "traffic patterns" in a classroom

Classrooms with well-arranged activity areas and good physical boundaries give children cues about the traffic pattern in the room (Kritchevsky & Prescott, 1977). The *traffic pattern* refers to the flow of movement in an early childhood classroom. Early childhood DAP classrooms encourage children to move about the room through logical traffic patterns. Good traffic patterns are created with *open pathways* that clearly lead to areas and make it easy for children to move between areas (Colbert, 1997).

Figure 4–6   One example of how to create boundaries between activity areas. Other figures of the preschool classroom show that the teacher has used shelves and other dividers as boundaries. (Source: Adapted from Alward, K. R. [1973]. *Arranging the Classroom for Children*. San Francisco: Far West Laboratory for Educational Research and Development. Reprinted by permission.)

Make pathways wide enough for wheelchairs, long enough to make moving between areas easy, and short enough to discourage running. Regulate traffic by making only one entrance to a center, and develop a closed circuit around the room with the pathway so that children may stop off at each center if they wish (Bowers, 1990).

Create Attractive, Sensory-Rich Activity Areas

Soft architecture is the type that is designed to respond to the needs of the individuals using the space. Children who spend a large part of their day in a room have a right to spend that time in a clean, attractive, and sensory-rich space. This does not mean that the space has to be extravagently designed but we should strive for an aesthetic, pleasing, and serene environment. Create such an environment by paying attention to some seemingly commonsense things such as lighting and the sensory environment. Here are several specific and practical suggestions:

Strive for a sensory-rich but uncluttered classroom

Many early childhood teachers do a good job of adding interesting items to the classroom, but it is also important to weed out items that have served their purpose. A cluttered, disorderly room is unpleasant and distracting. Eliminating clutter helps children focus on new material because the number of stimuli to which they must attend is decreased (Alexander, 1996; Marion, 1995).

Example: Miss Hume realized that lots of the children in her class were fascinated by all the butterflies in the area, so she encouraged the study of butterflies. After adding a beautiful book on butterflies; two large, color photographs; and several real butterfly models to the science area, she was puzzled at the children's lack of interest. A close look at the science corner showed that the butterfly book was on the table with old cups of seeds, the rock collection, a magnet, and a magnifying glass. The pictures had been pinned to a somewhat cluttered bulletin board, and the butterflies had been dwarfed by a large, green plant.

After clearing the science table and the bulletin board, Miss Hume set out only "butterfly" things—the collection of butterflies, books, and the magnifying glass. She arranged the pictures of butterflies attractively on the bulletin board so that they were the central focus. She also placed a picture of butterflies on the door of the classroom with a note to parents to "join us in learning about butterflies."

Modify the lighting

Skillful use of lighting is an indirect method of guidance. Many schools are equipped with bright lights; although it is desirable to have adequate lighting, it can also be boring, stressful, and overstimulating to be in a harshly lighted room for an extended time. Classrooms are often equipped with only one or two light switches, giving adults only two options: all the harsh lights on or all of them off. Teachers can request that dimmer switches be installed so that they can control the intensity of lighting in different sections of the room.

Modify ceiling height or floor level

Create safe, cocoonlike spaces that define the areas in a classroom. Many schools, for example, build a safe, inexpensive platform (Figure 4–7) to give some variety to the flatness of a room. Children use platforms for a variety of activities. My university lab school also also made good use of the space *under* a platform to house the manipulative/writing areas.

Further define an activity area by draping strips of cloth across and between dowel rods hung from the ceiling. This strategy softens an area and room and actually makes the ceiling appear to be lower. This strategy is especially useful when a private, quiet, semienclosed activity area is desired.

Example: Miss Hume, in her first year at her school, was disappointed that the children did not seem to enjoy the reading area. She followed Colbert's advice (1997) and drew a floor plan of the reading area and decided that she needed to make some changes. A major change was to use bookshelves to better separate the reading area from other areas. She added a fluffy carpet and large pillows that are designed to lean against a wall. She then added to the cozy feeling by suspending cloth across two rods hanging from the ceiling. The children loved it, and reading activity soared!

Modify the sensory environment

Make your classroom pleasant and attractive by creating visual, auditory, olfactory, and textural interest.

Figure 4–7 A platform set in a corner against the wall in a kindergarten classroom. (Source: Adapted from Alward, K. R. [1973]. *Arranging the Classroom for Children.* San Francisco: Far West Laboratory for Educational Research and Development. Reprinted by permission.)

Create visual interest. Enhance the aesthetic appeal of your early childhood classroom by keeping it clean and by adding well-chosen, inexpensive items such as paintings, posters, safe green plants, photographs of the children, cloth hangings, and artwork.

Create auditory interest. We have already discussed the importance of a calm and peaceful environment in which children are free to move and to talk but not to make excessively loud noise. You will easily be able to use sound to create a pleasant environment in such a calm environment. How pleasant and relaxing it is for children to be able to hear their favorite composer's music when they arrive at school. Other sounds—new musical instruments, a gerbil gnawing a box or scratching around in his bedding, a mobile tinkling, or the hum of the computer—can help create a pleasant, relaxing atmosphere if the children are tuned in to the sounds and are not distracted by unnecessary noise.

Create olfactory interest. Scary, hurtful, fun, and joyful memories are often triggered by either bad odors or wonderful fragrances—the disinfectant smell of the hospital, the fragrance of the lilac bush in bloom as we brushed by it, the garden after a rainfall, fresh oranges shared with a friend on a summer day.

Think of all the ways you could make your room pleasant through attention to fragrance. Eliminate unpleasant odors by maintaining cleanliness. Add pleasant aromas from safe sources to your classroom. Bake bread, muffins, and cookies, and vary ingredients, urging children to identify aromas. Put peppermint extract in the play dough, inexpensive scented soap in the bathroom, safe flowering plants in the room or yard.

Create textural interest. Putting carpeting on the floors or walls and covering bulletin boards with cork or burlap are two things you can do almost immediately. Then the fun begins when you hang a child's large collage of cloth scraps or when you create a touch wall with an expanse of corrugated paper and other materials, or when you hang fabric wall hangings. Developmental appropriateness means attending to the needs of individual children; children with impaired sight will benefit from a room rich in textures.

CURRICULUM, ACTIVITIES, AND MATERIALS IN A DAP EARLY CHILDHOOD CLASSROOM

Curriculum

It is important that the curriculum for young children match how young children think and learn (Bredekamp & Rosegrant, 1992). Hart et al. (1997) have written an excellent chapter on integrated developmentally appropriate curriculum. They and others teaching those in early childhood are concerned about the emphasis on instruction for young children that is merely a copy of the type of formal instruction used in upper elementary grades. Charlesworth (1985) warned that this type of skill-based instruction does not meet the developmental needs of young children.

Developmentally appropriate practices view children as the source of the curriculum, and teachers who are good at observing children's development in all areas can develop activities that nurture children's growth in those areas (Williams, 1994). Teachers who have DAP classrooms believe that young children learn in an active, not a passive, way. They believe that young children *construct* or build knowledge as they interact with people and things (Piaget, 1952; Vygotsky, 1978). Therefore, teachers in DAP classrooms tailor the curriculum to meet the needs of every child.

Teachers in DAP classrooms offer options to children and allow children to participate in ways that best suit the child's learning style. The DAP curriculum is integrated rather than being compartmentalized into separate areas. Teachers provide experiences that require children to be actively involved. Play is an integral part of the DAP curriculum and is valued by teachers inside as well as outside the classroom (Hart, 1993; Hart et al., 1997).

Activities

After designing a DAP physical environment, you will look to children for cues about the curriculum and then design activities that meet the children's needs. Early childhood activities are developmentally appropriate when:

1. There is a wide, but not overwhelming, variety of age-appropriate activities that occur throughout the day.
2. Children know that some activities will occur at the same time each day.
3. Children are required to be actively involved and engage in concrete experiences.
4. Children choose their own activities from among the large number of activities set up by the teacher.
5. Children have options about when and how to complete activities.

You will have an opportunity to use these criteria in the case study analysis at the end of the chapter.

Materials

We know that one of the major ways in which we influence children is by providing materials and equipment (Chapter 2). Teachers in DAP classrooms provide appropriate materials with which children work and play. Appropriate materials, as we know from some older research, refer to a moderately rich assortment of exploratory and safe items that encourage competent, independent behavior in children (Stallings, 1975; Wachs & Gruen, 1982; White & Watts, 1973). These materials reflect the developmental level of the children and the goals of the school or learning center.

The National Association for the Education of Young Children (NAEYC) publishes a fine book that will help you select materials for children from birth to age 8. It is written by Martha B. Bronson and is titled: *The Right Stuff for Children Birth to 8: Selecting Play Materials to Support Development.* It is a user-friendly handbook with clear descriptions of what children are like at each age, including very concrete information on what they enjoy doing. You will see at a glance the play materials that enhance children's development in the different areas at each age. (Order #312, ISBN: 0-935989-72-2 from NAEYC, 800-424-2460)

It is also important for teachers to have specific skills in managing materials (Bowers, 1990). Management of classroom materials refers to how well they are gathered, whether they work well, how well organized and displayed they are, and whether they are available to the children. See Figure 4–8 for a rating scale on managing materials.

DAP CLASSROOMS FOR INFANTS AND TODDLERS

Brief Summary of Infant/Toddler Development

Developmentally appropriate physical environments are based on the developmental level of the children using them. This section briefly summarizes child development during the first three years of life (Fogel, 1984). Adults support infant/toddler development first by understanding infant/toddler development and then by designing the physical environment to be safe, cozy, and appropriate for the care and education of each child in the group (Fu, 1984).

Very young infants, up to 3 or 4 months, spend most of their time getting bodily and physiologic systems in order. Parents and teachers spend a lot of their time with new infants holding and rocking the baby, giving them tactile stimulation, and helping them establish a schedule of eating, sleeping, playing, and exercising.

A caregiver's touch seeks to help moderate the production of a hormone that affects an infant's reaction to stress. Institutionalized Romanian orphans without such attention exhibit wide fluctuations of that hormone level. Abnormal levels of the hormone have been linked to changes in a part of the brain involved with learning and memory (Rubin, 1997).

As time goes on, infants are gradually able to cope with slightly more complex stimulation because they continue to develop in all of the domains—physical,

Rating Scale: Classroom Management of Materials

Use this rating scale to evaluate classroom management of materials and equipment in this early childhood classroom. Rate each item with the scale: "1" indicates the lowest rating you can give, "5" is the highest rating you can give. A space is provided for comments.

The teacher has taken leadership in gathering materials.   1   2   3   4   5

Comments:

All materials needed for an activity are there.   1   2   3   4   5

Comments:

Materials appear to have been gathered well in advance of the activity.   1   2   3   4   5

Comments:

Equipment is correctly sized for children using it.   1   2   3   4   5

Comments:

Equipment works well.   1   2   3   4   5

Comments:

Children will be able to use the materials without a lot of adult help.   1   2   3   4   5

Comments:

Equipment is clean.   1   2   3   4   5

Comments:

Materials are organized logically.   1   2   3   4   5

Comments:

Items within centers are stored so that they are easy for the children
to get to and then put away.   1   2   3   4   5

If children are expected to clean up after an activity, then this teacher
appears to have thought through and has provided necessary items.   1   2   3   4   5

If children are expected to set up an activity, then necessary materials are available.   1   2   3   4   5

Comments:

Materials not intended for children's use are stored out of their reach.   1   2   3   4   5

Comments:

Figure 4–8   Rating scale: classroom management of materials.

motor, cognitive, social, and emotional. An example is the rapid perceptual and motor development in infancy that allows the infant to engage in one-on-one interactions, to play with any of hundreds of "things" in her physical environment, and to experience the pleasure of these new abilities.

Infants are partners in social interaction from the moment they are born. But there are important changes in their interaction with others as their cognitive development changes during the first year or so of life. Older infants and toddlers realize or seem to "sense" their status as partners in social interaction and realize that they "cause" things to happen.

The changes in cognitive development in the first 3 years are dramatic. By her first birthday, an infant has a better sense of the permanence of objects, that is, that Mom and Dad still exist even if she cannot see them. She now understands the value of words and has become a real "communicator." Perception and memory change and affect her understanding of such things as emotions. Emotional development is tied to cognitive development over the next few years, and toddlers will develop fears and some anxiety. Infants and toddlers can begin to deal with these uneasy feelings if they have understanding caregivers to help them.

Ever-changing cognitive and emotional development allow very young children to begin to see themselves as separate individuals and to be conscious of the "self," a phenomenon that grows as infants and toddlers interact with others. Motor skills advance, enabling toddlers to act in an increasingly autonomous way. Development during this period and in the next few years allows toddlers to experience the joy of living, to begin to understand the world around them, and to develop feelings of competence and confidence.

An infant's environment should support her development, and the next section describes supportive infant/toddler environments.

Supportive Physical Environments for Infants/Toddlers

Fogel (1984) believes that it is not possible to even think about infants without also considering the child's environment. He identified two types of environments—the *physical environment* and the *caregiving environment*—for children from birth to age 3.

The physical environment includes all objects and situations, such as how clean and safe a home or center is; the types of toys and how available they are; the size and nature of the home or center; the adequacy of nutrition, health care, and sanitary practices; and the variety of objects and settings that an infant or toddler experiences. The caregiving environment includes caregiver behavior as the caregiver interacts with the baby. This section will describe supportive physical environments first and then will describe supportive caregiving environments.

The physical environment affects infant/toddler cognitive development

Perception and memory, problem-solving, spatial relations, perspective-taking, planning strategies. All of these are a part of cognitive development and this section focuses on this area of development in infants and toddlers. Teachers in DAP infant/toddler classrooms use child development and information about a child's family and culture as the basis for planning curriculum, activities, and materials.

Teachers in DAP infant/toddler classrooms understand that they are not "baby-sitters" but teachers. They believe that how they structure the physical environment has a major impact on an infant's or toddler's cognitive development. They know that even the youngest infants are active information-processing people who need the right type of stimulation for optimal development. They know that infant and toddler cognition and learning is enhanced in a DAP classroom.

Problem-solving in infants and toddlers. Children's cognitive development is enhanced when children actively explore their surroundings. We want infants and toddlers to begin to be able to solve problems based on their safe explorations. Therefore, an infant or toddler's cognitive development is affected by how well teachers design and then manage the physical environment. For example, children in their second and third years have better problem-solving skills and engage in more exploratory behavior when teachers and parents provide certain types of objects for them.

Spatial relations and perspective-taking. These skills develop over a period of years, but the development begins in infancy. Our goal is to create the type of environment in which the youngest children have a good chance of developing a good sense of spatial relations. We also want to help them begin to understand that they are separate people from others and that they can have an effect on their environment. Young children develop better spatial relations and perspective-taking in well-organized and peaceful environments than in chaotic, stressful environments.

Learning to plan strategies. A child's ability to figure out new ways to do things and to plan effective strategies is related to the type of play materials parents and teachers provide. Children are better able to figure out how to do things and to plan effective strategies when teachers provide play materials appropriate to their developmental needs, interests, and abilities at an appropriate time.

Implications: What this means for teachers and caregivers. The principles of DAP classrooms apply here. Draw implications from the information just given and you will see that it would be wise to plan the physical environment so that it enhances cognitive development during infancy and toddlerhood.

- *Provide a variety of safe inanimate objects for infants.*
- *Provide objects that are responsive to an infant's actions,* such as busy boards, nesting blocks, and shape sorters.
- *Avoid noise, confusion, and overcrowding in environments for infants and toddlers.*
- *Organize the physical environment well.* Develop activity areas to meet the specific developmental needs of infants and toddlers.
- *Provide age-appropriate play materials for infants and toddlers.*
- *Introduce and emphasize certain forms of environmental stimulation at specific ages* (Figure 4–9).

Designing Physical Environments for Infants/Toddlers

Infants and toddlers are usually in Piaget's first stage of cognitive development, the sensorimotor stage, and take in information and act on their world through sensory

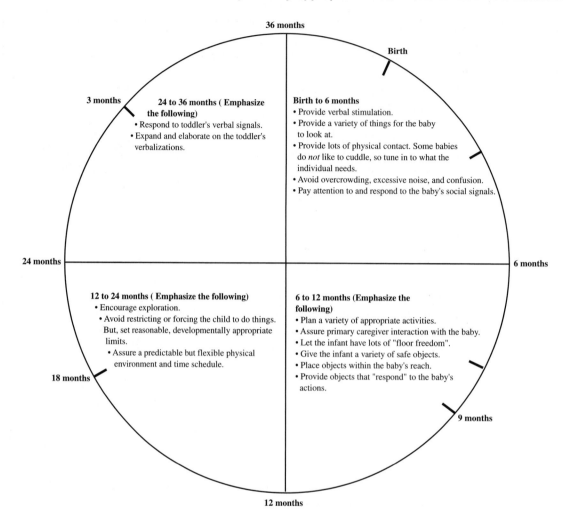

Figure 4–9   It's important to "time" environmental stimulation for infants and toddlers well. (Sources: Laliberte [1997]; Wachs & Gruen [1982]; White House Conference, reported in the *New York Times* [April 1997].)

and motor schemes. Very young children learn through experimentation and repetition, and teachers encourage their learning by providing a safe and stimulating physical environment and an emotionally supportive caregiving environment. Sensitive teachers take advantage of routine situations such as eating, bathing (Bredekamp, 1987; Bredekamp & Copple, 1997), diapering, and dressing to help very young children feel safe and learn at the same time.

Well-organized infant and toddler rooms contain activity areas but are not just scaled-down versions of classrooms for children 3 to 8 years old. Infants and toddlers should be able to practice sensorimotor activities in a well-designed space: clean, spacious bathing and dressing areas; crawling, scooting, walking in safe, open areas; pushing, pulling, rolling, emptying, and filling safe, clean toys; climbing on

Figure 4–10 Infant and toddler rooms should be divided into activity areas, but the areas must meet the specific needs of our youngest children. (Sources: King, Oberlin, & Swank [1990]; Wilson [1990]; and Bredekamp [1987] give excellent suggestions on specfic and developmentally appropriate activities for infant/toddler centers.)

Rattle, Reach, and Roll: Activity Areas for Infants

- Well-designed and maintained diapering, dressing areas
- Comfort corner (soft spot)
- Pleasant eating area
- Rattle, reaching, and sensory areas
- Manipulative area
- Interaction-game area
- Exercise mat
- Sensory table
- Reading

Explorers: Activity Areas for Toddlers

- Well-designed and maintained eating, toileting, dressing, and sleeping areas
- Music
- Private space
- Block
- Dramatic play
- Creative arts
- Large muscle
- Sensory table (e.g., water, sand)
- Play dough table
- Reading
- Comfort corner (soft spot)
- Small muscle

safe structures; gazing at objects at their level; and doing active things like finger painting or playing with water. Figure 4–10 suggests appropriate activity areas based on the infant's or toddler's level of development.

Supportive Caregiving Environments for Infants/Toddlers

The caregiving environment includes a caregiver's behavior as she interacts with an infant or toddler. A DAP caregiving environment is intertwined with the physical environment and together they enhance an infant's or toddler's development. Chapter 2 described different styles of caregiving and explained that the authori*tative* style is the one most likely to enhance an infant's or toddler's development in different domains. An infant or toddler teacher with an authori*tative* caregiving style has expectations for a young child and is also highly responsive to an infant's or toddler's needs.

Supportive teachers of infants and toddlers take a lot of responsibility for infants because our youngest children cannot function on their own. Authori*tative* caregivers understand, for example, that babies and toddlers cannot control themselves, have limited memory, and are limited in how they tell us what they need. Responsive teachers anticipate what babies and toddlers need and know when and how to gradually adjust support. They also know how to transfer control to children as children reach certain stages of development.

Examples: Ms. Corelli, head teacher in the toddler room, understands that her children have not yet achieved self-control. She believes that her job is to model self-control and to gradually transfer control to the toddlers. She does this when setting limits by giving positively worded statements such as "Hit this ball," rather than just restricting a toddler and saying what *not* to do.

Mrs. Goldberg, head teacher in the infant room, realizes that babies cannot stop crying just because somebody tells them to. But she knows that babies cry for lots of different reasons and that there are some things she can do to help a baby who is crying. She also gives this information to the parents of the infants (see Parent Talk. Babies Often Cry When They Are . . .).

Parent Talk. "Babies Often Cry When They Are . . ."

Your baby does not cry to annoy you but she does cry because something is wrong. Crying is a baby's way of communicating some of her needs. Try to figure out what might be causing her to cry. Your baby cannot stop crying just because you tell her to. Here are the main reasons that your baby cries and some things you can do to help the baby. "Babies often cry when they are . . ."

- **Hungry.** Babies often cry when they're hungry. If it has been at least 2 hours since she was fed, see if she is hungry.
- **Lonely.** If a baby calms down and stays calm as soon as you pick her up, she missed you! A baby's need for closeness is real. You can't spoil a baby by cuddling her when she needs it.
- **Cold or hot.** Feel the baby's back or tummy to see if she is too cold or too hot.

Adjust her clothing to make her comfortable. Dress a baby as warmly as you dress yourself, or one layer warmer.

- **Overstimulated.** Give her calm and quiet. Rocking her in a dimly lit room may help.
- **Undressed.** Put a cloth on her tummy until you redress her.
- **Startled.** A baby may move suddenly, startle, and cry. Wrapping a blanket securely around her and holding her securely may calm her.
- **In need of a diaper change.**
- **In pain.** A baby might be ill or uncomfortable because a pin is pricking her or because her clothes have sharp tags or zippers.
- **Sleepy.** Some babies need to fuss a bit before sleeping.

Source: Parenting the First Year. Wisconsin Children's Trust Fund, 110 E. Main St., Suite 614, Madison, WI. Adapted from the newsletter for the first month of life.

Case Study Analysis: Discovering DAP in Activities

Both Miss Hume and Mr. Pelander (chapter opening case studies) have developed activities based on principles of DAP. As a result, children in their classrooms are very likely to develop self-control, independence, and competence. Analyze the case studies by finding examples of how both Miss Hume's preschool and Mr. Pelander's third-grade classrooms meet the criteria for developmentally appropriate activities.

(continued)

Both classrooms have a wide, but not overwhelming, variety of age-appropriate activities that occurred throughout the day.
Examples for the preschool classroom:
Examples for the third-grade classroom:

Both classrooms schedule activities so that they occur at the same time each day.
Examples (preschool):
Examples (third grade):

Both teachers emphasize activities requiring the active involvement of the children.
Examples (preschool):
Examples (third grade):

Both teachers encourage children to choose their own activities.
Examples (preschool):
Examples (third grade):

REFLECTING ON KEY CONCEPTS

1. Suppose that you are explaining to a friend that early childhood is defined as birth through grade 3. The friend says, "That's strange. What could all those ages have in common?" Illustrate by referring to the principles of designing DAP early childhood classrooms, that is, what do all DAP early childhood classrooms have in common?

2. "H-m-m. That's interesting," says your friend, "but does it make any difference if a child's classroom is 'developmentally appropriate' or not?" What would you tell this person about the value of DAP early childhood classrooms?

3. Now suppose that you are giving a tour of your preschool classroom for a parent who is thinking about enrolling his child in the school. You point out each small-group learning center, the individual learning center, the large-group area, and the private space. Explain why you have organized the classroom into activity areas and tell the parent about what goes on in each area. The parent asks you why the block area is placed next to the dramatic play area and why the books are next to the puzzle area. What would you say?

4. You meet a person who teaches eighth grade and you start talking about curriculum. "So," says your friend, "just what do you early childhood teachers teach? Do you just drill them on numbers, colors, and shapes?" You realize that this person does not understand young children or how they learn and want to treat this as a teachable moment. Briefly explain the meaning of a DAP approach to curriculum for early childhood.

5. Name four of the most important things to remember about managing materials in an early childhood classroom. Why do these four seem most important to you?

6. Why is it so important to understand infant and toddler development before one can design a DAP environment for this age group?

7. How does a classroom for infants and toddlers differ from a classroom for older early childhood children?

APPLY YOUR KNOWLEDGE

Finding DAP in an Early Childhood Classroom. Request permission to visit an early childhood classroom for preschool, kindergarten, first-, second-, or third-grade children. As a guest in the classroom your goal is *not* to criticize but to look at how the teacher has designed activity areas, how the areas are bounded, the traffic patterns in the classroom, and the management of materials in the classroom.

Practice professionalism by making suggestions for change *after* you leave the classroom. Keep information on the classroom confidential. If you share information in a class, remove information that could identify the teacher, class, or school from your work. Present any suggestions in a positive way so that you are merely suggesting things that would make a good classroom even better.

1. **Activity Areas**
   - Draw a simple floor plan of the classroom. Include the toilet area for children, doors to the outside and to hallways, small-group learning centers, large-group area, private areas, and boundaries between areas. Label each area clearly.
     Private Area. Explain whether and how the private space in this classroom meets the criteria for private spaces. Suggest any changes needed.
     Large-Group Area. Explain whether and how the large-group area in this classroom meets the criteria for large-group areas. Suggest any changes needed.
     Small-Group Learning Centers. Number of centers: _____ Explain whether and how the small-group learning centers in this classroom meet criteria for this type of activity area. Suggest any changes needed.
     Individual Learning Center(s). This classroom (does or does not) have individual learning centers. Explain how these centers meet the criteria for this type of activity area.

2. **Boundaries and Traffic Pattern**
   - Describe the boundaries used to separate activity areas from one another in this classroom. Which areas were especially well bounded? Why? Which areas would benefit from having more effective boundaries?
   - Describe the traffic pattern in this room using information on "good traffic patterns" from the chapter. How could this room's traffic pattern be made even better?

3. **Management of Materials in the Classroom**
   - Use the rating scale (Figure 4–8) to evaluate classroom management of materials and equipment in this early childhood classroom. After you are done with the rating scale, name three ways in which this classroom's management of materials would most benefit from a change in how materials are managed.

4. **Suggestions for Change**
   - Draw a second floor plan for this classroom. Clearly show your suggestions for change in your drawing. If, for example, you note that the classroom does not have quite enough small-group learning centers, then decide where you would put them and draw them on your "after" floor plan.

References

Alexander, N. (1996). How to organize your classroom. *Early Childhood News, 8*(4), 28–30.

Alward, K. R. (1973). *Arranging the classroom for children.* San Francisco: Far West Laboratory for Educational Research and Development.

Bowers, C. (1990). Organizing space for children. *Texas Child Care Quarterly,* Spring, 3–10, 22.

Bredekamp, S. (Ed.) (1987). *Developmentally appropriate practice in programs serving children from birth through age 8.* Washington, DC: NAEYC.

Bredekamp, S., & Copple, C. (Eds). (1997). *Developmentally appropriate practice in early childhood programs: Revised.* Washington, DC: NAEYC.

Bredekamp, S., & Rosegrant, T. (Eds.). (1992). *Reaching potentials: Appropriate curriculum and assessment for young children* (Vol. 1). Washington, DC: NAEYC.

Burts, D., Hart, C., Charlesworth, R., Fleege, P., Mosley, J., & Thomasson, R. (1992). Observed activities and stress behaviors of children in developmentally appropriate and inappropriate kindergarten classrooms. *Early Childhood Research Quarterly, 7,* 297–318.

Caples, S. (1996). Some guidelines for preschool design. *Young Children, 51*(4), 14–21.

Charlesworth, R. (1985). Readiness: Should we make them ready or let them bloom? *Day Care and Early Education, 12*(3), 25–27.

Charlesworth, R., Hart, C., Burts, D., & DeWolf, M. (1993). The LSU studies: Building a research base for developmentally appropriate practice. In S. Reifel (Ed.), *Advances in Early Education and Day Care: Perspectives on Developmentally Appropriate Practice, 5,* 3–28.

Colbert, J. (1997). Classroom design and how it influences behavior. *Early Childhood News, 9*(3), 22–30.

David, T., & Weinstein, D. (1987). The built environment and children's development. In C. Weinstein & T. David (Eds.), *Spaces for children: The built environment and child development.* New York: Plenum Press.

Fogel, A. (1984). *Infancy: Infant, family, and society.* St. Paul, MN: West Publishing.

Fu, V. (1984). *Infant/toddler care in centers.* In L. Dittmann (Ed.), The infants we care for. Washington, DC: NAEYC.

Gandini, L. (1993). Fundamentals of the Reggio Emilia approach to early childhood education. *Young Children, 49*(1), 4–8.

Hart, C. (1993). *Children on playrounds: Research perspectives and applications.* Albany, NY: State University of New York Press.

Hart, C., Burts, D., & Charlesworth, R. (1997). *Integrated developmentally appropriate curriculum.* In C. Hart, D. Burts, & R. Charlesworth (Eds.), *Integrated curriculum and developmentally appropriate practice: Birth to age 8.* New York: State University of New York Press.

Howes, C. (1991). Caregiving environments and their consequences for children: The experience in the United States. In E. Melhuish & P. Moss (Eds.), *Day care for young children.* New York: Routledge.

Jones, E., & Prescott, E. *Environments for young children.* Washington, DC: NAEYC, Film #806.

King, M., Oberlin, A., & Swank, T. (1990). Supporting the activity choices of two-year-olds. *Day Care and Early Education, 17*(2), 9–13, 67–70.

Krogh, S. (1995). *The integrated early childhood curriculum* (2nd ed.). New York: McGraw-Hill.

Kostelnik, M. (1992). Myths associated with developmentally appropriate programs. *Young Children, 47*(4), 17–23.

Kritchevsky, S., & Prescott, E. (1977). *Environments for young children: Physical space.* Washington, DC: NAEYC.

Laliberte, R. (1997). Inside your baby's brain. *Parents, 72*(9), 48–53.

Marcon, R. (1993). Socioemotional versus academic emphasis: Impact on kindergartners' development and achievement. *Early Child Development and Care, 96*, 81–89.

Marcon, R. (1994). Doing the right thing for children: Linking research and policy reform in the District of Columbia public schools. *Young Children, 50*(1), 8.

Marion, M. (1995). *Guidance of young children* (4th ed.). New York: Merrill/Prentice-Hall.

Myhre, S. (1993). Enhancing your dramatic play area through the use of prop boxes. *Young Children, 48*(5), 6–19.

New York Times (1997, April 28). Nurturing development of the brain. *New York Times, 146*(50776), A14.

Olds, A. R. (1977). Why is environmental design important to young children? *Children in Contemporary Society, 11*(1), 58.

Pelander, J. (1997). My transition from conventional to more developmentally appropriate practices in the primary grades. *Young Children, 52*(7), 19–25.

Pelander, J. (1998, February 3). Personal communication.

Petrakos, H., & Howe, N. (1996). The influence of the physical design of the dramatic play center on children's play. *Early Childhood Research Quarterly, 11*, 63–77.

Piaget, J. (1952). *The origins of intelligence in children.* New York: International Universities Press.

Rubin, R. (1997). The biochemistry of touch. *U.S. News & World Report, 123*(18), 62.

Stallings, J. (1975). Implementation and child effects of teaching practices in followthrough classrooms. *Monographs of the Society for Research in Child Development, 40* (78).

Vygotsky, L. (1978). *Mind in society: The development of higher psychological processes.* In M. Cole, V. John-Steiner, S. Scribner, & E. Souberman (Eds. & Trans.). Cambridge, MA: Harvard University Press.

Wachs, T. D., & Gruen, G. E. (1982). *Early experience and human development.* New York: Plenum.

White, B. L., & Watts, J. C. (1973). *Experience and environment: Major influences on the development of the young child* (Vol. 1). Englewood Cliffs, NJ: Prentice-Hall.

Williams, L. (1994). Developmentally appropriate practice and cultural values: A case in point. In B. L. Mallory & R. S. New (Eds.), *Diversity and Developmentally Appropriate Practices* (pp. 155–65). New York: Teachers College Press.

Wilson, L. C. (1990). *Infants and toddlers* (2nd ed.). New York: DelMar.

Part 2

Special Topics in Child Guidance

Part One helped you learn the essential elements in DAP child guidance. If you adopt a developmentally appropriate child-guidance philosophy and learn DAP guidance strategies, you will be prepared to help children with five special issues that all children face:

- Stress
- Self-esteem
- Anger
- Aggression
- Prosocial behavior

There are five chapters in Part Two and each will help you apply your knowledge of DAP child guidance to one of these topics.

Chapter 5. Guiding Children in Times of Stress. This chapter focuses on the positive when describing children and stress. You will read about the nature of stress and how it affects children.

The main focus is to help you develop knowledge and skills for helping children cope with specific stressful events.

Chapter 6. Guiding Children Toward a Healthy Sense of Self and Self-Esteem. Child guidance using DAP helps children develop a healthy and balanced sense of self and self-esteem that is firmly rooted in a strong set of personal values. The chapter does not give you a set of "cute activities," but it does give you several practical suggestions on how to use DAP child guidance to guide children toward healthy self-esteem.

Chapter 7. Guiding Young Children's Understanding and Management of Anger. *Young children feel and express anger but they do not understand it.* That is an extremely important concept to keep in mind as you work with children. This chapter will help you apply DAP child guidance so that you can help angry children begin to understand and manage this strong emotion.

Chapter 8. Understanding and Guiding Aggressive Children. Anger and aggression are related, but they are two different issues. This chapter will help you understand how some children become excessively aggressive. It also focuses on applying DAP child guidance to help aggressive children develop more positive ways of dealing with others.

Chapter 9. Prosocial Behavior: Guiding Its Development. One of our tasks as early childhood educators is to nurture the roots of compassion, generosity, helpfulness, and cooperation in the children we teach. When we nurture these positive traits, we actually give children an alternative to aggression. This chapter willl help you understand how a child's development affects prosocial behavior and what teachers can do to guide its development.

Chapter 5

Guiding Children in Times of Stress

After reading and studying this chapter, you will be able to

✿ Define resiliency and explain its origin in children. Define stress for young children and explain it as a child–environment relationship.
✿ Identify two major sources of stress for children and give examples of each.
✿ List the stages of the stress response and summarize the elements of each stage.
✿ Explain how young children's developmental limitations makes it difficult for them to know how to cope with stress on their own.
✿ List and give examples of general guidelines for helping children cope with stress.
✿ Analyze a case study in which a teacher attempts to buffer the effect of stress for a child.

"Growing up means meeting a variety of challenges, many of which can cause stress."
(McCracken, 1986)

Case Study: Joseph's New School

Wednesday, 5:30 P.M.

Mr. Fong waited for Joseph, a new child in his kindergarten, and Joseph's father to arrive. "Hello, Joseph. I'm pleased to meet you," said Mr. Fong. To his father he said, "Please come in and we'll all look around Joseph's new classroom." "This is where you hang your coat. I've printed your name on your locker already, Joseph." He showed the pictures of the children in the class and took Joseph's picture to place with the others. He pointed out areas in the classroom and asked Joseph about the areas of the classroom at his other school. Mr. Fong showed Joseph the children's bathroom, where the 5-year-old demonstrated that he knew how to turn on faucets, use the new type of soap dispenser, and get paper towels. Joseph looked at the toileting area, which was in a room right next to the classroom. "You can go to the bathroom whenever you want to," said Mr. Fong. "Your other teacher told me that you usually had a carton of milk for snack. Here you can still have milk if you want it, but you can also choose juice."

Mr. Fong asked Joseph about his favorite activities (building with blocks, puzzles, and singing). Mr. Fong told Joseph that the children played with blocks and puzzles every day and that everyone would be learning a new song tomorrow. Then they looked in the nap room, and Joseph smiled when he discovered that he already had a cot with his name on it. The teacher gave Joseph's father a copy of his class schedule so that Dad would have a clear idea of how the day was structured. "Why don't you look this over and just talk casually with Joseph about the flow of the day. It might help him make the transition."

"Thanks," said Dad, "for meeting with us so late in the day. Can you think of anything else that I can do to help Joe make this move to a new school?" "Yes, there is," Mr. Fong replied. "I have a children's book on moving. You can borrow it if you'd like. Joseph might like to read it with you. And here's a short handout on how you can prevent stress from this move for Joseph. These things have helped other parents and children who are new to our school."

Thursday Morning

Joseph stood next to his locker while all the new faces swirled around him. Mr. Fong decided to let him watch the other children for a while, but brought him one of the unit blocks to hold while he looked. Soon he brought Justin over to Joseph and said, "Justin, would you please show Joseph the rest of the blocks and explain how we put them away?" Mr. Fong explained the playground rules to Joseph when they went outside, and at naptime Joseph knew that he had a cot with his name on it.

Children are not immune to stress. They face stress-inducing situations every day, like the one that Joseph and his family now face with the move to a new home and school. This chapter focuses on resilience and stress during early childhood. You will learn about how children become resilient, the origins of stress and how it affects children, stages of responding to stress, what it takes to cope effectively, and why young children have a difficult time coping with stress on their own. On a practical level, you will learn some general guidelines for helping children with stress and then will learn about how to help children who are facing one of many possible specific stressors—moving. Let's turn first to the nature of resilience and stress in young children.

RESILIENCE AND STRESS IN YOUNG CHILDREN

Resilience in Young Children

Many children in our classrooms face adversity in their homes and communities (Weinreb, 1997). These are the "high-risk" children about whom we worry so much. What we know, though, is that many, but certainly not all, children who face multiple and severe risks overcome the odds and show great *resilience*. Resilience is a set of qualities enabling a child to adapt successfully in spite of risk and adversity. A person who is resilient is socially competent, can solve problems, can reflect critically on issues, is autonomous, and has a sense of purpose (Benard, 1995).

Children develop resilience in their families, schools, and/or communities. If you looked inside the institutions that help children become resilient, what would you see that separates them from families and classrooms in which children do not become resilient? One of the major observations that you would undoubtedly make is a resiliency-building family or school provides three major *"protective factors"* that help a child successfully navigate the bumpy waters of a high-risk environment. These three protective factors are caring relationships, high expectations, and opportunities for participation. Resilient children have been able to connect with at least one caring and compassionate person, often a teacher who serves as a good model of confidence and positive action.

It is this type of relationship through which a child can learn to understand and manage potentially stressful events. Let's turn now to the topic of stress. There is a lot that early childhood professionals can do to help all children, including the high-risk children, cope with stressful events and to develop resilience.

Definition of Stress

Stress is a relationship, not an "event"

Stress is a relationship between a child and his environment; it involves his understanding and evaluation of some event and his ability to cope with the event. A child is most likely to feel stress when he cannot understand, evaluate, or cope effectively with some internal or external event. He then feels overwhelmed by the inability to cope and the stress that results from it (Holroyd & Lazarus, 1982). Children often feel stress when conditions keep them from achieving any of several fundamental needs—security, bonding, acceptance, status, meaning, and mastery (Zimbardo, 1982).

Some people view stress as a life event that is generally considered stressful, such as moving, starting a new school, having a parent die, or having parents going through a divorce. While these life events often result in stress, they are not in themselves a stress. There are merely life events (Zegans, 1982). They create stress only if a child does not understand the event, cannot evaluate the event, or does not have the skills for effectively coping with the life event.

For example, many people believe that moving is automatically a stressful life event for young children (Jalongo, 1986b). It would probably be more accurate to call moving a potentially stressful event; it has the potential to create stress but

One of the major factors that helps children become resilient are caring relationships.

whether it does depends on a child's understanding of and ability to cope with the move.

Stress for children can be acute or chronic

Children can experience *acute* stress. Acute stress occurs quite suddenly, but tends to subside as suddenly as it arose, like a visit to the emergency room to have a broken arm set or a visit from the firefighters to put out a fire. The impact of the event on a child depends on how the child appraises the event and on how others deal with the event. The trip to the emergency room to have a broken arm set will have little impact if parents buffer the experience for a child. On the other hand, one instance of being sexually molested can have a long-lasting impact if parents and professionals deal with the incident poorly.

Children can also experience *chronic* stress, which is the type of stress that continues for some time. The children in your classes come from a variety of backgrounds, and the chances are very good that, in any one year, several of the children will experience chronic stress from such things as an illness, child abuse, irresponsible or inept parenting, long-term bitterness after divorce of parents, seemingly never-ending daily hassles, and loneliness or not having friends. The effects of chronic stress seem to accumulate to cause problems (Bullock, 1997), even for children who are well adjusted (Honig, 1986).

Sources of Stress for Children

There are two major sources of stress for young children: internal and external sources. Some are *internal* sources because they come from within the child (Honig, 1986). Others are *external* sources because they originate outside the child.

Internal sources of stress

Internal sources of stress include such things as pangs of hunger in an infant who is being neglected, shyness (Zimbardo, 1982), or headaches (Sargent, 1982). Emotions may also be internal sources of stress. Anxiety, anger, jealousy, guilt, and even joy are potentially stressful for children if parents and teachers do not help them understand and deal with these emotions. Children do not automatically understand and know how to deal with an emotion like anger (Kuebli, 1994; Marion, 1997; Marion, Barby, Dahl, & Friske, 1998).

Example: Bill has experienced a lot of anxiety over almost always being chosen last in pickup games of basketball in his neighborhood park. His dad has not helped Bill deal with his feeling and Bill has begun to avoid the park because of the stress that being chosen last has caused him.

External sources of stress

Other potential sources of stress for children are external; that is, they come from the child's environment. Some of these external sources of stress are:

- Inept or harsh child-guidance practices
- Child abuse or neglect (Gale, Thompson, Moran, & Sack, 1988)
- Anger-arousing social interactions (Fabes & Eisenberg, 1992; Marion, 1994, 1997; Marion et al., 1998)
- Loneliness or not having friends (Bullock, 1997)
- Developmentally inappropriate classrooms (Burts, Hart, Charlsworth, Fleege, Mosley, & Thomasson, 1992; Hyson, Hirsh-Pasek, Rescorla, & Cone, 1991)
- Divorce (Amato, 1997)
- Joint custody arrangements (McKinnon & Wallerstein, 1987)
- Blended families (Skeen, Robinson, & Flake-Hobson, 1986)
- Moving (Jalongo, 1986b; Prestine, 1997)
- Going to a new school with new children, some of whom might be aggressive (Furman, 1986; Kerbow, 1996)
- Poor quality child care (Matlock & Green, 1990)
- Daily hassles for parents (Crnic & Greenberg, 1990)
- Living conditions that are overcrowded
- Illness and hospitalization (Bull & Drotar, 1991; Stuber, Nadar, Yasuda, & Pynoos, 1991)
- Death (Furman, 1986)

How Stress Can Affect Children

Stress can affect children in a variety of ways. A child might experience physical changes such as a racing heart, dry throat, headaches, or even ulcers. Children also show us that they are overwhelmed with a stressor through their behavior. They might cry, have a great deal of difficulty concentrating, or might be aggressive or withdrawn. Stress can exhibit psychological effects, as when a child is depressed or highly anxious.

These physical, behavioral, or psychological changes are symptoms that something is wrong in a child's world and the human body goes into action when a person comes face-to-face with some sort of stress. The body's major goal when a child responds to stress is to maintain **homeostasis,** that is, to return the body to, and keep it in a constant, stable condition.

Returning and keeping the body at a steady, constant state is the job of the brain, which controls the body's responses to stress. The brain receives messages about the stressor from all parts of the body and its task is to prepare the body for either "fight" or "flight," that is, to prepare the child to get away from the stressor or to deal with it in some way. The brain prepares a person's body to deal with stressors by increasing breathing rate, heart rate, and blood pressure; by dilating air passages; by shunting blood to skeletal muscles; and by increasing production of certain hormones.

Stress can eventually play a major role in disease. Stress is related to an increased risk of disease in a number of ways (Stein, Keller, & Schleifer, 1981; Zegans, 1982).

- Stress upsets a child's immune system response. A child whose immune system is compromised is less resistant to infections. For instance, the number of white blood cells decreases when a child is overwhelmed by a stressful event. These cells protect the body from infections, and a child who is chronically stressed, say from child abuse, is likely to have a lowered resistance to infectious diseases (Hole, 1981).
- Stress causes the body to produce either too much or far too little of certain hormones.
- Stress interrupts a child's sleep patterns; this has a negative effect on a variety of the body's functions.

As a teacher, you can fully expect to experience firsthand a child's reactions to stress. You might wonder why a child suddenly has problems focusing on projects or why a young child seems to be so aggressive. You will wonder why some children are so withdrawn or seem to be so highly anxious in certain situations. Children are not the only ones affected by their reactions to stress; teachers and centers or school systems are affected as well.

STAGES IN RESPONDING TO STRESS

Children go through a series of stages when they respond to a stressor, and each stage places different demands on a child's body (Zegans, 1982). This section describes each of these three stages—alarm, appraisal, and searching for a coping strategy.

Alarm

A child stops what he is doing and "orients" toward or focuses on the potentially stressful event. This is the stage in which a child perceives the situation and is aware of or remembers any danger.

Examples: Ben, 7 years old, stood in the doorway of his new classroom and scanned the room. His mother had moved once again, and Ben was in yet another new school, his third new school in 2 years.

Lee looked up from his game, startled, when his mom said, "Your father will be here to pick you up soon, Lee." Lee's parents had joint custody of him after their divorce and Lee had come to dread visits to his dad's. His dad had remarried and Dad's new wife had a child 2 years older than Lee. This child called Lee names and Dad didn't stop the hurtful behavior of the older child.

Appraisal

The stage of *appraisal* is complex and involves reviewing what this event meant in the past. Ben, for example, thought "I was scared when I went to the last new school, but the teacher helped me find things." Children also try to figure out to cope as Ben did: "Maybe the new teacher will help me find things."

There are several things that affect a child's appraisal of a potentially stressful event. One is developmental level in terms of memory and perception. Infants and very young children will obviously not be able to perceive and remember or evaluate a stress-inducing event like a much older child or an adult would. Positive self-esteem is another thing that affects an older child's appraisal. Older children with positive self-esteem have a much more positive view of stress-inducing events and their ability to cope with the stressor.

Example: Ben, who has a positive and realistic view of himself, appraised the situation and said to himself, "The teacher in my last school told me that I know how to make friends and that other children like me."

Searching for a Coping Strategy

The third stage in responding to stress involves searching for some sort of coping strategy. Children, like all of us, do not always cope effectively with stress-inducing events. Children have a better chance of coping successfully when they believe they can control or master the event (Levine, Weinberg, & Ursin, 1978). Controlling or mastering an event depends, first, on whether the child is familiar with and understands an event, and second, on whether he can generate successful coping strategies. The following possibilities were outlined by Zegans (1982).

1. *A child is familiar with an event, has actively dealt with it in the past, and used a good coping strategy.* This is the best-case scenario, because a child has already successfully dealt with a similar stress-inducing event and would very likely think that he could master the current event.

Example: Thad was to get his first barbershop haircut. Thad has been to the shop lots of times with his father whenever Dad got haircuts, and Thad occasionally got to sit in the big chair on his own. The barber has demonstrated how he uses the things used in haircutting, such as a comb, scissors, and towel.

2. *A child is familiar with an event, has actively dealt with it in the past, but used an ineffective coping strategy.* In this case, the strategy did not work because it was applied incorrectly or was not a good strategy in the first place. This would make a child somewhat wary of the same or a similar stressful event in the future because he has not figured out how to cope.

Example: Lennie, 4 years old, was in the hospital again. He saw the hospital as a frightening place because nobody explained any of the procedures during his last visit.

3. *A child is familiar with a stressor but has not really dealt with it firsthand.* The child only passively dealt with the stressor through secondhand experience, and the secondhand source of information had an impact on his level of emotional or physiological arousal.

Example: Phillip was Ben's friend in Ben's old neighborhood. Phillip's family had never moved, but Phillip observed Ben's reactions to having to move to another new school. Phillip is somewhat familiar with what happens when somebody moves but has an incomplete understanding of the process.

4. *A child is totally unfamiliar with a stressor.* This is a case in which a child has never dealt with such an event, is now thinking about it for the first time, and does not yet have a coping strategy. Just how upset, physically or emotionally, he gets because of the stressful event depends on whether adults help him understand the event and whether they help him figure out how to cope effectively with the stressor.

You can be most helpful to a child who is dealing with a stressful event for the first time in a couple of ways. Consider changing the situation. You can eliminate the stressful event altogether as one mother did by taking the new dog from down the block back to his own yard after he ambled into her yard.

When the stressor is inevitable and cannot be eliminated, do something to help a child understand the meaning of an unfamiliar event. Give the unfamiliar situation meaning by helping a child understand as much as he is capable of understanding. If you use this strategy, you will be acting as a "buffer" to a stressful event. Think of this as "demystifying" the stressful event, making it less mysterious for a child.

Examples: When Tony's family moved (something they had never done before), they did not know anyone in their new neighborhood. Dad took Tony for a "get-acquainted" walk and met the new neighbors.

Josiah's first trip to the emergency room had all the earmarks of a "stressful event" when his parents ran to the car with him seconds after he fell off the swing and broke his arm. In the car Mom kept her composure so that she could help Josiah because she realized how frightened he was. "Remember the hospital? We're going there now, to a special room called the emergency room. A doctor is waiting for you and she'll take a special picture so she can see your arm's bone. Then she'll fix the bone. Mom and Daddy will stay with you. And then we'll all come home. It'll be OK."

The next section of the chapter will focus on the concept of coping with stress, first by explaining the concept of coping. Then we will look at how a child's level of development affects his ability to effectively cope with stressful events.

COPING EFFECTIVELY WITH STRESSORS

What Is *Coping?*

Suppose that you have a flat tire on a major interstate highway, obviously a potentially stressful event for almost anybody. You pull safely to the side of the road and catch your breath. You tell yourself, "Stay calm. I know how to change tires and I have all the equipment that I need to change this tire. I even have flares for safety." What you have done in the process of thinking through your predicament is to have *coped.* You looked inside yourself and found your knowledge that you needed to change the tire and to keep yourself calm.

A person who copes looks for something inside or outside himself to come to terms with stressors (Haan, 1982). In the flat tire example, you coped by searching within yourself for the resources (knowledge) that enabled you to deal with the crisis. At other times a person looks for something outside himself to deal with a stressor.

Example: Another person also has a flat tire but calls a garage with his cell phone. He has coped by looking outside himself for the resources (the garage) that he needed.

Our goal in working with children is to help them to cope as effectively as possible with the stressors that they face. One thing that might help you is to remember that coping does not necessarily mean a child will have a happy or successful outcome. Some situations like child abuse make it very difficult for a person to achieve a "successful" solution (Haan, 1982).

Different ways of coping with stressful events

There are many ways of coping with stressful events. There is no "one-size-fits-all" coping strategy, and you will quickly learn to recognize different patterns in different children and in other adults. No one way is best for every person, and it is probably wise not to force any specific method of coping with stress on anybody.

Some people cope by getting information on the stressor. Someone who copes with stress in this way searches his memory bank for information on how he has dealt with a similar stressor. A person might also look for information outside himself—from other people, self-help groups, a therapist, formal classes, books, pamphlets, movies, television, magazine articles, videos, or the Internet. Bookstores usually stock a lot of self-help books that people read for information on almost any stress-inducing event. Early childhood teachers give information on different stressors when they read well-written books to children about specific stressors like death or moving.

Early childhood teachers give information by reading books about such specific stressors as death or moving to children.

Others cope by taking direct action. Some people escape from a stressful event by choosing to leave the scene. Leaving can be a healthy way to take direct action and to cope. The withdrawal can be temporary, as when a parent leaves a room to "cool off" rather than yell at or hurt a crying baby. Such a person chooses either to return to further deal with the stressor or to cope by permanently withdrawing. A person who withdraws as a way of coping might either announce their plan to leave or might just leave without notice.

Example: Rachel, 5 years old and in kindergarten, was tired of hearing Levi tell her and the other girls that they didn't know how to do certain things because they were girls. She was weary from irritation at not being allowed to play with certain toys when Levi was around. She dealt with the stress of her irritation by announcing, "You can just play by yourself, Levi. I'm not going to play with you anymore!" She then left the science table.

Others take direct action by arguing or asserting their rights. This implies that the person understands that there is probably some injustice that has affected him and is now causing him some stress. You will read in Chapter 7 that asserting one's rights by "using words" is a good way to deal with the stress of anger.

Example: Rachel was clearly upset when Levi sat on her carpet square. She took direct action this time by asserting her rights and "using words" as her teacher had recommended: "Hey, Levi. That's my carpet square! You can get your own."

Another way to cope is to restrain one's movements or actions. A person might control his actions because he understands that it would be the most sensible way to deal with a stressor. For example, a teacher instructed a child who did not have friends in class on how to make friends and taught him how to join a group. Specifically, the teacher showed the child how to control his movement and control his tendency to just push his way into the group. The next day he practiced and controlled his actions by waiting and observing what the other children were doing before joining them.

It is possible for children to also control their actions out of fear or anxiety. Children who are abused often try to be as quiet as possible around the abuser, hoping to seem to disappear and not be noticed.

Still others cope with stress by denying or avoiding the problem. As you remember from your study of psychology, denial is a basic defense mechanism that protects us by allowing us not to face certain situations or to remember unpleasant events.

Example: Elena, 8 years old, is the fourth child in a family of seven children and her parents are migrant farm workers. All of the school-age children in Elena's family change schools frequently as the family moves from one worksite to another. Elena, clearly upset by the turmoil of constant moving, has begun to deny that the family is about to move again as a way of coping with the stress.

Abusive families and children who are abused will often deny that abuse is even occurring. Denial, in fact, is one of the hallmarks of an abusive family system. Denial does not solve problems, however, and people who are in denial often cope with their problem by engaging in some unhealthy activity such as gambling, overeating, drinking, or taking drugs.

Children's Developmental Level Affects Their Ability to Understand and Effectively Cope with Stressors

Guiding children effectively in times of stress requires that we understand what it takes for optimal coping. Then we have to remember what children are like during early childhood in terms of their cognitive, physical, social, and emotional development. Their development in all of these areas affects whether they have what it takes to cope with stressors on their own or whether they need our guidance in order to cope.

This section lists and explains what it takes to cope successfully (Haan, 1982) and then examines developmental considerations. It focuses on why an infant, toddler, preschooler, kindergarten or primary school-age child's developmental level makes it difficult for him to cope well with stressors on his own.

- *Coping well requires the ability to openly examine options.* A person who can openly examine different options has the basic cognitive ability to consider at least two things at one time. A person who can openly examine different options can also "keep an open mind" and take a perspective that might be different from his own perspective.

  Young children are not as capable as older people in taking different perspectives (see Chapter 1 for a discussion of perspective-taking) and they usually focus on only one thing at a time. They often focus on the stress-inducing situation itself and are not able to focus on examining different options.

- *Coping well requires that a person move from problem to solution by inventing creative options.* A person would have to be able to come up with creative ways of solving a problem, for example, "I'm locked out of my car. How can I solve this problem?" To do this, a person would have to be able to move from thinking about the problem to thinking about and then creating a solution. The person would also have to be able to look at an array of different solutions and categorize or classify groups of options.

  Young children have difficulty seeing how things can change because they tend to focus on the "before" and then the "after," but cannot seem to focus on how they could get from before to after. So during early childhood, children have difficulty creating solutions because of their inability to deal with the process of change. The children we teach also have limited classification skills and would not be able to look at a number of solutions and then classify them into logical groups.

- *Coping well requires that a person be able to effectively manage unpleasant or disturbing emotions.* This implies a person can pay attention to and understand emotions like anxiety, fear, or anger that are often associated with stressful events. He can evaluate what those emotions mean for him: "I'm anxious about giving this speech because my grade depends on how well I do today." A person who can manage emotions effectively and appropriately has learned good strategies for managing the emotions: "I am well prepared for the speech and I know how to do deep-breathing prior to beginning to speak."

  Young children have emotions and they certainly express them, as any teacher knows. But young children tend not to understand their emotions or be able to deal with them (Kuebli, 1994). The research on anger tells us that children are not able to understand or deal with anger until a certain age, and then only if they have had good models and instruction in managing anger (Marion, 1997; Marion et al., 1998).

- *Coping well requires that a person understand how his reactions will affect the situation.* Again, this would imply that the person could think of more than one thing at one time—his reaction, the stressful event, how his actions might affect the situation, and how another person might feel about his actions. It implies that the person has a broad enough knowledge and experiential base from which to draw the understanding.

  A young child usually is not able to understand how his reactions to a stressor will affect the situation. He does not understand, for example, that if he reacts to the stress induced by anger by hitting somebody, that the other child will likely be angry in turn.

  Young children in general have a limited knowledge base, and some of the children we teach have an even more restricted knowledge base than others their age. Young children have less knowledge and experience to draw from when they face a stress-inducing event such as the death of a grandparent or moving.

- *Coping well requires that a person be able to think purposefully.* Such a person would be able to think about what is obvious about a stressful event but also be able to acknowledge and think about what is not so obvious or what might be hidden. Thinking purposefully brings together a person's conscious and preconscious thoughts. When you start to think purposefully, you demonstrate that you know that you have thoughts and that you can think about those thoughts—you can "think about thinking."

Example: Starting college for the first time is usually fairly stressful for many students. The ability to think about this stress purposefully, however, enables an older person to cope successfully with the stress of college life. He would be able to think about the obvious, such as where everything is and how to register for courses. He would also be able to think about what is less obvious, such as his anxiety about meeting new people and making friends, because he understands the concept of anxiety and can think about it.

Young children are not able to consciously reflect—think about thinking—on such things as how they feel, why others do things, or how others feel. Young children tend to focus on the obvious—their own upset—and cannot reflect on the less obvious psychological aspects of stressful situations.

GUIDING CHILDREN AS THEY EXPERIENCE STRESS

General Guidelines

Children gradually learn how to manage stress, and then only if we actively teach and encourage them to practice stress management. Many young children's families model, teach, and reward poor coping skills. The parents themselves in these families often do not know how to manage stress, so it would be nearly impossible for them to teach helpful strategies to their children. These children will come to your classroom having already learned poor coping skills. Other children, fortunately, learn more helpful coping skills.

What follows are general guidelines for encouraging young children to develop good coping skills. After studying the general guidelines, you will have an opportunity to read about a specific experience that is very likely to cause great stress for young children.

Use good classroom management strategies to create a low-stress environment

Taking the time and effort to create a developmentally appropriate physical environment will result in a low-stress (not stress-free) classroom. Develop appropriate activities and make sure all materials are appropriate. Use positive child-guidance strategies when dealing with discipline encounters.

Learn and model responsible stress management

Children need teachers to model calm, thoughtful approaches to dealing with daily hassles. This is especially true for children whose parents deal ineffectively with their own daily hassles, because such children have had poor models of how to deal with life's minor problems (Honig, 1986; McBride, 1990).

Acknowledge and learn about the variety of stressors in children's lives

This chapter lists several of these stressors and then describes one of them in greater detail. You cannot learn about every single stressor and how to help children deal with each in one chapter in a textbook, but you can learn the general principles, learn about one or two specific stressors, and then make a commitment to continuing education in this area.

Act as a "buffer" between a child and a stressful event

You are most helpful to young children who cannot manage stressful events on their own if you guide them through the process of coping and if you act as a buffer. Give them opportunities to talk about their concerns, but avoid being meddlesome. Encouraging discussion prepares children for the stresses of new experiences.

Give emotional support through reflective listening, also called **active listening**. When children are embroiled in a stress-producing event, we can best help by listening to their problem without judging, evaluating, or ordering them to feel differently.

Teach relaxation strategies

Relaxation is a good stress-reduction technique for children. Children who can actively control their bodies by deliberately relaxing one or more body parts have a strategy that they can use when they are under stress. You will undoubtedly have to remind them to use the relaxation strategy, because they tend to focus on one thing—their problem—and do not think about how to cope when they are under stress.

The "rubber band" stretch is a good example to use with all children and is doubly useful for children who are very upset. It tends to decrease stress through slow breaths and by stretching arms out like tight rubber bands and then bringing the rubber bands back to hang limply next to the body. A child is more likely to be ready to work on the stress-inducing issue after he is somewhat relaxed.

Learn and teach good coping skills

This often involves direct instruction, and specific strategies will depend on the particular stressor that a child is facing. For example, if a child does not have friends, then you might consider teaching him how to approach other children. If a child is under stress because of a lot of anger, you would do well to teach him how to deal with anger and how to do deep-breathing. Use books to teach about specific stressors (Jalongo, 1986a; Marion, 1997).

The next section describes a specific major stressor for many young children—moving/going to a new school. This particular stressor was chosen for this chapter because almost all early childhood teachers directly confront the issue of children moving away from or to their classrooms. Teachers who understand such specific stress-inducing events as moving have a strong base for helping children deal with such issues.

Guidelines for Helping Children Who Face the Specific Stressor of Moving

We live in a mobile society. By the end of early childhood (end of third grade), one in six of the nation's third-graders had changed schools at least three times since beginning public school (Department of Education [DOE], 1994).

Some groups, such as migrant children, urban low-income, or abused children, move even more frequently than others. For example, 58 percent of one sample of urban low-income students changed schools at least once (Mehana & Reynolds, 1995). Kerbow (1996) also described the high mobility in large urban settings, noting that in Chicago there were clusters of schools tied together by the students they exchange from year to year. Abused children move twice as frequently compared with other children (Lang, 1996). Migrant children, who can move several times in one year, are especially vulnerable to stress from moving (Prewitt Diaz, 1989).

As a teacher you will experience frequently and firsthand the effects of a mobile society just as teachers have for the last several decades. Teachers start the school year knowing that some of their children will move to a new school and that they are likely to get new students anytime during a year. Teachers witness the stress that moving often produces in children, families, and schools (Lash & Kirkpatrick, 1990).

Why moving is stressful for many young children

Moving to a new area is among the most stress-inducing experiences that a family faces, and moves are especially difficult for preschool and primary-grade young children (American Academy of Child & Adolescent Psychiatry [AACAP], 1998; Cornille, 1993; Kutner, 1994). Moving, for children, is a type of loss just as is death or a parent's divorce (Gerlach, 1992). A child loses friends, a home, and a school, the losses often resulting in feelings of sadness and anxiety or even anger. Moving is stressful for many young children because:

- *Moving interrupts friendships and children lose social support.* Children who move to a new area or a new school often think that everybody at school or in the new neighborhood is in a group or has a best friend (AACAP, 1998; Lang, 1996). Children who lose friendships are likely to go through a mourning process for those friendships, and having somebody dismiss or laugh at the loss intensifies the sadness over the loss. If a child is shy or aggressive or has poor social skills, then the move and the need to make friends will be even more difficult and stressful.

  Many children lose the support of older people, too. Moving away from trusted teachers, a cub scout leader, Sunday school teacher, relatives, and neighbors means that a child will not have these adults to turn to for support.

- *Moving elicits unpleasant emotions.* Children, like all of us, experience anxiety and sadness when they move (Prestine, 1997). Young children, however, do not understand their emotions and do not know how to manage them on their own. So added to an already stressful situation of moving is the stress that goes along with emotions that cannot be managed.

- *Moving interrupts the separation process for certain ages.* Moving is especially troublesome for children during early childhood because they are in the process of separating from parents, adjusting to adults other than their parents in centers and schools, and adjusting to peers (AACAP, 1998). Relocating often pushes young children to return to a more dependent relationship with parents than is warranted, thereby interrupting the normal separation process.
- *Moving requires children to adjust to a new curriculum in school and different teacher expectations.* Children often find that they are behind on some subjects or might be ahead in others; this often results in boredom or anxiety (AACAP, 1998; Lang, 1996). Children can withstand the stress if their parents and teachers give them the support that they need. But many children who move most frequently are the least likely to get the help that they need to manage the stress of curriculum changes (DOE, 1994). Their families and schools are often not prepared to give them the support they need.

  For example, Prewitt Diaz (1989) studied the culture of migrancy and noted that there is a survival-oriented way of thinking among migrants of different ethnic and cultural backgrounds. This survival-orientation makes it alarmingly difficult for migrant children to do well in school. Migrant children are negatively affected by many things; among the most important is the fragmented education received between moves and the low self-esteem related to the trauma of constant moving.

  Abused children also move much more frequently than do most children; Lang (1996) reports that the frequent moving accounted for many problems in English and reading. Frequent moves also account in part for abused children having to repeat grades.
- *Moving interrupts school and social services.* Kerbow (1996) noted that some public school systems, such as those in Chicago, are undergoing reforms that center on promoting greater local school autonomy. Greater local autonomy is based on the assumption that children will attend one specific school consistently enough so that the school can make a difference in the child's achievement. Urban low-income children who frequently change schools lose the benefit of any school or social services that go along with such school reform.

Act as a "buffer" between a child and the stress of moving

Schools, teachers, and policy-makers can buffer the stress of moving and changing schools. Moving and changing schools, a potentially stress-inducing event, does not have to automatically have a negative effect on children. With proper support, moving can be a positive growth experience for children (AACAP, 1998). Teachers, directors/principals, schools, and policy-makers must take the first step and make a conscious effort to help children who are about to move away from or who have just transferred to their center or school (Dubow, 1993; Prestine, 1997).

Buffering the effects of moving and changing schools is important for all children, but it is crucial for children who move frequently (DOE, 1994). The DOE's report underscored the urgency of the need to help children who change schools frequently. It reported that these children will continue to be low-achieving in math and reading and may have to repeat grades unless a greater effort is made to help them when they change schools. For example, one of the major changes the DOE recommended is that states implement a more effective student record transfer system. Similarly, child-care centers could help children who change centers by transferring a child's records to the new center after parents give approval.

When a child moves away from your school/classroom. Consider doing some of the following things to help a child deal with the stress of moving away from your classroom. Our goal is to acknowledge our regret at his leaving and help the child find the strength from within to enable him to deal with his feelings and uncertainties about the move. Another goal is to work with parents so that they can also help their child cope with a move.

- Talk with him about moving away and help him understand something about his new school. It would help greatly if you would take the effort to find out where he is going, the name of his school, and his new teacher. Present this information in a positive way.
- Listen carefully and encourage him to talk about his feelings about moving away. Avoid being intrusive, however, and do not force a child to talk about feelings.
- Help him say "good-bye" to his school in a low-key and positive way.
- Give the child a picture of the entire class with him included.
- Make sure that his records are up-to-date and accurate, and make sure that the records are transferred quickly to the new school.
- Follow your center's or school's policy about contacting the new school so that you can give positive information to the new teacher about the child. The goal here is to help the new teacher make the child's transition as smooth as possible.
- Work with the child's parents. Answer their questions and give them information that will enable them to help their child make the move with as little stress as possible (see the Parent Talk box).

When a child moves to your school/classroom. Consider the following suggestions as you welcome a child who is moving to your classroom. Your goal is to open your classroom circle to let this new child in. Adding a new member to a family or a classroom involves adjusting the boundaries to admit that person.

- Obtain the child's file and read it carefully. Follow your school's policy if you need to contact the previous teacher for clarification on any issues.
- Do a home visit if that is possible and if you have done them for the rest of the children. Home visits are a good way to get to know the child.
- Familiarize the child and family with the new school. Invite them to come to school for a tour so that the new school is not so new on the child's first day.

- Make sure that the child and his family know the schedule in your room. Give them a handout of your schedule and encourage parents to talk about his new classroom's schedule.
- Create a space for a new child by preparing a locker or cubby, cot for napping, and any other individualized area or material. Create his space before he arrives, if at all possible.
- Take a new group picture with the new child included. Do this on the first day the new child enters your room.
- Walk through your classroom's and center or school's routines, for example, bathroom, snack or lunch, getting on the bus, waiting for parents. Take your class through the fire safety drill so that everyone, including the new child, knows the procedure. Get the child to tell you about how the new routines are different from or similar to those in his old school.
- Talk with the child and find out what he likes to do in school.
- Include the child in activities of his new room at his pace.
- Request that other children in the class act as guides for the new class member. Be specific in your requests: "Joe, please walk with Robert to the lunchroom. He will be sitting next to you, and I thought that you could show him how the lunch is served in our school," or "It's time to put the carpet squares down for group time, Cindy. Please help Jean choose her carpet square and then sit next to her during her first group time with us."
- Be sure that every child wears a name tag so that a new class member can get to know names.
- Read a book about moving with the child or with the class.
- Listen carefully for the feelings that the new class member has about moving. Acknowledge them and avoid commanding him to feel differently.
- Work with parents. Please see the Parent Talk box for information that you can use with parents to help them buffer the effect of moving on their children. Your school might have a formal policy or program in place through which you can help children who are moving away. Even if there is no formal program, you can do some things to help parents decrease the stress of moving for their children.

Parent Talk. Moving to a New Home? How to Help Your Child Cope with the Move.

Moving is a busy, stressful time for parents who have to buy and sell a house or rent a new apartment, then move the family's possessions, make arrangements for child care and new schools, say good-bye to friends, and finally get acquainted with the new setting and neighbors. Help parents of the children you teach learn some simple but powerful and practical strategies for helping their children adjust to a move. Offer these strategies to parents of children who are either leaving or

(continued on next page)

who are new to your classroom or school. A simple handout with this information might well be the most efficient way to reach parents in the midst of a move.

Explain and listen. Explain clearly to your child why the move is necessary. Are you being transferred? Are you starting school in another section of the state? Is the home you've been building finally finished? Is his school closing? Your child will understand the reason for the move if you state it simply and clearly. Get feedback from your child about what you've explained. Listen closely, clarify anything that your child didn't seem to understand, and "listen for feelings" like fear or anxiety.

Read. Read a book about moving with your child (Jalongo, 1986a). A picture book will help children understand the process of moving and deals with some of their feelings.

Familiarize and describe. Acquaint your child with the new area as much as possible. Visit the new area and take your child on a tour of the new house and neighborhood. Consider visiting the public library or parks. Familiarize children with their new home by using maps of the area or photos of a new house or apartment building. Consider taking the local newspaper early to acquaint your child with the comics section if he has a favorite cartoon.

Describe something about the new area that your child might like such as a pool, a pond with ducks, an amusement park. Give the information in a positive, "upbeat" way, but do not force your child to be enthusiastic.

Get involved. After the move, get involved with your children in activities of the new community such as synagogue or church, parent's group at school, YMCA, family education and support program, or volunteer groups such as the humane society.

This information was adapted from two sources:

American Academy of Child & Adolescent Psychiatry, *Children and family moves* (1998). A Family Fact Sheet available on the Parenthood Web. May be reproduced and given to parents if the Academy is cited.

Prestine, J. (1997). *Helping children cope with moving: A practical resource guide for "Moving Is Hard."* Kids Have Feelings, Too Series. Fearon Teacher Aids, 299 Jefferson Road, PO Box 480, Parsippany, NJ 07054-0480.

Case Study Analysis: Buffering Joseph's Move to His New School

Analyze the chapter opening case study to decide how well Mr. Fong, the teacher, buffered the effect of Joseph's move to his new kindergarten. Use the suggestions in the section of the chapter called "When a child moves to your school/classroom" as a guide for your analysis.

1. Identify, from your perspective, the three most helpful strategies that Mr. Fong used.
2. If you had to choose the single most important thing that Mr. Fong did to help Joseph, what would you choose? Why?
3. If you were the teacher, what would be one additional thing that you would have done? Why? Which of the strategies used would you have eliminated and why would you not have used it?
4. Now, give your overall evaluation of how well Mr. Fong has "cushioned" or "buffered" Joseph's move to his new school. Mr. Fong did a(n) _____ job (excellent, good, adequate, barely adequate, quite bad).

REFLECTING ON KEY CONCEPTS

1. Describe a *resilient* child. Please describe the circumstances under which a child is most likely to experience stress from any life event.
2. "Stress?" asks a friend of yours who is unfamiliar with early childhood. "What do children have to be 'stressed' about?" Talk to this person about acute and chronic stress and about the two major sources of stress for young children. Also tell that person about how stress can affect young children.
3. Alarm, appraisal, searching for a coping strategy: all of these are stages of responding to stress. What sorts of behaviors would you look for in a child at each of the stages?
4. What does it mean when we say that a person has coped with a stressful event? What does it mean to say that coping does not necessarily mean that a person has come to a happy or successful conclusion?
5. What does it take to cope well with stressors? Use your knowledge of child development to explain why young children have such a difficult time coping well with stressors on their own.
6. Given your response to Question 5, explain why teachers and other professionals have to buffer the effect of potentially stressful events for young children and give several specific ideas for helping children cope with stress.

APPLY YOUR KNOWLEDGE

Get a start on developing some expertise in one thing that can cause stress for children. Do you want to know more about how death, divorce, hospitalization, child abuse, child neglect, harsh parenting, not having friends, or loneliness cause stress for some children? Choose a specific stressor and then prepare yourself to help children deal effectively with it by doing the following application activities.

1. Surf the Net and other resources. Here are some suggestions: the ERIC database on the Internet is an excellent resource for early childhood information. Also use one of the other searching mechanisms to find information on your chosen stressor. Visit or call the Extension Service in your county and ask the family or child life specialist for written information on your topic. Collect magazine articles about your stressor. Make copies of the information, study the information, and organize it in a file for later use.
2. Children's books. Develop an annotated bibliography of children's books about the stressor you have chosen. Find and read at least four children's books. Give a brief synopsis of each and then explain how you would use it to help children deal with that specific stressor.
3. Your portfolio and interview. Let others know that you have knowledge, skills, and materials for teaching children how to begin to cope with this specific stressor. Decide how to place information in your professional portfolio.

Then role-play being interviewed for a teaching position. The director/principal looks over your portfolio, pauses, and asks you, "I see that you've studied about how children deal with _____ [moving, death, divorce, etc.]. How would you see yourself using this information if you're hired to teach in this school?" Be prepared to explain how you would use the material you've gathered in your teaching and with parents.

References

Amato, P. (1997). Life-span adjustment of children to their parents' divorce. In E. Junn & C. Boyatzis (Eds.), *Annual editions: Child growth & development.* (pp. 149–169). Sluice Dock, Guilford, CT: Dushkin/McGraw-Hill.

American Academy of Child & Adolescent Psychiatry (1998). Children and family moves, *A Family Fact Sheet,* Internet, Parenthood Web.

Benard, B. (1995). Fostering resilience in children. *ERIC Digest,* EDO-PS-95–9 (http://ericps.crc.uiuc.edu/eece/pubs/digests/1995/benard95.html). University of Illinois at Urbana-Champaign: *ERIC Digest,* Clearinghouse on Elementary and Early Childhood Education.

Bull, B., & Drotar, D. (1991). Coping with cancer in remission: Stressors and strategies reported by children and adolescents. *Journal of Pediatric Psychology, 16*(6), 767–782.

Bullock, J. R. (1997). Children without friends: Who are they and how can teachers help? In E. Junn & C. Boyatzis (Eds.), *Annual editions: Child growth & development* (pp. 121–125). Sluice Dock, Guilford, CT: Dushkin/McGraw-Hill.

Burts, D., Hart, C., Charlesworth, R., Fleege, P., Mosley, J., & Thomasson, R. (1992). Observed activities and stress behaviors of children in developmentally appropriate and inappropriate kindergarten classrooms. *Early Childhood Research Quarterly, 7,* 297–318.

Cornille, T. (1993). Support systems and the relocation process for children and families. *Marriage & Family Review, 19*(3–4), 281–298.

Crnic, K., & Greenberg, M. (1990). Minor parenting stresses with young children. *Child Development, 6*(5), 1628–1637.

Department of Education (Migrant Education Program), (1994). Elementary school children: Many change schools frequently, harming their education. Report to the Honorable March Kaptur, House of Representatives. Washington, DC: author. *ERIC Digest,* No. EC369526.

Dubow, E. (1993). Development and evaluation of a school-based stress and coping curriculum. *ERIC Digest,* No. ED360051.

Fabes, R., & Eisenberg, N. (1992). Young children's coping with interpersonal anger. *Child Development, 63*(1), 116–128.

Furman, E. (1986). What nursery school teachers ask us about: Psychoanalytic consultations in preschools: Stress in the nursery school. *Emotions and Behavior Monographs,* No. 5, 53–68.

Gale, J., Thompson, R., Moran, T., & Sack, W. (1988). Sexual abuse in young children: Its clinical presentation and characteristic patterns. *Child Abuse and Neglect, 12*(2), 163–170.

Gerlach, K. (1992). Stress in children bibliography. *ERIC Digest,* No. ED367662.

Haan, N. (1982). The assessment of coping, defense, and stress. In L. Goldberger & S. Breznitz (Eds.), *Handbook of stress: Theoretical and clinical aspects.* New York: Free Press.

Hole, J. (1981). *Human anatomy and physiology.* Dubuque, IA: Wm. C. Brown.

Holroyd, K., & Lazarus, R. (1982). Stress, coping, and somatic adaptation. In L. Goldberger & S. Breznitz (Eds.), *Handbook of stress: Theoretical and clinical aspects.* New York: Free Press.

Honig, A. S. (1986). Research in review: Stress and coping in children. In J. B. McCracken (Ed.), *Reducing stress in young children's lives.* Washington, DC: NAEYC.

Hyson, M., Hirsh-Pasek, K., Rescorla, L., & Cone, J. (1991). Ingredients of parental pressure in early childhood. *Journal of Applied Developmental Psychology, 12*(3), 347–365.

Jalongo, M. R. (1986a). Using crisis-oriented books with young children. In J. B. McCracken (Ed.), *Reducing stress in young children's lives.* Washington, DC: NAEYC.

Jalongo, M. R. (1986b). When young children move. In J. B. McCracken (Ed.), *Reducing stress in young children's lives.* Washington, DC: NAEYC.

Kerbow, D. (1996). Patterns of urban student mobility and local school reform. *ERIC Digest,* No. ED402386.

Kuebli, J. (1994). Research in review: Young children's understanding of everyday emotions. *Young Children, 50*(3), 36–47.

Kutner, L. (1994). "Good-bye, house." *Parents, 69*(4), 106–109.

Lang, S. (1996). Maltreated children move more often, do worse in school. *Human Ecology Forum, 24*(3), 24.

Lash, A., & Kirkpatrick, S. (1990). New perspectives on student mobility. Final report. *ERIC Digest,* No. ED322608.

Levine, S., Weinberg, J., & Ursin, H. (1978). Definition of the coping process and statement of the problem. In H. Ursin (Ed.), *Psychobiology of stress.* New York: Academic.

Marion, M. (1994). Encouraging the development of responsible anger management in young children. *Early Child Development and Care, 97,* 155–163.

Marion, M. (1997). Research in review: Guiding children's understanding and management of anger. *Young Children, 52*(7), 62–67.

Marion, M., Barby, S., Dahl, D., & Friske, J. (1998). Helping children manage the strong emotion of anger. *Early Childhood News,* January-February, pp. 6–12.

Matlock, J., & Green, V. (1990). The effects of day care on the social and emotional development of infants, toddlers and preschoolers. *Early Child Development and Care, 64,* 55–59.

McBride, A. (1990). The challenges of multiple roles: The interface between work and family when children are young. *Prevention in Human Services, 9*(1), 143–166.

McCracken, J. B. (1986). *Reducing stress in young children's lives.* Washington, DC: NAEYC.

McKinnon, R., & Wallerstein, J. (1987). Joint custody and the preschool. *Conciliation Courts Review, 25*(2), 39–47.

Mehana, J., & Reynolds, A. (1995). "The effects of school mobility on scholastic achievement." Paper presented at the Biennial Meeting of the Society for Research in Child Development, Indianapolis, IN (March 30–April 2).

Prestine, J. (1997). *Helping children cope with moving: A practical resource guide for "Moving Is Hard."* Parsippany, NJ: Fearon Teacher Aids.

Prewitt Diaz, J. (1989). The effects of migration on children: An ethnographic study. *ERIC Digest,* No. ED327346.

Sargent, J. (1982). Stress and headaches. In L. Goldberger & S. Breznitz (Eds.), *Handbook of stress: Theoretical and clinical aspects.* New York: Free Press.

Skeen, P., Robinson, B., & Flake-Hobson, C. (1986). Blended families. In J. B. McCracken (Ed.), *Reducing stress in young children's lives.* Washington, DC: NAEYC.

Stein, M., Keller, S., & Schleifer, S. (1981). The hypothalamus and the immune response. In H. Weiner, M. Hofer, & A. Stunkard (Eds.), *Brain, behavior and bodily disease.* New York: Raven.

Stuber, M., Nadar, K., Yasuda, P., & Pynoos, R. (1991). Stress responses after pediatric bone marrow transplantation: Preliminary results of a prospective longitudinal study. *Journal of the American Academy of Child and Adolescent Psychiatry, 30*(6), 952–957.

Weinreb, M. (1997). Be a resiliency mentor: You may be a lifesaver for a high-risk child. *Young Children, 52*(2), 14–20.

Zegans, L. (1982). Stress and the development of somatic disorders. In L. Goldberger & S. Breznitz (Eds.), *Handbook of stress: Theoretical and clinical aspects.* New York: Free Press.

Zimbardo, P. (1982). Shyness and the stresses of the human condition. In L. Goldberger & S. Breznitz (Eds.), *Handbook of stress: Theoretical and clinical aspects.* New York: Free Press.

Chapter 6

Guiding Children Toward a Healthy Sense of Self and Self-Esteem

After reading and studying this chapter, you will be able to:

- Define self-esteem and explain how it is a part of the self-system.
- List, explain, and give an example of the three building blocks of self-esteem.
- Explain how social interaction affects the development of self-esteem.
- Tell in your own words how adult acceptance and support affect a child's self-esteem.
- List, explain, and give examples of specific adult practices that affect a child's self-esteem.
- Analyze the case study.
- Acknowledge the importance of helping children develop a strong moral compass as well as a healthy and balanced self-esteem.

Sticks and stones may break our bones, but words will break our hearts.
(Fulghum, 1988, p. 18)

Case Study: Self-Esteem

Mrs. Apodaca, an early childhood consultant, works with teachers on understanding the issue of self-esteem. She first likes to find out what teachers currently believe about self-esteem and then likes to observe in their classrooms before making recommendations. Here are some samples from her visits.

Preschool Classroom

"I want my children," the teacher said, "to feel good about themselves but I *don't* believe in doing a lot of cute activities focusing on self-esteem. I also think it's *in*appropriate to give them a lot of empty praise and flattery." Mrs. Apodaca watched this teacher treat her class with great respect, use positive guidance strategies, and give them positive meaningful feedback instead of empty flattery. For example, the teacher expressed appreciation for a child's effort: "Clara, you walked across the balance beam gracefully."

Kindergarten Classroom

"I want to help my children," said the teacher, "to realize that a big part of themselves [and self-esteem] is tied to helping and working cooperatively with others." She and the children had placed a large display on one wall titled "We are a class filled with helpers." Under the sign was a group picture of the class. Then the teacher had taken pictures of small groups of children working together or helping each other. She made sure that each child was included in a picture. Each group picture was displayed, and there was a brief description of how they had worked or cooperated with each other.

First-Grade Classroom

"My main goal," said the teacher, "is to boost the self-esteem of the children." During the classroom observation, Mrs. Apodaca heard lots of praise but for trivial things. Every child who came down the slide heard the teacher say, "Good job!" Whenever any child hung her coat on a hook the teacher said, "way to go!" Each child in the class made a book called "This Is Me!" The books consisted of duplicated pages asking a child to provide facts such as "My favorite thing to eat is . . .," "I want to buy this when I go to the store . . .," or "I want a birthday cake that looks like this . . . ." This teacher also made an "I am special because . . ." book for each child. The children completed the sentences on each page, for example, "I am special because my favorite color is . . ." or "because I have _____ hair."

Second-Grade Classroom

"I think," said the teacher, "that the children will do well in school when they feel good about themselves. Lizzie and Gordy are having trouble with the new math concept. But math really isn't as important as how these children feel about themselves, so I'm not going to focus on their trouble with math." The principal, when asked about this teacher's approach, was astounded. He pulled the children's records and showed the consultant the teacher's note to the parents that these two children were doing excellent work in math.

Third-Grade Classroom

"I think," wrote the teacher, "that *real* self-esteem grows from real effort and persistence, not from getting a smiley face slapped on every little thing that you do. Real self-

(contiued)

esteem is *earned.*" This teacher's approach to working with a child having trouble with math was to individualize his instruction so that the child could learn the concepts at her own pace. He talked with the parents about the issue: "June understands most of the math concepts but is having difficulty with two specific concepts. I'm certain that she can master these, and we are working on it. Here's a sample of how she is improving. One of June's best qualities is her persistence, which will work well for her."

ou can easily see that teachers differ in their views on self-esteem and how to foster it. Self-esteem has become a major issue in the early childhood field and you, like the case study teachers, will be squarely faced with making decisions about this issue. Our goal as early childhood professionals is to help children develop a healthy sense of self and self-esteem. This chapter will help you with these decisions by explaining what a healthy sense of self and self-esteem is and how it develops. You will identify some of the major issues regarding self-esteem, for example, can positive self-esteem ever be a bad thing? Then you will learn about appropriate and practical strategies that foster healthy self-esteem as well as a strong moral compass. You will have a chance to analyze the case study and will learn how to present some of this information to parents. Let's first focus on what self-esteem is and how it develops.

THE NATURE AND DEVELOPMENT OF SELF-ESTEEM

Parts of the "Self-System"

The *self* is like a family system in that it is made up of many parts, and the parts form a whole. Just as a family system is different from any of the individual members of the system, the self-system is different from any of the parts that go into making it up. This section describes the separate parts or components of a child's self-system. The parts are *self-referential behaviors, self-concept, self-regulatory behaviors, and self-esteem.* The children who you teach began to develop their sense of self while they were infants and continue to develop this concept throughout their lives. The self is a cognitive structure that a human literally and gradually builds or constructs inside her head (Curry & Johnson, 1990; Harter, 1983).

Self-referential behaviors

Self-referential behaviors include viewing the self as separate from others and as an active, independent causal agent. Infants gradually learn that they are separate from other people, and this learning occurs as the infant's perceptual system develops during the first year of life. Self-referential behavior emerges during infancy and toddlerhood and continues to develop during early childhood. A child must be able to refer to her *self* and herself as separate from others and as capable of causing things to happen before she can ever develop self-esteem.

Self-concept

Self-concept is the knowledge that a child acquires about her *self*. Children go through a long process of learning about the self. Children gradually gather information about themselves, such as physical appearance, physical abilities, gender, intellectual abilities, and interpersonal skills. Such knowledge gathering goes on at about the same time as more general changes in cognitive development.

Example: Six-year-old Patrick did one of the classic Piagetian conservation experiments with his teacher and said, "You have the same amount of water in that short glass as you have in that tall glass . . . because the short glass is so fat that it holds just as much as the tall glass." (Conservation is one of the more general changes in cognitive development.) During the same week the teacher heard Patrick say to his friend Jake, "Yeah! We're boys and we'll always be boys. They're girls [pointing to a group of girls] and they're always going to be girls." (This is called *gender constancy;* children understand that gender remains the same when they understand the concept that some things remain the same, despite apparent changes.)

A child's set of ideas about himself affects how he behaves (Harter, 1983). For example, a 6-year-old boy who believes that washing dishes is "girl's work" is very likely to refuse to comply or at least protest when his father tells him to wash dishes. And a 7-year-old girl who views her *self* as someone who can run fast would more likely enter a race than her friend who believes that she cannot run fast.

Self-regulatory behaviors

Self-regulatory behaviors are those behaviors that allow us to control our impulses, tolerate frustration, and put off immediate gratification. You can expect to see the beginnings of self-regulation or self-control in children who are about 24 months old and will notice that they become better able to use certain strategies to regulate their own behavior as they get older. This is the part of the self that enables children to stop themselves from hurting somebody, to think before acting, or to use words instead of hitting. Parents and teachers can use guidance strategies that help children use such strategies.

Example: A preschool teacher had been working on helping 4-year-old Lucy use words instead of hitting when Lucy was angry. She wanted Lucy to control the impulse to strike out when angry. So the teacher said, "Lucy, just as soon as you know that you are angry, put up your STOP sign and say to yourself, 'Stop! Use words. Don't hit.'"

Self-esteem

Self-esteem is like self-regulation, self-concept, and self-referential behavior because it is one part of the self-system. Self-esteem is also different from the other parts of the self-system. You have heard the old saying, "She is held in high esteem," which indicates that somebody thinks highly of another person. The same thing is true for a child as she pays attention to all the information that she gathers about herself. A child will stand back and make some sort of judgment about the self. When we speak about a child's self-esteem we are talking about that part of the self through which she evaluates the self (Coopersmith, 1967; Harter, 1983; Tafarodi & Swarm, 1995).

Ideas About Self-Esteem to Remember

1. High self-esteem can mean *confident and secure,* but it can also mean *conceited, arrogant, narcissistic, and egotistical* (Baumeister, 1996). It is important that we help children develop self-esteem that is realistic, positive, and healthy. It is important that children earn self-esteem by meeting the demands of authori*tative* caregivers and that we not artificially boost their view of themselves (Lerner, 1996). We do not want to do anything that will give children inflated self-esteem, that is, unrealistic positive views about the self and excessive pride (Curry & Johnson, 1990).

2. Healthy self-esteem is earned (Lerner, 1996). One of the things that people with healthy self-esteem have learned is that they cannot just wish for competence, they have to work for it. They have learned that they have to make things happen through their own effort rather than trying to force or manipulate others into doing things for them. People with healthy self-esteem have earned a positive self-evaluation through hard work that results in increased competence. Lerner (1996) believes that children who do not have to live within limits and who are congratulated for mediocre work do not develop healthy self-esteem.

3. Self-esteem is a dynamic process that goes on throughout a lifetime. The wonderful thing about being an early childhood professional is that we are present as children start to evaluate themselves (Bakley, 1997) and we can help children develop a healthy and balanced view of themselves. Children's initial self-esteem develops slowly in early childhood, tends to be stable and long-lasting, and provides a secure foundation for further growth and development.

THE BUILDING BLOCKS OF SELF-ESTEEM: COMPETENCE, CONTROL, AND WORTH

What is it in the self that a child examines and evaluates so that she can develop her self-esteem? We do know that self-esteem is not just one overall global concept but that it can be broken down into distinct parts. Every child builds self-esteem as she observes and evaluates several different parts or dimensions—competence, control, and worth or significance to others (Coopersmith, 1967; Curry & Johnson, 1990; Harter, 1983).

Competence

We all need to feel competent, that we can meet demands for achievement (Harter, 1982; Tafarodi & Swarm, 1995; White, 1959). Children who have an honest and balanced sense of themselves can look at themselves in a number of areas and make realistic judgments about how they are doing in an area. It is possible to feel extremely competent in one area and only moderately competent in another area and still have positive self-esteem.

Example: Nita is 5 years old and is very competent socially, that is, she gets along with adults and other children. She makes friends easily and knows how to get her parents' or teacher's attention without whining. She deals with angry feelings in a nonaggressive way. She is only moderately competent in physical skills but seems to enjoy them anyway because her mother and father have never made fun of her physical skills.

Other children have a far less balanced view of themselves. They might not recognize their competence in an area and might even dwell on poor performance in some other area. Children with a negative view of their competence in some area might have had their lack of ability pointed out by adults. Some children have even been humiliated for being competent in an area.

Example: Veronica is 5 years old and loves and is very good in physical activities. Her mother, however, calls Veronica a tomboy when she gets physically active. Mom has begun to dress her daughter in frilly dresses that make it impossible for Veronica to climb or jump. Veronica has begun to think about her physical skills in a negative way, even though she is skillful.

How a child is motivated has a big impact on how she achieves. Some of the children you will teach will be primarily interested in understanding something new or in acquiring some new skill. They will be oriented toward learning (Elliott & Dweck, 1988), fail at some things, or make mistakes; they will not just give up but will try to overcome the problem (Mischel, 1981).

Example: June, the third-grader in the chapter opener case study, realized that she did not understand the new math concept. She did not get upset but instead said to her teacher, "I don't understand this. Can you help me?"

Other children will be motivated differently. You will deal with some children who go to great lengths to avoid having anybody make unfavorable judgments about their competence (Wine, 1982). They dread making mistakes and often react to them by giving up a project instead of trying again, practicing, and overcoming the problem. Their confidence is often undermined by the adults in their lives.

Some children have the confidence that they can achieve their goals, while others expect that they will not be able to achieve their goals even when they have the capacity to do so (Elliott & Dweck, 1988). Children who expect to perform well on challenging tasks are able to analyze the skills needed for effective performance (Meichenbaum & Asarnow, 1982). Children who expect to be able to perform well are realistic when analyzing a task and are not overly optimistic (Janoff-Bulman & Brickman, 1981). They do not overestimate the difficulty of a task and don't say "I can't do it" (Dweck & Leggett, 1988).

Control

We all deal with the issue of control throughout our lives (Wong, 1992). Another part of self-esteem is called ***control,*** which refers to the degree to which a person feels responsible for outcomes in her life or the degree to which she attributes events to sources beyond her control (Connell, 1980). Some children believe that they can "get things done," and that it is their actions that influence whether they do achieve a goal. They also believe that they can decide how much effort to expend in achieving their goals—that they have control over their effort. They have a positive and healthy view of control.

Example: Mrs. Apodaca observed an interaction between 4-year-old Christine and the preschool teacher that will very likely help Christine develop a positive view of her control. Christine was doing a science experiment—adding food coloring to white play dough to change the color of the dough. She was trying to match a light blue color on a chart but added far too much coloring. The teacher said, "You have a problem. What do you think would happen if you took this big glob of white dough and mixed it with your small glob of dark blue dough? Why don't you try mixing the two? It will take a lot of squishing and squashing!" Christine pummeled and pushed the dough until she got the light color that she wanted. She smiled and called out, "Look! I made the color of the sky!" The teacher then said, "You really worked hard at mixing that dough, Christine."

It is hundreds of such interactions that show children that they can, indeed, control many of the outcomes in their lives. Many children have been discouraged from viewing themselves as "in control." Authori*tarian* teachers or parents, for example, exert a lot of arbitrary control over their children, discouraging children from making decisions and from engaging in verbal "give and take" with adults. Abusive parents go even further and model an extremely rigid, external type of control. It would be quite difficult for children from these types of families to evaluate themselves as being in control of what happens to them in certain circumstances. These children tend not to think that their own actions influence whether they achieve goals.

Kemple (1995) suggests a child's sense of control or efficacy is a critical aspect of her self-evaluation or self-esteem. She further suggests that a shy child's lack of assertiveness, lack of initiative, and unwillingness to take risks reflect her limited sense of control.

Worth

Completing the circle of self-esteem is the part called *worth* or *significance to others*. This refers to a generalized sense of one's own social worth (Tafarodi & Swarm, 1995). This generalized sense is built on a child's evaluation of how much she likes herself, whether she judges herself to be liked or loved by peers and parents, and whether she believes she is accepted by and deserving of attention from others. Some children see themselves as accepted, well liked, and deserving the attention of others. Others see themselves as unloved and unworthy of attention.

HOW DOES SELF-ESTEEM DEVELOP?

Self-Esteem Develops in a Social Context

Any child's view of herself develops in a social context or setting. Infants come into this world with a basic temperamental style, and physical, psychological, and emotional characteristics. These characteristics influence that baby's behavior and also influence the reactions of adults to the infant. The self that an infant eventually experiences depends on both of these things—the interaction of the child's characteristics and behavior with other people (Anderson & Hughes, 1989; Brazelton, 1997; Curry & Johnson, 1990; Tafarodi & Vu, 1997).

This implies that both a child and an adult have an active part in a child's developing sense of self, that a child's sense of self is not just a mirror image of the adult's attitude toward that child. But there is one thing that you might consider as you work with young children: You have a greater share of responsibility in any interaction with a child.

Example: The caregiver in the infant room at a child-care center noticed that Amelia, 5 months old, cried a lot and was generally fussy. The caregiver thought that Amelia might have a difficult temperamental style. The caregiver thought, "Hmm, how can I help Amelia?" To this caregiver's credit, she recognized her responsibility to figure out how to mesh her responses with the baby's style.

Example: The teacher in the preschool room knew that Kenneth had been physically abused by his biological parents and was now in foster care. Kenneth's negative view of his worth and control was clearly shown in his many angry outbursts

The "self" that a baby comes to know depends on the interaction of the infant's characteristics and behavior of other people.

with other children. Understanding that Kenneth's sense of self was at stake, the teacher spent considerable effort helping him acquire a more accurate and positive view of his self.

How Adults Influence a Child's Self-Esteem

Parents, grandparents, aunts, uncles, brothers, sisters, cousins, neighbors, and teachers make up a child's social environment, and a child's opinion about her competence, control, and worth develops out of close involvement with these persons (Curry & Johnson, 1990). Adults observe children, have attitudes about them, interact with them, and interpret a child's behavior and characteristics. Children evaluate the self and develop self-esteem, to a large extent, because of the attitudes of others who are important to them. Parents and teachers are among the significant others who affect children's self-esteem because young children believe that adults possess a superior wisdom and children tend to rely on adult judgments (Harter, 1983).

The process that adults use to influence children's self-esteem is similar to the process that a computer programmer uses to develop information output. Computer programmers feed data into the computer (Figure 6–1). Significant adults feed data to the child through words, facial expressions, and actions, telling a child what the adult's attitude toward the child is. The adult data say such things as:

"You sure have lots of friends!"
"You're so gentle with Sam [the puppy]. I'll bet he feels safe with you."
"I like being with you."
"It's OK to feel angry when somebody takes something that belongs to you."

You know the old saying, "garbage in, garbage out."

Figure 6–1 Poor computer programs result from careless programming. Similarly, negative self-esteem in children results from degrading, demeaning adult behavior.
(Source: Stone, M. *Data Processing: An Introduction.* Reprinted from INFOSYSTEMS, copyright © 1978 by Hitchcock Publishing Company.)

> "It was thoughtful of you to whisper when you walked past the baby's crib when she was sleeping."
> "That game was fun. Let's play it again sometime."
> "You tell funny jokes. Grandma would love to hear that one!"

The adult data can, unfortunately, also say such things as the following:

> "No wonder nobody plays with you!"
> "You're really a lazy person."
> "Yuck! What muddy colors you used for painting."
> "Don't bother me. Play by yourself."
> "Grow up! Stop whining because she took your puzzle."
> "Why don't you stop cramming food into your face? You're fat enough already."
> "You know something? I wish you'd never been born!"

This data, taken in over a period of years, influences a child's evaluation of the self. The child's concepts of herself are put together with her physical and psychological characteristics to influence her future behavior (Curry & Johnson, 1990), which then influences the adult's attitudes and behavior once again. Computer scientists emphasize, as the cartoon implies, that if input is "garbage" then we can expect output to be "garbage" as well. Similarly, adults who feed a child "garbage" messages that convey demeaning, degrading adult attitudes can fully expect that child's self-esteem to be "garbage," too. *Garbage in, garbage out.*

Now that you know how children develop a sense of self, which includes self-esteem, it is important that you know how to influence, but not determine, a child's self-esteem. The most important thing that you can do to help children develop healthy self-esteem is to adopt an authoritative caregiving style. Adults who are authoritative tend to use specific appropriate practices as they interact with children, and these strategies influence a child's self-esteem. The next section describes several appropriate practices that will help you guide children toward a healthy and balanced sense of self and self-esteem.

GUIDING CHILDREN TOWARD HEALTHY SELF-ESTEEM

Adults use specific practices that affect a child's self-esteem. Authori*tative,* supportive adults use strategies that enhance, or help to improve, children's development of healthy and positive self-esteem. Nonsupportive adults use strategies that demean children and contribute to the development of negative self-esteem.

Practices That Guide Children Toward Healthy and Balanced Self-Esteem

Believe in and adopt an authoritative caregiving style

An authoritative caregiving style—high in both demandingness and responsiveness—is related to higher levels of compliance (obedience), helpfulness, and cooperation, and to lower levels of aggression. As you might suspect, an adult's caregiving style also affects a child's self-esteem. Parents and teachers are most likely to help children develop healthy self-esteem when they use a mixture of acceptance, affection, expectations, and limits on children's behavior and effort (Bednar, Wells, & Peterson, 1989; Hales, 1979a, 1979b; Lamborn, Mounts, Steinberg, & Dornbusch, 1991). You can review this style by reading Chapter 2 in this text.

Plan appropriate activities that focus on self-esteem

You really do not need to plan a lot of "cute activities" that are intended to boost self-esteem. In fact, cute activities are frequently developmentally inappropriate, as were the activities in the first-grade classroom in the chapter opening case study. The "This Is Me!" book focused the children's attention on themselves as consumers and the "I am special because . . ." book focused on trivial things about each child.

Katz (1993) believes that children are most likely to develop healthy self-esteem when they participate in activities for which they can make real decisions and contributions. Katz and Chard's work (1989) on the project approach helps the child focus on real topics, environments, events, and objects that are deserving of a young child's time and effort. Developmentally appropriate activities help a child see herself as connected to others, as a hard worker, as kind and helpful, and as a problem solver. These are enduring traits that will help children develop a healthy sense of self and self-esteem.

Example: Take another look at the chapter opening case studies and you will see an example of this. The kindergarten teacher's emphasis on her group as "a class filled with helpers" is a very good example of this approach. This teacher is guiding the children toward self-esteem that is based on being connected to others in a meaningful way, not on some self-centered emphasis on trivial characteristics.

Express genuine interest in children and their activities

Engage in joint activities willingly. Adults who show an interest in children believe that a child's activities—whether it is playing with measuring cups, finger painting, playing computer games, building a campsite, or playing in sand—are valid and interesting for the child (Kuykendall, 1991). An adult communicates her belief that the child is a person worthy of the adult's attention by demonstrating concern about a child's welfare, activities, and friends. Children tend to be competent, both academically and interpersonally, when significant adults communicate genuine interest in them (Harter, 1983; Heyman, Dweck, & Cain, 1992; Sheridan, 1991).

Coopersmith (1967) found that parents of both high and low self-esteem children spent the same amount of time with their children. He explained this puzzling finding by saying that the mothers of high self-esteem children spent time willingly with their child and seemed to enjoy the interaction. Mothers of low self-esteem children, on the other hand, appeared to spend time with their children grudgingly.

Give meaningful feedback to children

Giving feedback to children is one of the basic ways through which adults influence children. Feedback from adults about how a child has performed a task is an important source of information about the child's competence (Bandura, 1981). Adults who encourage credit-taking focus on what a child has done well, thereby helping her recognize her competence, one of the dimensions of self-esteem.

Example: The preschool teacher, who knew that Sarah recognized and could name a square and a circle but did not know the name for a triangle, placed a large square, circle, and triangle on a bulletin board and had the same shapes in a box. "You know the names of some shapes, Sarah. Reach into this box, take out one shape, and put it on top of the same shape on the board. When Sarah correctly matched squares, the teacher said, "You're right!" When Sarah matched the triangular shapes she simply said, "You've matched the triangles!"

Some people use empty praise and flattery, thinking that such feedback will boost self-esteem. We are most likely to help children develop a healthy sense of self and self-esteem when we use what Katz (1993) calls *meaningful feedback in the form of appreciation* rather than empty praise and flattery. ***Appreciation*** is meaningful positive feedback that is directly related to what a child has made an effort to do or is interested in. This is an appropriate practice that will help a child build a healthy view of her competence.

Example: Mrs. Apodaca, the consultant, observed the third-grade teacher use appreciation as feedback. Bennie was working on a project about mammals and had a specific question. The teacher brought in a new reference book in response to the question. This teacher was helping Bennie develop healthy self-esteem based on increased understanding of a specific concept.

"Jenna, I saw you talking quietly to the birds." This teacher is expressing appreciation for Jenna's effort and avoids empty praise and flattery. This practice is likely to enhance the child's self esteem.

Acknowledge pleasant and unpleasant feelings

The real test of support of a child worthy of attention comes when a child is sick, hurt, unhappy, angry, jealous, fearful, or anxious. Authori*tative* adults believe that all feelings are legitimate (they do not, however, let children hurt others when expressing the feelings). Chapter 7 focuses on the strong emotion of anger.

Demonstrate respect for all family groups and cultures. Avoid sexism and judging physical attributes

An abiding belief that all children are valuable must come through clearly to children in our words and actions. It is important that children observe us demonstrate authentic respect for both genders, for children with different abilities, and for various family groups and different cultures (Bakley, 1997; Beane, 1991).

Examples: The kindergarten teacher, Mrs. Apodaca observed, needed help in carrying a bale of hay. She asked for two strong children and then chose a girl and a boy. This teacher knows her class well. Several children live in single-parent families and one child lives with her grandmother. When discussing the topic of families, she showed pictures of each child's family and said, "There are lots of people in some of your families, and some of your families are small."

Teach specific social skills

Some children have serious problems with social skills that interfere with their having positive experiences. Consequently, their evaluation of themselves suffers and they are likely to develop a negative view of their competence, control, and worth—self-esteem. Rather than artificially boosting self-esteem, Curry and Johnson (1990) recommend teaching such children real skills as a way of giving them positive social experiences with others. For example, they might need to learn how to take turns, how to ask for something, how to enter a group, how to respond to someone's anger.

To summarize, there are many appropriate practices that you can use to guide children toward a healthy and balanced sense of themselves and self-esteem. Many of the children you will teach, however, come from families that use inappropriate and even hurtful practices. Such practices do *not* help children gain accurate self-knowledge or self-control. When important adults use such practices, they bruise a child's self-esteem by degrading and demeaning children.

The next brief section describes these degrading practices so that you will know just how some of the children in your care have been treated. Children incorporate negative opinions into their sense of self; you might well see a child's negative view of herself reflected in her behavior. Your job with these children will be to keep this in mind as you strive to reflect a more positive view of those children.

Practices Likely to Contribute to Unhealthy Self-Esteem

Nonsupportive adults use negative discipline

Nonsupportive adults control, are sarcastic, threaten, use harsh punishment, and humiliate children. Negative discipline has a negative effect on self-esteem. It leaves children lacking in self-confidence, feeling inadequate and incompetent, and derogating (belittling) themselves (Anderson & Hughes, 1989).

Nonsupportive adults do not set limits well

Some adults set almost no limits, some set too many limits, and many adults do not know how to clearly state even reasonable limits. Poorly defined or poorly stated limits are not helpful to children because the child has no way of knowing whether a behavior is appropriate or inappropriate. He is left to guess and frequently guesses "wrong."

Nonsupportive adults fail to emphasize self-responsibility

They do not take the time necessary to help children assume responsibility. Chores are either not specified or, even if they are specified, there is no penalty for not doing them. Nonsupportive adults also often fail to require children to take responsibility when they have hurt someone or damaged property.

Nonsupportive adults are overly critical

Constant negative feedback is degrading because it communicates the adult's belief that the child is incompetent. Younger children, who rely heavily on adult opinion, feel incompetent when they are constantly criticized. Children who are criticized by adults and who live in a negative verbal environment tend to judge themselves negatively, including judgments of their goodness (Heyman et al., 1992; Kostelnik, 1988).

Nonsupportive adults deny children the right to have feelings

Denying feelings is akin to denying a child's self because even unpleasant feelings are real and are a part of the child. The implication is that if my feelings are bad, then I'm bad, too.

    Example: "Janna! You're not angry. You really like the new shirt, don't you?" Janna obviously did not like the shirt and was angry, but this adult is denying her the right to her feelings.

Nonsupportive adults do not like spending time with children

Example: Marty asked his mother to show him how to make chocolate chip cookies. Feeling obligated, Mom did teach him, but at the same time clearly communicated resentment, annoyance, and irritability by talking quickly and answering Marty's questions abruptly. Marty is likely to conclude that he cannot be very likable because his own mother does not like to do things with him.

Nonsupportive adults are judgmental and sexist

Example: Mrs. Olsen allows only boys to use woodworking tools and allows only girls to bathe dolls.

Nonsupportive adults show contempt for some family or cultural groups

Example: Several of the children in Mrs. Olsen's class live in single-parent families. Vernon lives with his grandmother, and another child lives in a foster home. Mrs.

Olsen demonstrated her insensitivity when she had children bring in pictures of families. Looking at Vernon's picture of him and his grandmother at the park, the teacher said, "Too bad that you don't have a family, Vernon."

CHILDREN NEED A STRONG MORAL COMPASS

A compass can be a lifesaving instrument because it indicates direction. Likewise, a strong moral compass or direction finder gives direction and guides behavior. This chapter is *not* a collection of "feel good about me" activities. Helping children develop healthy and balanced self-esteem takes so more than a collection of activities, although appropriate activities can enhance self-esteem. Damon (1991) notes that too strong an emphasis on the development of self-esteem in young children can lead to self-centeredness if children are not also helped to develop a strong, objective moral compass that guides their behavior (Baumeister, 1996; Damon, 1991; Lerner, 1996).

Without this moral referent, even children who have positive self-esteem cannot acquire a stable sense of right and wrong. Using positive discipline, setting appropriate limits, requiring children to be self-responsible, and teaching them that some things are wrong are excellent ways to help them develop this moral compass (Buzzelli, 1992).

A final thought: Self-esteem is fundamental to mental health, but children also need other things that are even *more* basic, such as prenatal care, food, pure water, shelter, and immunizations (Grant, 1994; Greenberg, 1991; Children's Defense Fund, 1994). Children whose most basic needs are not met cannot develop a healthy sense of self and therefore cannot develop healthy self-esteem.

Case Study Analysis: Self-Esteem

Analyze the case study at the beginning of the chapter by answering the following questions. You will find it useful to refer to information from the chapter to support your responses.

1. Suppose that you were in Mrs. Apodaca's place as the consultant. Write a brief report on the differences between the second- and third-grade teachers' approaches to self-esteem development in children. Which teacher is most likely to help children develop a balanced and healthy view of themselves? Why?
2. What, according to the research, is a likely outcome of the first-grade teacher's emphasis on boosting self-esteem on her children's self-esteem? What do you think that the consultant will suggest about this teacher's praise? Why?
3. Explain why the preschool teacher's feedback is likely to be much more effective in guiding children toward healthy self-esteem.

Parent Talk. Parents, Infants, and Toddlers—Architects of Self-Esteem

Pete Henriquez was amused by the postcard from the Parents of Infants support group. They were going to talk, the note said, about their baby's self-esteem at the next support group meeting. "Self-esteem? Yenoris [his daughter] is only 1 month old. Why should I think about her self-esteem now?" Pete and his wife went to the meeting as usual and were surprised that infancy was an important time for Yenoris's developing sense of self. They learned that self-esteem is a structure built as active newborns, infants, and toddlers interact with responsive parents. The group talked about some practical things that parents can do to help their infants build this thing called self-esteem (Curry & Johnson, 1990).

Early Infancy

Make the environment predictable, secure, and gentle. Be flexible, not rigid, about feeding schedules. Make routines predictable and regular. Talk to the baby about what you are doing during diapering and feeding. Pay attention to baby's cues and respond appropriately, for example, respond to cries quickly and appropriately.

4 to 9 months

Play games. Traditional games like "Where are baby's toes?" or 'Peek-a-boo" help infants distinguish themselves from others. Use routine times to play word games.

Encourage play with appropriate toys. Offer safe and clean toys. Do not overwhelm a baby with too many toys at one time. Try offering a toy just outside baby's reach to encourage an infant to reach. Talk with pleasure about individual toys, "Oh! Look at this pretty blue cube." Encourage babies to grasp toys and offer toys that make a sound, and then focus on that sound. Remember: Your interaction with your baby is more important than any toy.

9 to 15 months

Create an environment that children can manage. Infants manage best in small groups and when there is a moderate, not overwhelming, amount of stimulation. Provide simple props for pretend play—dressup clothes, pots, pans, dolls. Play games that help young children develop self-awareness, such as, "Simon Says." "Simon says touch your nose. Simon says hold Daddy's hand."

15 to 24 months

Children struggle for autonomy and adult responses to this struggle influence a child's view of herself. Structure the environment and activities to give children as much control as is safe and possible. Short songs, finger plays, or walks around the block are all appropriate. Toys should encourage active manipulation, problem-solving, and talking: blocks, play dough, telephones, books with short stories.

Decide how to look at the child's struggle for autonomy. You are most likely to foster all dimensions of self-esteem if you approach this period as a healthy and normal period rather than as a contest of wills and as a power struggle. For example, do state limits but state them as positively as possible, "Walk in the house," rather than "Don't run!" Be prepared for your child to now test some of those limits.

24 to 36 months

Continue to provide safe and appropriate toys and to encourage children to play. Communicate genuine respect through words and actions. Give fair and honest feedback about a toddler's feelings and actions, for example, "It really is hard to wait for the basket of crackers," or "I can see that you are upset about Mike taking your block. Let's think of some words to use to tell him that you're angry."

REFLECTING ON KEY CONCEPTS

1. How are self-referential behaviors, self-concept, self-regulatory behaviors, and self-esteem alike? How is self-esteem different from the other parts of the self-system?

2. True or False? Explain each of your answers.
   a. Positive self-esteem means that a child will always be confident and secure.
   b. Healthy self-esteem is *earned.*

3. Suppose that you are talking to a parents' group and are explaining what self-esteem is. What would you tell parents about the parts or dimensions of self-esteem?

4. "Garbage in, garbage out." Explain this statement to the parents as a way to help them understand how they influence but do not determine their child's self-esteem.

5. Choose two of the appropriate strategies for helping children develop healthy and balanced self-esteem. Explain why each is considered an appropriate practice. Give an example different from the one in the chapter.

6. Why is it more important to help children develop a strong moral compass and base of values than it is to just plan activities to help children feel good about themselves?

APPLY YOUR KNOWLEDGE

1. Observe architects of self-esteem—an adult and a young child interacting with each other for a couple of hours. Consider observing a relative or a teacher and her children. Focus on the practices that the adult uses that will likely help the child develop a healthy and balanced self-esteem. Write specific examples of the appropriate practices and be prepared to present your analysis to your classmates.

2. Conversation with an expert. Invite a professional who works with abused children to speak to your class. Ask this professional questions that will help you understand why abused children are likely to be highly anxious, compulsive, withdrawn, or overly hostile. Explain how abuse helps to create negative (unhealthy and unbalanced) self-esteem in children, for example, how does abuse affect a child's evaluation of her competence, control, and worth?

3. Problem for you to solve: Identify a more appropriate practice.

For each situation, state specifically how someone has been demeaned. Explain how the adult could just as easily have used a more appropriate practice to enhance, rather than demean, the child's self-esteem.

Situation: The music teacher stared out at the first-grade class and said, "That was terrible. John, come up here. I want all of you to listen to John. He's the only child in this class who can sing!"

Who has been demeaned?
How could the adult have enhanced self-esteem?

Situation: Sam, the class's pet hamster, died during the night, and the aide found Peter crying after he heard the news. "Come on, Peter. Stop crying. You know that big boys don't cry."

How has Peter been demeaned?
In what way has this adult been sexist?
How has the adult demeaned girls as well as boys?
How could this adult have enhanced self-esteem?

Situation: Dad and Jenna were in a restaurant and Dad asked if Jenna wanted spaghetti or pizza. "Pizza," said Jenna. Dad turned to the waiter and said, "Well, I think she'll have spaghetti."

How has Jenna been demeaned?
How could Dad have enhanced self-esteem?

Situation: Three-year-old Gerry correctly matched all the colors in the color-matching activity and named two of the six colors. His teacher said, "Well, you have some work to do. You still have trouble with the names of these colors."

How has Gerry been demeaned?
How could the adult have enhanced self-esteem?

RESOURCES FOR SPECIFIC ACTIVITIES

Center for Applied Psychology, Inc. (1993). *The building blocks of self-esteem.* This is a catalog of games and other materials for building healthy and balanced self-esteem. Available from Center for Applied Psychology, Inc., P.O. Box 1586, King of Prussia, PA 19406 (800-962-1141).

Greenberg, P. (1991). *Character development: Encouraging self-esteem and self-discipline in infants, toddlers, & two-year-olds.* Washington, DC: NAEYC. This is a wonderful resource for teachers of infants and toddlers. It contains practical suggestions for fostering self-esteem and self-discipline in very young children.

Katz, L. (1989). *Family living: Suggestions for effective parenting.* Washington, DC: Office of Educational Research and Improvement. Available from ERIC Clearinghouse on Elementary and Early Childhood Education, University of Illinois, 805 West Pennsylvania Ave., Urbana, IL 61801 (catalog no. 205).

National Black Child Development Institute. (1991). *The spirit of excellence: Resources for black children ages three to seven.* Washington, DC: Author. Available from NBCDI, 1023 15th St. NW, Suite 600, Washington, DC 20005.

References

Anderson, M., & Hughes, H. (1989). Parenting attitudes and the self-esteem of young children. *Journal of Genetic Psychology, 160*(4), 463–465.

Bakley, S. (1997). Love a little more, accept a little more. *Young Children, 52*(1), 21.

Bandura, A. (1981). Self-referent thought: The development of self-efficacy. In J. H. Flavell & L. D. Ross (Eds.), *Development of social cognition.* New York: Cambridge University Press.

Baumeister, R. (1996). Should schools try to boost self-esteem? Beware the dark side. *American Educator, 20*(2), 14–19, 43.

Beane, J. (1991). Enhancing children's self-esteem: Illusion and possibility. *Early Education and Development, 2*(2), 153–160.

Bednar, R., Wells, M., & Peterson, S. (1989). *Self-esteem: Paradoxes and innovations in clinical theory and practice.* Washington, DC: American Psychological Association.

Brazelton, T. B. (1997). Building a better self-image. *Newsweek,* special edition, Spring/Summer, 76–77.

Buzzelli, C. (1992). Research in review: Young children's moral understanding: Learning about right and wrong. *Young Children, 47*(5), 47–53.

Children's Defense Fund. (1994). The state of America's children. Washington, DC: Author.

Connell, J. P. (1980). *A multidimensional measure of children's perceptions of control.* Unpublished master's thesis, University of Denver.

Coopersmith, S. (1967). *The antecedents of self-esteem.* San Francisco: W. H. Freeman.

Curry, N., & Johnson, C. (1990). Beyond self-esteem: Developing a genuine sense of human value. *Research Monograph* (Vol. 4). Washington, DC: NAEYC.

Damon, W. (1991). Putting substance into self-esteem: A focus on academic and moral values. *Educational Horizons, 70*(1), 12–18.

Dweck, C., & Leggett, E. (1988). A social-cognitive approach to motivation and personality. *Psychological Review, 95*(2), 256–273.

Elliott, E., & Dweck, C. (1988). Goals: An approach to motivation and achievement. *Journal of Personality and Social Psychology, 54*(1), 5–12.

Fulghum, R. (1988). *All I really need to know I learned in kindergarten.* New York: Ivy Books.

Grant, J. (1994). *The state of the world's children, 1994.* New York: UNICEF.

Greenberg, P. (1991). *Character development: Encouraging self-esteem and self-discipline in infants, toddlers, & two-year-olds.* Washington, DC: NAEYC.

Hales, S. (1979a). "Developmental processes of self-esteem." Paper presented at the Society for Research in Child Development, San Francisco, CA.

Hales, S. (1979b). "A developmental theory of self-esteem based on competence and moral behavior." Paper presented at the Society for Research in Child Development, San Francisco, CA.

Harter, S. (1982). The perceived competence scale for children. *Child Development, 53,* 87–97.

Harter, S. (1983). Developmental perspectives on the self system. In P. Mussen (Ed.), *Handbook of child psychology* (Vol. 4). New York: Wiley.

Heyman, G., Dweck, C., & Cain, K. (1992). Young children's vulnerability to self-blame and helplessness: Relationship to beliefs about goodness. *Child Development, 63*(2), 401–415.

Janoff-Bulman, R., & Brickman, P. (1981). Expectations and what children learn from failure. In N. T. Feather (Ed.), *Expectancy, incentive, and action.* Hillsdale, NJ: Erlbaum.

Katz, L. (1993). Self-esteem and narcissism: Implications for practice. *ERIC Digest.* ED358973.

Katz, L., & Chard, S. (1989). *Engaging children's minds: The project approach.* Norwood, NJ: Ablex.

Kemple, K. (1995). Shyness and self-esteem in early childhood. *Journal of Humanistic Education & Development, 33*(4), 173–183.

Kostelnik, M. (1988). Children's self-esteem: The verbal environment. *Childhood Education, 65*(1), 29–32.

Kuykendall, J. (1991). *Early childhood development series.* Fairbanks, AK: Cooperative Extension Service.

Lamborn, S., Mounts, N., Steinberg, L., & Dornbusch, S. (1991). Patterns of competence and adjustment among adolescents from authoritative, authoritarian, indulgent and neglectful families. *Child Development, 62*(5), 1049–1065.

Lerner, B. (1996). Self-esteem and excellence: The choice and the paradox. *American Educator, 20*(2), 9–13, 41–42.

Meichenbaum, D., & Asarnow, J. (1982). Cognitive-behavior modification and metacognitive development: Implications for the classroom. In P. C. Kendall & S. D. Hollon (Eds.), *Cognitive-behavioral interventions: Theory, research, and procedures.* New York: Academic Press.

Mischel, W. (1981). Metacognition and the rules of delay. In J. H. Flavell & L. D. Ross (Eds.), *Social cognitive development: Frontiers and possible futures.* New York: Cambridge University Press.

Sheridan, M. (1991). Increasing self-esteem and competency in children. *International Journal of Early Childhood, 23*(1), 28–35.

Tafarodi, R., & Swarm, W. (1995). Self-liking and self-competence as dimensions of global self-esteem: Initial validation of a measure. *Journal of Personality Assessment, 65,* 322–342.

Tafarodi, R., & Vu, C. (1997). Two-dimensional self-esteem and reactions to success and failure. *Personality and Social Psychology Bulletin, 23*(6), 626–636.

White, R. W. (1959). Motivation reconsidered: The concept of competence. *Psychological Review, 66,* 297–333.

Wine, J. D. (1982). Evaluation anxiety: A cognitive-attentional construct. In H. W. Krohne & L. Laux (Eds.), *Achievement, stress, and anxiety.* Washington, DC: Hemisphere.

Wong, P. T. (1992). Control is a double-edged sword. *Canadian Journal of Behavioural Science, 24*(2), 143–146.

Chapter 7

Guiding Young Children's Understanding and Management of Anger

After reading and studying this chapter, you will be able to:

✿ List and describe the three components of anger and explain how children can feel and express anger without understanding it.

✿ Identify types of interactions in early childhood settings that are likely to elicit anger, and describe children's responses to each.

✿ Identify and explain how several factors affect how a child expresses anger.

✿ List, explain, and give examples of developmentally appropriate strategies adults can use to guide children's expressions of anger.

✿ Analyze a case study on anger in an early childhood classroom and apply your knowledge to specific anger-related exercises.

"Unpleasant feelings are like weeds. They don't go away when we ignore them; they grow wild and take over."
(Beattie, 1987, p. 144)

Case Study: Anger in an Early Childhood Classroom

Ted

"Remember to use words, Ted, to tell Sam that you're angry," said Mr. Sanchez. Ted, almost 5 years old, paused briefly and then replied, "Oh, yeah, . . . that's my paint. Give it back! I'm mad because you took it." Mr. Sanchez sighed with relief. Saying, "Use words" seems so simple, but was not so with Ted, who has learned from his family and from television to express anger aggressively. This was March and he has been working with Ted all year on expressing his anger in direct nonaggressive ways. At times he has been extremely frustrated but lately knows that Ted has made some major changes and is beginning to understand his feelings and to express his anger in more responsible ways.

Here are some samples from the teacher's anecdotal records for Ted; the observations are recorded at least weekly throughout the year for each child. These observations come from September and the first two weeks of October:

September 7: Ted and Sam had both been building separate block structures. Sam reached for a curved block on the shelf, but was interrupted by Ted, who grabbed the block and said, "I want that block for my tower."

September 11: Lydia walked into the dramatic play area and started to put on a firefighter's hat when she heard Ted say, "Hey, you get out of here. Girls are stupid and you're not allowed to play with a fireman's stuff!"

September 21: I noticed that Ted left the bathroom without washing his hands. I reminded him to "scrub away the germs." He continued to walk away and ignored the classroom rule. "Ted, please come back and wash your hands." Ted walked back to the bathroom, glaring at me as he turned on the water.

October 5: Ted seemed to be upset when Laurie turned around suddenly and bumped into him. He shoved her away with both arms and hissed, "Get out of my way!"

Lydia

Mr. Sanchez noticed almost immediately that Lydia's style of expressing anger or irritation was very different from Ted's. Lydia has learned a different lesson about how to show angry feelings from her family, and she now deals with the normal everyday anger-arousing situations in her classroom directly and nonaggressively. Here are the observations that Mr. Sanchez made early in the year.

September 9: Lydia was just about to take the plate of carrots being passed around the table when Jenny grabbed it. "Hey," said Lydia, a questioning look on her face, "it was *my* turn next. Give me the plate."

October 5: I reminded Lydia to put her puzzle back in the rack as she was leaving the puzzle table. She pursed her lips and frowned at me but then brightened and said, "Okeydokey!" I have heard her Dad say that to her!

October 6: Ted put his face right up next to Lydia's while they were standing next to a wagon. He grabbed the handle of the wagon from Lydia's hand and pushed her away. She said nothing to him but came over to me and said, "It was my turn with the wagon and Ted took it."

THREE COMPONENTS OF ANGER: STATE, EXPRESSION, AND UNDERSTANDING

Anger is believed to have three components, including the emotional state, the expression, and the understanding of the emotion.

Anger as an Emotional State

The first component of anger is the emotional state of anger. *Anger* is an emotion—an affective state, or feeling experienced when a goal is blocked or needs are frustrated (Campos & Barrett, 1984). Children are likely to experience the emotional state of anger when they encounter an obstacle to attaining any significant goal and when they think that the obstacle will be difficult to remove. A major function of the emotional state of anger is to restore progress toward a goal because angry individuals generally act to eliminate obstacles to a goal. Even the youngest children (including infants and toddlers) seem to have an appreciation of a goal blockage, and such an appreciation is possible long before they can consciously reflect on the feeling of anger (Campos & Barrett, 1984). The emphasis in this chapter is on anger in early childhood settings. Children often feel angry when their goals are blocked by other children or by teachers.

Example: A toddler felt angry when her goal of playing with a specific toy was blocked after her teacher put her in a high chair and the toy was out of reach.

Example: Four-year-old Jeb felt angry when his goal of finishing a painting was blocked after another child took the paint he needed to complete his work.

What sorts of things tend to bring on the feeling of anger?

Young children face several types of stress-producing anger provocations in their daily interactions (Fabes & Eisenberg, 1992). One of the most common interactions in early childhood classrooms that provokes anger is a *conflict over possessions,* which involves someone taking or destroying the target child's property or invading their space. Most conflicts over possessions take place between a child and another child.

Example: Rachael left the puzzle she had been working on to get a drink of water. Sandra sat in Rachael's chair and began putting the puzzle together. Rachael returned and declared that the puzzle was hers. The girls had a conflict over the puzzle and each became angry.

Physical assault is the second most frequently observed cause of anger in early childhood settings and involves something done to a child's body, for example, pushing or hitting. This chapter emphasizes child-to-child physical assault, but children can be and are physically assaulted by adults, as Ted often is by his Dad. Some forms of physical assault are classified as child abuse in most state laws on child abuse.

Example: Solee, a second-grader, had her goal of playing safely blocked when George pinched the skin on her arm and told her to get away from the table so that he could do his math worksheet.

Verbal assault involves teasing, insults, or degrading or demeaning statements and blocks a child's goal of psychological safety. *Rejection* provokes anger when a child is ignored or not allowed to play. Again, degrading comments or rejection by adults are forms of emotional child abuse (Garbarino, Guttman, & Seeley, 1986).

Example: LaShan is in third grade and has just moved to a new school. He has a severe speech defect, for which the school provides therapy. But the older children have begun to insult and tease him during recess.

Anger over *issues of compliance* arise when a child is asked or forced to do something that he or she does not want to do. In this case, a child's goal for independence will seem to have been blocked by a teacher's request for compliance. Almost all anger over issues of compliance occur between a teacher and a child.

Example: Mr. Sanchez had given a warning for cleanup outside and now it was time to put the sand toys away. "I don't want to go inside," shouted Jeanette, an angry look on her face, when Mr. Sanchez reminded her to put the toys away.

Expression of Anger

The second component of the anger experience is its expression, and this unpleasant emotion is first expressed in infancy. Children who believe that an important goal has been blocked attempt to cope by expressing the anger that they feel. Infants encounter many events that elicit the feeling of anger (Karraker, Lake, & Parry, 1994), which they express with their faces and voices (Stenberg, 1982). Anger can be expressed in many ways, and early childhood teachers have observed one or more of the following behavioral coping strategies in their classrooms: venting, active resistance, revenge, expressing dislike, avoidance, and adult-seeking (Fabes & Eisenberg, 1992).

Often children *vent* to express anger through facial expressions, crying, sulking, or talking but do little to try to solve a problem or confront the provoker. Some people think of venting as "blowing off steam."

Example: Jake and Jim, 8 years old, were angry about the number of math problems that they had to do for homework and vented their anger by complaining all the way home from school.

Some children *actively resist* when angry by physically or verbally defending their position, self-esteem, or possessions in nonaggressive ways.

Example: Roberto responded with active resistance when Linda tried to take the scoop from him as he worked at the sand table: "That's mine. You can't have it, Linda!"

Children *express dislike* by telling the offender that he or she cannot play or is not liked because of an incident.

Example: Laurie was hurt and angry when Ted pushed her (chapter opener case study). Later, when Ted wanted to sit at her table for snack she said, "You can't sit here, Ted. We don't like you."

Other children express anger with *aggressive revenge* by physically or verbally retaliating against the provoker with no other purpose evident. They use name-calling, pinching, hitting, or threatening to express their feeling.

Example: After snacktime the children went to the playground. Ted, steaming from Laurie's comment at snacktime, was hanging from the climbing gym when Laurie rode by on her trike. He sang out, "Laurie is stupid. Laurie is stupid."

Other children express anger through *avoidance* or attempts to escape from or evade the provoker, while others use *adult-seeking* to let us know how they feel. Adult-seeking involves seeking comfort from a teacher or telling a teacher about an incident.

Early childhood teachers see the whole range of possible responses. Most young children express anger nonaggressively through active resistance, but some children express their anger aggressively. Teachers strive to use child-guidance strategies that help all children express angry feelings in socially constructive, not destructive, ways. They understand that children develop ideas about how to express emotions (Lewis, 1989; Michalson & Lewis, 1985; Russel, 1989) through social interaction, watching television or movies, playing video games, and reading books (Honig & Wittmer, 1992). Some children who express anger aggressively have learned a negative aggressive approach to expressing anger (Hennessy, Rabideau, Cummings, & Cicchetti, 1994) and then resort to using aggression in classrooms when confronted with everyday anger conflicts (Huesmann, 1988). One of the major challenges to early childhood teachers is to permit and encourage children to acknowledge angry feelings while helping them learn to express anger in a positive and effective way.

Factors that affect the expression of anger

Age and gender. Teachers can expect younger children to express anger more often than do older children and can expect differences in how boys and girls express anger. Girls are more likely to use active resistance, but boys tend to vent or to use mildly aggressive methods (Fabes & Eisenberg, 1992; Zeman & Garber, 1996; Zeman & Shipman, 1996). Socialization practices may account for the sex differences (Davis, 1995; Underwood, Coie, & Herbsman, 1992). For example, Malatesta and Haviland (1982) found that mothers showed different reactions to anger in children as young as 3 months old by responding to girls' anger with an angry expression but to boys' anger with sympathy.

Perceived control. Another factor that affects the expression of anger is whether children think that they have some degree of control in an anger-arousing conflict (Levine, 1995; Zeman & Shipman, 1996). Children tend to view themselves as having more control in a conflict with other children and use more direct strategies such as active resistance. Young children tend to view themselves as having much less control when their anger is provoked by the teacher and therefore indirectly express anger by venting (Fabes & Eisenberg, 1992). Children also use more sophisticated reasoning to justify their choices of action with peers than they use with adults. Piaget (1970) suggested that a child's peer interactions, which are based on mutual relations, may foster moral development more than do interactions with adults, in which the difference in power is clear to many children. Some children express anger toward a popular child who provokes anger in much the same, indirect, way as they do toward an adult (Fabes, Eisenberg, Smith, & Murphy, 1996).

This occurs because children tend to see themselves as having far less control in angry interactions with popular children.

Understanding of Anger

The third component of the anger experience is understanding. A person who understands children's feeling of anger can interpret and evaluate the emotion. The puzzling thing about anger in early childhood is that a child's understanding of anger develops later than the other two components (Michalson & Lewis, 1985). That the three components of the anger experience develop at different times explains why children in early childhood settings can feel and express anger but not understand it. Because the ability to regulate the expression of anger is linked to an understanding of the emotion (Zeman & Shipman, 1996) and children's ability to reflect on their anger is somewhat limited, children need guidance from teachers and parents first in understanding and then in managing their feelings of anger.

Factors contributing to understanding and managing anger

Memory. A person can understand any emotion only when he or she can pay attention to it and basic cognitive processes such as memory undergird the gradual development of the understanding of anger. Memory improves substantially during early childhood (Perlmutter, 1986), and this enables young children to better remember aspects of anger-arousing interactions.

Young children feel and express anger but do not understand this unpleasant feeling.

What happens, though, when parents and teachers try to help children gain a more helpful perspective on anger-arousing interactions? Do children remember the new ideas or do they revert to an old unhelpful perception? One study found that young children can remember an *in*correct perception that had been replaced by a more accurate perception of events (Freeman, Lacohee, & Coulton, 1995), the memory of a wrong notion merely repressed to allow the use of a new idea. In terms of anger understanding, children who have developed unhelpful ideas of how to express anger (Miller & Sperry, 1987) can retrieve the earlier unhelpful strategy even after teachers help them gain a more helpful perspective on anger conflicts. This implies that teachers will probably have to remind some children, sometimes more than once or twice, about a less-aggressive way of expressing anger.

Language. Talking about emotions helps young children gain a greater understanding of the feeling (Brown & Dunn, 1996), and preschool emotion understanding seems to be tied to overall language development (Denham, Zoller, & Couchoud, 1994). Acquiring word labels for and naming the emotion of anger, then, is an important part of understanding anger. Two- to 5-year-old children are aware of the correspondence between many facial expressions and their emotion word labels but generate very few labels before age 3 (Michalson & Lewis, 1985). Some of the difficulty that young children have in labeling emotions is related to

Talking about anger helps children understand this emotion.

how their families discuss anger-arousing incidents (Miller & Sperry, 1987). Some parents use moral talk (i.e., they accuse, threaten, or insult the perpetrator, assert their own rights, or defend themselves) and their children tend to talk about angry conflicts in the same way.

Example: Ted's father was angry about how long he had to wait in the drive-through at the bank and said, "Who do they think they are? I ought to go right in there and tell the manager what I think about this place." At school, Ted was angry when George wouldn't give him one of the puppets. Ted said, "I'm gonna get my dad to beat you up! He'll make you give me a puppet."

Ted fails to label his anger, but he does use language to talk about George's unfairness. Ted uses moral talk, not emotion talk, and has, like many children, adopted this style of talk by observing his parents talk about anger-arousing events. Other children have heard emotion talk (i.e., talk about feelings or labeling feelings) and they tend to use similar language when talking about anger-arousing conflicts.

Example: Lydia, the child from the chapter opening case study, was sitting on the porch with Mom when her father came home from a fishing trip. Dad hadn't caught any fish. Mom said, "Oh, George! It's no big deal." Dad said, "Hey, I was looking forward to grilling some fish for all of us, and I'm a little disappointed that I didn't catch anything. Plus, I'm irritated that you would tell me 'It's no big deal.'" Mom said, "Sorry, honey. I know you're disappointed."

At school the next day, Lydia and Jessica were in the dramatic play area. Jessica pushed Lydia out of the way so that she could get to the prop box first. Lydia stopped and put her hands on her hips and said, "I'm irritated, Jessica, that you pushed me. Don't do that anymore." Early childhood teachers can expect to see individual differences in children's ability to identify and label angry feelings because their family systems model a variety of approaches to talking about emotions.

Self-referential and self-regulatory behaviors

The development of self-referential and self-regulatory behaviors during early childhood also sets the stage for understanding and managing anger and other emotions. *Self-referential behaviors* include viewing the self as separate from others and as an active independent causal agent. *Self-regulation* refers to controlling impulses, tolerating frustration, and postponing immediate gratification.

Self-referential behavior emerges during infancy and toddlerhood, and continued development of the self during early childhood further enables children to think about themselves and events, such as anger-arousing interactions (Harter, 1983). Self-regulation or control appears at around 24 months, and children become better able to use certain strategies with which they regulate their own behavior, including how they express anger, as they get older (Kopp, 1989). A child's budding ability to control the self provides a base for early childhood teachers and parents who develop strategies to nurture children's emerging ability to regulate how they express angry feelings.

IMPLICATIONS FOR GUIDING CHILDREN'S EXPRESSIONS OF ANGER

Teachers can give children the gift of a healthy approach to dealing with anger by guiding their understanding and management of anger. Some children in our classrooms have learned unhelpful and aggressive approaches to anger management, while others have learned a more direct, nonaggressive approach. The guidance practices described here will help children understand and manage angry feelings in a direct and nonaggressive way (Marion, 1993, 1994, 1997).

Create a Safe Emotional Climate

The leader in a parent education class on anger management asked the parents what happened in their families when they, as children, expressed anger.

This teacher has planned a "thinking puppets" session on appropriate ways to respond to anger-arousing events.

"My dad used to get so mad at me when I was angry, even if my anger had nothing to do with my father," said Marv.

"How did you feel when he got mad?" asked the leader.

"It scared me to see him get so mad that I just stopped telling him when I was upset."

The leader asked, "Did you ever talk about what it was that you were angry about in the first place?"

"No. And you know what? I ended up taking care of Dad by pretending nothing was wrong, even if I was seething about something," said Marv. "I've never thought about this before!"

Others noted that their parent criticized or even punished them for being angry or expressing anger. The root of their anger was never dealt with and resolved. They were punished or criticized for feeling angry. Their anger was shamed and the emotional climate was not safe.

The hallmark of a safe emotional climate is that it permits children to acknowledge all feelings, both pleasant and unpleasant, and does not shame anger. They are not told to hide feelings, and they know that they will not be criticized for having the feeling, whatever it is. If Jamal has sad feelings when the gerbil dies, then he knows that he can express them without fear. If James expresses tender feelings by gently stroking his puppy when it visits, nobody laughs or calls him a sissy. If Mary is irritated when somebody takes her puzzle, then she will feel safe in knowing that her teacher will not also become angry just because Mary is mildly irritated.

Healthy classroom systems, like healthy family systems (Minuchin, 1974), have clear, firm, and flexible boundaries. Adults who most effectively guide an understanding and responsible management of anger convey a simple, firm, consistent message (Baumrind, 1996) acknowledging a child's right to feel anger while prohibiting expressing anger in destructive or hurtful ways.

Example: Mr. Sanchez watched 4½-year-old Ted get ready to hurl a shovel at Bob after Bob ran over Ted's sand structure. The teacher was quick enough to grab the shovel, and said, "Ted! No throwing! I won't allow you to hurt children when you're mad." (The teacher then dealt with Bob's aggression.)

Model Responsible Anger Management

Adults influence children through modeling, and adults are powerful models of how to manage anger. Children's understanding of emotions is damaged and they experience great stress when adults show a lot of anger (Cummings & Cummings, 1988; Denham et al., 1994). Therefore, adults who are most effective in helping children manage anger well model responsible anger management.

How to model responsible anger management

Children need good examples (models) from parents and teachers of how to responsibly manage anger:

- *Acknowledge and accept your own angry feelings.* You will show children that you trust yourself and that you think anger is a normal experience.

- *Give yourself permission to feel angry when you are angry.* You will be modeling several important things: that you feel the emotional energy of anger, that you do not think that you have to justify your feelings, that anger simply is, and that there is nothing wrong with this or any other emotion.
- *Take responsibility for your own feelings and avoid blaming others for causing your feelings.* In this way you will show children that you understand that anger often covers some other feeling, as in the following example.

Example: Mr. Sanchez took responsibility for his adult anger when he said, "I feel scared when you run into the street, John, and then I feel angry." Notice that the teacher does *not* say "You made me angry, John." Nobody makes us feel anything. Yes, John did something that was inappropriate, but it was the adult's angry feeling, and John observes his teacher "owning" the feeling.

- *Make decisions about how to deal with anger. Avoid simply venting emotional energy.* Venting anger, or blowing off steam, is an ineffective way to manage angry feelings. John's teacher knew that it would be much more helpful for John to observe an appropriate way to deal with the situation that was causing the feeling, so he modeled for John how to determine and then to ask for what one needs from the person who is the target of the anger.

Example: He decided to say what he wanted from John by firmly restating the playground limit of staying inside the fenced area. He also used indirect guidance to manage the environment better by moving the handle on the gate up higher so that the children could not reach it from the inside.

Help Children Develop Self-Regulatory Skills

Teachers of infants and toddlers realize that the children in their care have a very limited ability to regulate themselves and therefore do a lot of the self-regulation "work" for these very young children. For example, teachers put appropriate winter clothing on toddlers who otherwise would not remember to dress appropriately. As children get older, adults who use positive child-guidance strategies gradually transfer control of the self to children in order to help them develop healthy self-regulatory skills. For instance, after having taught the limits prohibiting hurting others when one is angry, a teacher would restate that expectation for self-control to individuals as needed. Such a transfer is facilitated by the use of authoritative caregiving and positive affective sharing in day-to-day social exchanges with adults (Baumrind, 1996; Hart, DeWolf, Wozniak, & Burts, 1992).

Teach Children to Use Words to Describe Angry Feelings

Help young children produce a label for their feeling of anger by teaching them emotion talk, that they are having a feeling and that they can use a word to describe their angry feeling. It is fair to say to children, "Use your words . . .," only after helping them learn the specific words. Do not assume that a child knows how to label a feeling. He might have come from a family where parents tell stories about how they reacted to anger, say, in the grocery store or on the freeway, but never actually discuss angry feelings.

Example: Teacher: "Lindy, you seem to be feeling very angry. You can use words to tell George how you feel. Say, 'George, I'm angry because you won't give me a puppet.'"

Teachers would never expect children to automatically know the names of each new animal in a zoo unless somebody had told them the name. Similarly, we should not expect children to know the labels for all the feelings they may have unless we help them learn the label. Teaching word labels for feelings is just like teaching word labels for anything else—colors, animals, shapes, plants.

Help Children Expand Their Feelings Vocabulary

Anger is a complex emotion with many levels of emotional energy, ranging from minor irritation to rage. Help children understand that at times one can feel "a little angry" and at other times feel "very, very angry." After children have learned to use a word for angry feelings, encourage them to increase the number of labels or words they can use to describe the specific feeling they are having.

Many children will describe anger as feeling *mad*. Build their feelings vocabulary by adding synonyms to the list—words like *angry, irritated, annoyed, furious, irate, enraged, upset*—that help them more accurately describe the level of emotion. Make a permanent record, for example, a book or chart (Figure 7–1) listing different words for angry feelings and refer to it when discussing anger. (You can do the same thing with other feeling words, too.)

Example: "I think that the librarian was a little annoyed when we were late for our library period." "It seemed to irritate you when Pete took the block again." "I noticed that you seemed angry when Amy put a big blob of red paint on your paper." "Mr. Rogers seemed upset when he discovered that the puppy was lost." "That man was furious when his neighbor walked on the fresh cement."

Use Active Listening When Children Are Having an Anger Conflict

Young children understand anger and other emotions best when adults explain emotions (Denham et al., 1994). Help children begin to reflect on anger-arousing

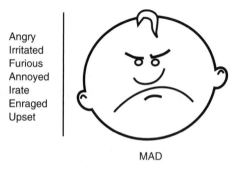

Angry
Irritated
Furious
Annoyed
Irate
Enraged
Upset

MAD

Use a chart as a permanent record, listing different words for angry feelings. Refer to it when discussing anger.

events by giving them opportunities to discuss them. When children are embroiled in an anger conflict, be helpful by listening to them without judging, evaluating, or ordering them to feel differently. Discussing their angry feelings and interactions with an adult who listens actively helps children begin to understand the meaning of the interaction and prepares them for dealing more effectively with similar events in the future.

Plan Discussions About Anger

At "cooler" times, when children are not engaged in anger-arousing interactions, teachers can plan activities involving discussions about anger to teach more effective anger management skills. Make up scenarios or situations and then encourage children to generate a direct nonaggressive response: "What could you do if you were washing your hands and somebody pushed you out of the way?" or "Here's a picture of a child who is upset because somebody just called her a stupid girl. What do you think that she should do?" Or use the thinking puppets, as Mr. Sanchez did.

Example: Mr. Sanchez planned a discussion about anger for large-group time. "This thinking puppet is angry because this other puppet pinched him. Help him think about what he could do."

Use Appropriate Books and Stories About Anger Management

Bibliotherapy refers to using literature to promote mental health and would be an appropriate way to help young children deal with the stress producing emotion of anger. Books dealing with the emotion of anger can help a child cope more effectively with this strong emotion. Reading crisis-oriented books, including those about anger, serves three purposes. First, children get information about anger from well-chosen books on the topic. Second, they are encouraged to make connections between what they hear about this emotion in school and their life outside school. Third, a child is more likely to view her own feelings of anger as natural and normal when a teacher plans, reads, and follows up on a story about anger (Jalongo, 1986).

Guidelines for choosing books on anger

There is a motto that seems appropriate here: *First of all, do no harm.* This is a time to be extra careful about the books that we read to children because we can do harm if we use a badly written book on anger. Some children's books on anger do not help children understand or manage anger well. Follow selection guidelines for choosing any picture book (Jalongo, 1986) but be sure that the book meets additional, specific selection criteria for books about anger (Marion, 1995, 1998). Evaluate books on anger by answering these questions:

1. How well does this book clarify or expand vocabulary on anger?
2. Does this book identify the specific event that seemed to elicit the anger?
3. How well does this book convey the idea that feeling angry is a natural and normal experience?

4. How effectively does this story present nonaggressive strategies for managing the anger?

5. Does this book tend to show how to manage anger in an optimistic way?

Children's books about anger

- Barshun, R. N., & Hutton, K. (1983). *Feeling angry.* Elgin, IL: Child's World.
- Carle, E. (1977). *The grouchy ladybug.* New York: Harper & Row.
- Duncan, R. (1989). *When Emily woke up angry.* Hauppauge, NY: Barrons.
- Mayer, M. (1983). *I was so mad.* Racine, WI: Western Publishing.
- Noll, S. (1991). *That bothered Kate.* New York: Puffin.
- Riley, S. (1978). *What does it mean?* Angry. Elgin, IL: Child's World.
- Simon, N. (1974). *I was so mad!* Chicago: A. Whitman.

Suggestions on using a book on anger

Sharply focus on anger throughout the lesson by developing specific introductory remarks to motivate thinking and help children to concentrate on the topic of anger. Prepare specific comments and questions to use when reading the book. Prepare a thoughtful follow-up. Avoid merely asking children to relate the chronological events of the story. Instead, clarify information presented on how to manage anger responsibly. Concentrate on reviewing concepts or vocabulary relating to anger. Most important, communicate your acceptance of anger as a natural and normal emotion, and your approval of managing anger in a direct, nonaggressive way.

Teach Children How to Deal with the Stress of Anger

It is important for adults to teach children how to deal with the stress that almost always accompanies anger. Anger is a useful but stressful emotion, and managing anger responsibly returns the body to a normal state. Not dealing with anger maintains a stressful state. Encouraging responsible anger management may also have positive long-term effects. Researchers are finding a connection between chronic hostility and anger and poor health and damaged relationships. Cynical hostility is marked by frequent anger, and this high level of stress and hostility has consistently been the factor that best discriminates between adults with coronary heart disease and those without coronary heart disease (Baughman, 1992; Johnson, 1992). Anger and hostility also make it difficult to function effectively in groups, whether in school or at work. Teaching responsible anger management to young children, then, may help to prevent some of these problems.

Two of the most helpful stress reduction strategies are relaxation training and deep-breathing exercises. Both strategies allow children (and adults) to get the autonomic nervous system under control, gain control of breathing, get the heart rate back to normal, stop shaking, calm down and actually think about the feeling, and refrain from doing anything irrational while in a highly stressed state.

Parent Talk. Building Anger Management Skills and Emotional Intelligence in Children

The children in our centers and classrooms exist in a family system (Bronfenbrenner, 1979). The work that we do in teaching anger management to children will be more effective if we acknowledge and work with a child's family as well as with a child. When you help parents understand how to help their children manage anger, you will also be helping parents build in their children what Goleman (1995) calls *emotional intelligence*. There are several ways in which you can do this efficiently and effectively.

One of the best things to do is to offer information to parents about helping children understand and manage anger and build emotional intelligence. Consider using the same strategies that you use when talking with parents about other areas of the curriculum or other concerns. For example:

- Write a newsletter article about learning to use words to label anger.
- Plan a group-based parent education session to explain some of the things you have done to help children manage anger nonaggressively.
- Introduce the thinking puppets to parents and explain how they are used in discussion about anger with the children.
- Display books on anger management at the meeting, say how you have used them with the children, and invite parents to also read the books. Do the same thing with books on emotional intelligence.
- Explain how you use the chart with the words for anger and give a handout of the same chart to parents so that they may have a reference.

Work with Other Professionals

Teachers are trained to teach but usually are not trained as therapists and are therefore not expected to know how to deal with extremely angry children whose anger springs from abuse or neglect or other major emotional problems. We help these children best when we seek the counsel of professionals trained to help angry children and their families. Consider getting the advice of such a professional when you suspect that a child needs help beyond normal classroom interventions and lessons. This mental health professional can also give you advice on how to talk to parents about a possible referral for the family or for the child.

RESOURCES FOR PARENTS ON EMOTIONAL INTELLIGENCE

Azerrad, J. (1997). *Anyone can have a happy child: How to nurture emotional intelligence.* New York: M. Evan.

Chapman, D. (1996). *Playwise: 365 fun-filled activities for building character, conscience, and emotional intelligence in children.* New York: G.P. Putnam's Sons.

Myers, D. E. (1996). *Heartful parenting: Connected parenting & emotional intelligence.* Mesa, AZ: Blue Bird Publishing.

Shapiro, L. E. (1997). *How to raise a child with a high EQ: A parent's guide to emotional intelligence.* New York: Harper Collins Publishers.

RESOURCES FOR TEACHERS ON EMOTIONAL INTELLIGENCE

Goleman, D. (1996). *Emotional intelligence.* New York: Bantam Books.

Salovey, P., & Sluyter, D. J. (1997). *Emotional development and emotional intelligence: Educational implications.* New York: Basic Books.

(Video) *Emotional intelligence—A new vision for educators.* Daniel Goleman Presents, 1996.

Case Study Analysis: Anger in an Early Childhood Classroom

Both Ted and Lydia, in the case study at the beginning of this chapter, felt anger. They both expressed anger. Analyze this case study by answering the following questions.

1. Identify the interactions in which each child felt angry because of a conflict over possessions and by a compliance issue with the teacher. Name the strategy that Ted and Lydia used to express their angry feeling in each instance.
2. Which of these children do you think probably has a greater amount of stress related to angry conflicts? Please explain your answer.
3. How have Ted's and Lydia's families influenced each child's ability to use words to express angry feelings?
4. Briefly describe how the families of these two children have modeled how to express anger and how it has affected Ted's and Lydia's behavior in their classroom.
5. After reading the chapter, give at least one example of how you think that Mr. Sanchez has created a safe emotional climate in his classroom.

REFLECTING ON KEY CONCEPTS

1. As an early childhood professional, which of the components of anger— feeling, expression, or understanding—will you be *least* likely to see in young children? Why?
2. You are the leader of a parent education group whose topic is "Responsible Anger Management." You want to tell parents about the things that seem to elicit the feeling of anger in young children and how children typically express anger. What would you tell the parents?
3. Please name and briefly explain to the parents some of the things that will make it easier for their children to understand and manage their anger as their children get older.
4. Why is it so important to teach children how to use word labels for their feeling of anger? Why can you expect the children with whom you work to show individual differences in their ability to use word labels for emotions?
5. Choose three of the guidance strategies for helping children manage angry feelings described in this chapter that you would most like to help the parent education group understand. Briefly explain each of them.

APPLY YOUR KNOWLEDGE

1. Choose one of the observations that Mr. Sanchez made of Ted in the chapter opener case study. Using the information in the "implications" section

of the chapter, explain how he could have effectively dealt with how Ted expressed his anger. Be specific. Explain your solution thoroughly. Write out the words that you would have Mr. Sanchez use. Be prepared to role-play your solution.

2. Pick a children's book dealing with anger and analyze its content using the information in the section on choosing books on anger. Present your analysis to your fellow students. If the book meets the guidelines for choosing books on anger, arrange to read the book to a group of children. Write a brief lesson plan detailing how you will present the book to the children and get the plan approved by the children's teacher.

3. Select one of these early childhood age groups: toddlers, younger preschoolers, older preschoolers and kindergarteners, or primary school children. Then plan a developmentally appropriate activity that will teach children in that age group to use words to express angry feelings.

References

Baughman, D. (1992). Heal thyself: Reducing the risk of heart disease. *Optimal Health, 4*(2), 1, 4.

Baumrind, D. (1996). Parenting: The discipline controversy revisited. *Family Relations, 45,* 405–414.

Beattie, M. (1987). *Codependent no more.* San Francisco, CA: Harper & Row.

Bronfenbrenner, U. (1979). *The ecology of human development.* Cambridge, MA: Harvard University Press.

Brown, J. R., & Dunn, J. (1996). Continuities in emotion understanding from three to six years, *Child Development, 67*(3), 789–803.

Campos, J., & Barrett, K. (1984). A new understanding of emotions and their development. In C. Izard, J. Kagan, & R. Zajonc (Eds.), *Emotions, cognition, and behavior.* New York: Cambridge University Press.

Cummings, E., & Cummings, J. (1988). A process-oriented approach to children's coping with adults' angry behavior. *Developmental Review, 8,* 296–321.

Davis, T.L. (1995). Gender differences in masking negative emotions: Ability or motivation? *Developmental Psychology, 31*(4), 660–668.

Denham, S. A., Zoller, D., & Couchoud, E. Z. (1994). Socialization of preschoolers' emotion understanding, *Developmental Psychology, 30*(6), 928–937.

Fabes, R., & Eisenberg, N. (1992). Young children's coping with interpersonal anger. *Child Development, 63,* 116–128.

Fabes, R., Eisenberg, N., Smith, M., & Murphy, B. (1996), Getting angry at peers: Associations with liking of the provocateur. *Child Development, 67*(3), 943–958.

Freeman, N., Lacohee, H., & Coulton, S. (1995). Cued-recall approach to 3-year-olds' memory for an honest mistake. *Journal of Experimental Child Psychology, 60*(1), 102–116.

Garbarino, J., Guttman, E., & Seeley, J. (1986). *The psychologically battered child.* San Francisco, CA: Jossey-Bass.

Hart, C., DeWolf, M., Wozniak, P., & Burts, D. (1992). Maternal and paternal disciplinary styles: Relations with preschoolers' playground behavioral orientations and peer status. *Child Development, 63,* 879–892.

Harter, S. (1983). Developmental perspectives on the self-system. In E.M. Hetherington (Ed.), *Socialization, personality and social development, Vol 4. Handbook of child psychology* (pp. 275–385). New York: Wiley.

Hennessy, K., Rabideau, G., Cummings, E. M., & Cicchetti, D. (1994). Responses of physically abused and nonabused children to different forms of interadult anger. *Child Development, 65*(3), 815–829.

Honig, A., & Wittmer, D. (1992). *Prosocial development in children: Caring, sharing, and cooperation: A bibliographic resource guide.* New York: Garland Press.

Huesmann, L. (1988). An information processing model for the development of aggression. *Aggressive Behavior, 14*(1), 13–24.

Jalongo, M. (1986). Using crisis-oriented books with young children. In J. B. McCracken (Ed.), *Reducing stress in young children's lives.* Washington, DC: NAEYC.

Johnson, E. H. (1992). "The role of anger/hostility in hypertension and heart disease." Speech presented February 25 at the University of Wisconsin–Stout, Menomonie, WI.

Karraker, K., Lake, M., & Parry, T. (1994). Infant coping with everyday stressful events. *Merrill-Palmer Quarterly, 40,* 171–189.

Kopp, C. (1989). Regulation of distress and negative emotions: A developmental view. *Developmental Psychology, 25,* 343–354.

Levine, L. (1995). Young children's understanding of the causes of anger and sadness. *Child Development, 66*(3), 697–710.

Lewis, M. (1989). Cultural differences in children's knowledge of emotional scripts. In C. Saarni & P. Harris (Eds.), *Children's understanding of emotion* (pp. 350–357). Cambridge, England: Cambridge University Press.

Malatesta, C., & Haviland, J. (1982). Learning display rules: The socialization of emotion expression in infancy. *Child Development, 53,* 991–1003.

Marion, M. (Spring 1993). Responsible anger management: The long bumpy road. *Day Care and Early Education,* 4–9.

Marion, M. (1994). Supporting the development of responsible anger management in children. *Early Child Development and Care, 97,* 155–163.

Marion, M. (1995). *Guidance of young children.* Columbus, OH: Merrill/Prentice Hall.

Marion, M. (1997). Research in review: Guiding young children's understanding and management of anger. *Young Children, 53*(1), 62–67.

Michalson, L., & Lewis, M. (1985). What do children know about emotions and when do they know it? In M. Lewis & C. Saarni (Eds.), *The socialization of emotions* (pp. 117–139). New York: Plenum.

Miller, P., & Sperry, L. (1987). The socialization of anger and aggression. *Merrill-Palmer Quarterly, 33*(1), 1–31.

Minuchin, S. (1974). *Families and family therapy.* Cambridge, MA: Harvard University Press.

Perlmutter, M. (1986). A life-span view of memory. In P. B. Baltes, D. L. Featherman, & R. M. Lerner (Eds.), *Life-span development and behavior* (Vol. 7). Hillsdale, NJ: Erlbaum.

Piaget, J. (1970). Piaget's theory. In P. Mussen (Ed.), *Carmichael's manual of child psychology.* New York: Wiley.

Russel, J. A. (1989). Culture, scripts, and children's understanding of emotion. In C. Saarni & P.L. Harris (Eds.), *Children's understanding of emotion* (pp. 293–318). Cambridge, England: Cambridge University Press.

Stenberg, C. (1982). *The development of anger facial expressions in infancy.* Unpublished doctoral dissertation, University of Denver.

Underwood, M., Coie, J., & Herbsman, C. (1992). Display rules for anger and aggression in school-age children. *Child Development, 63,* 366–380.

Zeman, J., & Garber, J. (1996). Display rules for anger, sadness, and pain: It depends on who is watching. *Child Development, 67*(3), 957–974.

Zeman, J., & Shipman, K. (1996). Children's expression of negative affect: Reasons and methods. *Developmental Psychology, 32*(5), 842–850.

Chapter 8

Understanding and Guiding Aggressive Children

After reading and studying this chapter, you will be able to:

✿ Define aggression and list and describe different forms of aggression.
✿ Explain age and gender differences in aggression.
✿ Explain, from a systems or ecological perspective, how children become aggressive.
✿ List, discuss, and give examples of specific guidance strategies that prevent or control aggression.

"You first learn violence within the family." Violence "is learned early and learned very well . . . violence is preventable."
(American Psychological Association [APA], 1993)

Case Study: Aggression in Mrs. Spencer's School

Mrs. Spencer has been a second-grade teacher in a public school for children ages 4 through 8 for 10 years. She knows most of the families and also realizes that some of the children in the school will have a problem with aggression. Some of this aggression is easy to deal with but other aggression—like Ben's—is more difficult to manage. Her school's principal received help for the teachers in learning about children's aggression and then how to guide them effectively. The school's and Mrs. Spencer's goal is to protect children and to help aggressive children find a better way to communicate and get what they need.

Here is a small sampling of some of the aggression-related behaviors that this teacher has seen during the first 4 weeks of the school year:

- Ben is a 7 year-old in Mrs. Spencer's class. She noticed after only a few days in school that Ben often got what he wanted through aggression. For example, when she saw him grab a marker (the aggressive act) from John, she turned to John and suggested a way for John to deal with Ben's aggression. "John, you were using the marker. Please tell Ben that it's your turn."
- Her class was in the computer lab and Mrs. Spencer heard the argument that Ben and Charlene had about whose turn it was at the computer. Ben pinched Charlene (the aggression) and told her to move. "No pinching, Ben," said the teacher, "because that hurt Charlene." Then she talked to both children: "Looks like we have a problem here. Two children and only one computer. What do you think that we could do about this problem?"
- Mrs. Spencer was supervising on the playground and noticed Josie, a kindergarten child, having trouble waiting for her turn pulling the wagon. The 5-year-old girl went over to the child with the wagon and simply pushed him out of the way and took the handle (the aggression). Mrs. Spencer fell in step with Josie as Josie walked away, took the wagon handle, and said, "It looks like you really want your turn, Josie, but you know the school's rules—wait for your turn and no pushing, grabbing, or hurting people to get a turn. It hurts people when you push them. Your name is next on the list, and Tom is just about finished. Tell me one thing that you could do while you are waiting."
- Ben and Joseph were working on their stories when Mrs. Spencer heard Ben say, "Let's go look at the list of words on the wall to see how to spell that word" (no aggression). Relieved to see Ben act in a helpful way and to see something other than aggression, she said to Ben, "You really helped Joseph, Ben. Thanks."

At this point you probably have some questions about Ben, Josie, their aggression, and Mrs. Spencer's responses. This chapter should help you understand what aggression is like in children during the early childhood years. The chapter will also help you understand that some aggression, like Josie's, is fairly typical in young children but that other children like Ben use aggression far too frequently. You will learn about how Ben developed his high level of aggression. And you will learn the guidance strategies that Mrs. Spencer and the other teachers use to help aggressive children.

Let's look first at the concept of aggression—what it is (the definition), different forms of aggression, and gender differences in aggression.

UNDERSTANDING AGGRESSION

Aggression Is . . .

Aggression is a problem-solving behavior that is learned early in life, is learned well, and is resistant to change (Eron, 1986). Aggression is any behavior that injures or diminishes a person or animal in some way or damages or destroys property. Aggression can take several forms—physical, verbal, or psychological and emotional harm. The attack can be direct or indirect, impulsive or well-planned (Berkowitz, 1993; Parke & Slaby, 1983; Potter, Vaughn, Warren, Howley, Land, & Hagemeyer, 1995).

Examples: In Iowa in 1997 three 18-year-old men broke into an animal shelter for cats and slaughtered all the cats living there. A man in Menomonie, Wisconsin, in 1992 tied a dog to his pickup truck and dragged the dog until it was mutilated and dead (both were premeditated, direct, physical aggression).

Jessie, 8 years old, has a father who calls his son "dummy" (verbal, psychologically harmful aggression).

The same 8 year old delivered a karate-like hit to another child's chest (direct, physical aggression). He had seen the same action (also direct, physical aggression) on *The Mighty Morphin Power Rangers* show.

One child kicked down another child's block structure (physical, direct aggression that damages property).

Aggression may well be one of those behaviors that is in the eye of the beholder (Duhs & Gunton, 1988). Connor (1989) discovered that not everybody agrees on the definition of aggression. She showed 14 videotaped incidents of the play behavior of 4- and 5-year-old children to male and female college students, preschool teachers, and preservice preschool teachers. In the videos, children played with three different types of toys: regular toys such as dolls and trucks, miniature war toys such as "action" characters, and war toys such as commando sets and cowgirl guns.

Whether observers thought any of the types of play constituted aggression depended on whether that person had engaged in war-toy play, the person's gender, and whether he worked in a preschool setting. The point? Teachers in your school are likely to have slightly different definitions of aggression. It would be a good idea to develop a common definition of aggression so that your group will be much more likely to deal with aggressive behavior consistently and effectively.

Aggression is not the same thing as anger. Anger is an emotion, a feeling. Aggression is a behavior. Children who are angry might behave aggressively, but not always. And children can be aggressive without being angry. It is for these reasons that anger and aggression are dealt with in separate chapters in this text.

Forms of Aggression

This section describes three forms of aggression: *instrumental, hostile,* and *accidental.* As an early childhood teacher you will see instrumental and accidental aggression from your children fairly often, but will see hostile aggression far less frequently. This section also describes several factors that seem to influence how an adult or child shows aggression.

Instrumental aggression

Instrumental aggression is any behavior that is aimed at obtaining or getting back some object, territory, or privilege (Hartup, 1974). This type of aggression is linked to simple goal-blocking. A child who uses instrumental aggression is usually not even angry with the person blocking her goal, she simply wants to remove whatever is blocking her goal and tends to do something that hurts the other person to achieve her end.

Example: Four-year-old Donna wanted to sit on the yellow carpet square at circle time. When she saw that Linda was already sitting on the yellow square (Linda was blocking Donna's goal), Donna sat down right next to Linda and started to bump her. "Stop it," said Linda. Donna did not stop. In fact, she bumped Linda even harder and pushed her off the yellow carpet square (instrumental aggression).

You can expect to see a lot of instrumental aggression in early childhood children as they go about trying to get what they want. This is the most common form of aggression during early childhood and we have known this for many decades. Research from the 1930s (Dawe, 1934) and 1970s (Hartup, 1974) demonstrated that young children have most of their conflicts over space and resources (toys and

Janet wanted the basket of pencils (her goal). Sandy (middle child) had the basket, thus blocking Janet's goal. Janet used instrumental aggression when she grabbed the basket and met her goal. Instrumental aggression is very common in early childhood classrooms.

other equipment), and there tends to be little hostility involved. They push their way into line, grab things from others, yell "It's *my* turn!" and even bite (quite common in very young children).

Does this mean that early childhood teachers should let children get what they want by pushing, grabbing, or biting? Certainly not. Children should not be allowed to use aggression to get what they need or want. If Donna is allowed to push people around as she did with Linda and get what she wants, then she will have been rewarded for aggression. In the carpet square incident, her teacher decided to acknowledge that Donna had a goal but refused to let her use aggressive tactics to achieve her goal.

Example: Donna's teacher said, "Donna, I want you to move to another carpet square. Linda was sitting on the yellow square. You are not allowed to push other people around."

What should the teacher do if Donna whines, argues, or pouts? This teacher has done exactly the right thing in stopping the instrumental aggression and should simply ignore any whining, arguing, and pouting and should politely, calmly, and firmly restate the limit that Donna move to another carpet square.

Hostile aggression

Hostile aggression often looks like retaliation or revenge to an onlooker. It is quite different from instrumental aggression because the hostile aggression involves anger at a person; it is person-oriented aggression. It is not merely an attempt to remove something blocking attainment of a child's goal.

A person who is aggressive in a hostile way usually thinks that her ego has been threatened or that her self-esteem has been bruised. She will likely think that the other person has done something to her on purpose. Such a belief is the root of the physically or psychologically hostile aggression and this type of aggression often looks like retaliation or revenge to an onlooker. This type of aggression tends to increase with age (Feshbach, 1970; Hartup, 1974; Szegal, 1985).

Example: Two 8-year-olds, Samuel and Theng (pronounced Teng), worked on their science project together. Samuel's parents almost constantly criticize their son and frequently call him a "dummy." When Theng offered to help Samuel solve a problem with Sam's part of the project, Samuel perceived the offer as a sign that Theng thought him incompetent (perceived threat to self-esteem). Samuel did not say a word, but later, on the playground, waited for Theng to run past him and then tripped him (hostile aggression).

Rely on your knowledge of child development to explain why hostile aggression tends to show up in older children, adolescents, and adults but not very often at all in young children (Hartup, 1974; Szegal, 1985). This change in how children can express aggression parallels a more general change in their cognitive structure. Preschool children are usually in the second of Piaget's stages of cognitive development, the preoperational stage, and one of the major characteristics of this stage is a trait called *egocentricity.* As you read in Chapter 1, egocentricity refers to a child's inability to take another person's perspective and refers to being centered on one's own perspective. A young child is focused on her own needs and wants and usually does not understand as well as an older person that someone else has just as much right as she does, for example, to sit on a yellow carpet square.

An older child, in a different Piagetian stage, becomes less egocentric and better able to understand another person's intentions, including mean-spirited intentions to embarrass him. People do, however, make mistakes about the intentions of other people, as Samuel did with Theng's offer of help, but it is a person's perception of reality that matters, even if the perception is a faulty one. Samuel acted on his perception, faulty as it was, and he reacted with hostile aggression.

Accidental aggression

Accidental aggression is unintentional aggression (Feshbach, 1970) and is common in many early childhood classrooms. This type of behavior usually occurs when one child unintentionally annoys or hurts another child. The second child often behaves aggressively as a response. Accidental aggression is particularly common in poorly designed or crowded spaces.

Example: It was crowded in the coatroom of Mrs. Spencer's classroom. Ethan hung his up his coat and then turned around to leave the room but crashed into Andy (accidental aggression). Andy reacted by yelling at Ethan.

The real problem with accidental aggression is that the injured child (Andy) often retaliates in a hurtful way. Young children are not very good at distinguishing between accidental and intentional aggression and do not have the skills needed to deal effectively with strong feelings.

Here are some practical ideas for guiding children involved in accidental aggression:

- Help children learn to distinguish between accidental and intentional injury. They will be far less likely to retaliate when they understand that the damage was not on purpose.

Example: Mrs. Spencer said to Andy, "It's crowded in the coatroom, Andy, and Ethan bumped into you because it was so crowded just now. I really don't think that he meant to bump you."

- Expect some of the inevitable bumping, pushing, or shoving as young children learn how to live and work with others. Teach your children how to manage their feelings (Chapter 7).
- Practice good space management. We are responsible for making the classroom as safe as possible and we can prevent a lot of this type of aggression through good space management. (See Chapter 4 for more information about managing the physical environment.)

Example: Mrs. Spencer came up with a plan to rearrange the coatroom to give the children a bit more space. She also decided to limit the number of children allowed in the coatroom.

Gender Differences in Aggression

There are clear differences in aggression between boys and girls and these differences are evident during early childhood (Darvill & Cheyne, 1981; Maccoby & Jacklin, 1980). These researchers predict that we will see evidence of these sex differences in a group of young children in the following ways:

1. Boys will show more aggression than the girls.
2. Boys will be both physically and verbally more aggressive than the girls.
3. Older boys will be more likely than older girls to counterattack when physically attacked.
4. There will be more aggressive interactions between pairs of boys than between boy–girl or girl–girl dyads.

Cummings, Iannotti, and Zahn-Waxler (1989) supported these findings. In their studies of aggression in 2- and 5-year-old children they noted a gender difference in aggression. Their work also tells us that these gender differences in aggression were stable. Boys were not only more physically aggressive but their aggression was stable, that is, it stayed about the same for boys during the early childhood years.

Just how do those gender differences in children affect how they express aggression? One of the major explanations lies in how we socialize boys and girls for aggression. Our culture has clearly defined attitudes about girls, boys, and aggression, and we can easily observe these attitudes by looking at different child-rearing tactics used with boys and girls. Parents tend to use more physical punishment with boys than with girls, and boys might adopt these aggressive methods in interaction with others (Block, 1978). Some parents expect, permit, and then encourage aggression in boys. Parents also manage the environments of boys and girls differently by choosing different toys for girls and boys, clearly designating some toys for boys; these "male" toys, such as guns or action figures, are *aggressive cues,* items that seem to elicit aggressive play. Boyatzis, Matillo, and Nesbitt (1995) found that boys committed more aggressive acts than girls after watching an aggressive television show.

HOW CHILDREN BECOME AGGRESSIVE: A SYSTEMS/ECOLOGICAL APPROACH

Children are not aggressive when they are born, and not all children act aggressively as they get older. If we want to effectively guide aggressive children then we must acknowledge how complex the social behavior aggression is. There are many forces that seem to work together to shape aggression in certain children; keeping this in mind will help you as you search for ways to help the aggressive children in your care.

The most complete explanation of how children become aggressive is a *systems* or *ecological approach* (Bronfenbrenner, 1979). Professionals taking this approach acknowledge that a child is embedded in a variety of social systems and believe that these systems work together to shape a child's aggression (Huesmann, 1988). A child quite frequently first learns about aggression in her *family system.* Almost equal in importance to a family's influence is the media, that is, television, videos, and movies in helping children learn aggression. The child's *peer group* is a system that teaches and reinforces aggression. Families and peer groups are themselves embedded in a larger setting, the *community and culture,* and it is the teachings from these settings that families learn and pass on to their children. Let's take a look now at how aggression is learned, maintained, and modified in these systems.

Aggressive Families Teach Aggression to Children

This section describes how aggressive families teach children to be aggressive. Families play a critical role in the acquisition, maintenance, and modification of children's aggression (Parke & Slaby, 1983). Some children exist in violent families, and it is here that they receive lessons in how to hurt other people and animals. Some families become violent because members of the system develop aggressive patterns of interacting with one another. Adults in many aggressive family systems deal with anger irresponsibly; are authoritarian and nonsupportive; manage their children's environment poorly; and use ineffective, often harsh, discipline techniques.

Children acquire aggressive scripts when they observe family aggression

Aggression is a learned behavior, and children learn aggression in their families. Aggression within a family system is called *intrafamilial aggression.* Children in aggressive families have many opportunities to observe their parents using aggression to resolve conflicts. These children acquire *aggressive scripts* much like the scripts that actors use to memorize their parts. They acquire these scripts by observing their parents who model aggression. Over time, aggressive children have collected a set of scripts for social behavior. The aggressive children you will teach have a collection of scripts that tell them to behave aggressively in certain interactions.

These scripts for aggressive behavior get activated under a number of circumstances, for example, when a child's memory has been jogged. An aggressive script can also be called up when a child is exposed to specific cues, such as war toys or aggressive videos. Children who continue to observe aggression acquire even more aggressive scripts for calling up in the future, and the newly observed aggression may well trigger the recall of existing aggressive scripts. In addition, a child who practices these scripts is much more likely to recall them in the future.

Aggressive family systems use a coercive process

If we could observe an aggressive child's family we would see that the family uses a specific process to teach aggression and then to maintain it. The family also uses the same process to increase aggression. Patterson (1982) observed definite family interaction patterns that he termed a *coercive process.* Knowing that some of your children come from families using such a process for teaching aggression should help you understand the origin of the children's aggression. These are the steps that aggressive families use for teaching aggression.

1. *One system member does something aggressive.* For example, Ben hit his brother.
2. *A second system member is likely to respond in an equally hurtful way.* Ben's brother hit him back.
3. *The unfriendly interaction continues and escalates in intensity.* Ben responded by pushing his brother and the brother pushed back. Ben hit him again and the brother cried.
4. *Other system members are drawn into the process.* Dad heard the children fighting, raced to the backyard, grabbed each child, and yelled at them to stop the fighting.

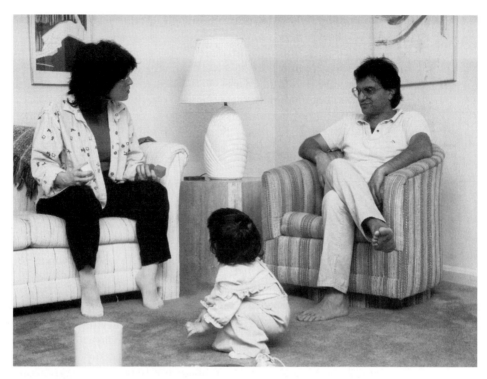

Cathy is acquiring aggressive scripts by watching her parents argue.

5. *One system member eventually withdraws the aversive or unpleasant stimulus and breaks the cycle of aggression for a short time.* Dad retreated to the house, proud of having stopped the fighting. The problem? Dad thought he succeeded in stopping the aggressive behavior of his children (actually, the children's aggressive behavior will probably increase). Dad has been negatively reinforced for slapping his children and is highly likely to slap them again in future interactions.

6. *System members reinforced for aggression victimize the same members of the system in future interactions.* Ben will be very likely to use aggression with his brother because the brother cried. Likewise, Dad was reinforced for aggressive discipline and will very likely use negative discipline strategies toward both children because he mistakenly believes these tactics to be effective.

Members of families caught up in this coercive process train each other to use aggression (Herrenkohl, Egolf, & Herrenkohl, 1997). They help each other develop aggressive scripts that will be played back again and again. Dad has a script that says, "Yell, slap, hit when the children fight." He models aggression by yelling at Ben and his brothers. Ben and his brother reinforce Dad for using such aggressive discipline strategies by temporarily stopping their fighting. Ben has learned how to hurt his brother, and his brother is on his way to becoming a victim. Herrenkohl et al. (1997) did a study that lasted 16 years—a longitudinal study—and found that preschoolers whose parents used harsh discipline showed a lot of aggressive behavior when they were adolescents.

Not all families go through this process. Both the parents and the children in aggressive families have specific characteristics that partially explain why only certain families use this process (Patterson, 1982). Parents in aggressive families tend to be high in demandingness but low in responsiveness (authori*tarian*) and tend to have ineffective guidance skills. Aggressive children show little self-control, are impulsive, and are generally noncompliant. Aggressive children do not respond very well to reinforcers and are not very responsive to social stimuli (Parke & Slaby, 1983).

By the time you get such a child in your classroom or center, she will have gone through hundreds of unpleasant interactions with parents who do not know much about children or child guidance and who use poor guidance strategies. This child will have reacted with noncompliance and impulsivity. The interactions will have been frustrating for both parent and child, and the result will be that you will have an aggressive child in your class who will challenge you as you try to figure out how to help her.

An authoritarian caregiving style fosters aggression

Members of aggressive family systems are not very responsive to each other. Recall that parents in the authoritarian and the permissive-by-default styles are low in responsiveness. They are neither sensitive to nor supportive of their children, and their caregiving style sets the stage for heightened aggression in children in a number of ways (Feshbach, 1970; Parke & Slaby, 1983).

1. These unresponsive adults often ignore and fail to meet their child's basic psychological needs for protection, love, affection, nurturance, play, and self-esteem. Unmet needs result in frustration, and frustrated, angry children frequently act aggressively if other conditions are present.

2. Adults low in responsiveness are ineffective teachers of social behaviors because they model and teach ineffective interactional skills such as irresponsible anger management and aggression. They reward aggressive behavior and fail to teach more appropriate behavior because they do not know how or what to teach. Their children tend to be low in self-control or self-restraint, and children who are not self-controlled are likely to react with aggression under many circumstances.

3. Adults in aggressive systems tend to use not just one or two negative discipline strategies but a whole cluster of negative discipline tactics, and it is this group of factors that contributes to aggression. You read about these negative strategies in Chapter 2: using physical discipline; failing to set appropriate limits; inconsistency in discipline; using humor as a weapon; using sarcasm, shame, nattering, or nagging; and using hurtful forms of punishment.

4. Adults in aggressive systems indirectly influence aggression through their management style. This adult managerial role is probably just as important

as the adult's direct role because children spend more time interacting with the inanimate environment than they do with people (Parke & Slaby, 1983). Parents in aggressive systems provide many cues that elicit aggression—lots of televised violence and toy guns. Other adults consciously avoid providing such cues.

Examples: Ben's parents (Ben is in Mrs. Spencer's second-grade class) are authori*tarian* and do not supervise their children very well or monitor their activities. Ben, for example, is allowed to watch as much television as he wants, and he watches plenty of televised violence. He owns several toy guns and frequently plays his brother's video game "Shoot the Rabbit."

David is also 7 years old. His parents seem to be authori*tative* and supervise their son fairly closely. They make an effort to monitor how much television he watches. They try to eliminate as much televised aggression as they can, and try to help Dave understand the violence if he does see it. They look for interesting toys that do not serve as cues for aggression (Carlson-Paige & Levin, 1990).

Aggressive Peers Teach Aggression

Aggression has its roots in a child's family, but aggression is also learned, maintained, and modified in a child's peer group. The children in your center or class will influence each other's aggression in several ways (Parke & Slaby, 1983).

Peers model aggression

Researchers first studied how children learn from peer models more than 30 years ago (Hicks, 1965). What they discovered was that young children learn just as effectively from models who were their own age, that is, were peers as they do from other types of model and that the effect of the modeling lasted for at least six months after observing the model.

Example: Lonnie, 5 years old, plays with other children who are 5, 6 and 7 years old. He has observed one of these children extort lunch money from one of the girls, has watched his friend Bert twist another child's arm until that child gave up a turn, and has observed yet another friend push one of the smaller children off the climbing structure. Lonnie's peer group shows a lot of aggression and the research tells us that Lonnie can learn how to be aggressive simply by watching his friends.

Peers reinforce aggression

Peers also reinforce other children's aggression. Aggressive children lack certain social skills, such as the ability to resolve conflict. Aggressive, unpopular children solve conflicts with peers through aggressive means and do not seem to know how to resolve conflict in a positive way (Bullock, 1991). Patterson, Littman, and Bricker (1967) studied a child's reactions to being attacked by another child. Some children cried, others withdrew from the attacker, and still others gave in to their attacker. Such responses from a victim of aggression actually reinforce an aggressive child.

A child's peer group influences the development of aggression

Example: Sue gave up her turn on the seesaw when Ben pushed her off. Other children, however, did not give in and tried to get adult help. Lew called the teacher and said, "Ben pushed me!"

Sue reinforced Ben's aggression by "giving in." Ben, the aggressor, is very likely to continue to aggress on this child, but he will also very likely seek out a new victim in the case of the children who refused to give in to him.

Peers teach how to avoid being a victim

Example: Jim is a relatively passive child who has frequently been the victim of Ben's aggression. After being hit several times, pushed out of the way, and having his puzzle dumped, Jim did nothing. One day when Ben pushed Jim out of place at the slide, Jim counterattacked and shoved Ben. The number of attacks against Jim declined, and he realized that he could avoid being a victim by behaving aggressively.

Yes, Jim does need to learn to defend himself, but he also should be taught responsible anger management. He has learned that aggression is a powerful tool.

Peers regulate aggression by setting norms

Peer groups influence aggression of members of the group by *setting norms* about the expression of aggression. Some peer groups, such as gangs, have norms that demand that members use aggression in order to be a group member. Other groups might forbid aggression through their norms.

Television Affects the Development of Aggression

There is *"absolutely no doubt that higher levels of viewing violence on television are correlated with increased acceptance of aggressive attitudes and increased aggressive behavior."*
(APA, 1993)

Teachers and parents have many years of research available to them showing that children watch a lot of television, that they watch an excessive amount of violence, and that heavy viewing of television violence has major behavioral effects. Along with family and peer group, we should regard television as a major socializer of children's aggression (Boyatzis et al., 1995; Kuttschreuter, Wiegman, & Baarda, 1989; NAEYC, 1990; National Television Violence Study Council [NTVSC], 1997). Television is so pervasive in our society that it would be foolhardy to ignore how it affects the development of a child's aggression (Parke & Slaby, 1983).

How does television and video violence affect children's aggression?

Conclusion #1: Television can and does increase subsequent aggression in children. This conclusion comes from basic research and reports of professional groups (APA, 1985, 1993; Primavera, Herron, & Javier, 1996; Funk, 1992; Lefkowitz, Eron, Walder, & Huesmann, 1972).

Conclusion #2: Televised violence increases a child's passive acceptance of aggression by others. Not only do children themselves become more aggressive when they watch televised violence, but they also more readily accept violence by others. Children are most likely to relax their standards if they view violence as effective, justified, reinforced, and commonplace (Eron & Huesmann, 1987; NTVSC, 1997). Television and video violence is presented in precisely this fashion.

Television violence influences children in four ways: making them want to imitate what they see, reducing learned inhibitions against violent behavior, desensitizing them to violence through repetition, and increasing arousal (Black & Newman, 1995; Gunter & McAleer, 1990).

How much television do children watch?

By 1988 almost all American homes (98%) had one television, and more than 50 percent had at least one extra television, the extra set used mainly by children (Nielsen Company, 1988). In that same year, more than 50 percent of American homes had a video cassette recorder, and about 33 percent had cable programming (Stipp & Milavsky, 1988). So, American children have access to a wide range of programming—regular broadcast stations, hundreds of cable stations, and whatever other video programming is allowed in their homes.

It will come as no surprise to you, then, that children watch a lot of television. Television-viewing habits develop in early childhood, and, in spite of large individual differences in how much television children watch (Huston, Rice, Kerkman, & St. Peters, 1990), 2- to 18-year-old children watch television for an average of 28 hours per week (Nielsen Company, 1988). Parents even expose infants (6 months) to an average of 1 hour of television per day. Many children spend more time watching television than they do anything else, including exercising, playing, reading, and interacting with friends or family (Gunter & McAleer, 1990; Huston et al., 1990).

Many parents express concern about the effects of televised violence on their children. In one study, parents were as concerned that televised violence may contribute to fear and passivity in their children as they were that television might promote aggressiveness (Ridley-Johnson, Surdy, & O'Laughlin, 1991). At the same time, though, many of the same concerned parents place very few restrictions on children's viewing. They restrict neither the amount of television their children watch nor the content of the programs.

How is violence portrayed on television?

American television programming shows violence as a common form of social interaction. Gerbner, Gross, Morgan, and Signorielli (1986) monitored televised violence over a 13-year period and found that violence was frequently and consistently portrayed on television; 80 percent of the programs monitored contained violence that occurred at a rate of 7.5 incidents per hour. Children's television contains an especially high level of violence, with almost 18 violent incidents per hour in more than 90 percent of these shows. Children's cartoon programs have high concentrations of violence. The NTVSC (1997) spotted more than 800 high-risk cartoons.

Children see a distorted view of violence on television (Mustonen & Pulkkinen, 1993; NTVSC, 1997; Potter et al., 1995). Real violence is dirty—people bleed, jaws are broken, people are stabbed, dogs are mutilated, animals and people suffer and die. Real violence is not funny, but televised violence does not show real violence. Televised violence is distorted, because it depicts shootings, fighting, knifings, and murder as clean, justified, effective, rewarded, and humorous. "Good guys" are allowed to use violence as a way of punishing "bad guys." "Good guys" are just as violent as the "bad guys."

Our children see violence on television and in videos as a good way to get what they want or to attain goals. Children's television shows that violence is an effective way to get things and to get things done. The children see that "good guys" get what they want by hurting others, and that they are actually rewarded for being violent. Less than one aggressive act out of six is punished in any form; twice that number are rewarded (Potter et al., 1995).

Televised violence is often depicted as humorous. Children's television is especially guilty of connecting violence and humor (Parke & Slaby, 1983). Violent cartoons are frequently accompanied by laugh tracks. Linking violence and laughter tells children that "violence is funny."

How well do children understand televised violence?

Young children do not seem to understand violence in the same way that an older child does (Collins, 1983). Collins, Wellman, Keniston, and Westley (1978), wanting to know what children of different ages would remember about violence on television, showed a program containing violence to children in kindergarten, second, fifth, and eighth grades. Kindergarten and second-grade children remembered either an aggressive act alone or the aggressive act and its consequences. For example, they would remember that a detective successfully extracted information from a victim by threatening to shoot her (aggressive act). Fifth- and eighth-graders also understood and remembered the motives of an aggressor.

Children acquire aggressive scripts by watching violence on TV or in videos

In the section on learning aggression in families, we saw that children acquire scripts from their families that tell them how to behave in social situations. They also acquire these powerful scripts by watching aggression in movies, videos, and television (Boyatzis et al., 1995; Mortimer, 1994). The Boyatzis research group investigated the effects of *The Mighty Morphin Power Rangers* on children's aggressive behavior. The National Coalition on Television Violence (NCTV) called this program the most violent children's program it had ever studied, averaging 211 violent acts per hour (Kiesewetter, 1993). Most of the aggression in the show is severe and hostile, rather than instrumental. Most of the violence in the show is intended to harm or kill another character. The researchers were alarmed at the power of the Mighty Morphin Rangers to increase aggression. The children in the study who watched only a single episode were immediately and significantly more aggressive after the show. This show had helped children write a script for social behavior that says, "Hit, punch, kick, hurt."

STRATEGIES FOR GUIDING AGGRESSIVE CHILDREN

Early childhood teachers are challenged when guiding aggressive children. Some aggression is normal as young children learn to live with others, but other aggression has developed in an aggressive family and is much more deeply rooted in a child and, therefore, much more difficult to work with. There are a number of strategies described in this section for guiding aggressive children. You will notice that most of the strategies focus on helping individual children in a classroom setting. Two small sections describe how beneficial it is to also work with a child's family and to focus on events in the child's larger community.

Work with Individual Children

Set and clearly communicate limits prohibiting aggression

Create a nonpermissive atmosphere by establishing limits against hurting or disturbing others or damaging toys or equipment and firmly, but gently, enforcing limits. You will begin to help children see that other people have a right to be safe and secure. You will help them develop values and internal controls about the rights of others.

   Example: When Mrs. Spencer restated a limit—"Ben, I know that you want to sit in that chair, but I can't just let you push Pete off. I want you to sit in this chair"—she clearly communicated her refusal to tolerate Ben's aggression.

Reduce exposure to aggression-evoking cues and aggressive models

Turner and Goldsmith (1976) wanted to know if children's aggression would increase if toy guns were available. They observed preschool children during free play. In some of the play sessions toy guns were available, but in other sessions the toy guns were replaced by airplanes. Aggression was much more evident when guns were present. Children frequently act aggressively when certain stimuli associated with aggression are available.

In this case, effective guidance calls for limiting the number of models of aggression to which children are exposed. One of the best ways to do this is to limit the amount of violent television a child watches. Another is to carefully screen and select movies, books, pictures, and other media.

Watch television with children and comment on aggressive program content

We need to be realistic and accept the fact that the children we teach will watch television. Teachers and parents can still be proactive by decreasing the amount of television watched, monitoring what children watch, watching with them as much as possible, and teaching them how to understand what they watch (Primavera et al, 1996).

Example: While John was watching television, his father said, "Why do you think that man kicked his neighbor's car, John? . . . Yes, I think he was mad at him for driving his car over the flowers. That still doesn't make it OK to kick his neighbor's car." Ben (chapter opener case study) watched the same movie, but he watched it by himself.

Children who watch televised violence with adults and hear a negative evaluation of the violence, as John did, tend to be less aggressive than such children as Ben, who watch the same aggression alone (Eron, 1986; Singer, 1987).

Encourage children to be empathic

Teach aggressive children how the person they have victimized is feeling. Don't just ask how the aggressive child *thinks* that the other might feel. Tell them.

Example: "Oh, Susan! You've torn Sarah's painting. I think she's sad because she is crying."

Susan was being encouraged to be empathic. Children who are trained to be more empathic tend to be more sensitive to another's feelings and to be less aggressive (Feshbach & Feshbach, 1982).

Encourage consequential thinking

Help children develop a value system that encourages them to treat others with respect and to refrain from hurting others (APA, 1993). One way to help children develop a respectful attitude is to teach them *consequential thinking,* the understanding that a consequence of aggression is that somebody gets hurt or something is damaged. Consequential thinking is one key to changing or preventing aggressive behavior. A good way to encourage consequential thinking is to give gentle but direct instruction in thinking about consequences.

Example: Ben was learning to train his puppy in 4-H, and the dog trainer was watching. Ben yanked the puppy's collar when the puppy did not sit on command. The trainer said, "Hold it, Ben. You hurt Rusty when you yank his collar like that. He looks real scared to me. Let me show you the 'sit' command again."

This adult is trying to arouse empathy in Ben for Rusty by "feeding back" the puppy's fear and she is also teaching Ben the consequences of aggression—that someone gets hurt. Ben will be less likely now to yank the puppy's collar because the trainer has helped him think about the consequences of his actions.

Avoid a common, but misguided, tactic to say, "Ben, how would you like it if somebody pulled you like that?" Adults who use this tactic want children to think consequentially, but their method misses the mark. Young children do not know how the other person felt, so they will not be able to figure it out on their own. Do not expect them to automatically know this unless you say many times when they are young, "That hurt," "You broke that when you stepped on it," or "It hurts somebody's feelings when you call them names."

A word of caution. Not everyone reacts to pain feedback by becoming less aggressive. For highly aggressive children, another person's or animal's pain is merely a signal that the aggression "worked," and these children show little or no sorrow for hurting another person or animal. The person who dragged the dog to death bragged about it: "Yeah, I kept going until he [the dog] stopped squealing!" This person heard and fully understood the suffering he caused, but he did not stop, even when the dog was so obviously hurt.

Teach more positive behavior

Assertiveness, negotiation, cooperation, sharing, helping—all of these behaviors are incompatible with or contrary to aggression. We can essentially crowd out aggressive behaviors by teaching children how to cooperate or be assertive in place of acting aggressively. Aggressive children have a limited number of ways of dealing with interactional problems. We can be very helpful by enlarging their set of responses so that they have a greater choice when faced with an issue (Middleton & Cartledge, 1995).

Example: Mrs. Spencer made a real effort to plan and teach nonaggressive behavior. So, when the children worked on projects, she encouraged them to help each other. She did a skit about one child needing help at the computer and another child offering help.

Recognize and encourage cooperative behavior and language

When David helped another child with a math problem, Mrs. Spencer said, "You really helped Joseph, David. Thanks." Mrs. Spencer has discovered that it is very effective to notice and then to encourage nonaggressive behavior (Brown & Elliot, 1965) when she sees it in children who are usually aggressive. The school's guidance counselor also encouraged her to ignore some of Ben's aggressive language, too. She started ignoring such language as "I'm going to punch you in the nose!" and instead listened carefully for verbally cooperative statements such as "Let's put this puzzle together!"

The counselor taught Mrs. Spencer to encourage such cooperative language by saying something like, "Ben, I heard you ask Sue if you could work with her on the big puzzle." Slaby and Crowley (1977) found that verbal aggression decreased and cooperation increased when teachers noticed and reinforced such cooperative statements.

Step between children involved in an incident, ignore the aggressor, and pay attention to the victim

Some children persist in their aggression in spite of very well developed and well stated limits.

Example: Mrs. Spencer, at recess, saw Nathan push and bump his way (the instrumental aggression) across one of the climbing structures. Mattie bruised her elbow when she slammed against a bar after Nathan bumped her. The teacher decided to attend to Mattie, the victim, and to ignore Nathan, the aggressor—for the moment. She recommended that Mattie use an assertive way of dealing with Nathan's instrumental aggression: "Mattie, you were on the climber first. Please tell Nathan that he has to wait for you to move out of the way."

This is an effective strategy, first, because Mrs. Spencer did not reinforce Nathan's aggression. She did not allow Mattie, his victim, to give in to the aggression. Second, Mattie learned how to cope with conflict by being assertive. Third, other children observed that aggression would not be tolerated, that aggression is not an effective method of interacting with friends, and that it is good to be sympathetic with a victim (Parke & Slaby, 1983).

Encourage responsible anger management

Children who are aggressive are usually not very good at managing strong emotions such as jealousy or anger. Prevent some of the aggression that comes from this source by teaching children how to understand and manage their strong feelings (Marion, 1997). See Chapter 7 for specific strategies for teaching children how to understand and manage anger.

Use Early Childhood Family Education to Teach Families About Aggression

A teacher concentrates on working with children in a classroom. Teachers are not therapists and are not trained to do therapy with aggressive families. However, early childhood teachers know how important it is to have a good relationship with and to work with parents and families. Early childhood teachers work with families by giving information and advice about any number of issues (Marion, in press). Consider giving information and advice about issues such as the link between harsh discipline and children's aggression, positive discipline strategies (Marion, 1992), the role that television plays in children's aggression, and how to mediate their child's television or video watching. (Please see the Parent Talk box.)

Focus on the "Larger Picture" of Aggression at the Community Level

We can work with individual children who are aggressive and we can also do parent education to help families deal with aggression. That is a wonderful start. Early childhood professionals can also think about the "bigger picture" by keeping in mind the idea that families are embedded in communities, that families do not exist in a vacuum. Each family of a child we teach is heavily influenced by its community. It is, after all, the community that establishes laws and makes policy that affects families.

There are several practical and realistic things that early childhood professionals can do to decrease aggression at a community level. An individual teacher would not be able to do all of the following activities but might consider joining with others to do one or two to help decrease aggression within her community:

- Join and support the efforts of your professional organization to document and curb violence and aggression. The NAEYC, for example, has had a national-level committee examining violence in the lives of children and provides information to its members on this topic (NAEYC, 1990).
- Understand television ratings systems and explain them to parents in your center or school. The ratings system developed in 1997 was seen as unnecessarily confusing.
- Urge lawmakers to require your state to fund child abuse prevention programs. Wisconsin has been doing this for several years now and these programs serve early childhood families in every part of the state. Child abuse and other aggression in families are largely determined by the availability of community support systems. Aggression within families tends to decrease when families have access to positive support systems. The Wisconsin Children's Trust Fund (1996) required that grant proposals contain a method for helping families build social support systems.
- Know how to refer families of aggressive children to the appropriate community agency.
- Plan anti-aggression activities for the Week of the Young Child, sponsored by the NAEYC each spring. For example, prepare a display of books for parents to read to children that emphasize nonaggressive solutions to problems. Hold a conflict-resolution workshop open to all community parents.

Parent Talk. Recommendations for Parents from the National Television Violence Study (1997)

The researchers offer good recommendations to parents who can begin immediately to change the way they think about violence on television and the way they make decisions about their children's viewing.

- **Take an active interest in your children's television viewing and watch and discuss programs with them.** Parental involvement is essential. Watch and discuss television with children and you will prevent many of the harmful effects that can occur and help make viewing a learning experience. You will help your children interpret story lines, recognize stereotypes, and discriminate what is real from unreal on television.

(continues on the next page)

- **Be aware of the three risks associated with viewing television violence.** The first risk: learning aggressive attitudes and behaviors. The second risk: fear and viewing the world as a fearful place. The third risk: becoming desensitized to violence.
- **Consider the context of violent depictions in making viewing decisions for children.** Your child is most likely to be harmed by violence on television when humor is used along with the aggression, when violence is morally condoned, when violence doesn't have any serious negative consequences, when violence is rewarded, and when heroes or good characters act violently.
- **Consider your child's developmental level when making viewing decisions.** Very young children are less able to distinguish fantasy from reality on television. Your preschooler or primary-grade child will identify strongly with superheroes and fantastic cartoon characters and will learn from and very likely imitate their violence.

Do not make the mistake of dismissing cartoon violence because it is unrealistic. Punishment of the violence should be shown within the violent scene, not at the end of the program, if the punishment is to be effective.
- **Recognize that certain types of violent cartoons pose particularly high risk for young children's learning of aggression.** Closely monitor cartoons because some of them are "high-risk." A show that is labeled high-risk is especially likely to teach your child aggressive attitudes and behaviors. What should you look for?—a cartoon or program that features an attractive character who engages in violence that is condoned and that does not result in any serious consequences to the perpetrator.
- **Recognize that some types of ratings might make a program more attractive to your child.** The research shows that current rating systems might actually make a program more attractive to your child. Be prepared to supervise his or her viewing even more closely.

Case Study Analysis: Aggression In Mrs. Spencer's School

Analyze the case study at the beginning of the chapter (Mrs. Spencer's school) by answering the following questions.

1. There were three examples of aggressive behavior in the case study. Identify the type(s) of aggression and then give a reason for your choice. Is the aggression you identified typical for the ages of the children? Why or why not?

2. Mrs. Spencer used a specific strategy in each example in the case study, including the behavior that was *not* aggression. Using information from the chapter, explain what her strategy was in each instance and say why it was appropriate for that incident.

3. Ben, as seen in both the case study and throughout the chapter, is a highly aggressive child. From the information presented in the text, please explain how Ben has very likely become so aggressive.

REFLECTING ON KEY CONCEPTS

1. Reflect on the concept of aggression by answering these "True/False" questions:
   a. True or False? Anger and aggression are the same thing? Why or why not?
   b. True or False? Young children's aggression is usually instrumental in nature. Explain your answer.
   c. True or False? Hostile aggression usually shows up in children as they get older. Explain your answer.
   d. True or False? Research has demonstrated that there are very few differences in how boys and girls show aggression. Explain your response.
2. Name two specific ways in which aggressive families foster aggression in young children. Explain how a child's peers can teach her to be aggressive and summarize television's influence on aggression in young children.
3. Choose at least three of the strategies for guiding aggressive children presented in this chapter and explain why they would be effective either in stopping or preventing children's aggression.

APPLY YOUR KNOWLEDGE

1. Watch at least one hour of television that is aimed specifically at young children. On a sheet of paper, break that hour into 10-minute segments. In each of the segments keep a tally of the number of times that you see an act of aggression—any act of aggression—and total it at the end of the hour. Write a brief description of each act of aggression.
2. Visit a toy store. Find several examples of toys and describe those that you think would serve as aggressive cues, that is, would likely bring out aggression in young children. Were these toys designated for a specific gender?
3. Write the script for a puppet play about an incident of instrumental aggression. Use an example different from those in the chapter. Write in a part for a teacher who guides the aggressive child(ren) to use a more effective way of getting what they want or need. Be prepared to put on your brief play for your class or for a group of children. (Get permission from the children's teacher first and also get approval for your play.)

References

American Psychological Association. (1985). *Violence on television.* Washington, DC: APA Board of Ethical and Social Responsibility for Psychology.

American Psychological Association. (1993). *Violence and youth report.* Washington, DC: APA Commission on Violence and Youth.

Berkowitz, L. (1993). *Aggression: Its causes, consequences, and control.* Philadelphia: Temple University Press.

Black, D., & Newman, M. (1995). Television violence and children. *British Medical Journal, 310,* 273–274.

Block, H. (1978). Another look at sex differentiation in the socialization behaviors of mothers and fathers. In J. Sherman & F. L. Denmark (Eds.), *The future of women: Future directions of research.* New York: Psychological Dimensions.

Boyatzis, C., Matillo, G., & Nesbitt, K. (1995). Effects of *The Mighty Morphin Power Rangers* on children's aggression with peers. *Child Study Journal, 25*(1), 45–57

Bronfenbrenner, U. (1979). *The ecology of human development.* Cambridge, MA: Harvard University Press.

Brown, P., & Elliot, R. (1965). Control of aggression in a nursery school class. *Journal of Experimental Child Psychology, 2,* 103–107.

Bullock, J. (1991). Supporting the development of socially rejected children. *Early Child Development and Care, 66,* 15–23.

Carlson-Paige, N., & Levin, D. (1990). *Who's calling the shots? How to respond effectively to children's fascination with war toys.* Philadelphia: New Society Publishers.

Collins, W. A. (1983). Social antecedents, cognitive processing, and comprehension of social portrayals on television. In E. T. Higgins, D. N. Ruble, & W. W. Hartup (Eds.), *Social cognition and social development.* Cambridge, England: Cambridge University Press.

Collins W. A., Wellman, H., Keniston, A. H., & Westly, S. D. (1978). Age-related aspects of comprehension and influence from a televised dramatic narrative. *Child Development, 49,* 389–399.

Connor, K. (1989). Aggression: Is it in the eye of the beholder? *Play and Culture, 2*(3), 213–217.

Cummings, E. M., Iannotti, R. J., & Zahn-Waxler, C. (1989). Aggression between peers in early childhood: Individual continuity and developmental change. *Child Development, 60*(4), 887–895.

Darvill, D., & Cheyne, J. A. (1981). *Sequential analysis of responses to aggression: Age and sex effects.* Paper presented at the Society for Research in Child Development, Boston, MA.

Dawe, H. C. (1934). An analysis of two hundred quarrels of preschool children. *Child Development, 5,* 139–157.

Duhs, L., & Gunton, R. (1988). TV violence and childhood aggression: A curmudgeon's guide. *Australian Psychologist, 23*(2), 183–185.

Eron, L. D. (1986). Interventions to mitigate the psychological effects of media violence on aggressive behavior. *Journal of Social Issues, 42*(3), 155–169.

Eron, L. D., & Huesmann, L. R. (1987). Television as a source of maltreatment of children. *School Psychology Review, 16*(2), 195–202.

Feshbach, S. (1970). Aggression. In P. Mussen (Ed.), *Carmichael's manual of child psychology* (Vol. 2). New York: Wiley.

Feshbach, N. D., & Feshbach, S. (1982). Empathy training and the regulation of aggression: Potentialities and limitations. *Academic Psychology Bulletin, 4,* 399–413.

Funk, J. (1992). Video games: Benign or malignant? *Journal of Applied Developmental Psychology, 12*(1), 63–71.

Gerbner, G., Gross, L., Morgan, M., & Signorielli, N. (1986). Living with television: The dynamics of the cultivation process. In J. Bryant & D. Zillman (Eds.), *Perspectives on media effects.* Hillsdale, NJ: Erlbaum.

Gunter, B., & McAleer, J. (1990). Children and television—The one eyed monster? London: Routledge.

Hartup, W. W. (1974). Aggression in childhood: Developmental perspectives. *American Psychologist, 29,* 336–341.

Herrenkohl, R. C., Egolf, B. P., & Herrenkohl, E. C. (1997). Preschool antecedents of adolescent assaultive behavior: A longitudinal study. *American Journal of Orthopsychiatry, 67*(3), 422–432.

Hicks, D. J. (1965). Imitation and retention of film-mediated aggressive peer and adult models. *Journal of Personality and Social Psychology, 2,* 97–100.

Huesmann, L. (1988). An information processing model for the development of aggression. *Aggressive Behavior, 14*(1), 13–24.

Huston, A. C., Rice, M. L., Kerkman, D., & St. Peters, M. (1990). Development of television viewing patterns in early childhood: A longitudinal investigation. *Developmental Psychology, 26,* 409–420.

Kiesewetter, J. (1993, Dec. 17). Top kids show also ranks as most violent. *The Cincinnati Enquirer,* A1.

Kuttschreuter, M., Wiegman, O., & Baarda, B. (1989). Aggression, prosocial behaviour and television viewing: A longitudinal study in six countries. *Pedagogische Studien, 66*(10), 377–389.

Lefkowitz, M., Eron, L. D., Walder, L. O., & Huesmann, L. R. (1972). Television violence and child aggression: A follow-up study. In G. A. Comstock & E. A. Rubinstein (Eds.), *Television and social behavior: III. Television and adolescent aggressiveness.* Washington, DC: U.S. Government Printing Office.

Maccoby, E., & Jacklin, C. N. (1980). Sex differences in aggression: A rejoinder and reprise. *Child Development, 51,* 964–980.

Marion, M. (1992). Community coordinated family education and support center. Grant proposal. Funded. Madison, WI: Wisconsin Children's Trust Fund.

Marion, M. (1997). Research in review: Guiding young children's understanding and management of anger. *Young Children, 52*(7), 62–67.

Marion, M. (In press). *Early childhood family education.* Columbus, OH: Merrill/Prentice-Hall.

Middleton, M. B., & Cartledge, G. (1995). Effects of social skills instruction and parental involvement on the aggressive behaviors of African American males. *Behavior Modification, 19*(2), 192–211.

Mortimer, J. (1994). How TV violence hits kids. *Education Digest, 60*(2), 16–20.

Mustonen, A., & Pulkkinen, L. (1993). Aggression in television programs in Finland. *Aggressive Behavior, 19,* 175–183.

National Association for the Education of Young Children. (1990). NAEYC position statement on media violence in children's lives. *Young Children, 45,* 18–21.

National Television Violence Study Council (1997). National television violence study, executive summary. J. Federman (Ed.), Santa Barbara, CA: Center for Communication and Social Policy.

Nielsen Company. (1988). 1988 Nielsen report on television. Northbrook, IL: Author.

Parke, R. D., & Slaby, R. G. (1983). The development of aggression. In P. Mussen (Ed.), *Handbook of Child Psychology* (Vol. 4). New York: Wiley.

Patterson, B. R., Littman, R. A., & Bricker, W. (1967). Assertive behavior in children: A step toward a theory of aggression. *Monographs of the Society for Research in Child Development, 32* (Serial No. 113).

Patterson, G. R. (1982). *Coercive family processes.* Eugene, OR: Castilia Press.

Potter, J., Vaughan, M., Warren, R., Howley, K., Land, A., & Hagemeyer, J. (1995). How real is the portrayal of aggression in television entertainment programming? *Journal of Broadcasting and Electronic Media, 39*(4), 496–517.

Primavera, L., Herron, W., & Javier, R. (1996). The effect of viewing television violence on aggression. *International Journal of Instructional Media, 23*(2), 137–151.

Ridley-Johnson, R., Surdy, T., & O'Laughlin, E. (1991). Parent survey on television violence viewing. *Journal of Developmental and Behavioral Pediatrics, 13*(1), 53–54.

Singer, J. L. (1987). Is television bad for children? *Social Science, 71*(2–3), 178–182.

Slaby, R., & Crowley, C. G. (1977). Modification of cooperation and aggression through teacher attention to children's speech. *Journal of Experimental Child Psychology, 23*, 442–458.

Stipp, H., & Milavsky, J. R. (1988). U.S. television programming's effects on aggressive behavior of children and adolescents. *Current Psychology: Research and Reviews, 7*, 76–92.

Szegal, B. (1985). Stages in the development of aggressive behavior in early childhood. *Aggressive Behavior, 11*(4), 315–321.

Turner, C., & Goldsmith, D. (1976). Effects of toy guns and airplanes on children's antisocial free play behavior. *Journal of Experimental Child Psychology, 21*, 303–315.

Wisconsin Children's Trust Fund. (1996). *Request for proposals.* Madison, WI: Author.

Chapter 9

Prosocial Behavior: Guiding Its Development

After reading and studying this chapter, you will be able to:

✿ Define prosocial behavior.
✿ Identify, describe, and give an example of types of prosocial behaviors.
✿ List developmental building blocks of prosocial behavior. Explain the role of each.
✿ Explain the benefits of encouraging prosocial behavior in children.
✿ Identify, describe, and observe developmentally appropriate strategies that foster prosocial behavior.
✿ Apply your knowledge to real-world situations and analyze case studies.

"Who raises altruistic children? . . . parents
who themselves are highly concerned about the welfare of others."
(Shaffer, 1993, p. 547)

Case Studies: Prosocial Behavior

Miranda

Three-year-old Miranda lives on a farm with her parents and three older brothers. When Dad takes care of his houseplants, Miranda's regular job is to help by misting the plants needing moisture. After lunch her 16-year-old brother handed her plate to her and said, "Take your plate over to the dishwasher, Miranda. Thanks!" She helped her mother feed the barn cats and watched as her mom picked up Puddles, a cat whose leg was cut. Mom said, "O-o-h, come here and let me take care of your cut. Get that cloth for Mommy, Miranda. I'll bet that Puddle's leg hurts, and I think she might be afraid, too. So, we have to tell her it's going to be OK."

Steve

Five-year-old Steve lives with his mom and dad. Within a one-month time frame this is what he witnessed: Mom and Dad really shared the housework. He watched *Mr. Rogers' Neighborhood* when Mr. Rogers talked about working together and showed what it meant. Steve and his dad and uncle made cookies for the child-care center's bake sale, and Dad helped a neighbor fix the gate on his fence. "Glad to help!" was Dad's reply to the neighbor's thanks. Mom took Steve with her when she showed Humane Society slides on taking good care of pets at the local elementary school and when she took vegetables from their garden to the food pantry and quietly said, as they drove away, "There are a lot of people who don't have enough to eat, Steve. I like sharing the vegetables from our garden. "

John

Seven-year-old John lives with his dad in a single-parent family. "It's time to plan 'Project Winterizing,' John," said Dad, as they sat down at the table with hot chocolate and a pad of paper. "There are some special things that have to be done in the yard before winter, and I don't have time to do them all by myself. Let's list them. I'll do some of the chores, and then I want you to do some, too. We'll get this done a lot more quickly if we work together. We'll go out for pizza for dinner when we finish.

"Let's figure out which things would be done first, second, and third, and then go get the equipment ready that we need. And I'll show you how to cover the rosebushes so that the cover stays put." They shook hands as they headed off to the garage. "Project Winterizing is under way!"

In August 1996 an amazing thing happened at the Brookfield Zoo near Chicago. Binti Jua, a female lowland gorilla, rescued a 3-year-old human child who had fallen into the gorilla enclosure at the zoo. She took the boy into her arms and stayed with him near a door until the zookeepers arrived. She kept the child safe and away from the other gorillas. Binti Jua's actions touched off a storm of debate about whether altruistic behavior can be seen in anything other than the human species. Her behavior typifies the type of behavior discussed in this chapter; it is called prosocial behavior.

As an early childhood educator, you will rightly be concerned about encouraging children to act prosocially, that is, to be helpful, cooperative, and generous in a world determined to show quite another set of values—violence, hatred, mean-spiritedness, stinginess, and aggression. Some children, Miranda, Steve, and John, for example, come from healthy family systems that foster moral development by showing concern for and responding to the needs of family members. But many children come from less healthy family systems in which interactions leave people feeling degraded or demeaned, where adults refuse to respond to the needs of others, and in which compassion is rarely, if ever, demonstrated.

This chapter focuses on the development of *prosocial behavior,* or concern for others, and will target major issues in this area. First, we'll focus on what prosocial behavior is and what you are likely to see in an early childhood classroom. Then the focus shifts to figuring out what motivates people to share, help, and cooperate. This chapter emphasizes how development in a couple of important areas is the key to enabling children to act prosocially. Finally, you will learn some very practical and effective strategies for guiding children's sharing, helping, and cooperation. Let's turn now to understanding prosocial behavior.

UNDERSTANDING PROSOCIAL BEHAVIOR

What Is Prosocial Behavior?

Prosocial behavior is behavior that is intended to benefit another person or animal. Prosocial behavior is made up of several smaller groupings of behaviors or actions that you are likely to see when children or adults act prosocially (Naparstek, 1990). Figure 9–1 shows that these smaller groupings of prosocial behaviors are sharing, helping, and cooperating.

Sharing, helping, and cooperating are all prosocial behaviors and are alike because they are intended to benefit someone else. At certain times each might be used to meet somebody's physical needs as when a child willingly shares a blanket

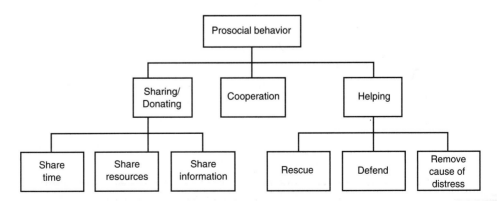

Figure 9–1. Prosocial behavior

with another child or when one child helps another find a shovel hidden in the sandpit. At other times sharing, helping, and cooperating are also used to meet another's emotional needs.

Example: Miranda's mother (chapter opener case study) asked Miranda to help the hurt cat by reassuring it.

People are different in how clearly they communicate what they need in the way of assistance. Sometimes, a person's or animal's need for assistance is plain and unmistakable, as when a child can easily tell that his friend needs help because the friend has dropped an entire box of beads for stringing on the floor. In other cases, though, needs are not as evident and are more difficult to figure out, as when one child, too shy to openly request a chunk of play dough, stands quietly by the play dough table looking longingly at the dough but does not say what he wants.

Forms of Prosocial Behavior

Sharing

Every early childhood teacher has heard, "Teacher, he won't share!" Many early childhood teachers worry when children refuse to share, because they understand how important prosocial behavior is. Parents, too, want to know how to help children learn to share. Sharing, then, is an important issue in early childhood settings. A child who shares owns something, or at least currently has possession, and decides to let somebody use the item or even gives ownership of the item to the other person (Beauvais, 1982). People can share or donate materials, information, or time.

Examples: Tim shares his glob of paste with Simon at the collage table (sharing materials).

Tim's father works as a volunteer firefighter (donating time).

Christina, a third-grader, showed a new child in the class where things were in the cafeteria and library (sharing information).

Sharing in the early childhood years is an important but puzzling part of a young child's positive social interactions. For preschool children, prosocial behavior is usually not highly self-sacrificing, that is, it requires little risk (Eisenberg, Wolchik, Goldberg, & Engel, 1992; Radke-Yarrow, Zahn-Waxler, & Chapman, 1983). Young children's sharing quite often takes the form of simply offering objects to other children or adults during social interaction (Eisenberg, Cameron, Tryon, & Dodez, 1981; Eisenberg et al., 1992).

Sharing is certainly a prosocial behavior when it is intended to benefit another person, but sharing also seems to serve another important purpose for young children in social interaction. Offering things to others—often viewed as sharing—is one way that a young child has to initiate social contact and then to keep the interaction going once it has started (Hay, 1979). So, children might share at times to meet somebody's physical needs but they are also likely to offer things to others as a way of meeting their own need for contact with others.

Examples: Justin, almost 4 years old, counted out half of his orange slices and shared them with another child who was not supposed to be in school that day but who had arrived at snacktime and for whom food had not been prepared (sharing to meet physical needs).

Justin (on the right) said, "Come on over and play with the water, Charlie." This form of sharing is a way for young children to meet their need for social contact.

The next day, Justin asked his friend to join him in play at the water table: "I have a water wheel, Charlie. Come on over and play with the water wheel in the water" (offering something to initiate an interaction).

Helping

Helping is another major category of prosocial behavior that you will see quite often in preschool children (Grusec, 1991). Their helping behavior can indeed be prosocial because it benefits somebody. There are different forms of helping, some of them simple everyday acts of kindness. Another form of helping which prevents someone from getting hurt is called an act of *rescue* (Marcus & Leiserson, 1978). Some people help by defending others, and others help by removing the cause of someone's distress.

Examples: Steve's dad (chapter opener case study) helped his neighbor fix his garden gate (simple act of kindness).

Later that afternoon Steve stopped the garden gate just as it was about to close on his sleeping cat's tail. Whew! (rescue).

Steve's father had helped him once by taking a splinter out of Steve's foot (helping by removing the cause of Steve's distress).

Helping and sharing occur more frequently in dealings with other children than do other prosocial behaviors (Eisenberg et al., 1981). Many researchers believe that children's willingness to help or share is heavily influenced by whether their teacher and parents value prosocial behavior (Eisenberg et al., 1992) and by whether these adults model prosocial behavior (Moore & Eisenberg, 1984) (e.g., helping a child pick up toys or sharing a snack with a child).

Cooperation

You can expect some of the children you teach to play cooperatively as research demonstrated more than 60 years ago (Parten, 1932). In cooperative play, children follow one another around and make mutual suggestions about what to do next. This interest in others and in playing and working cooperatively with them is seen as a form of prosocial behavior when the cooperation is used to benefit someone or a group. Cooperation is a form of prosocial behavior in which people work together to get a job done and when their motive is altruistic.

Examples: Terri and Robin cooperated by carrying a heavy bucket of water to the outdoor painting area.

Mr. Pellini's kindergarten cooperated when they worked together to plant a small garden.

Tim's father (volunteer firefighter) cooperated with the other firefighters to demonstrate the station's equipment to Tim's class.

Helping is one form of prosocial behavior that you will see quite often in the preschool years.

What Motivates People to Act Prosocially?

What you see when someone acts prosocially is a *behavior.* What you do not always know is their motivation for behaving that way. People share, help, or cooperate for a variety of reasons, some of them altruistic (self*less*) and some of them for self-interest. These reasons include:

- Genuine feelings of empathic concern
- The ability to imagine the inner experience of someone in need
- A sense of responsibility for relieving the other's distress
- A need for social approval
- External pressure
- Relieving one's own sadness, anger, or guilt
- A desire for social interaction

Think about such a person as Mother Teresa, who spent her entire adult life among the poorest people in Calcutta, India, ministering to their needs. Her life was an endless string of selflessness and prosocial behavior. She seemed to have been motivated by an unusually high level of ability to take their perspective combined with the ability to imagine the inner experience of a leper or a starving person. She was empathic and she seemed to have a sense of responsibility for relieving their distress. Most people would probably agree that someone like Mother Teresa was a good example of selfless altruism. Batson & Shaw (1991) believe that real prosocial behavior exists only when a person has altruistic motives.

Now think about another person, one who volunteers many hours in a nursing home. Is this prosocial behavior? On the surface, yes, because he is helping people. When questioned about why he does this work, he said, "It'll look great on my resume." This person's helping benefits others but he is motivated by his own needs and not so much by the needs of those he helps. His motives are not altruistic and therefore his actions are not real prosocial behavior (Batson & Shaw, 1991).

The same thing seems to hold for Jessie, who has been ordered by a judge to do 70 hours of community service as a part of his sentence. Jessie grumbles about having to do the work at the soup kitchen and only does the work that looks like prosocial behavior because he has been ordered to do it. His actions are not altruistic and therefore not true prosocial behavior.

Focus on Development to Understand Prosocial Behavior

Childhood is such a brief span of time. What happens during this short time that can turn an infant who knows nothing about helping, sharing, or other prosocial behaviors into a child who is capable of selfless altruism and prosocial behavior? The answer is *development.* As you know from studying child development, there are different areas of development; advances in these areas enable children to help, share, or cooperate with others (Zahn-Waxler, Radke-Yarrow, Wagner, & Chapman, 1992). A young child cannot act prosocially unless this development occurs.

Our concern as early childhood and parent educators is to understand when children acquire cognitive and emotional competencies and skill development, and

Figure 9–2. The area of overlap of all three competencies will yield prosocial behavior (shown in shaded area).

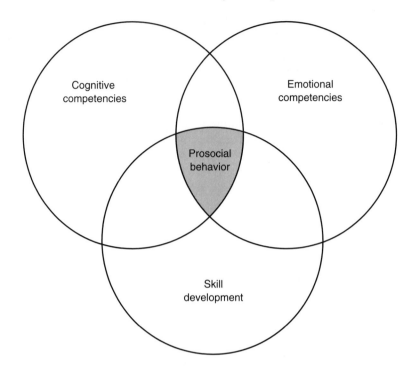

then to understand how these elements come together to enable a child to share, help, or cooperate. Having one or two of these competencies is not enough; a child needs all three. It is only when all three overlap that a child will be able to act in a prosocial way. Let's turn now to these cognitive, emotional, and skill developments (Figure 9–2).

Cognitive competencies

A child must have several cognitive competencies before he can act prosocially (Bohlmeyer, 1989). First, a child must realize that he is an individual and that he is separate from other individuals (Bengtsson & Johnson, 1992; Berthenthal & Fischer, 1978; Hoffman, 1987) if he is ever to think about another person's or animal's needs. A child must also be able to take another's perspective, that is, think about what that person would say that he needs (Rheingold & Emery, 1986; Selman, 1980) and be able to reflect on the victim's inner experience (Bengtsson & Johnson, 1992). A child must also be able to see himself as a person who can make things happen (Kuebli, 1994)—"I can help Ginny by sharing my blocks with her." He must have good enough language skills to describe how others might be feeling and to describe how he himself feels, for example, "My kitty was afraid of the loud noise and so I held her." (Bretherton, Fritz, Zahn-Waxler, & Ridgeway, 1986). A child's memory must be sophisticated enough to allow him to keep another person's need in mind long enough to act on that need.

Example: Steve and his mother (chapter opener case study) were shopping one day when Steve recalled something that he had seen at the food pantry: "There was a little boy at the food pantry the other day, Mom, and he didn't have any gloves. He can't play in the snow. Can we buy some gloves for him?"

All of these abilities have their roots in early childhood. We first see glimmers of these abilities in older infants and toddlers, and that allows the youngest of our children to begin to act in ways that appear to be helpful or cooperative. These cognitive competencies, however, are not fully developed in very young children. For instance, young children are not very good at reflecting on another person or an animal's inner experience of needing something. They tend to focus on readily observable, external characteristics of people. As they get older, children tend to focus more and more on another person's internal psychological perspective (Bengtsson & Johnson, 1992).

Example: Jimmy, age 11, and Celine, his 4-year-old sister, saw a neighbor child fall off his bike and break his arm. Celine said, "John was crying real loud, Mom!" Jimmy demonstrated an older child's ability to reflect on another's inner psychological perspective when he said, "Yeah, he cried. I think that he must have felt really scared when the ambulance came."

Typically, developing toddlers and young preschoolers continue to develop these skills throughout the preschool and elementary school years and that is what enables them to act in ways that are closer to true prosocial behavior as they get older (Bengtsson & Johnson, 1992; Miller, 1996; Perlmutter, 1986; Selman, 1980). An example is older children who are much better at taking another's perspective (Dixon & Moore, 1990; Selman, 1976) than are younger children. This cognitive ability makes them more capable of figuring out what another person or animal needs.

Emotional competencies

It is not enough for a child to have developed all of the cognitive competencies just described in order for him to act in a truly prosocial way. Children also need to have specific emotional competencies, and such emotional competencies develop quite slowly (Kuebli, 1994). To act prosocially, children must have the emotional capacity to respond to another's needs or distress. They must have developed *empathy*.

A child who shows empathy is responding to another person's emotional state. The heart and soul of empathy is that a child's emotional state is similar to the other person's situation. But, like most other aspects of development, empathy develops slowly and is affected by a child's level of cognitive development. Cognitive processes influence whether empathy will be stimulated in the first place. Cognitive processes also influence the quality of a child's empathic response as well as how intense the response is (Bengtsson & Johnson, 1992; Hoffman, 1987).

The road to high-level empathy starts in infancy. In fact, some researchers think that human children are biologically prepared for empathy (Hoffman, 1975). A very young baby responds to the emotions of others (Sagi & Hoffman, 1976) and seems to be able to discriminate between his mother's different emotions and, in some cases, can imitate these emotions (Termine & Izard, 1988). Very young infants

Donald has already developed many of the cognitive and emotional competence he needed before he could act prosocially—helping his friend build a tower.

also respond to the affective states of the caregiver; for example, they can respond to the unpleasant feelings that go along with their mother's depression (Cohn, Campbell, Matias, & Hopkins, 1990). Along with essential cognitive competencies, then, the emotional competencies enabling a child to know how another might be feeling begin to develop very early in life.

This budding ability to pick up on another person's emotional state is not real empathy, though. Hoffman (1987) said that we should look at how a child's emotional response to someone's situation is affected by his ability to take that person's perspective. Very young children seem to be able to pick up on another person's need, a beginning level of empathy. They can have this feeling without a cognitive sense of the other as an individual separate from themselves and without the ability to take the person's perspective. Later, when they do recognize the other as separate and distinct from themselves and when they develop better perspective-taking skills, they can also demonstrate real empathy.

In a study of prosocial behavior in 10- and 11-year-olds, Bengtsson and Johnson (1992) found that some children had a high level of empathy for a victim and were able to take both the victim's and the victimizer's point of view, as shown in the next example.

Example: The children in the study were given an example of a little girl turned away by force when entering a room where her older sister and a friend were playing. Some children showed ***extended empathic reasoning*** by showing empathy for the little girl as well as understanding of the victimizer "I didn't like the way they pushed the little girl out of the room, but I can also understand that they wanted to be left alone while playing."

Children who reasoned like this about another person's situation showed the highest levels of prosocial behavior. These were 10- and 11-year-olds, not young children. We know that children in the early childhood stage are not capable of reasoning like this. It takes several years for children to develop high-level empathy and the ability to think about the perspective of both a victim and a victimizer. Some children never develop this high level of empathy. Getting older is an important element in developing empathy but, by itself, getting older is not enough.

Skill development

Suppose that a child has high-level perspective-taking skills and is empathic. This child will be much more likely to actually share, help, or cooperate with someone if he also knows how to help, that is, if he has the skills for prosocial behavior. If Sam, for instance, wants to share something with his friend, Sam must have the social skill of approaching another child and must also know what to say as he offers something. Zahn-Waxler et al. (1992) believe that young children have a better chance of developing such skills if they have had a firm attachment to their primary attachment figures and have experienced sharing, turn-taking, and cooperation with their parents. As early childhood teachers, we can also influence children's willingness to share, help, and cooperate by teaching the skills that they need for acting prosocially.

Example: Sydney was having trouble putting on her parka. Janet could put on her parka easily and watched Sydney struggling. "Janet," Mr. Pellini said quietly, "you could really help Sydney by showing her how you lay your jacket on the floor and then flip it over your head."

IMPLICATIONS: GUIDE CHILDREN'S PROSOCIAL BEHAVIOR BY USING DEVELOPMENTALLY APPROPRIATE STRATEGIES

Kontos and Wilcox-Herzog (1997) described the positive effect of good adult–child relationships on a child's development. Prosocial behavior develops largely because of the relationships children experience. We early childhood educators can make it possible for kindness, compassion, and generosity to flower by understanding the developmental level of the children we teach, by helping our children understand how others feel, and by showing them how to share, help, or cooperate. Consider using the following practical and developmentally appropriate strategies to help children learn to act prosocially.

Model Prosocial Behavior

In terms of generous, helpful behavior, the research shows that what a child sees is what the child does. Modeling prosocial behavior is a powerful way to encourage it in children (Marcus & Leiserson, 1978; Oliner & Oliner, 1988). But children do not imitate all models.

Several factors determine whether a child will imitate any model. Children are more likely to imitate a *powerful* model—a person who controls resources—and children usually perceive parents and teachers as powerful because caregivers do control resources (Mussen & Eisenberg-Berg, 1977). They are also more likely to imitate an authoritative model, one who is highly responsive to their needs but who also makes expectations known.

Children are more likely to imitate a *consistent* model, that is, a model who "practices what he preaches." For example, children whose families talk about generosity or volunteering and then actually give or volunteer are very likely to share or donate (Bryan & Walbek, 1970).

Children are more likely to imitate models who *give without grumbling,* who are quietly and effectively generous, cooperative, and helpful, and who are genuinely pleased to be able to help someone else and not seem to expect anything in return (Midlarsky & Bryan, 1972). Children are more likely to act prosocially if they vicariously experience the same good feeling as the model.

Honig and Wittmer (1991) advise you to provide models of prosocial behavior by arranging regular viewing of prosocial media and video games, because programs whose messages emphasize cooperation, helping, and sharing promote these behaviors in children (Stout & Mouritsen, 1988). A major study analyzing 190 other studies found that prosocial programming does have powerful effects on children's prosocial behavior (Hearold, 1986).

Encourage Children to Develop Helpful Emotional Scripts

A growing body of research on emotions reveals that young children are able to identify another person's distressed state and the situation that produced the distress (Fabes, Eisenberg, McCormick, & Wilson, 1988; Michalson & Lewis, 1985). Children seem to organize their understanding of the emotional state of others in the form of *emotional scripts* that they learn by the age of 6 years (Russell, 1989). These scripts include information about the appropriate emotion for the child and the emotion or affective state of another person or animal in specific situations (Lewis, 1989). Children learn emotional scripts as they interact with parents, siblings, teachers, and others; as they watch television; and as they have books read to them.

Example: Derek is an overweight 5-year-old. At snacktime Adam snickered when Derek took one of the snacks: "Hey, Derek. You're so fat! You don't even need to eat." Mr. Pellini, the teacher, took Adam aside and said, "Adam, it hurts somebody's feelings when you make fun of them. I think that Derek probably feels bad because you called him fat. In this classroom I will not allow you to make fun of others."

Adam's teacher is helping him develop an emotional script by helping him understand how Derek probably felt in this particular situation. Reading stories about sharing was found to be another excellent way to help children learn emotional scripts. This strategy increased children's willingness to share and their ability to take another person's perspective (Trepanier & Romatowski, 1981). The experimental group had nine children's books focusing on sharing read to them at a rate of three per week. They discussed sharing, its relationship to the feelings of the characters, and the causes of the feelings.

State Expectations for Prosocial Behavior and Accept Children's Help When Offered

Children learn to be prosocial in families and in classrooms when adults ask them to cooperate, help, share, or give comfort or by actually accepting a child's offer of help or cooperation (Child Development Project, 1988, 1991; Schenk & Grusec, 1987; Swanson, 1988).

Examples: Mr. Pellini said to two children, "Louie and Portia, I'm going to need some help taking the trikes and wagons out of the shed. I want both of you to come with me and help."

The next day Louie approached Mr. Pellini when he was in the shed getting trikes out: "Can I help you again today, Mr. Pellini?" The teacher replied, "That would be wonderful, Louie. Sure!"

Adults, as socializing agents, have the responsibility to help children learn *norms of social responsibility.* One of these norms deals with prosocial behavior. The norm tells children that they are expected to help or cooperate with others (Bryan, 1975), and Mr. Pellini has actually told the children that they are expected to help someone else. It is difficult, if not impossible, for children to learn this norm of socially responsible behavior unless we teach it to them.

Communicate your expectations that children are an important part of a family or classroom system by assigning age-appropriate responsibilities to them. Authori*tative* adults, high in demandingness and responsiveness, assign household chores and tasks. This might have accounted for Baumrind's (1971) finding that children in these families were the most cooperative when observed at school. Rheingold (1982) discovered, however, that some parents were often reluctant to accept their child's offer of help even though the child offered to help fairly often. The parents seemed to prefer to do the task at hand by themselves rather than guide the child through the process.

Responsibilities should be assigned to children based on their developmental ability. A 3- to 4-year-old child can certainly mist plants, feed or water pets, clean out her own locker at school, place toys back in the spot where they belong, help set and clean tables for meals, hang up her own clothes, and take good care of books, games, and other materials. Older children should be expected to regularly help with yardwork and housework. They can carry out trash, rake leaves, shovel snow, make centerpieces for a dinner table (it is pleasant to be assigned a creative task occasionally), help plan menus, cook simple meals under supervision, wash dishes, write things on the shopping list, and wash the car. Children who grow up on farms and ranches are regularly assigned chores that are real contributions to the functioning of the unit.

Use Positive Discipline Strategies

Adults who use positive discipline strategies have an authori*tative* style of caregiving. Two traits that characterize this style are high demandingness and high responsiveness. For several reasons, this style of caregiving tends to foster prosocial behavior (Swanson, 1988).

1. *Adults who use positive discipline clearly communicate their expectations about helping, sharing, and cooperating.* Because these parents or teachers make their expectations of the child's cooperation clear, they are more likely to get that cooperation than are adults who threaten punishment if the child does not help.

2. *Adults who use positive discipline encourage children to take someone else's perspective,* and children are more likely to be cooperative, helpful, or compassionate if they understand another's perspective.

   Examples: The teacher watched 3-year-old Cheryl take the Raggedy Andy doll from another child. "No, Cheryl. Mary wants to play with the doll, too, and she had it first."

   Mr. Pellini heard the commotion near the gerbil's house and said, "Whoa! You're making so much noise that the gerbils look really afraid. Play more quietly when you're around the gerbils."

   A word of caution. Emotionally vulnerable, depressed caregivers in one study overemphasized their child's responsibility for others' problems, leading children to believe that they had created problems for which they were not responsible at all (Zahn-Waxler, Kochanska, Krupnick, & McKnew, 1990). So, while children need to learn that they are responsible for their own behavior, they should not be held responsible for things beyond their control.

3. *Adults who use positive discipline give suggestions on how to help, cooperate, or share.* Stating expectations is an excellent strategy, but adults can be even more helpful if they also give specific suggestions on how to help or cooperate with someone. This means that adults have to do some skill development by telling or showing children specifically how they can help or cooperate with someone.

   Example: Mr. Pellini said to Vinnie, "Here, Vinnie. I'm going to hold this tricycle steady, and your job is to squirt just a little oil right here, on the spots where the wheels join the trike's body. We'll fix that squeak together."

4. *Adults who use positive discipline tell children what to do.* They try to avoid telling children what not to do. Some adults all too frequently tell children what not to do, such as "Don't throw the towel on the floor," "Don't hold your fork like that," "Don't wiggle around," and "Don't pick your nose!" Authoritative adults prefer to tell children what to do, such as "Hang the towel on the rack," "Hold your fork like this, Jane," "Stand still so that I can brush your hair," and "Tonya, use this tissue to clean your nose." We will be much more successful in helping children share, help, and cooperate if we tell them what to do rather than harping on what not to do (Cain, 1987; Olejnik & McKinney, 1973).

Verbally Label and Discuss Prosocial Behavior

All of the following examples come from Mr. Pellini's kindergarten.

   Examples: He said to the children who made applesauce, "We all worked together to make the applesauce, and it's going to be a good snack for the rest of the group."

The aide said to two children after cleanup, "You did a fine job of cooperating. You put all the blocks on the shelf and cleared the space for group time."

Mr. Pellini showed a short segment of *Mr. Rogers' Neighborhood* and then led a discussion: "It was kind of Mr. Rogers' visitor to help him build the shelves. How could we tell that his friend wanted to help? How could you tell that his friend was happy about helping? What did Mr. Rogers say that made you think he was grateful for the help?"

In each example, the teachers made an effort to *verbally label* prosocial behavior, and Mr. Pellini planned a discussion of the television episode on helping as a part of the lesson plan. There are a number of ways to teach children about cooperation and helpfulness, and talking about prosocial behavior is an excellent but often neglected technique (Honig & Wittmer, 1991).

We acknowledge the need to help children learn to label lots of things, such as, "You picked up the red square" or "This animal is called a timber wolf." We consider this a part of direct instruction, one of our basic responsibilities as teachers and one of the processes through which we influence children. We should not hesitate to also label acts of kindness and compassion as a way to teach children about these traits.

You will more effectively foster sharing, helping, and cooperating if you use certain types of verbal labels. Statements that would be considered mere preaching, such as "It is good to give," are not very effective in encouraging prosocial behavior. Instead, use statements focusing on how a child's sharing, helping, or cooperation affects others (Grusec, 1991). Our examples showed adults noting how acts of kindness or cooperation affected others ("It's going to be a good snack for the rest of the group," "You . . . cleared the space for group time").

Practice Prosocial Behavior

Suppose that Luke learns how to help and cooperate by observing models and by hearing the behaviors labeled. Does that mean that he will automatically perform the prosocial behavior? No, but chances that he will actually perform cooperative, helpful acts that he has seen modeled increase when his parents and teachers set up opportunities for him to *practice the desired behavior* (Child Development Project, 1988, 1991; Orlick, 1981; Rogow, 1991; Solomon, 1988). Orlick's (1981) work with preschool children demonstrated that children taught to play cooperative games were later more cooperative in other settings. In addition, the cooperative game training resulted in increased sharing. (You will get a chance to write a lesson plan for using such games with young children in the Apply Your Knowledge section at the end of this chapter.) Rogow's (1991) work suggested a variety of ways for teachers to facilitate the practice of prosocial behavior of children with a variety of disabilities

Give children the chance to practice by planning activities focusing on prosocial behavior. Teachers and parents can do a variety of things to ensure that children have an opportunity to practice prosocial behavior. Plan specific activities focusing on concepts of *sharing, helping, and cooperating*. Plan these activities just as you would math, science, language arts, and social studies activities. Write a lesson plan, for example, with the objective being that children practice cooperation.

Recognize and Encourage Prosocial Behavior

Once you have modeled and labeled prosocial behavior, it is important that you recognize a child's efforts to share or help and then encourage his efforts (Honig & Pollack, 1988; Schenk & Grusec, 1987).

Examples: "You put your painting in your cubby, Jim, just as you agreed to do. That's great!" said Mr. Pellini.

"You two did a fine job of putting the sand toys away. You followed my suggestions about where to place each toy," noted the aide as she held the hands of both children and smiled.

"Each of you had a second helping because Rudy took my suggestion and broke his second cookie so that he could share it with Christina and George!" The teacher clapped his hands softly, "Good thinking, Rudy." (Rudy, by the way, basked in the warm glow of success.)

In each case a supportive, authori*tative* adult used either social reinforcement (smiles, verbal praise), more tangible rewards (favorite stickers), or a combination of the two. Effective *praise* is a form of social reinforcement. The praise in each example was specific and descriptive; that is, it was informative to the child. It was appreciative but did not evaluate a child's character. The praise was given almost immediately after the act of prosocial behavior and was sincere. It was used to recognize successful completion of an agreed-upon task (putting a painting in a cubby, breaking a cookie). It was not used to manipulate. The praise was also accompanied by appropriate physical contact or nonverbal communication.

How frequently should adults use reinforcement?

How often do adults actually reinforce prosocial behavior? One study found that 4- and 5-year-olds in a preschool received positive feedback for spontaneous prosocial behavior only about 30 percent of the time (Eisenberg et al., 1981). In contrast, Grusec (1982) found that 4-year-olds with nonworking mothers were reinforced for prosocial behavior about 80 percent of the time. Grusec (1991) found that young children were as likely to receive praise and social approval as they were to receive no response at all.

Consider reinforcing a group of children for prosocial behavior whenever possible because, as Bryan (1975) showed, group-administered rewards are consistently more effective in fostering cooperation and friendliness and in decreasing competitive behavior than are rewards given to individuals. There are several ways in which adults can recognize the efforts of a group of children for prosocial behavior.

Examples: Mr. Pellini read the class's favorite story to the whole group after all the children cooperated on the "litter patrol" on the playground. "You all worked together so well, and the playground looks terrific!"

All the children in Mr. Pellini's school held a carnival and then donated the money they made to the Humane Society to sponsor a cage for an entire year. The principal gathered the entire group together in the cafeteria and read a letter of thanks from the director of the Humane Society. It said, "Your generous donation will pay for food and care for cats in this cage for one year. Thank you for helping the animals."

A student teacher sang a short song with the children at group time about how each child had acted prosocially during the morning's activities (to the tune of "Mary Had a Little Lamb"):

Lynn and Bob cleaned the gerbil house,
the gerbil house, the gerbil house.
Lynn and Bob cleaned the gerbil house
when they came to school.

Anne Marie put away her trike,
put away her trike, put away her trike.
Anne Marie put away her trike
when she came to school.

Then the student teacher said, "I saw Antonio and Anna sharing the flannelboard pieces. And I saw Olivia help Steven separate his orange sections at snacktime. Let's sing about that."

This student teacher did not just pull this activity "out of the air" or "do it off the top of her head." She planned it. She had written a lesson plan for it, and to carry it off well she had to carefully observe how each child showed prosocial behavior during the self-selected activity period.

Reinforce cooperation, not competition

Make sure that you are actually recognizing and encouraging cooperation, not competition. Some teachers form groups, for example, and pit one group against the others (e.g., at cleanup, for reading the largest number of picture books, for bringing in the most for a food drive). Although group members do have to work together, their goal in these examples is to beat another group, and they may easily lose sight of their real goal—to gather food for a food drive, to read, or to work together to clean up.

WHAT ARE THE BENEFITS OF ENCOURAGING PROSOCIAL BEHAVIOR?

Chances are that you, like most adults, would probably agree that it is a good thing to encourage young children to help and cooperate with others. If you value prosocial behavior and then take the time and effort to teach and encourage prosocial behavior then you will likely see the following outcomes (Marcus & Leiserson, 1978).

- Increased competence. A child who helps somebody tends to view himself as more competent, believing that "I am capable of helping" after having cooperated with, helped, complimented, or shared something with another person. Children have a strong need to feel competent (White, 1959) and finding out that he can indeed help someone will motivate a child to act that way again in the future.

- Mutual helping (Marcus, 1977). Children who act prosocially also tend to receive help from other children and adults, whereas children who do not willingly help others receive little assistance in return.
- Shared work. A family or classroom is a system, and there is work to do if any system is to operate smoothly. As members of families and classrooms, children have an obligation to share in the work of the system, whether the work involves farm or ranch chores, shoveling snow, setting tables, washing paint cups, putting away trikes, or getting out math workbooks.
- Pleasant, friendly, relaxing atmosphere. When children are appropriately encouraged to share, help, and cooperate, the general atmosphere of their home, classroom, or other setting is simply more more inviting (Edwards, 1992).

Parent Talk. Raising a Prosocial Child: Tips for Parents

At some point in your teaching career a parent will complain that his child refuses to share things and will ask you what to do about it. You'll think immediately about the same child who just the day before willingly moved over to make room for someone during grouptime (shared space). And you'll remember having observed him in the sandpit sharing one bucket with another child. Here are some tips that you can give parents for encouraging such thoughtful and kind behavior in their child. Encourage parents to:

Observe children sharing and helping. Parents sometimes miss the very behavior that they want to see. So, encourage parents to watch their child closely, in school if necessary, for times when their child does share and help. Consider sitting with the parent during the observation.

Provide cooperative games and play materials (Grineski, 1989; Kaiser, 1995). Tell parents that these games, and not competitive games, encourage sharing, cooperation, and helping. Make children's books emphasizing prosocial behavior available to parents, and emphasize the value of such stories in developing sharing, helping, and cooperation.

Arrange regular viewing of prosocial movies and videos. Label examples of sharing, helping, and cooperating (Honig & Wittmer, 1991). Help parents understand the power

of modeling in teaching prosocial behavior; remind them that films provide vivid and effective models of all kinds of behavior. Plan a parent meeting or write a brief handout on how to choose appropriate videos, show clips of good videos, and give them a list of suggested movies and videos showing prosocial behavior. Encourage parents to look for advertising that emphasizes prosocial behavior (Stout & Mouritsen, 1988) and teach parents to make appropriate comments about the helping, sharing, and cooperation in such ads.

Have the child participate in prosocial behaviors. The idea here is not to force altruism but for the child just to observe and participate with a parent who shares, helps, or cooperates but does not preach. For example, at Christmastime pick a needy child's name from the tree at a local department store (you'll find such trees in a variety of stores). The parent buys the desired gift with his own money but takes the child along to the store to help pick out the gift. Tell parents not to force a child to spend his own money. That idea can bubble up later and will then be true generosity. Tell parents to make the whole process low-key and tell them not to preach.

Give children appropriate and manageable household responsibilities. Help parents understand how meaningful such work is in fostering sharing, helping, and cooperation. Being

(continues on the next page)

immersed in a family in which everybody does their fair share of the work is an extremely effective strategy.

Recognize and then encourage the results of all this teaching. Parents will see an increase in their child's prosocial behavior if they use some of these strategies. Bolster their confidence as they learn to encourage prosocial behavior in their children. For example, give them three specific ways of showing or telling their child that they recognize the child's efforts: "You were very helpful when we made cookies today, Amanda" or "It was kind of you to share your sand toys with Jess!" or "I noticed that you and the other two children worked together to build that sand castle. That's what I call cooperation."

CASE STUDY ANALYSIS: PROSOCIAL BEHAVIOR

Each of the three children in the chapter opener case studies, Miranda, Steve, and John, have families that encourage prosocial behavior. Find evidence of and explain how they do this by analyzing each case study.

Miranda: Miranda's family is helping her understand how important it is to share, help, and cooperate. Find evidence of this by pointing out the times when Miranda was given some responsibility for specific chores, such as household tasks. Explain how her mother helped her understand how someone else might be feeling.

Steve: Steve's parents were good models of prosocial behavior. Explain how they were consistent, were genuinely pleased about helping, and were nurturant and supportive models.

John: John's father has a positive authoritative caregiving style that is likely to encourage John to act prosocially. Find evidence of this style by explaining how clearly Dad communicated his expectations that John would share in the work, how he helped his son understand his point of view about the work, and how Dad gave specific suggestions on how John could help.

REFLECTING ON KEY CONCEPTS

1. How are the prosocial behaviors of sharing, helping, and cooperation alike? Which of these behaviors are you most likely to see in an early childhood classroom? When is behavior that appears to be sharing not true prosocial behavior in young children?

2. Give an example, different from the one in the text, of a person who demonstrates true prosocial behavior and justify your example by saying what this person's motivation was. Do the same thing with a person who appears to act in a helpful way but whose motivation is more self-centered.

3. Explain to someone who has not studied this chapter how important it is for a child to develop in certain ways before it is even possible for him to act prosocially. Describe these areas of development and give some specific examples. Explain, using Figure 9–2, why all of these areas have to overlap before a child can act prosocially.

4. Choose at least three of the strategies for fostering prosocial behavior and explain why they would help a child share, help, or cooperate.

5. As the director of a large child development center, it is your job to explain to aides why the school encourages prosocial behavior. What would you tell them?

APPLY YOUR KNOWLEDGE

1. Label or Discuss Prosocial Behavior. All of these situations occurred in Mr. Pellini's class. For each situation help him generate at least one statement or question that focuses the children's attention on the prosocial nature of the activity. Emphasize the sharing, helping, or cooperating and how it affects someone else.

   Situation: During grouptime Mr. Pellini showed a newspaper photo of rescue workers cleaning oil from a duck caught in an oil spill.

   I would say this to emphasize prosocial behavior:

   Situation: Mr. Pellini divided his group into pairs and each pair of children planted a green bean plant in a small vegetable garden outside their school.

   I would say this to emphasize prosocial behavior:

   Situation: Shannon, working with white play dough, decided to make it pink by mixing in some red dough but found that Eli was using all the red dough. She asked Eli for some, and Eli said, "OK" and broke off a chunk for her. Then, Eli got interested in the color mixing and suggested that they mix all of their dough together. Together, they pummeled and pushed the dough. Eli gleefully said, "Hey, Mr. Pellini, look at our BIG ball of pink!"

   I would say this to emphasize prosocial behavior:

2. Practice Prosocial Behavior. Write a lesson plan centered on one of these activities designed to help children practice sharing, helping, or cooperating. If you are working at a practicum site, seek permission to carry out the plan. Get your plan approved by the teacher before you do the activity.

   Activity: Game: Tug of Peace (Kreidler, 1984)

   Children are in a circle. Lay a rope in a circle inside the children's circle. The objective is for all children to raise themselves to a standing position by pulling on the rope. Briefly discuss how they worked together.

   Activity: Using Puppets

   Do this short puppet story about helping or cooperation. One puppet, Sam, has trouble placing paper on an easel.

   - Amanda: "What's the matter, Sam?"
   - Sam: "I can't reach the clip for the paper."
   - Amanda: "Maybe I can reach it." (She clips the paper onto the easel.) "There, it's done."
   - Sam: "Thanks for helping."

Place the puppets in a learning center after this demonstration. Encourage children to practice what they observed. Encourage them to take both roles—helper and the one helped—so that each has a chance to practice helping.

Activity: Circle Game: Sharing (adapted from Smith, 1982)

This is a good game to play when children are learning each other's names, but you can also use it whenever you'd like to emphasize kindness and generosity. Children sit in a circle. You, the adult, hold a bowl of nutritious cookies. Take one cookie out of the bowl and say, "I want to share this cookie with Josie," and then give the cookie to Josie (the child to her left). Then it's Josie's turn to share with the person sitting to her left by sharing the bowl of cookies with that person.

Activity: Game: Cooperative Musical Chairs (Kreidler, 1984)

Place chairs in a circle. Children slowly circle the chairs to music. When the music stops, children scramble for a seat. Then one chair is taken away. The objective is for every child to get a seat every time the music stops. Tell the children that they may share a seat with no more than one other child. Contrast this version with the version in which the objective is to shut others out of a turn. (Safety rules: Don't take more than half the chairs away. Permit only two children to share one chair.)

Activity: Making Pudding (small-group activity)

Children work in pairs. Give one child in the pair a spoon, an empty paper cup and a plastic container with a lid containing enough dry instant pudding mix for two children. Give the other child a measuring cup with just enough milk to mix pudding for two children, a spoon, and an empty paper cup. Emphasize working together and cooperating by noting the need to share resources if they want to make and eat pudding.

RESOURCES FOR SPECIFIC ACTIVITIES

Honig, A., & Wittmer, D. (1991). *Helping children become more prosocial: Tips for teachers.* Available from ERIC Document Reproduction Service. Contains numerous examples of cooperative games and activities.

Kreidler, W. (1984). *Creative conflict resolution.* Evanston, IL: Scott, Foresman. Also contains lots of good examples of cooperative games and activities.

Ragow, S. (1991). The dynamics of play: Including children with special needs in mainstreamed early childhood programs. *International Journal of Early Childhood, 23*(2), 50–57. Suggests several ways for teachers to encourage participation of children with a variety of special needs in prosocial play activities.

Schmitz, D. The design and implementation of 40 manipulative tasks to develop cooperation in a kindergarten class at Palmer School. ERIC Document Reproduction Service.

Smith, C. A. (1982). *Promoting the social development of young children: Strategies and activities.* Palo Alto, CA: Mayfield Publishing Co. Provides a sound theoretical framework for more than 100 strategies and activities. An excellent addition to your professional library.

Spivack, G., & Shure, M. (1989). Interpersonal cognitive problem solving (ICPS): A competence-building primary prevention program. *Prevention in Human Services, 6*(2), 161–178. Description of a competence-building program for preschool, kindergarten, and first-grade children. Concise outline of the ICPS program based on the kindergarten/first-grade script. Describes problem-solving skills training using a lesson from a program script.

References

Batson, C. D., & Shaw, L. L. (1991). Evidence for altruism: Toward a pluralism of prosocial motives. *Psychological Inquiry, 2*(2), 107–122.

Baumrind, D. (1971). Current patterns of parental authority. *Developmental Psychology Monograph, 4*(1, Pt. 2).

Beauvais, C. (1982, April). *Sharing in preschool: A naturalistic observation.* Paper presented at the Annual Meeting of the Western Psychological Association, Sacramento, CA.

Bengtsson, H., & Johnson, L. (1992). Perspective taking, empathy, and prosocial behavior in late childhood. *Child Study Journal, 22*(1), 11–22.

Berthenthal, B. I., & Fischer, K. W. (1978). The development of self-recognition in the infant. *Developmental Psychology, 14,* 44–50.

Bohlmeyer, E. (1989, April). *Age differences in sharing as a function of children's ability to estimate time and motivational instructions.* Paper presented at the Biennial Meeting of the Society for Research in Child Development, Kansas City, MO.

Bretherton, I., Fritz, J., Zahn-Waxler, C., & Ridgeway, D. (1986). The acquisition and development of emotion language: A functionalist perspective. *Child Development, 57,* 529–548.

Bryan, J. H. (1975). Children's cooperation and helping behaviors. In E. M. Hetherington (Ed.), *Review of child development research* (Vol. 5). Chicago: University of Chicago Press.

Bryan, J. H., & Walbek, N. H. (1970). Preaching and practicing generosity: Children's actions and reactions. *Child Development, 41,* 329–353.

Cain, S. H. (1987). The relationship of role-taking, temperament, and parent behaviors to prosocial behaviors in children. Unpublished master's thesis, Wake Forest University, Winston-Salem, NC.

Child Development Project. *Description of Program.* (1988). Palo Alto, CA: Hewlett Foundation.

Child Development Project. *Summary of Findings to Date.* (1991). Palo Alto, CA: Hewlett Foundation.

Cohn, J. F., Campbell, S. B., Matias, R., & Hopkins, J. (1990). Face-to-face interactions of postpartum depressed and nondepressed mother–infant pairs at 2 months. *Developmental Psychology, 26,* 15–23.

Dixon, J.A., & Moore, C.F. (1990). The development of perspective-taking: Understanding differences in information and weighting. *Child Development, 61,* 1502–1513.

Edwards, C. (1992). Creating safe places for conflict resolution to happen: Beginnings. *Child Care Information Exchange, 84,* 43–45.

Eisenberg, N., Cameron, E., Tryon, K., & Dodez, R. (1981). Socialization of prosocial behavior in the preschool classroom. *Developmental Psychology, 17,* 773–782.

Eisenberg, N., Wolchik, S., Goldberg, L., & Engel, I. (1992). Parental values, reinforcement, and young children's prosocial behavior: A longitudinal study. *Journal of Genetic Psychology, 153*(1), 19–37.

Fabes, R. A., Eisenberg, N., McCormick, S. E., & Wilson, M. S. (1988). Preschooler's attributions of the situational determinants of others' naturally occurring emotions. *Developmental Psychology, 24,* 376–385.

Grineski, S. (1989). Children, games, and prosocial behavior—insight and connections. *Journal of Physical Education, Recreation, and Dance, 60*(8), 20–25.

Grusec, J. (1982). The socialization of altruism. In N. Eisenberg (Ed.), *The development of prosocial behavior.* New York: Academic Press.

Grusec, J. (1991). Socializing concern for others in the home. *Developmental Psychology, 27*(2), 338–342.

Hay, D. F. (1979). Cooperative interactions and sharing between very young children and their parents. *Developmental Psychology, 15,* 647–653.

Hearold, S. (1986). A synthesis of 1043 effects of television on social behavior. In G. A. Comstock (Ed.), *Public communications and behavior* (Vol. 1). New York: Academic Press.

Hoffman, M. L. (1975). Developmental synthesis of affect and cognition and its interplay for altruistic motivation. *Developmental Psychology, 11,* 607–622.

Hoffman, M. L. (1987). The contribution of empathy to justice and moral judgment. In N. Eisenberg & J. Strayer (Eds.), *Empathy and its development* (pp. 47–80). Cambridge, England: Cambridge University Press.

Honig, A., & Pollack, B. (1988). Effects of a brief intervention program to promote prosocial behaviors in young children. ERIC No. ED316324, available from ERIC Document Reproduction Service.

Honig, A., & Wittmer, D. (1991). *Helping children become more prosocial: Tips for teachers.* ERIC No. ED343693, available from ERIC Document Reproduction Service.

Kaiser, J. (1995). Adult choice of toys affects children's prosocial and antisocial behavior. *Early Child Development and Care, 111,* 181–193.

Kontos, S., & Wilcox-Herzog, A. (1997). Research in review: Teacher's Interactions with children: Why are they so important? *Young Children, 52*(1), 4–12.

Kreidler, W. (1984). *Creative conflict resolution.* Evanston, IL: Scott, Foresman.

Kuebli, J. (1994). Research in review: Young children's understanding of everyday emotions. *Young Children, 49*(3), 36–47.

Lewis, M. (1989). Cultural differences in children's knowledge of emotional scripts. In C. Saarni & P. L. Harris (Eds.), *Children's understanding of emotion.* Cambridge, England: Cambridge University Press.

Marcus, R. F. (1977, March). *A naturalistic study of reciprocity in the helping behavior of young children.* Paper presented at the biennial meeting of the Society for Research in Child Development, New Orleans, LA.

Marcus, R. F., & Leiserson, M. (1978). Encouraging helping behavior. *Young Children, 33*(6), 24–34.

Michalson, L., & Lewis, M. (1985). What do children know about emotions and when do they know it? In M. Lewis & C. Saarni (Eds.), *The socialization of emotions.* New York: Plenum.

Midlarsky, E., & Bryan, J. H. (1972). Affect expressions and children's imitative altruism. *Journal of Experimental Research in Personality, 6,* 195–203.

Miller, P. (1996). Relations of moral reasoning and vicarious emotion to young children's prosocial behavior toward peers and adults. *Developmental Psychology, 32*(2), 210–219.

Moore, B.S., & Eisenberg, N. (1984). The development of altruism. In G. Whitehurst (Ed.), *Annals of child development* (pp. 107–174). Greenwich, CT: JAI Press.

Mussen, P. H., & Eisenberg-Berg, N. (1977). *Caring, sharing and helping.* San Francisco: W. H. Freeman.

Naparstek, N. (1990). Children's conceptions of prosocial behavior. *Child Study Journal, 20*(4), 207–220.

Olejnik, A. B., & McKinney, J. P. (1973). Parental value orientation and generosity in children. *Developmental Psychology, 8,* 311.

Oliner, S. P., & Oliner, P. M. (1988). *The altruistic personality: Rescuers of Jews in Nazi Europe.* New York: Free Press.

Orlick, T. D. (1981). Positive socialization via cooperative games. *Developmental Psychology, 17,* 426–429.

Parten, M. (1932). Social participation among preschool children. *Journal of Abnormal and Social Psychology, 27,* 243–269.

Perlmutter, M. (1986). A life-span view of memory. In P. B. Baltes, D. L. Featherman, & R. M. Lerner (Eds.), *Life-span development and behavior* (Vol. 7). Hillsdale, NJ: Erlbaum.

Radke-Yarrow, M., Zahn-Waxler, C., & Chapman, M. (1983). Children's prosocial dispositions and behavior. In P. Mussen (Ed.), *Handbook of child psychology* (Vol. 4). New York: Wiley.

Rheingold, H. L. (1982). Little children's participation in the work of adults, a nascent prosocial behavior. *Child Development, 53,* 114–125.

Rheingold, H. L., & Emery, G. N. (1986). The nurturant acts of very young children. In D. Olweus, J. Block, & M. Radke-Yarrow (Eds.), *The development of anti- and prosocial behavior.* San Diego, CA: Academic Press.

Rogow, S. (1991). The dynamics of play: Including children with special needs in mainstreamed early childhood programs. *International Journal of Early Childhood, 23*(2), 50–57.

Russell, J. A. (1989). Culture, scripts, and children's understanding of emotion. In C. Saarni & P. L. Harris (Eds.), *Children's understanding of emotion.* Cambridge, England: Cambridge University Press.

Sagi, A., & Hoffman, M. L. (1976). Empathic distress in the newborn. *Developmental Psychology, 12,* 175–176.

Schenk, V., & Grusec, J. (1987). A comparison of prosocial behavior of children with and without day care experience. *Merrill-Palmer Quarterly, 33*(2), 231–240.

Selman, R.L. (1976). Social-cognitive understanding. In T. Lickona (Ed.), *Moral development and behavior.* New York: Holt, Rinehart, & Winston.

Selman, R.L. (1980). *The growth of interpersonal understanding.* New York: Academic Press.

Shaffer, D. (1993). *Developmental psychology* (3rd ed.). Pacific Grove, CA: Brooks/Cole.

Smith, C. A. (1982). *Promoting the social development of young children: Strategies and activities.* Palo Alto, CA: Mayfield Publishing Co.

Solomon, D. (1988). Enhancing children's prosocial behavior in the classroom. *American Educational Research Journal, 25*(4), 527–554.

Stout, D. & Mouritsen, R. (1988). Prosocial behavior in advertising aimed at children: A content analysis. *Southern Speech Communication Journal, 53*(2), 159–174.

Swanson, K. A. (1988). *Childrearing practices and the development of prosocial behavior.* ERIC No. ED299552. Available from ERIC Document Reproduction Service.

Termine, N. T., & Izard, C. E. (1988). Infants' responses to their mothers' expressions of joy and sadness. *Developmental Psychology, 24,* 223–229.

Trepanier, M., & Romatowski, J. (1981, April). *Classroom use of selected children's books to facilitate prosocial development in young children.* Paper presented at the annual meeting of the American Educational Research Association, Los Angeles.

White, R. W. (1959). Motivation reconsidered: The concept of competence. *Psychological Review, 66,* 297–323.

Zahn-Waxler, C., Kochanska, G., Krupnick, J., & McKnew, D. (1990). Patterns of guilt in children of depressed and well mothers. *Developmental Psychology, 26,* 51–59.

Zahn-Waxler, C., Radke-Yarrow, M., Wagner, E., & Chapman, M. (1992). Development of concern for others. *Developmental Psychology, 28*(1), 126–136.

Part 3

Developing an "Eclectic" Approach to Child Guidance

Chapter 10: **Child-Guidance Theories and Their Strategies**

Chapter 11: **The Decision-Making Model of Child Guidance: An "Eclectic" Approach**

You have learned a lot of practical strategies in Parts One and Two of this book. The time will come when you will face a real discipline encounter and then you will have to decide how you will respond. For example, what will you do when a child in your class spits at other people? Put her in time-out? Ignore the spitting? Figure out what she seems to be getting with the spitting? Think about whose problem the spitting is? Deliver an I-message? Set limits on spitting?

As you can see, you have lots of choices, and the mark of a professional is the ability to make active, conscious decisions and to be able to articulate reasons for those choices. You do not have to be trapped into using the first "trick" that comes to mind. You can reject certain strategies, too, if they do not fit with your personal set of values and principles or with what you believe about child development.

There are two chapters in Part Three of this text. Both will help you with the child-guidance decisions that you will face when you work with children.

Chapter 10. Child-Guidance Theories and Their Strategies. This chapter describes three different theories of child guidance—Rogerian, Adlerian, and social learning. You can use each of these models as a guide for making decisions about how to handle different discipline encounters. You will notice that each offers specific child-guidance strategies that are consistent with the basic beliefs in the theory. For example, social learning theorists believe in using feedback and reinforcement, so the specific strategy *effective praise* comes out of this model.

You will read about the basic beliefs of each theory and then examine specific, concrete child-guidance strategies that come from the theory. You have already studied some of the strategies in Chapter 3 (also refer to the Appendix) and will now have a chance to match a strategy with the theory. You will have a chance to practice using the strategies in case study analyses. You will also probably find yourself saying, "Hmmm, I like that strategy," or "That strategy is not for me!" When you do, you are on the road to . . .

Chapter 11. The Decision-Making Model of Child Guidance: An "Eclectic" Approach. There are no nice, easy answers to discipline encounters. By this point in the book you should not be surprised to discover that there is no one right way to deal with any discipline encounter; there are many effective and positive approaches. You will get a chance to consider the "eclectic" approach which draws from many theories and strategies.

This chapter will help you understand the decision-making model of child guidance. You will be most effective in guiding young children when you make active conscious decisions about discipline encounters and when you look at discipline encounters merely as problems to be solved. You will have a chance to practice the decision-making approach right in the chapter.

Chapter 10

Child-Guidance Theories and Their Strategies

After reading and studying this chapter, you will be able to:

- ☼ Define terms associated with the Adlerian, Rogerian, and social learning models.
- ☼ List and explain the major principles of the three models.
- ☼ Explain how a responsible, authoritative adult could choose any of the three models.
- ☼ List, give examples of, and describe some of the major strategies used in each model.
- ☼ Explain how each model views the use of punishment.
- ☼ Name the form of punishment under which time-out is classified, explain the function of time-out, explain why time-out does not teach anything, and explain why time-out should be used only rarely, if at all.

"A theory . . . can be likened to a lens . . .
[It] filters out certain facts and gives a pattern to those it lets in."
(Thomas, 1992, p. 4)

Case Studies: Theories and Child-Guidance

Child Guidance Based on Rogerian Theory

Mrs. Mason watched her third-graders choose teams for football practice. About five minutes later she saw Tony leaning against the fence watching the others play and said, "You're not playing." He turned his face to her while he tried to wipe away his tears. "They called me a runt and said to get lost!" Mrs. Mason stooped so that she could be closer and asked, "You want to play football and somebody called you a name and said to get lost?" Tony said, "Yeah, they don't want me to play because I'm so small." She nodded, saying, "They think that you're too small to play." Tony started to cry. Mrs. Mason took both his hands in hers and said, "You really seem to be feeling sad about this, Tony."

Child Guidance Based on Adlerian Theory

Miss Chen is a mentor to a new teacher who brought up the following issue, "Greg's mom told me that Greg was a problem eater, and now I know what she means. He hardly ever tries the snack, and I have to coax him to eat what we have for lunch. I decided to use the *try-a-bite* strategy and told him he'd have to stay at the lunch table until he tried a bite of everything. He did stay at the table but really never ate much at all and just kept staring at me. What am I supposed to do?"

Miss Chen did not criticize the teacher for using the ineffective strategy but instead asked the teacher how she felt when she had to coax Greg to eat and discovered that the teacher was angry. "Sometimes when we're angry with a child," said Miss Chen, "we tend to get caught up in a fight with them. I have an idea that might work if you'd like to try that instead of fighting with Greg."

Child Guidance Based on Social Learning Theory

Mrs. Worthley realizes that many of her 4- and 5-year-olds watch a television show called *Mighty Morphin Power Rangers.* She is concerned about the amount of violence to which they're exposed and does not want this type of aggression displayed in their classroom. She wants to help them understand another more important lesson—helping others.

She decided to encourage another type of powerful play. She collected old shirts and printed on them "Powerful Helpers". During grouptime, Mrs. Worthley introduced a puppet who was recruiting children to wear the shirts and become a Powerful Helper. She used the puppet to demonstrate how one person can be powerful by helping another person, and the class discussed the concept of helping. The next day, some of the children wore the Powerful Helper shirts and Mrs. Worthley guided them in finding someone who needed help.

After the small group of Powerful Helpers helped mop up spilled water, Mrs. Worthley said, "You worked together and you helped John mop up the water." At grouptime, she showed the class a chart titled "We Are Powerful Helpers!" Across the top were the names of the days of the week. "The Powerful Helpers worked hard today to help someone. Let's remember that by putting this sticker under today's name. Tomorrow, we'll put another sticker on the chart when the new group of Powerful Helpers has also helped someone. As soon as our class gets three stickers [printed on chart], we'll watch our favorite video." Mrs. Worthley drew a picture of the videotape on the chart. For each day that the Powerful Helpers helped somebody, Mrs. Worthley put a sticker on their chart and also verbally encouraged their accomplishment. As agreed, the children got to watch their video after three days of helping.

CHILD-GUIDANCE STRATEGIES MUST BE DEVELOPMENTALLY APPROPRIATE FOR ADULTS, TOO

In this chapter you will study three models of child guidance—Rogerian, Adlerian, and social learning. All three responsible teachers in the case studies use developmentally appropriate activities and have an appropriately set up classroom environment. Mrs. Mason explains behavior from a Rogerian perspective and chooses guidance strategies primarily from that model. Miss Chen explains behavior from the Adlerian perspective and chooses guidance strategies primarily from that model. Mrs. Worthley explains behavior from a social learning perspective and chooses guidance strategies primarily from that model.

All three teachers have an authori*tative* style: they are high in both demandingness and responsiveness. Each is warm and nurturing and has created a safe and secure classroom environment. Each is adept at setting good limits. Each is an excellent observer of children's behavior, and each firmly believes that adults in a child's world have an impact on how a child behaves—not total responsibility, but an impact. Each is articulate about the strategies she uses and understands why they reject other strategies. These teachers are effective because the positive guidance strategies they choose match their basic explanation of development and behavior.

Early childhood professionals have focused recently on the concept of developmentally appropriate practice for children. It is just as important that we focus on developmentally appropriate practice for adults (Vartuli & Fyfe, 1993) because teachers use positive strategies with children only when they understand and willingly accept them.

We adults tend to accept or reject strategies because of our basic theory about how children grow and develop. The recent debate in the early childhood profession about time-out has come about because professionals who reject one theory of child development also tend to reject the strategies (e.g., time-out) that have evolved out of that view.

Let's first examine Rogerian theory and how it has affected child guidance. Then we will turn to the Adlerian and the social learning models.

ROGERIAN THEORY AND CHILD GUIDANCE

Rogerian theory was formulated by Carl Rogers, who was born in 1902 in Chicago. Rogers studied to be a minister, but eventually he became an educational psychologist and worked in both clinical and academic settings. He counseled children and their parents at the Child Study Department of the Society for the Prevention of Cruelty to Children in Rochester, New York. Rogers was also a teacher. It was during the period from 1940 to 1963 that he developed and disseminated his views on counseling and therapy (Rogers, 1961).

Rogerian Concepts

The Rogerian model is based on beliefs about the nature of the self, and adults who use Rogerian-based child-guidance strategies believe that children have an active awareness of the self. They believe that a child develops a *self-concept*, which is a set of ideas about the self, and it is this self-concept that helps a child make sense of and operate effectively in a world of constant change.

Adults who are guided by Rogerian principles believe that children have the capacity for self-direction and that they can become increasingly able to control their own actions. These adults also believe that a child's perception of his experience is private, personal, and highly subjective because the events in a child's life have meaning as they are perceived by that child and not as perceived by anyone else.

Rogerians believe that humans have a tendency to develop all of their abilities, to actualize or realize their full potential. The ultimate goal for a human, in the Rogerian framework, is to become a fully functioning person, a person who is open to experience and aware of all his feelings—including the unpleasant ones, such as anger or jealousy. Fully functioning people do not feel shame for having unpleasant feelings.

Fully functioning people also tend to live fully in each moment because they perceive things accurately. Such children tend to be much less defensive in dealing with new people, experiences, and problems. Fully functioning people think for themselves and trust their ability to make decisions. They do not need other people to tell them how to act, because they have the ability to accurately appraise situations and they trust themselves to develop good solutions to problems (Rogers, 1957).

Rogerians believe that children move in the direction of becoming fully functioning people when they receive support, acceptance, and approval from others. Children begin to regard themselves as positive when they receive and internalize positive regard from important people in their lives. Children who do not receive support and acceptance from important adults may spend lots of time and energy trying to attain the elusive adult approval and may not have enough time or energy to work on becoming a fully functioning person (Rogers, 1961).

Applying Rogerian Concepts to Child Guidance

Problem ownership. Active listening. I-messages. No-lose method of conflict resolution. All of these are strategies taught in a program called *Parent Effectiveness Training*, widely known as P.E.T., a program of child guidance based on Rogerian theory. It was begun in 1962 by Thomas Gordon, who had been trained as a Rogerian therapist. Gordon's objective in starting the P.E.T. program was to teach adults some of the skills used by professional Rogerian counselors.

Mrs. Mason, the teacher in the case study at the beginning of this section, is an early childhood teacher who understands the Rogerian concepts and has created a classroom atmosphere in which Rogers (1957) would maintain that it will be quite possible for the children to move in the direction of becoming fully functioning persons.

Mrs. Mason has a warm and nurturing (not permissive) relationship with her children, and they seem to feel safe in her classroom. She has a great deal of respect for each child but is still open to all of her feelings about individual children. She does not deny these feelings but accepts them as real. Mrs. Mason is genuine, congruent, and integrated.

One of the things she has learned in workshops that teach how to apply Rogerian principles is to accept the existence of all kinds of feelings in children, not just the friendly, cooperative feelings. She understands a child's fear, rage, or jealousy but does not become tangled in those feelings and does not allow children to hurt others when they are angry. She has also worked on learning specific strategies for clearly communicating what she understands about a child's feelings and is also able to make a child feel understood (Thomas, 1992).

Mrs. Mason wants the children to be able to make good decisions. She believes that she can best help them by refusing to tell them how to solve problems that they themselves should be solving. Mrs. Mason does not believe she has to play a role or that she has to be a perfect teacher. She simply tries to put her beliefs and her understanding of the Rogerian model into practice when she has to deal with typical classroom discipline encounters.

The following section decribes some of the major child-guidance strategies that have grown out of Rogerian theory.

Guidance Strategies Used in a Rogerian-Based Program

Identify who "owns" a problem

The principle of **problem ownership** is a central concept in the P.E.T. model. Gordon teaches adults that problems or issues arise in all relationships and then teaches how to identify who owns the problem before deciding how to deal with the issue. At certain times the adult owns the problem and at other times the child owns the problem and at still other times there is no problem. Gordon's goal is to teach adults how to enlarge the area of no problems.

When the adult owns the problem. Adults find some child behavior irritating because a child is interfering with the adult's rights—for example, when a child interrupts a group lesson or a child leaves her bike in the driveway. In these cases the adult "owns the problem."

Authori*tative* caregivers use self-responsible, nonaccusatory communication skills; these are exactly the skills needed to defuse an adult-owned problem. An adult uses the P.E.T. skills to tell a child: "I have a problem, and I need your help." These skills also help adults learn how to encourage a child to modify his behavior out of respect for the adult's needs. You will read about one of these communication skills, sending I-messages, later in this chapter.

When a child owns the problem. Children own problems, too, when their needs are not met or when something hurts or humiliates them. For example, an infant cannot reach a toy, a toddler cannot fit puzzle pieces together, a 4-year-old is afraid of an injection, or a third-grader feels bad after somebody calls her a dummy. These are problems the child experiences, separate and independent from an adult's life. Therefore, the child owns the problem.

We can best help a child who owns a problem by using specific communication skills that send the following message: "You seem to have a problem. Do you need my help?" Active listening is the P.E.T. communication skill you will read about in this section.

When there is no problem. Some behaviors are not a problem. They represent what adults strive for in guiding children: the times when things seem to be going well. The goal in the P.E.T. program is to teach adults the skills that will help them enlarge the area of no problems.

Active listening

Example: Six-year-old Mark said, "I don't want to play cards with Grandpa. He makes fun of me."

Mark *owns* this problem. Active listening would be the strategy that an adult trained in the Rogerian framework would use to encourage Mark to solve the problem by himself. Active listening is a strategy used by professional counselors and taught to adults who take the P.E.T. or T.E.T. (Teacher Effectiveness Training) courses. (Figure 10–1 lists some things to remember and to avoid when using active listening with children.) Mark needs to know that his teacher recognizes his feelings, and active listening is an excellent way for his teacher to convey that understanding.

What will Mark's teacher accomplish if she chooses to listen actively to him? By listening closely, carefully, and accurately, she will discover his message. Listening without judging will communicate her recognition and acceptance of Mark and his feelings. She will also communicate trust in Mark's ability to work through his own problem and to find a solution by himself.

Think about the last time you had a problem and confided in someone who really listened. They did not deny your problem or your feelings. They did not

Figure 10–1. How to listen actively.

> **How to Listen Actively**
>
> Remember to:
>
> • Listen carefully.
> • Understand what the message means.
> • Listen for what the child is feeling.
> • Suspend judgment.
> • Merely feed back your perception of the child's feelings.
>
> Do not:
>
> • Interrupt the child.
> • Preach, give advice, order, or try to persuade the child to feel something else.

judge you. They did not offer you a quick solution, but they listened well and understood and accepted your feelings. You can show the same courtesy to children by listening actively.

Teachers are mandated reporters of child abuse according to their state's statutes on child abuse and neglect; therefore, it is essential that we know how to act appropriately when we suspect child abuse or neglect. These children might make indirect allusions to problems at home, and we will help them best when we listen actively without judging or acting shocked.

Example: Joyce and her teacher were playing a board game while Joyce waited for her dad to pick her up.

Teacher:	"I like playing games. Do you, Joyce?"
Joyce:	"Uh-huh. Uncle Charlie likes games, too."
Teacher:	"Uncle Charlie likes to play games?"
Joyce:	"He likes one game the best. We play when he baby-sits."
	(By this time the teacher was worried. She knew about the indicators of sexual abuse, and it was beginning to look as if Joyce was trying to tell her something.)
Teacher:	"There's one game that he really likes?"
Joyce:	"Yeah. But he told me that it's a secret game and I shouldn't tell anybody else that we play it."

This teacher has listened and responded well to frightening information. She has not closed the conversation down or denied the child's feelings. She has not preached, she has not acted shocked—she has listened actively. And she will follow her state's law on the reporting of this information.

Sending I-messages

Gordon (1970, 1974, 1978) believes that every member of the guidance system, adult as well as child, has a right to have his needs met. Children occasionally do things that interfere with the satisfaction of an adult's legitimate needs (e.g., an adult cannot get work done because of interruptions from a child, an adult must replant flowers run over by a child on a trike, or an adult has to clean paint brushes not cleaned by a child).

Sending an I-message is the communication strategy an adult should use when the adult, not the child, owns the problem and when a child has done something that is usually perceived as annoying, frustrating, or anger-arousing by the adult. I-messages should be simple statements of facts and should not accuse the child of creating the adult's feeling (Gordon, 1970). (Please see Chapter 3 and the appendix for details on how to state I-messages.)

No-lose method of conflict resolution

Rogerians will tell you to expect some conflict with children and not to deny it when it crops up. Rogerians believe that conflict is not necessarily bad, and that there are times in any relationship when conflict arises simply because the needs of

Ms. Antolini is using an I-message with Grace because the teacher "owns" a problem.

the people in the relationship do not match. Gordon teaches an approach to responsible conflict resolution called the *no-lose method of conflict resolution*. He also advises that we avoid the following two ineffective methods for resolving conflict (Gordon, 1970).

1. *I win, you lose.* Some adults see a conflict as a battle in which there has to be a winner and a loser. With this ineffective technique for trying to resolve conflict, the adult wins and the child loses. An adult who uses this method quite often resorts to using authori*tarian* strategies to win. Rogerians are adamantly opposed to resolving conflicts through this method.

2. *You win, I lose.* This is also an ineffective way to try to resolve conflict: the child wins and the adult loses. It is frequently used by adults who are permissive, who do not feel confident in following through with limits, and who do not know how to do problem solving. The adult usually feels discouraged—even angry—after such an episode and often ends up doing the task for which a child has responsibility.

To counter the idea that there has to be a winner and a loser when conflict arises, Gordon (1970) proposed a third, more responsible method of resolving the inevitable conflicts in a relationship. He called this the **no-lose** method of conflict resolution. One of the main goals of this approach is to teach adults to avoid the use of power so that nobody wins or loses and so that everybody gets their needs met. This method involves decision making by adult and child to achieve a mutually agreeable solution to a problem without resorting to the use of power. Children are more likely to carry out the solution to a conflict or problem if they have played a role in reaching the solution (Gordon, 1976).

Adults who use the no-lose method acknowledge that the child's needs are important and communicate trust in the child's ability to carry out decisions. Using this method, therefore, requires that adults truly accept the child's feelings and needs as valid and important. Adults who use this method must also be adept at active listening and sending I-messages.

3. *"No-lose" conflict resolution.* This method involves simple problem solving and negotiation in which both parties participate. It does not involve one person "giving in." The steps in this process are to:

- *Identify and define the conflict.* Avoid using accusatory statements ("We have a problem . . . ")
- *Invite children to participate in fixing the problem.*
- *Generate possible solutions as a group.* Accept a variety of solutions. Do not evaluate solutions during this brainstorming phase.
- *Examine each idea for its merits and drawbacks.* Decide which one to try. Thank everybody for brainstorming.
- *Work out ways of implementing the solution.*
- *Follow up to evaluate how well the solution worked.* If the solution worked, thank the group for their help in cooperating to solve the problem. If the solution did not work, ask the group to try to figure out why and to fine-tune the solution or to try another solution.

Case Study Analysis: Child Guidance Based on Rogerian Theory

Analyze the chapter opener case study involving Mrs. Mason by answering these questions.

1. Identify the "owner" of the problem in this case study. Is it Mrs. Mason? Tony? The rest of her third-graders? Or is there no problem? Use the information in the chapter to justify your response.

2. Decide how well Mrs. Mason has used active listening. Use Figure 10–1 and information from the section on active listening to make your decision. Support your decision with specific examples, for example, which statement showed that Mrs. Mason listened for what Tony was feeling? How could you tell that Mrs. Mason avoided preaching and trying to persuade Tony to feel differently?

ADLERIAN THEORY AND CHILD GUIDANCE

Alfred Adler was the founder of individual psychology. His life paralleled that of Sigmund Freud in many ways. Both were from Vienna, and Adler was born in 1870, only a few years after Freud. They both attended medical school and developed an interest in psychiatry, but they held divergent views on how the personality develops. Freud maintained that each person is primarily a biological being, while Adler believed that each person is primarily a social being. Freud believed that personalities are shaped by biological needs, but Adler maintained that personalities are shaped by individual social environments and interactions. And while Freud believed that people are driven by unconscious forces that cannot be controlled, Adler maintained that people actively and consciously direct and create their own growth (DiCaprio, 1974).

The Adlerian approach guides many adults in their interactions with children. These adults accept the basic concepts of Adler's theory and have learned specific positive child-guidance strategies based on these concepts. Adlerians do not believe in using punishment. They believe in figuring out what a child is getting out of a misbehavior and then changing their own reaction to the misbehavior to try to help a child make some changes. By offering safe, natural, and logical consequences, they allow children to learn from their behavior. (See Chapter 3 for a more detailed discussion of logical consequences.)

Adlerian Concepts

Each person has an individual style of striving for psychological strength

Adler believed that humans, with their long period of utter dependency, realize that they lack the physical strength of many other species and because of this tend to develop feelings of psychological inferiority and helplessness (Mead, 1976). Adler believed that people try to overcome a sense of inferiority with feelings of psychological strength.

Each child in your care develops a characteristic individual style of striving for the goal, that is, a core set of ideas about how to understand, predict, and have some control over his experiences. This life-style affects how a child deals with problems encountered in daily life. A child's characteristic style of dealing with the world and his place in it is established by the age of 4 or 5 (Dinkmeyer & McKay, 1988; Dreikurs, 1958).

Humans develop different levels of social interest

Social interest refers to a sense of being a vital part of the group, realizing one's role in a group's functioning. Adlerians believe that humans are primarily social beings and that achieving feelings of psychological strength is best done through cooperation with others (Adler, 1964). Consequently, a child with a high degree of social interest is willing to cooperate with other group members and contributes to the functioning of the group. A person with little social interest tends to do things that benefit the self but not necessarily other group members.

A child's self-esteem influences her level of social interest. Adlerians believe that a child who develops positive self-esteem (feelings of competence and self-worth) during childhood will develop a strong sense of social interest and will strive to cooperate with others, while a child who develops negative self-esteem will have a low level of social interest (Mead, 1976). In short, a child who likes and respects herself and is confident about her abilities is likely to become a person who will respect, work well with, and help others, while a child who is given little respect or who is treated as incompetent is likely to become a person who shows little respect for others and who refuses to cooperate with and help other group members.

A child's family influences her level of social interest. Every child is born with the capacity to cooperate, but Adlerians believe that cooperation must be nurtured by a child's environment. Parents, other caregivers, and teachers influence a child's level of social interest and cooperation because they create the atmosphere in which the child exists, an atmosphere in which cooperation with and respect for others can be valued, modeled, and encouraged. It can be a place in which hurting others is prohibited through reasonable, firmly enforced limits on behavior.

The accuracy of a child's personal perceptions affects her level of social interest. Adlerians believe that children play a large role in their development, that their interpretation or perception of their experiences is important. And children go about fitting into a group by following their own interpretation of the rules for group membership (DiCaprio, 1974; Dreikurs, 1958; Mead, 1976).

Some children are able to achieve a sense of belonging to their group by cooperating and making useful contributions. They make accurate interpretations

Many children make accurate interpretations about how to be a member of a group.

of the rules of group membership. Other children have a pattern of misbehavior and noncooperation because they interpret their world inaccurately. These children have a faulty perception of how to fit into the group and use ineffective approaches to gain a place in it.

Goals of Misbehavior: Attention, Power, Revenge, and Inadequacy

The chapter opener case study involving Miss Chen, a new teacher, and the picky eater Greg showed typical adult–child interactions that occur when a child has a faulty perception of how to fit into a group. Children like Greg have a faulty perception or mistaken goal on how to be a group member and seek group membership by (Dreikurs, 1958):

- Striving for undue attention from others
- Seeking power over others
- Hurting others through revenge
- Displaying inadequacy or incompetence

We will look at each of these issues from the child's faulty perception, what the child does, how the adult feels and usually reacts, and a better approach to the encounter.

Striving for undue attention

The child's faulty perception. Everyone, including a child, has a need for and a right to attention. Some children, however, make demands for undue attention from adults, indicating that they have the mistaken belief that they are important only when they are the center of attention. Getting the attention of others, then, is their mistaken goal.

What the child does. Attention seekers accomplish their mistaken goal by keeping adults busy. The child becomes skillful at using different attention-getting techniques. Some attention seekers are active mischief makers, in trouble all the time, but others are passive and get attention through laziness and demanding that things be done for them.

How the adult feels and usually reacts. Adults usually feel annoyed when children demand undue attention and tend to give in to the child's demands, but this reinforces both the attention-getting behavior and the child's faulty perception of how to become a member of the group (Mead, 1976). Other adults reinforce attention-seeking behavior by scolding the child.

A better approach. Adlerians believe in helping a child discover that he can be a valuable group member without having to be the center of attention. Here are specific steps to take when you are confronted with attention-seeking behavior; the basic ingredient is changing how you react to demands for undue attention (Mead, 1976).

1. *Ignore the impulse to give in to the attention-seeking behavior.*
2. *Acknowledge the child's request but let him know that he can complete the task.* Leave the area if necessary so that he can finish the job.

3. *Give the child attention when his behavior is more appropriate.*
4. *Encourage the child to take the perspective of others* by telling him their perspective and by helping him learn to cooperate.

Example: Just when Miss Chen received an emergency phone call from a child's parent, Kelly demanded her attention: "I found the book." Miss Chen said, "I'm talking to Jon's mom about something important. Read by yourself for now and I'll read to you later." Later, she stopped by the reading corner and said, "Thanks for helping me by waiting, Kelly. Let's read that book."

Struggling for power

The child's faulty perception. Some children think that they are important only when they demonstrate power over others. Their faulty perception is that their personal value comes from being in charge and showing others that they are the boss. For such a child a loss of power to an adult is the same as a loss of personal value.

What the child does. The child develops several techniques for involving adults in a power struggle and for gaining control over them. These children might have tantrums, be very disobedient, or, with older children, be very argumentative. Some power seekers are active and rebellious. Others are passive, striving for power through stubbornness, forgetfulness, and laziness.

How the adult feels and usually reacts. Adults often feel threatened or angry when confronted with a power-seeking child. Some adults feel that their authority has been challenged, and their first impulse is to fight back and remind the child that the adult is in power. Adlerians believe that some children are so skillful at the power game that adults do not even realize they are in a power struggle. Some adults resort to punitive, hurtful strategies in trying to reestablish authority and overpower the child.

Adults who allow themselves to be drawn into a power struggle with a child reinforce a child's power-seeking behavior. They do nothing to help power-seeking children clarify their faulty perception; they reinforce the child's faulty perception of how to become a group member. Mrs. Chen made this mistake with Amy.

Example: The teacher said, "Amy, you can have two more turns, and then I want you to park your trike." (Amy took several more turns, got off the trike, and ran over to the slide.) "Amy, it's time to come in. Please park your trike." (Amy got on the tricycle and rode it to the shed. She got off but did not put the trike inside. Instead, she walked toward the classroom.) The teacher glared at her and said, "Amy, for the last time, get over to the shed and put your trike inside." Amy replied, "No!" The teacher replied, "We'll see about that." Amy has controlled and manipulated her teacher, engaging her in a power struggle.

A better approach. Whether a child continues to play the power game depends largely on how important adults react. Children like Amy need adults to guide them toward more positive ways of becoming group members; they do not need adults as sparring partners. Adlerians maintain that adults who change their ways of reacting to a defiant child have the best chance of actually helping that child. The following are their suggestions (Dinkmeyer & McKay, 1988; Mead, 1976):

1. *Resist the first impulse to fight back.*
2. *Decide to respond differently.* You do not have to be drawn into a power struggle. You can choose to respond differently.
3. *Decline the child's invitation to argue or fight.* This will surprise a child, particularly if you have previously been locked in power struggles with him. A useful technique is to label the interaction as a power struggle.

Example: The teacher said, "It looks to me like you feel like fighting with me about the trike. I don't feel like fighting, so I'm going inside to watch the movie. You may watch it, too, when you put your trike away." (She refuses to fight back and communicates her intention to Amy.)

Getting revenge

The child's faulty perception. These children feel hurt, and their goal is to get even by hurting others. Like all children, they need recognition, but these children get it in quite a negative way. This is hostile aggression (discussed in Chapter 8) and is more often seen in children who are at the end of the early childhood period.

Example: Eight-year-old Tom was angry when Peter accidentally bumped into him and punched Peter on the arm. When Miss Chen asked Tom to put away the math manipulatives, he said, "You're not my boss! Stop telling me what to do because I hate you!"

What the child does. These children expend a lot of energy convincing people that they are not likable. The child works hard at getting even with those he perceives as having hurt him. The revenge may be active, in which the child is easily recognizable as a troublemaker, or the revenge may be passive. The passively vengeful child is quietly defiant.

How the adult feels and usually reacts. An adult who has been attacked by a child usually feels hurt and either backs away from the child or retaliates against the hurtful behavior. The typical adult reaction does not help a child bent on revenge. Retaliating or backing away reinforces both the child's hurtful behavior and his faulty perception: that he is a bad, unlikable person of little value who has to hurt others to be a part of the group.

A better approach. Do the unexpected and resist the first impulse to retaliate, give sermons, or back away. A child who seeks revenge has poor self-esteem and needs your help. Adlerians believe that you can best help this child by fostering positive self-esteem because he will value others enough to refrain from hurting them only when he feels valued.

Example: Miss Chen said, "You really are angry with me, Tom! I think that we need to talk about it."

Displaying inadequacy or incompetence

The child's faulty perception. These children feel completely discouraged and think they cannot do anything well. They believe they have nothing to contribute to the group, so they do not even try. They want to be left alone.

What the child does. These children let others know how inadequate they perceive themselves to be, with the hope of discouraging others from expecting much from them. They quietly work out a deal with adults in which the adult leaves the child alone and does not ask much of the child, just as the child asks very little of the adult. These children tend to act in an incompetent way.

How the adult feels and usually reacts. Adults are usually puzzled and frustrated when they interact with an intelligent child who has given up and acts as if he cannot do anything. Adults are often at a loss to help such a child. Their first impulse is often to highlight the child's errors, but this results in further discouraging the child. Many adults then perform the task for the child, which reinforces the child's faulty perception that he can be a group member only by demonstrating incompetence.

A better approach. Rely on knowledge of child development. For example, if a healthy 4-year-old should be able to zip his own coat, refrain from performing the task for him. Most important, learn how to encourage children who mistakenly believe that they have to demonstrate incompetence. Your role is to light the fire of self-confidence in the child so that he can solve problems and carry out tasks on his own.

Example: "I think you can zip your own coat. Put this part of the zipper into this part . . . Good . . . Now catch that little tab and pull it up. That's it . . . Z-Z-Z-ZIP!"

Case Study Analysis: Child Guidance Based on Adlerian Theory

This case study involved Miss Chen, another teacher, and Greg (the picky eater).
1. What made the teacher's initial strategy so ineffective?
2. Miss Chen and other Adlerians would say that Greg's behavior grew out of his "mistaken goal." What was his mistaken goal? Why did you select this mistaken goal and not some other?
3. Explain your Adlerian-based idea for guiding Greg more effectively (instead of using coaxing and forcing him to eat). Rely on information from the chapter for help.

SOCIAL LEARNING THEORY AND CHILD GUIDANCE

A major social learning theorist is Albert Bandura, who was born in 1925; this section focuses on his view of social learning theory (Bandura, 1977; Bandura & Walters, 1963). *Social learning theory* acquired its name because it emphasizes the social variables that determine a child's behavior (Thomas, 1992). A social learning theorist like Bandura has helped teachers understand the important role of imitation in child development. He has helped us understand that children are not just machines responding to stimuli. Social learning theorists believe that children are active in their own development, that they are affected by their environment but that they also contribute to producing their environment (Thomas, 1992).

This section of the chapter describes the major principles of social learning theory, describes two types of reinforcers, describes the process of extinction, emphasizes teaching more appropriate behavior, and closes with a look at social learning theory's view of punishment.

Social Learning Principles Applied to Child Guidance

Principle No. 1: Social learning theorists do not emphasize stages of development

Developmental theorists like Jean Piaget (1952, 1970, 1983) view development as a series of phases, or stages, each stage being qualitatively different from the ones before and after. In learning theory, however, development is not viewed as a series of stages but rather as a gradual accumulation of knowledge (Thomas, 1992).

Principle No. 2: Development occurs through learning from the environment

A major belief common to all branches of behavioral or learning theory is that human behavior is learned (Cairns, 1983; Fogel, 1984; Langer, 1969). All learning theorists believe that a child's behavior is gradually shaped as he interacts with his environment. For example, learning theorists believe that a child who treats dogs humanely has learned this behavior.

Principle No. 3: Most of a child's learning occurs through the process of modeling

Social learning theorists believe that learning takes place in and cannot be separated from a child's social setting. Social learning theorists demonstrated more than 30 years ago that children could learn new behavior by observing another person perform the behavior (Bandura & Walters, 1963). A child who treats animals humanely, the social learning theorists would insist, has learned this behavior by imitating his model's actions and words about how to treat animals.

Children learn from a variety of models: a real person who is physically present; real people on television, movies, or videos; cartoon characters; graphic representations of human figures in video games; models in books; or audio models (Maccoby & Martin, 1983; Stevenson, 1983; Thomas, 1992). Children become increasingly accurate in their ability to imitate a model as they grow older.

In the process of modeling, the actual content that is demonstrated for the child depends on the child's social environment. All children learn simple things such as vegetable preference, facial expressions, and table manners through observation. More complex social behaviors are also taught through modeling, with some social environments modeling behaviors like respectful treatment of others and assertiveness while other social environments model behaviors like aggression and selfishness.

Children are not just machines, automatically imitating every behavior that they observe. What accounts for a child's selectivity in who or what they imitate? Children imitate models who possess certain characteristics: they are powerful, more skillful than the child, have a lot of prestige, and are nurturing (Maccoby & Martin, 1983). The model's behavior may be positive (e.g., an ad in which an admired athlete says not to smoke or take drugs) or negative (e.g., an older brother who is a gang member).

An explanation of why children do not imitate all of their models is that children actually build a *prototype* of behavior after observing several models (Perry & Bussey, 1979). They observe a large number of models performing a certain type of behavior and then construct a prototype or composite of the behavior of the group. Then, when a child observes another model of the same type of behavior, he will imitate the model's behavior only if it matches his construction of what the behavior should be. Thus, social learning theorists believe that children are active in their development and not just passive recipients of every stimulus in their world.

Example: Joseph has observed lots of males in real life and on film and has constructed a prototype of how males act with babies: they hold them and smile, and they seem to like playing with them. Joseph imitated these models of male behavior with his infant sister. He then observed a friend's father refuse to change his infant's diaper or to feed the baby. The new model's behavior with infants did not fit Joseph's construction of "how males act with babies," and he did not imitate this model.

There are a variety of cognitive factors that determine whether a child will learn something after observing a behavior.

1. *Attentional factor:* A child must be able to pay attention to something before she can learn from it.
2. *Retentional factor:* A child must also be able to remember (retain information about) an event.
3. *Reproductive factor:* A child must be able to reenact the event.
4. *Motivational factor:* A child must want to learn the material even if he can discriminate, interpret, remember, and reproduce it (Bandura, 1969; Cairns, 1983; White, 1970).

Even though social learning theorists do not emphasize stages of development, they do acknowledge that a child's level of development plays a part in learning from models: for example, whether perceptual skills are sophisticated enough to enable a child to pay attention to; whether memory is well enough developed to enable her to remember; and whether motor skills are good enough to enable her to reproduce something she has observed.

Principle No. 4: Children learn complex behaviors in big chunks rather than in tiny steps

Some learning theorists believe that children learn things in tiny steps, with each step reinforced. But social learning theorists believe that children learn complex behaviors in big chunks (Thomas, 1992).

Example: After a unit called "Showing Kindness to Animals," Nick acted out in the dramatic play area outdoors the entire set of behaviors demonstrated or described by his teacher or by visitors or through videos.

Principle No. 5: Behavior can be changed if a child's social environment is changed

Social learning theorists believe that the most effective way to change (modify) a child's behavior is to alter the child's environment. Because they believe so strongly in the effect of the social environment, they place great emphasis on changing the social environment. In practice this means that people in the child's social environment might need to change how they respond to his behavior (Mead, 1976; Thomas, 1992).

Principle No. 6: Children do not need to be reinforced to learn a behavior

Example: Sam observed the Mighty Morphin Power Rangers fight in a way that he had never fought. Sam learned (acquired) the new behavior simply by observing the model. He did not need to be reinforced to learn how to fight like the Power Rangers; he only had to watch them and remember what he observed.

Principle No. 7: Reinforcement gives children information on the consequences of that behavior for the person who modeled it

Example: Then Sam listened to and observed his older brother cheer for the Power Rangers when they fought. Sam thought to himself, "Hmmm. Tommy liked how the Power Rangers fight."

How has reinforcement operated in Sam's observational learning? First, he learned how to fight like the Power Rangers by observing them. Then reinforcement entered the picture. Whether he actually imitated (reproduced) the behavior depended on how he looked at the consequences of that activity for the models. Social learning theorists would predict that Sam is highly likely to imitate the fighting because he heard and watched the cheering (positive consequences) for the Power Rangers (Bandura, 1977). Reinforcement, then, is feedback and is a basic process through which adults influence children.

Types of Positive Reinforcement: Effective Praise and Token Systems

There are different forms of positive reinforcement, and Mrs. Worthley (case study) believes in using them. She has made an effort to learn to use them ethically and effectively. The two forms she uses that are emphasized here are positive verbal reinforcement (praise) and token systems.

Effective praise

Effective praise is specific, descriptive, and appreciative but is not "gushy or mushy." When you praise, notice and then describe specifically what it was that a child did. Describe what you saw, heard, tasted, or touched. Relate the praise directly to the event. Avoid making judgments about what the child did and avoid making comments about the child's character, but let the child know that you appreciate what he has done.

Example: Mrs. Worthley walked over to the block area just after cleanup and said, "Thanks for putting away all the small blocks. You put each one in its own spot on the shelf, right behind the outline for the block." (She had set a limit on where to place the blocks, communicated the limit clearly, and has now noticed and encouraged the children's willingness to accept the limit.)

Effective praise is given as soon as possible after the event. Praise is most effective when it is delivered as soon as possible after a child performs a desired behavior and requires that you concentrate and make an effort to watch for, notice, and then immediately give feedback. There is a good reason for reinforcing as quickly as possible. Reinforcers give children information about the consequences of their behavior. Children make more accurate connections between their behavior and your feedback if the two happen close together.

Mrs. Worthley uses sincere and descriptive words of appreciation for efforts. "Danielle, you said to place the second block in the middle."

Example: Immediately after closing the storybook, Mrs. Worthley leaned forward and said, "Everybody could hear the story today because the whole class listened so carefully and sat so quietly."

Effective praise is sincere and rewards effort and small steps. If you choose to use praise, use honest and sincere praise. Your firmly grounded set of values and ethical standards and your respect for children will forbid you from giving insincere, phony, or perfunctory praise. When you think feedback would be helpful for a child, try to find something in a situation that you can praise sincerely and honestly.

You can foster persistence in children when you give feedback about a child's effort to complete difficult tasks. Children need to know that they control the effort that they put into a task, and you can help them increase their effort by giving feedback, specifically about effort (Dweck & Elliott, 1981).

Example: Mrs. Worthley watched Rick, who has a reputation for not being able to stay on task, work for 25 minutes with a small tray of wet sand. Rick's concentration was evident when he was not distracted by the noise in the dramatic play area. Rick drew in the sand with his finger and a small stick and then pressed designs into the sand. Mrs. Worthley has been working on helping Rick concentrate, and this is what she praised, quietly and quickly, without fanfare: "You've worked with the sand tray for almost the whole work period, Rick. That's what I call concentration."

Praise is even more effective when given along with appropriate physical contact or other nonverbal communication. Increase the impact of your verbal feedback by combining it with appropriate physical contact or other appropriate forms of nonverbal communication, such as nodding your head or smiling.

Pitfalls to Avoid: Ineffective Praise

There are several things that make praise or any type of reward ineffective. Authoritative adults make an effort to avoid the following forms of ineffective praise.

Avoid combining praise with some form of negative comment. Note the praise as well as the negative comment in the following example. Why do you think that this form of praise is so ineffective?

Example: Teacher to a kindergartner: "I'm glad to see that you've washed your hands. Maybe you can remember to do it again tomorrow."

Avoid praising only perfection. Some adults praise only perfection, but this is one way to decrease the effectiveness of praise. Instead of noticing and praising a child's effort to do something helpful, some adults attend only to some part of the job the child is not doing.

Example: Teacher to 5-year-old who is washing paintbrushes at the sink: "Kerry! You forgot to wipe the easel."

Avoid praising only completion of a difficult task. Children should be encouraged as they successfully complete each step in a difficult task.

Example: A classroom aide says nothing to a 3-year-old who is working with a difficult puzzle. She fails to encourage the child's effort to match colors or to finally fit two pieces together. Later that day the aide noticed the same child again having trouble with the puzzle. She said, "Here, let me do that for you."

Do not overdo praise. Children seem to adapt to a particular level of praise (Maccoby & Martin, 1983). An adult who uses praise indiscriminately will find it necessary to use even more because the child receiving such lavish praise becomes accustomed to it. Rewards that are given too frequently lose their reward value. Children come to expect to receive the reward, and if it is not offered they might think they are being punished. Many adults have been trapped into constantly having to escalate the value of treats so that children still view the treat as a reward. What often started out as a legitimate reward (e.g., a trip to their favorite restaurant for practicing a musical instrument) can become, in an adult's eyes, a bribe.

Do not give praise if it is not necessary. It is possible for rewards to backfire and negatively affect a child's motivation. Children who are spontaneously interested in an activity but are then rewarded for performing the activity may lose interest in the activity because they perceive the adult's reward as an attempt at control. The child's decreased interest is actually resistance to external control (Maccoby & Martin, 1983).

Example: Molly really liked sweeping the sand off the trikeway. She made designs with the broom, imitated the scrape-scrape sound of the sand on the sidewalk, and watched sand slide into the sandpit. Mrs. Worthley started to praise her work, and she stopped her sweeping.

Do not confuse rewards with bribes. Reinforcers and bribes are not the same thing. Here is an example of a bribe.

Examples: Julie whines when her mother is talking on the phone. Mother stops and says, "I'll give you some candy if you stop bothering me." Julie stops whining, and mother gives her the candy.

Julie's mother also gives bribes before a behavior occurs. She gave Julie a dime so that Julie would place her toys on the shelves in the family room.

Effective reinforcers are aimed at giving accurate information about the consequences of a behavior and are used to increase the chances that a child will imitate a behavior that she has witnessed. Julie's mom, on the other hand, has done nothing to teach more acceptable behavior. She has reinforced Julie's obnoxious behavior (whining) by giving a bribe of candy and will very likely have to continue to bribe Julie to keep her quiet.

All children need feedback. Some children deserve praise and encouragement but seem unable to accept it. How can you help a child who deserves praise but rejects it when it is given? A child who rejects praise may not feel comfortable receiving it because he has negative self-esteem and may feel unworthy of the praise. Such a child may not have received much praise in the past. It is important for you not to argue with the child about whether he deserves praise—just deliver the praise in a positive, matter-of-fact way. Ignore the child's rejecting behavior about the praise. Do not argue. Continue to praise appropriate behavior.

Tokens: Nonsocial, or tangible, positive reinforcers

Praise is a positive social reinforcer. Another class of positive reinforcers is called nonsocial or tangible reinforcers. Some authoritative adults make a deliberate attempt to modify a child's environment and therefore to help a child modify his behavior by using tangible rewards, or tokens, as positive reinforcement.

A token is an object, so the term *tangible* is applied. Some examples are a sticker, a smiley face, a star, a check, a plastic chip. An adult who decides to use a token system targets a specific behavior that he wants to see more of (e.g., cooperation), and a child earns a token for demonstrating that behavior.

Responsible, ethical adults realize that tokens are a means to an end, not an end in themselves. Tokens are merely a way to remind adults to give a child feedback for his efforts to behave appropriately. Responsible adults realize that tokens are a gimmick, that the tokens must be combined with appropriate social reinforcement, and that the tokens must be used ethically. They realize that effectively carrying out a token system requires concentration and special effort from adults. (Figure 10–2 describes how to use "tokens" ethically and effectively.)

Withdrawing a Reinforcer: Extinction

Suppose that you have been reinforcing a behavior. If you decide to take away that reinforcer, the behavior will very likely decrease or disappear. Please see the Parent Talk box for an example of a parent withdrawing a reinforcer, which leads to a decrease in problems at the child's bedtime.

Figure 10–2. How to use "tokens" ethically and effectively.

How to Use "Tokens" Ethically and Effectively

- **Reward small steps.** What was Mrs. Worthley's (chapter opener case study) overall goal for the children? How did she encourage/reinforce their small steps toward the bigger goal?

- **Reward often.** Considering the age of the children, explain why Mrs. Worthley rewarded the new behavior often enough.

- **Combine the token with a social reward** (smile, praise, encouragement). Mrs. Worthley uses tokens to remind herself to use social reinforcers. When did she combine tokens and social reinforcers?

- **Keep a record of tokens.** How did Mrs. Worthley do this?

- **Ask children what they would like to work for.** The item or activity used as the reinforcer (the thing for which the chart is traded) must be highly desirable and is best if chosen by the children within certain limits.

- **Spend tokens by letting the children exchange their tokens for the reward fairly often.** How well did Mrs. Worthley do on this criterion?

- **Do not take away tokens children have already earned as fines for undesirable behavior.**

- **Gradually fade out the use of tokens as the child shows willingness to use the behavior, but continue to give social reinforcers periodically.** One way to do this is to increase the time periods between tokens until the Child no longer gets a token.

Parent Talk. Tips for Dealing With Bedtime Hassles

Joel was driving to work and listening to a radio talk show on which a child development specialist was answering call-in questions from listeners. "Well . . . I have a question!" He pulled to the side of the road and dialed the show with his car phone. He explained that his 2-year-old son Josh had begun to have temper tantrums when Mom or Dad put him to bed at night. The specialist asked questions that revealed that Joel and his wife encouraged the tantrums by going to Josh's room when he screamed and by staying with him, often spending an hour in his room until he went to sleep.

"There are a few simple things that you can do to make bedtime less nerve-racking for you," said the child developmentalist. Here is what she recommended.

- First: Make bedtime pleasant by singing a song and reading a favorite story to Josh.

- Second: Tell Josh that after the story is done you will leave the room, close the door, and not come back (you will, of course, still monitor for safety).
- Third: Realize that Josh will likely scream and have his usual tantrum when you first try this, but do not go back to his room.
- Finally: Here's the good part! Be prepared for shorter and shorter tantrums as the days go by. Be patient and calm. Josh's tantrums will subside in about four to seven days.

Note that there was no punishment. Josh's parents did not do anything to Josh; they merely withdrew the reinforcer (lots of attention for a tantrum) they had previously given, and by so doing they helped Josh (Thomas, 1992).

Teaching and Strengthening More Appropriate Behavior

Example: Four-year-old Linda screeched whenever she was frustrated, and Mrs. Worthley had reinforced the screeching by occasionally paying attention to Linda when she screeched. The teacher decided to stop paying attention to the screeching by using extinction. She combined extinction with another procedure, strengthening a more appropriate behavior, which makes extinction even more effective.

The teacher taught and strengthened a behavior that is incompatible with screeching, one that cannot be done at the same time as screeching. Asking for things in a normal voice is incompatible with screeching. The teacher told Linda that she would listen to requests made in a normal voice but not to requests made with a screech. Then she demonstrated a normal voice. She gave encouragement for Linda's effort to use a normal voice and stopped paying attention to screeching.

Social Learning Theory's View of Punishment

Punishment is a procedure for weakening or eliminating behavior. It is one of the most widely used (and misunderstood) of all the strategies for influencing children (Richards & Siegel, 1978). Learning theorists are not opposed to using punishment to try to change a child's behavior. But responsible authoritative adults who believe in the social learning model refuse to use hurtful punishment.

There are several forms of punishment. Some forms of punishment hurt children and are never used by responsible, authoritative adults. But social learning theorists do approve of using other forms of punishment that they say do not seem to have negative side effects. I do *not* advocate using punishment. I will present here a brief summary of two major categories of punishment—*punishment by hurt* and *punishment by loss.* Effective child guidance requires that you have a good, broad knowledge base and this includes your need to know how some of the children in your care have been punished. You can then teach people how to use more positive strategies.

Punishment by hurt

Punishment by hurt is degrading and is never used by ethical professionals.

Examples: Mary swore, and her mom slapped her.

Danny reached across the table for the butter. Dad grabbed his wrist and shoved him back into his chair.

Danny's dog raced to the fence to bark at the neighbor, and Dad threw a tennis ball and hit the dog on the head.

Eighteen-month-old Ron bit his brother, and Ron's dad bit Ron.

Mary's, Danny's, and Ron's parents have used punishment by hurt to try to weaken behaviors that irritated them (swearing, reaching across the table, barking, biting). They did something to the child (and to the animal). They applied an aversive (hurtful) stimulus (slapping, grabbing, shoving, biting, and throwing the ball) after the undesirable behavior. As you know, there are many ways to punish by hurting, both physically and psychologically (ridicule, sarcasm), and all are unethical and irresponsible.

Hurtful punishment is firmly embedded in the repertoire of many parents and teachers because it only seems to work quickly and decrease obnoxious behavior. A person does not have to be very creative to use hurtful punishment. As you have learned, hurtful punishment has a negative effect on a child's development and on adult–child relationships. There are many positive, and ultimately more effective, ways to guide children, as you have learned in other sections of this text.

Punishment by loss: Time-out

Punishment by loss is also a procedure for weakening a behavior. An adult who uses punishment by loss ethically pays careful attention to the reinforcement a child receives for a behavior. The adult then removes or reduces the reinforcement. But the adult does not hurt the child; the child merely loses the positive reinforcement or has to wait a bit longer to receive the reinforcement.

Time-out. Professionals in early childhood education are quite concerned about the misuse of time-out. (Time-out involves removing a child from a place where he is reinforced for a behavior to a place where the reinforcers are no longer available.) Time-out, if carried out as specified, is, officially, punishment. Specifically, time-out is a punishment by loss (Shaffer, 1996). There is much controversy about time-out in the early childhood profession because it does not match many people's basic beliefs of why children behave as they do. Time-out is also controversial because so many others either do not understand how to use it, overuse it, use it incorrectly, or confuse it with other strategies, and do not understand that time-out is a form of punishment.

Time-out should be used rarely—even if one believes that it is an acceptable strategy—and only after a person understands how to carry it out well. Time-out should not be used with all children, and it must be supplemented with the teaching of more appropriate behavior. By itself, time-out does not teach. Some adults use it far more often than is warranted and do not teach more appropriate behavior.

Do not confuse time-out/punishment with the more positive strategy of cooling off or of withdrawing from a situation for a short time and then going back to solve a problem. Time-out is punishment by loss. The intention in time-out is to take away the reinforcement you have given a child. (Review Chapter 3 for suggestions on how to teach children to take themselves out of situations when necessary.)

Case Study Analysis: Child Guidance Based on Social Learning Theory

This case study involved Mrs. Worthley and her 4- and 5-year-old Powerful Helpers.
1. Another teacher in the school criticized Mrs. Worthley's approach and said, "Why go to all that trouble? She [Mrs. Worthley] should just put children who fight like Power Rangers in time-out for fighting and be done with it!" Respond to this person's criticism. Why will Mrs. Worthley's approach be better for the children in the long-run? Explain why time-out would not have been the most appropriate way to deal with the issue.

(continues on next page)

2. Mrs. Worthley verbally encouraged small groups of children and then encouraged the entire group instead of focusing on individual children for helping others. Even though it is good to encourage individuals for helping, explain why her strategy is an even more powerful one.

3. Mrs. Worthley has a somewhat relaxed but careful approach to using tokens. Give positive feedback to her about what she did well regarding tokens. Name one thing that you would suggest that she change to make her token system even more effective. Reviewing Figure 10–2 might help you with this question.

REFLECTING ON KEY CONCEPTS

1. Take the role of a teacher who uses Rogerian principles in guiding children. Name and explain at least two of the central concepts in this theory. Explain how the Rogerian theory and its strategies can help children become fully functioning people.

2. Take the role of a teacher who believes in the Adlerian approach to child guidance. You are doing a workshop for other teachers and your main goal is to explain this statement from that perspective: "Some children have inaccurate perceptions about how to be accepted in their group and display these mistaken goals by seeking group membership in inappropriate ways."

3. Take the role of a teacher who believes in the social learning approach to child guidance. You are talking with other teachers about Janet, a child who hits other children when she is angry. You state, "I think that Janet will be able to make some changes only if we change how we deal with her problems." How does your statement illustrate the social learning view of the role of a child's social environment in a child's behavior?

4. One of the teachers with whom you're talking asks, "I agree with you that we have to change how we deal with Janet. But how exactly do you think that we can change [i.e., what are some *specific* strategies that we would use]?" Name at least three specific strategies for this other teacher and explain how you would use them to help Janet use a less aggressive way of managing her anger.

5. "Oh, really!" says another teacher. "Why don't you just put Janet in time-out?" Explain to her why time-out would not be an appropriate way to deal with Janet's poor anger management.

APPLY YOUR KNOWLEDGE

1. Mrs. Mason (case study teacher) has noticed that, despite reasonable, clearly stated limits for cleanup time, some of her third-graders almost always fail to clean up after themselves. She has already delivered an I-message, but that did not solve the problem. She does not believe in using punishment, but she realizes that she must do something to resolve this conflict because she gets angry every time she looks at the messy tables or books tossed into heaps.

Demonstrate how the conflict over cleanup in Mrs. Mason's classroom would be solved by using all three methods of conflict resolution. Work with another person and develop a short role-play based on each of the three methods.

Role-Play #1: I win, you lose. Develop a short vignette that illustrates at least one specific strategy used by an adult who believed in using this method to solve the issue of proper storage of blocks.

Role-Play #2: You win, I lose. Again, develop a short vignette illustrating a specific strategy used by an adult who believed in using this method to resolve the same issue.

Role-Play #3: No-lose method. Demonstrate how Mrs. Mason would use each step in negotiating a solution to this problem using the no-lose method.

2. Use effective encouragement. Examine each of these situations. Write exactly what you would say to show appreciation for the child's efforts. Then say why your encouragement is effective.

- *Situation.* Lucy loves to finger paint. Today she painted with three colors, piling on colors until her paper was saturated. The paper dried with the colors blended into one another, making a muddy green-brown. She shows it to you proudly. Even though you do not personally like the outcome of her effort, you try to find something in this situation that you can honestly encourage: her delight in the feel of the paint as she smoothed it onto the paper? the fact that she covered every inch of paper? her concentration?

- *Situation.* John hung his sweater in his cubby this morning. He also placed his painting there. You've tried for about a week to encourage him to abide by the limit of keeping personal possessions in cubbies and he has finally done so.

- *Situation.* J. T. is a child in your class. He usually gets a lot of attention for things he should not do, and it is easy to disregard his efforts at cooperation. Yesterday, however, you observed him at the woodworking table. He had been there about 15 minutes when Lauren walked up to the table. She couldn't work because she didn't have goggles. J. T. said, "Here, Lauren. See if my goggles fit you. I'm done here."

References

Adler, A. (1964). *Social interest*. New York: Capricorn Books.

Bandura, A. (1969). *Principles of behavior modification*. New York: Holt, Rinehart & Winston.

Bandura, A. (1977). *Social learning theory*. Englewood Cliffs, NJ: Prentice-Hall.

Bandura, A., & Walters, R. H. (1963). *Social learning and personality development*. New York: Holt, Rinehart & Winston.

Cairns, R. B. (1983). The emergence of developmental psychology. In P. Mussen (Ed.), *Handbook of child psychology* (Vol. 1). New York: Wiley.

DiCaprio, N. S. (1974). *Personality theories: Guides to living*. Philadelphia: W. B. Saunders.

Dinkmeyer. B., & McKay, G. D. (1988). *Systematic training for effective parenting*. Circle Pines, MN: American Guidance Service.

Dreikurs, R. (1958). *The challenge of parenthood*. New York: Hawthorne Books.

Dweck, C. S., & Elliott, E. S. (1981). *A model of achievement motivation, a theory of its origins, and a framework for motivational development*. Unpublished manuscript, Harvard University.

Fogel, A. (1984). *Infancy*. St. Paul, MN: West Publishing.

Gordon, T. (1970). *P.E.T.: Parent effectiveness training*. New York: Peter H. Wyden.

Gordon, T. (1974). *T.E.T.: Teacher effectiveness training*. New York: David McKay.

Gordon, T. (1976). *P.E.T. in action*. New York: Peter H. Wyden.

Gordon, T. (1978). *P.E.T. in action*. Toronto: Bantam. (Published by Wyden in 1976.)

Langer, J. (1969). *Theories of development*. New York: Holt, Rinehart & Winston.

Maccoby, E. E., & Martin, J. A. (1983). Socialization in the context of the family: Parent-child interaction. In P. Mussen (Ed.), *Handbook of child psychology* (Vol. 4). New York: Wiley.

Mead, D. E. (1976). *Six approaches to child rearing*. Provo, UT: Brigham Young University Press.

Perry, D. G., & Bussey, K. (1979). The social learning theory of sex differences: Imitation is alive and well. *Journal of Personality and Social Psychology, 37*, 1699–1712.

Piaget, J. (1952). *The origins of intelligence in children*. New York: International Universities Press.

Piaget, J. (1970). Piaget's theory. In P. Mussen (Ed.), *Carmichael's manual of child psychology* (Vol. 1). New York: Wiley.

Piaget, J. (1983). Piaget's theory. In P. Mussen (Ed.), *Handbook of child psychology* (Vol. 1). New York: Wiley.

Richards, C. S., & Siegel, L. J. (1978). Behavioral treatment of anxiety states. In D. Marholin (Ed.), *Child behavior therapy*. New York: Gardner.

Rogers, C. (1957). The necessary and sufficient conditions of therapeutic personality change. *Journal of Consulting Psychology, 21*, 95–103.

Rogers, C. (1961). *On becoming a person*. Boston: Houghton-Mifflin.

Shaffer, D. (1996). *Developmental psychology*. Pacific Grove, CA: Brooks/Cole.

Stevenson, H. (1983). How children learn: The quest for a theory. In P. Mussen (Ed.), *Handbook of child psychology* (Vol. 1). New York: Wiley.

Thomas, R. (1992). *Comparing theories of child development* (3rd ed.). Belmont, CA: Wadsworth.

Vartuli, S., & Fyfe, B. (1993). Teachers need developmentally appropriate practice too. *Young Children, 48*(4), 36–42.

White, S. H. (1970). Learning theory tradition and child psychology. In P. Mussen (Ed.), *Carmichael's manual of child psychology* (Vol. 1). New York: Wiley.

Chapter 11

The Decision-Making Model of Child Guidance: An "Eclectic" Approach

Case Study: What Should We Do About the Cursing?

Some Questions about the Decision-Making Model of Child Guidance

What Is the Decision-Making Model of Child Guidance?

Do You Think That Everybody Can Use This Model?

It Seems As If an Adult is "Active" and Has to "Be on His Toes" in Such a Model. Is That True?

What Does "Eclectic" Mean?

I Don't Quite Understand Why I Have to Understand Child and Family Development to Deal with Discipline Encounters. Is It Really All That Necessary?

Using The Decision-Making Model

Steps in the Decision-Making Model

Case Study Analysis: The Decision-Making Model in Action

Practicing the Decision-Making Model

What the Decision-Making Model Means for Children

Reflecting on Key Concepts

Apply Your Knowledge

After reading this chapter, you will be able to:

✿ Explain the decision-making model and identify its building blocks.

✿ Analyze a case study to determine how well a teacher has used the decision-making model.

✿ Summarize the benefits of using the decision-making model for both adults and for children.

✿ Apply your knowledge of the decision-making model by writing a guidance plan intended to solve specific discipline encounters.

"Guidance is good!"
(NAEYC poster, #447)

Case Study: What Should We Do About the Cursing?

Mr. Alvarez is Gary's teacher and is the cooperating teacher for preschool/kindergarten-grade student teachers Olivia and Hector. They are having an end-of-the-day discussion about the day's events.

"OK," Mr. Alvarez said, "OK . . . So you've both noticed that Gary curses."

"I suggest time-out for Gary," responded Olivia.

"His father curses, too. I've heard him curse at Gary. Like father, like son!" added Hector.

"Could be, but let's try to avoid blaming because that won't help Gary," said Mr. Alvarez. "This is only a problem, so let's do some decision making and make a guidance plan."

Mr. Alvarez said, "First of all, he's 4½ years-old. To Gary, *!#! is just another word, and he's imitating his dad. Our goal is not to lay blame. All I want is for Gary to know that there are different words that he can use in school to express his feelings."

"So, to get us started," Mr. Alvarez said, "I want you to think about who really has a problem here—Gary or us?"

"Gary, of course!" sputtered Olivia, giving Mr. Alvarez a look of astonishment.

"Think about that, Olivia. What would the P.E.T. people say?" asked the teacher.

"Let me think . . . oh, oh, the P.E.T. people would probably say that I'm the one with the problem because when he curses I get upset."

"Correct," said Mr. Alvarez, "so let's help Gary find a different way to say what he feels."

Mr. Alvarez gave each student teacher a list of guidance strategies.

"Let's review some guidance strategies and make a guidance plan," he said. "Do you think that we've made it clear that cursing is not permitted here?"

"We've never really talked about it at all," responded Hector, looking at the list. "Maybe we need to actually **state a limit** about cursing?"

"You might be right. Does that sound OK to you, Olivia?" responded Mr. Alvarez. She nods.

"OK, limit-setting is our first item. Now, what do you think Gary gets from us when he curses?"

"Our attention!" said Olivia. "We all laugh!"

Mr. Alvarez said, "Attention for *in*appropriate behavior. What can we do instead?"

Olivia looks over the list. "Use **substitution** . . . let's give him a different word to use as a substitute and then **encourage** him for using the new word."

"Good. Substitution and encouragement is item number two in the plan. What if he forgets or even tests our limit and substitution?" asked Mr. Alvarez.

"Sounds like you don't want to use time-out," said Hector.

"Right," said Mr. Alvarez. "I just don't like using punishment and, anyway, limit setting and noticing the more acceptable word will work in the long run."

Hector said, "I think that we should all just stick to the limit and the substitution and not get all upset if he forgets or tests."

Mr. Alvarez responded, "Great idea, Hector! Item number three on our guidance plan for the cursing. Let's stop with three ideas and review our guidance plan. Set limit. Use substitution. Calmly restate the limit and substitution. We'll evaluate it in two days at the next staff meeting. I like how we made this decision."

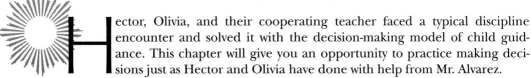

ector, Olivia, and their cooperating teacher faced a typical discipline encounter and solved it with the decision-making model of child guidance. This chapter will give you an opportunity to practice making decisions just as Hector and Olivia have done with help from Mr. Alvarez.

I have taught about the decision-making model since the fourth edition of this text was published. I decided to write the first part of this chapter in a question/answer format because my students have asked these questions several times and I thought that you might also like to think about them.

SOME QUESTIONS ABOUT THE DECISION-MAKING MODEL OF CHILD GUIDANCE

What Is the Decision-Making Model of Child Guidance?

It is a way of arriving at decisions about how to handle a variety of discipline encounters with children in a developmentally appropriate way. This chapter will help you use the positive strategies described throughout this book to make developmentally appropriate guidance plans with a logical, clear-headed approach. This approach will help you avoid getting caught up in emotion when faced with a discipline encounter. A guidance plan based on clear thinking and good decision making will help you effectively deal with a variety of discipline encounters—the typical ones as well as the more challenging ones.

Do You Think That Everybody Can Use This Model?

Developmentally appropriate child guidance and good decision making about discipline encounters does not come automatically. It is something that a person has to learn and practice. There are, essentially, three things that will help a teacher use this model successfully:

- An attitude that accepts the basic tenets of authoritative caregiving (Chapter 2)
- A specific knowledge base
- Specific child-guidance skills

Attitude

Professionals who have a deep-rooted respect for children and families are most likely to use a DAP approach to child guidance and most likely to be able to use the decision-making model well. A person who does not respect children and families will have a great deal of difficulty with child guidance.

A professional with a helpful attitude has a realistic perspective on the balance of responsibility in any interaction between them and a child of any age. He understands that he, the adult, has a much greater responsibility to recognize signals that children of different ages send.

Example: Mr. Alvarez understands that Gary's cursing is an example of imitation but is also an attempt to be recognized. Irritating? Yes. But the teacher understands that it is up to him to recognize Gary's attention-seeking. He also knows that only he, the adult, can control how he responds to this discipline encounter. He knows that Gary has a big part in this interaction but that the adult has the greatest share of responsibility for deciding how to handle things.

Knowledge base

A person who uses the decision-making model most effectively understands the DAP concept and understands the core concepts in child development, family studies, and child guidance. That is the knowledge base. Understanding what children are like at different ages and then understanding the impact of that child's family on her development and behavior, for example, will help you clarify your expectations of certain children.

Examples: Is it reasonable to expect a 6-month-old infant to stop crying just because someone tells him to stop?

How empathic can you expect an abused toddler to be?

How difficult is it for 3-year-old children to wait in line for the next activity?

How likely is it that a 4-year-old whose dad curses will say the same words?

Are kindergarten children able to understand emotions well enough to responsibly manage them on their own?

Will an aggressive preschool child outgrow his aggression by the time he is 6 or 7 years old?

How likely is it that an 8-year-old whose parents are permissive will willingly follow classroom rules and limits?

When a person can answer these developmental questions, then she has one of the key elements in using the decision-making model.

Skills

A professional who uses the decision-making model effectively also possesses specific child-guidance skills. He can use any one of a variety of DAP child-guidance strategies, the same ones you have learned in Chapters 3 and 10; they are also in the appendix. He has the skills to do good management of the layout of the classroom, the curriculum, activities, and materials. He understands current special topics in child guidance, for example anger or stress, and has the skills to help children deal with these issues.

It Seems as if an Adult Is "Active" and Has to "Be on His Toes" in Such a Model. Is That True?

Decision making requires a great deal of active involvement. Mr. Alvarez, for example, made an active, conscious, self-responsible decision about how best to help Gary. He did not just use the first strategy that popped into his head. He had to work at finding a solution. He deliberately walked the student teachers through the step-by-step process of choosing a strategy.

He has encouraged them to recognize their responsibility for choosing the adult behavior most likely to help Gary at this time, that is, to choose individually appropriate strategies. Choosing our adult behavior also means consciously rejecting certain strategies that do not fit our personal philosophy of guidance, as Mr. Alvarez rejected time-out.

What Does "Eclectic" Mean?

Wise early childhood professionals avoid the "one-strategy-fits-all" model. Instead, they adopt an *eclectic* approach, which means to select the most appropriate strategy for a specific child at a specific time. Mr. Alvarez, Hector, and Olivia, for example, selected strategies from all the strategies they knew, the mark of the eclectic approach to decision making.

An eclectic approach to decision making does not mean that you "go with the flow" or do "whatever works." On the contrary, an eclectic approach means that you understand different theoretical approaches, not just one. You know how to use a number of different strategies (Mr. Alvarez knows quite well how to use time-out) because you realize that each approach does offer appropriate strategies. A professional who relies on an eclectic approach also realizes that no single approach is appropriate for all children. Another thing that you do when you use the eclectic approach is justify your choices, not defensively, but in a logical fashion.

Like a skillful, well-equipped carpenter, a well-equipped teacher searches for and chooses the most appropriate tools available to the profession. A large pool of positive strategies will give you a great deal of flexibility in making good decisions about developmentally appropriate guidance.

I Don't Quite Understand Why I Have to Understand Child and Family Development to Deal with Discipline Encounters. Is It Really All That Necessary?

Yes. This is a textbook about working with real children in the real and complex world in which they live. There are some typical discipline encounters, like cursing, that are relatively easy to deal with. We all face such encounters, regardless of where we teach. But other children present us with discipline encounters that are tougher to deal with and challenge us as we guide the children affected (e.g., abused or neglected young children; children whose families move frequently; children whose family lives in poverty—real poverty; children from drug-infested areas; children whose neighborhoods ring with the noise of gunfire; children from permissive homes; and children whose parents model anger, aggression, and lack of empathy).

When you have your own classroom, you will be energized (exhausted on occasion!) by the often confusing, sometimes exasperating, wildly wonderful differences that make each of your children truly a unique person. You will meet a new group of individuals every year that you teach—children, yes, but individuals first.

Each infant to 8-year-old individual has a basic style or temperament and a rich personal history of interactions that have taught her how to be in this large world. All the children come from different families, each with its own scripts and rules, its own communication style, its own cultural history, its own view of how children should behave, and its own style of discipline. Some of these children will have parents who feel secure, who understand children and children's needs, who know how to communicate legitimate rules and limits, who know how to help children live within limits, and who know how to demonstrate their love and respect to that child.

Some of your children will have parents whose own needs for nurturance were never met and who cannot, as adults, meet their child's needs for nurturance and security. These parents do not understand how infants and children develop, are angry, and do not know how or refuse to take their child's perspective. They lack empathy for their children. These parents have very poor and ineffective child-guidance skills; for example, they do not know how to set limits effectively or how to help children accept limits. These parents do not know how to demonstrate the love that they feel for their child.

It is precisely because the children you teach are individuals that you should consider adopting an approach to guiding children that is as flexible as possible. The decision-making model is an individualized, personal model that allows you to determine the course of action most beneficial for a specific child in specific circumstances. The decision-making model allows you to combine your knowledge and personal strengths to deal more effectively with issues facing individual children.

USING THE DECISION-MAKING MODEL

The rest of this chapter will give you specific information on how to use the decision-making model and will give you some practice in using it.

Steps in the Decision-Making Model

There are specific steps that you take when you use the decision-making model. The steps include:

- Identifying the problem and problem ownership
- Paying attention to the "context" of the problem
- Choosing a positive child-guidance strategy
- Using and evaluating the strategy

These steps are relatively easy to learn and use. Please see Figure 11–1.

Use the steps in the decision-making model to analyze the chapter opener case study.

Case Study Analysis: The Decision-Making Model In Action

Use the list of steps in the decision-making model to evaluate the Alvarez team's use of the decision-making model of child guidance (chapter opening case study).
1. Determine whether and how well the teacher and student teachers carried out each step.
2. Name one or two things that you might have done differently.
3. How likely is it, from your perspective, that the teachers will be "successful" in dealing with this typical discipline encounter?

**Four Easy Steps in the Decision-Making
Model of Child Guidance**

1. Focus on the encounter as a problem to be solved.

Clearly identify the problem. Decide whether the child or the adult "owns the problem." Focus on solving a problem, not on blaming a child.

2. Examine the "context" of the problem.

Ask yourself how the child's age might be affecting her behavior. Ask how the child's family or the classroom physical environment, activities, or materials have contributed to the problem, not to place blame but simply to get a better picture of the context or setting in which the behavior has evolved.

3. Choose a guidance strategy.

Use *only* developmentally appropriate strategies, not punishment. Consult your list of guidance strategies given in in Chapter 3 and the appendix. Say why the chosen strategy is appropriate for this child at this time.

4. Use and evaluate the effectiveness of the strategy.

Figure 11–1.   Four easy steps in the decisions making model of child guidance.

The purpose of the rest of this chapter is to help you practice using the decision-making model of child guidance.

Practicing the Decision-Making Model

Decision-making issue No. 1: "Keep the sand in the pan, please!"

The discipline encounter. You are the head teacher in a preschool classroom for 4-year-olds. The children are interested in "writing" and you provide lots of materials for them to use for writing. Today, for example, you have placed two shallow pans of sand on the table in the writing center. Almost all the children used the sand trays to print their names or to print other letters. But you are getting frustrated with having to constantly remind the children to "keep the sand in the tray."

Using the steps in the decision-making model (Figure 11–1).

1. What is the problem?_____
    Whose problem is it—the children's or yours? _____

2. Examine the "context" of the problem. You see sand spilling out of the tray. How might a 4-year-old's motor development affect how he uses and moves sand around in a large cookie-sheet-sized tray? How has your setup of this activity affected the amount of sand flipped out of the trays (trays with very low sides are on the table, table is on the carpet)?

3. Choose a guidance strategy. You have simply been restating the limit of keeping sand in the tray, but that does not seem to be enough. Focus on changing something about the situation to really change things. What do

you think would be the effect of moving the table aside for a moment, placing a large sheet under the table, replacing the table, and then gently flicking any sand that spills under the table, later to be picked up in the sheet? Or what do you think would be the effect of using even larger pans, or pans with higher sides, or even using the sand table? What limits would you still need?

Which strategy would you feel most comfortable using?

a) From my perspective, the most effective strategy would be . . .
b) This strategy is age appropriate because . . .
c) I deliberately chose not to use _____ (name the rejected strategy) because . . .

Decision-making issue No. 2: "Outdoor cleanup time"

The discipline encounter. It's time for your classroom of kindergartners to go inside for story, and you notice that Levi and Dave have left the trucks out on the path again, instead of putting them in the spot designated for trucks. You and the staff have stated the limits clearly and positively, and the designated parking spots are easily accessible—you have managed the physical environment very well. Levi's parents are permissive-by-choice and do not set limits. Dave follows Levi's lead.

Using the steps in the decision-making model.

1. What is the problem? _____
   Whose problem is it—Levi's and Dave's or yours? _____
2. Examine the "context" of the problem. What is it about Levi's background that is probably contributing heavily to this encounter? How about Dave's personality and how it is contributing to the encounter?
3. Choose a guidance strategy. There are a lot of ways to deal with this encounter effectively. Here are some ideas to get you started.

   a) *You have set the limit. Explain why restating the limit is individually appropriate,* especially for Levi, who has never had to follow limits, and for Dave, who follows Levi's lead. Write the exact words you would use to restate the limit.
   b) *Explain how you could use the Adlerian strategy of logical consequences* to help the boys make better decisions about cleaning up. State the specific words you would use to present the choices to them and then to acknowledge and accept their choices. Avoid turning this experience into punishment by reviewing how to do logical consequences in Chapter 3 and in the appendix.
   c) *Explain how you could also use an I-message* (Rogerian approach) to help Levi and Dave understand your position. Write the I-message, including all three elements (again, see the appendix).
   d) *Explain how you could use the social learning approach's strategy called effective praise* to encourage the boys when they do cooperate. Write out the exact statements that you would use.

e) *Explain how you could use the social learning approach's strategy called a token system to help you follow through with the limit.* Review information on token systems in Chapter 10 and the appendix. Keep it simple, but be specific and draw the chart that you would use. Write the script that you might follow when you first tell the boys about the system. Be prepared to role-play the explanation.

f) *Explain why punishment (time-out, response cost) is not an appropriate choice* in this case. Explain why ignoring this problem is also not appropriate in this case.

Which strategy would you feel most comfortable using?

a) From my perspective, the most effective strategy would be . . .

b) This strategy is age appropriate because . . .

c) I deliberately chose not to use _____ (name the rejected strategy) because . . .

Decision-making issue No. 3: "Smashing pumpkins"

The discipline encounter. You are a second-grade teacher. Some of your children, including Quincy and Eddy, are working on a project about pumpkins, the interest having arisen after they read a newspaper story about a farmer's having grown a very large pumpkin. Both Quincy and Eddy are famous for their temper outbursts, and you keep a close watch on them. They were working together writing a "news-paper story" about their decorated pumpkins when you heard them start to yell at each other. You were on your way to their work station when Eddy picked up Quincy's pumpkin and slammed it to the floor, smashing it into small pieces. Quincy responded by grabbing Eddy's pumpkin.

You said firmly, "Put the pumpkin down, Quincy. Do it now."

Quincy glared at you and, saying nothing, threw the pumpkin at the wall, smashing the fruit into a slimy mess.

Using the steps in the decision-making model. This is an anger management issue. You might find it helpful to refer to Chapter 7 when making a decision about this encounter.

1. What is the problem?_____
   Whose problem is it: Quincy's, Eddy's, Quincy's and Eddy's, or yours?_____

2. Examine the "context" of the problem. These are 7-year-old children whose families use fairly harsh discipline and whose lives are chaotic. Quincy is a neglected child and the city human services department is working with his parents. You have been working on anger management with both boys but they occasionally forget your lessons, like today.

3. Choose a guidance strategy. Continue to focus on helping these boys manage anger. Avoid punishment and help them save face.

   a) You will probably be angry immediately after this encounter. How will you get your emotions in check before dealing directly with Quincy and Eddy?

b) This a "hot" time, with anger flaring. This is not the time to preach or admonish; it is the time to talk with the boys. Will you separate them before you talk to them? Why or why not?

c) What will you say and how will you act with each boy? What will you do if one of them tries to deflect the topic by accusing the other boy? How will you get him to focus only on his own behavior and reaction to the situation?

d) How do you think you might follow up on this incident, say, the next day when they have both cooled down a bit? This might be a good time to do another anger management activity. Describe at least two things that you could do.

e) Why is it an inappropriate strategy to force the boys to apologize to each other? Why is it highly inappropriate to use punishment, for example, time-out? Why is it also inappropriate to ignore this incident?

Which strategy would you feel most comfortable using?

a) From my perspective, the most effective strategy would be . . .

b) This strategy is age appropriate because . . .

c) I deliberately chose not to use _____ (name the rejected strategy) because . . .

What the Decision-Making Model Means for Children

Adults who adopt the authoritative style of caregiving (Chapter 2) realize that a big part of their job is to create a safe and secure emotional climate for children. They realize that they influence but do not determine a child's behavior. When you actively make decisions about discipline encounter plans, you set the stage for lots of good things to happen.

Investing time and effort in developmentally appropriate child guidance and the decision-making model of child guidance is an investment that will yield a very good return. Using the decision-making model helps children:

- Feel safe and secure
- Develop healthy self-esteem and a strong moral compass
- Honor and respect themselves and others
- Develop healthy self-control
- Learn how to deal with a variety of stresses
- Understand and deal effectively with a variety of feelings: anger, sadness, love, jealousy
- Walk a mile in another person's shoes—or an animal's tracks—to be empathic
- Be cooperative, helpful, and generous
- Learn when to be assertive
- Become self-responsible
- Become a competent partner in the dance of interaction

(a)
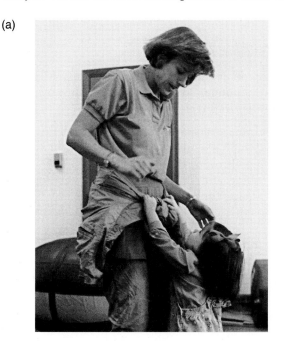
(b)

(a) Toddlers, decision making and discipline encounters (b) Primary age, decision making and discipline encounters

REFLECTING ON KEY CONCEPTS

1. Suppose that you decide to do a parent meeting and your main goal is to explain your school's commitment to developmentally appropriate child guidance. You use the term *decision-making model of child guidance* and one father stops you. He asks, "What exactly is that all about?" What will you say to him?

2. Another parent says, "But, everybody makes decisions. What's so special about this school's decision making and discipline or guidance?" How will you explain that the teachers have actually had to study and learn a couple of important things before they had "what it takes" to make developmentally appropriate decisions about discipline encounters? Tell this parent about the most important things that form the foundation of the decision-making model.

3. You use the work "eclectic" to describe your approach to choosing a guidance strategy in any discipline encounter, and Dad #1 stops you again. "Eclectic? What in the world do you mean?" What would you say to him?

APPLY YOUR KNOWLEDGE

Self-Test: Making Your Own Guidance Plan

Use Figure 11–1 to arrive at a developmentally appropriate child-guidance strategy for each of the following discipline encounters. Go through the first three steps just as you have for the discipline encounters in this chapter.

- An abused toddler who bites other children.
- Five-year-olds in a multiage grouping getting younger children to do inappropriate things (e.g., swearing, throwing things).
- Third-graders, lined up, pushing and shoving while they wait for their school bus. They have been waiting for 20 minutes.
- Three- to 5-year-olds pushing other children while changing activities (e.g., going outdoors).
- A 4-year-old who spits at other people.
- A 4-year-old, whose family consistently uses physical discipline (hitting, pinching), who hits the teacher when the teacher tries to use even a positive strategy like restating a limit.
- A 7-year-old who tattles.
- Third-graders, 8 years old, who deface library books.

Reference

National Association for the Education of Young Children (1998). Poster #447: *Guidance is Good!* Washington, DC: NAEYC.

Appendix

Review: Major Positive Discipline Strategies

This appendix reviews the major positive discipline strategies described in this text. First, you will read a list of the major strategies. Then each strategy is presented in outline form, along with suggestions of things to remember and to avoid when using the strategy.

Every strategy outlined here is described in more detail in other chapters, mainly Chapters 3 and 10. There is a notation in parentheses next to the name of a strategy that will tell you which chapter presents a detailed discussion of the strategy.

List of major strategies:

1. Help children preserve their dignity and save face.
2. Set limits well.
3. Change something about a situation.
4. Identify problem ownership.
5. Teach more appropriate behavior.
6. Give signals or cues for appropriate behavior.
7. Support children in using more appropriate behavior by:
    * teaching new behavior that is self-rewarding.
    * identifying mistaken goals and using encouragement.
    * using effective praise.
    * using tokens.
8. Ignore behavior when it is appropriate to do so.
9. Redirect very young children's behavior: Diversion and distraction.
10. Redirect older children's behavior: Substitution.
11. Use active listening.
12. Use I-messages.
13. Use logical consequences.
14. Resolve conflict through problem solving.
15. Manage strong emotions responsibly.
16. Withdraw from certain situations (not time-out).

1. HELP CHILDREN PRESERVE THEIR DIGNITY AND SAVE FACE (CHAPTER 3)

Purpose of the strategy: To treat children respectfully no matter what positive strategy is used. Children are likely to feel embarrassed in spite of well-done positive discipline.

How can adults do this?

1. Rely on your abiding respect for children and your perspective-taking skills, and think about how you would want somebody to handle things if they had just told you to calm down or that you had done something wrong.
2. Once you are finished with the positive discipline strategy, let the episode become history and allow the child to get on with things. Do not keep preaching or explaining.

3. Do not pull out your power. Avoid saying, "I told you so."
4. End the interaction quickly, simply, and gracefully. Quietly tell the child, especially if you've helped her calm down, "Let's go back and play now."
5. Help children deal with the root of the upset. Some children might be ready to talk about the emotion-arousing incident, but others need to wait before discussing it. Either way, schedule a time for talking about the original problem with the child. Do what is developmentally appropriate for this child at this time.

2. SET LIMITS WELL (CHAPTER 3)

Purpose of the strategy: State expectations for desired behavior. Clarify boundaries or limits on behavior.

Appropriate limits: Never arbitrary, limits focus on important things and are developmentally appropriate.

Effective limit setting:

1. Focus the child's attention, use appropriate nonverbal cues.
2. Speak naturally and slowly enough so that the child hears limit, use concrete words and short sentences, tell the child what to do, use suggestions, give choices when possible.
3. Give very few suggestions at a time.
4. Allow the child enough time to process information and complete the task.
5. Effectively repeat limit if necessary.
6. Give short, simple reasons for limit (before stating limit, after stating limit, or after the child complies).

Things to avoid in setting limits:

1. Avoid abstract words or phrases.
2. Avoid emphasizing what not to do.
3. Avoid ordering or commanding.
4. Do not give choices when the child should not have choice.
5. Avoid giving chain of limits.
6. Avoid rapid repetition of limits.
7. Avoid playing the "Why" game with the children.

3. CHANGE SOMETHING ABOUT A SITUATION (CHAPTER 3)

Purpose of the strategy: Indirectly guide a child by determining what the adult can do about a situation that will help a child be safe or to help the child behave more appropriately.

Ways to change something about a situation:

- Increase options available to a child: introduce new ideas, introduce new materials, forestall predictable problems.
- Decrease options available to a child: Limit choices, change activities.

4. IDENTIFY PROBLEM OWNERSHIP (CHAPTER 10)

Purpose of the strategy: Determine whether a problem is owned by an adult or by a child so that appropriate follow-up can be used.

- When an adult owns a problem: Use strategies focusing on self-responsible, nonaccusatory skills (e.g., I-messages).
- When a child owns a problem: The child's needs are the ones thwarted. Use active listening when a child owns the problem.

5. TEACH MORE APPROPRIATE BEHAVIOR (CHAPTER 3 FOR MAJOR DESCRIPTION, CHAPTER 10 FOR FOLLOW-UP)

Purpose of the strategy: Teach appropriate behaviors and deemphasize inappropriate behaviors. Means that adults must pinpoint behavior considered appropriate.

Method used: Several methods can be used. With young children modeling is effective (i.e., demonstrate desired behavior, such as hand-washing, table manners, social skills such as introducing oneself, using words instead of hitting to express anger).

Steps in teaching more appropriate behavior:

1. Identify inappropriate behavior (e.g., whining).
2. Name a more appropriate behavior (e.g., asking for things in a normal voice).
3. Model more appropriate behavior (e.g., model a normal voice for the child).

6. GIVE SIGNALS OR CUES FOR APPROPRIATE BEHAVIOR (CHAPTER 3)

Purpose of the strategy: To help children remember to use the appropriate behavior.
Steps in giving signals or cues:

1. Identify behavior for which you will use a signal or cue (e.g., asking for something in a normal voice).
2. Figure out what would be a logical signal for new behavior (e.g., quiet verbal reminder, "normal voice, please," hand signal).
3. Observe the child for when appropriate behavior should be used (e.g., asking to join other children).
4. Give signal just before new behavior should occur and not after a child has forgotten (e.g., just before the child asks for something).

7. SUPPORT CHILDREN IN USING MORE APPROPRIATE BEHAVIOR:

a. Teaching New Behavior That Is Self-Rewarding (Chapter 3)

Purpose of the strategy: To avoid using external reinforcement.
Steps in teaching self-rewarding behavior:

1. Identify inappropriate behavior (e.g., not washing hands after toileting).
2. Identify more appropriate behavior (e.g., hand-washing after toileting).

3. If possible, think about setting up the situation so that it is attractive enough for child to continue without further reinforcement (e.g., using a soap that smells wonderful or that turns colors when used for scrubbing hands).

b. Identifying Mistaken Goals and Using Encouragement (Chapter 10)

Purpose of the strategy: Identify a child's faulty perception of how to fit into a group. Be aware of what a child does to accomplish mistaken goal (seek undue attention, power, revenge, or demonstrate inadequacy). Explain how an adult usually feels and reacts. Outline a better way to deal with a child who has any of the four mistaken goals.

Steps in changing how you react to demands for undue attention:

1. Ignore the impulse to give in to the attention-seeking behavior.
2. Acknowledge the child's request, but let her know that she can complete the task. Leave the area if necessary so that she can finish the job.
3. Give the child attention at times when her behavior is more appropriate.
4. Encourage a child to take the perspective of others by telling her their perspective and by helping her learn to cooperate.

Steps in changing how you react to a child who seeks power:

1. Resist the impulse to fight back.
2. Decide to respond differently. You do not have to be drawn into a power struggle. You can choose to respond differently.
3. Decline the child's invitation to argue or fight. This will surprise a child, particularly if you have previously been locked in power struggles with her. A useful technique is to label the interaction as a power struggle.

Steps in changing how you react to a child who seeks revenge:

1. Resist impulse to retaliate or give sermons.
2. Focus on helping this child change her view of herself from a person who she thinks is not valued to the view that she is a good, worthwhile person (i.e., encourage development of self-esteem, the missing ingredient).

Steps in changing how you react to a child who demonstrates inadequacy:

1. Focus on what a normal child of this age should be able to do (e.g., should a 3-year-old be able to put on her own coat?).
2. Refrain from performing the age-appropriate task for her.
3. Encourage a child who mistakenly believes she has to act as if she is incompetent (e.g., tell her that she can carry out the task, demonstrate how she can do it, encourage her to try).

c. Using Effective Praise (Chapter 10)

Purpose of the strategy: A form of positive reinforcement. Gives information on the consequences of a behavior for the person who modeled or performed it.

Elements of effective praise:

1. Notice and describe specifically what it was a child did. Relate verbal praise directly to behavior. Convey your appreciation, but avoid making judgments about the child's character.
2. Give praise as soon as possible after a child performs a behavior.
3. Be sincere and honest. Try to find something in a situation that you can praise sincerely.
4. Encourage a child for her effort and small steps.
5. Combine praise with appropriate forms of nonverbal communication (e.g., nod of head, smile, pat on back).

Avoid these things when using praise:

1. Do not combine praise with a negative comment.
2. Do not praise only perfection.
3. Do not focus on what the child is not doing.
4. Avoid praising only completion of a multistep task.
5. Do not overdo praise or use it indiscriminately.
6. Do not give praise if it is not necessary.
7. Do not confuse praise or other rewards with bribes.

d. Using Tokens (Chapter 10)

Purpose of the strategy: To modify a child's environment by giving feedback for effort so that a child may more easily modify her behavior. A social learning concept.

Things to remember about using tokens effectively:

1. Give a token often.
2. Give tokens for small steps toward a bigger goal.
3. Combine tokens with social reinforcers (smile, praise).
4. Keep a record of tokens. Chart should define desired behavior, specify number of tokens to be earned to get reward, define how tokens are to be spent.
5. Ask the child what she considers to be a reward; reward should be desirable to the child; best if chosen by the child, within certain limits.
6. Let the child exchange tokens for a reward fairly often.
7. Do not take away tokens as fines for "backsliding."
8. Gradually fade out use of tokens as the child shows willingness to use appropriate behavior, but continue to give periodic social reinforcers.

8. IGNORE BEHAVIOR WHEN IT IS APPROPRIATE TO DO SO (CHAPTER 3; ALSO CALLED EXTINCTION [CHAPTER 10])

Purpose of the strategy: Eliminate payoff for inappropriate behavior (i.e., stop attending to and reinforcing inappropriate behavior). Goal is to weaken inappropriate behavior by changing the way an adult reacts to the behavior.

Do not ignore certain behaviors:

1. Do not ignore behavior that endangers anyone, including the child herself.
2. Do not ignore behavior that damages or destroys property or that could potentially damage or destroy property.
3. Do not ignore rude, embarrassing, intrusive, or unduly disruptive behavior.

Guidelines for ignoring behavior:

1. Pinpoint behavior to be ignored.
2. Tell the child you will no longer pay attention when she acts in this way.
3. Be prepared. It takes time to effectively use the ignore strategy (e.g., be prepared for a bigger and better whine before it decreases).
4. Decide to thoroughly ignore the behavior—don't mutter to yourself under your breath; don't make eye contact; don't communicate with the child verbally or with gestures.
5. Teach and encourage more acceptable behavior along with the ignore strategy.

9. REDIRECT VERY YOUNG CHILDREN'S BEHAVIOR: DIVERSION AND DISTRACTION (CHAPTER 3)

Purpose of the strategy: To distract a very young child from a forbidden or dangerous activity and then involve the child in a different activity.

Things to keep in mind:

1. Understand that responsible caregivers perform most of an infant's or a young toddler's ego functions.
2. Avoid a power struggle when stopping dangerous behavior.
3. Be prepared to act quickly when working with infants and toddlers. This requires constant supervision and observation even in a babyproofed area.

Steps in using diversion and distraction:

1. Identify for yourself the things that you do not want a baby or toddler to do because the activity is dangerous (e.g., playing with an electrical outlet, even if it is covered).
2. Tell infant or toddler not to do whatever it is that is dangerous (e.g., "No playing with the outlet, Sara").
3. Immediately do something different to distract infant or toddler from forbidden activity (e.g., roll ball to Sara the instant you tell her not to play with the outlet).

10. REDIRECT OLDER CHILDREN'S BEHAVIOR: MAKING SUBSTITUTIONS (CHAPTER 3)

Purpose of the strategy: Form of redirection in which an adult shows a somewhat older child (over age 2^1/2 years) how to perform the same activity or type of activity but in a more acceptable, safer way.

Steps in using substitutions:

1. Specify activity needing a substitution (e.g., outdoors, zigzagging through sandbox when others are playing there).
2. Develop substitution, a similar activity, or same activity done more safely (e.g., zigzagging through set of tires laid flat on ground).
3. Present substitution to child (e.g., "Looks like you want to do an obstacle course, but not in the sandbox. Try zigging and zagging through these tires").
4. Be prepared for a testing of your substitution. Resist getting drawn into a fight or power struggle. Respond to testing with positive discipline: continue to make the substitution calmly and with goodwill (e.g., if two children run back through the sandbox, say "Tom and Jim, the obstacle course is the set of tires, not the sandbox").

11. USE ACTIVE LISTENING (CHAPTER 10 FOR MAIN DESCRIPTION; CHAPTER 3 FOR BRIEF DESCRIPTION)

Purpose of the strategy: Careful, accurate listening to feelings of a child. Conveys an adult's recognition and acceptance of a child and the child's feelings. Communicates an adult's trust in the child's ability to work through her own problem.

Things to remember about active listening:

1. Listen carefully.
2. Do not interrupt.
3. Try to understand what the message means.
4. Listen for what the child is feeling.
5. Suspend judgment.
6. Avoid preaching, giving advice, or trying to persuade the child to feel differently.
7. Merely feed back your perception of the child's feelings.

12. USE I-MESSAGES (CHAPTER 3)

Purpose of the strategy: Give information; communicate feelings in respectful way; give the child chance to change behavior (a Rogerian concept).

Steps in constructing a good I-message:

1. Name exact behavior causing the problem. Give observable data about the child's behavior—what you see, hear, touch, smell, taste (e.g., "Adam, I see that the puzzles you used are still on the table").
2. Tell the child how his behavior tangibly affects you. Did it cost you time, money, effort to do the job he should have done ("and that meant that I had to put the puzzles away just before snack")?
3. Tell the child how you felt (remember, do not accuse the child of causing your feeling) ("I felt annoyed that I had to do two jobs").

Things to avoid in constructing I-messages:

1. Avoid accusing and blaming the child.
2. Do not induce guilt.
3. Avoid telling the child that he caused your feeling.

13. USE LOGICAL CONSEQUENCES (CHAPTER 3)

Purpose of the strategy: Safe consequences that would not have occurred naturally. Consequences are designed by adult.

Things to remember about logical consequences:

1. The child must understand the exact nature of the issue and how you feel.
2. Consequence should be logically related to the unsafe or inappropriate behavior.
3. Make consequence one that you can really accept and that the child will likely view as fair.
4. Time the consequence well.
5. Use a friendly, firm, nonthreatening tone of voice.

Steps in using logical consequences:

1. Respectfully restate expectations and tell the child how to change things. Give the child a choice; offer alternatives (e.g., "We are here for story. You can sit next to Sue and listen to the story without pushing her, or you can sit with Mrs. Doren and listen to the story. You choose.").
2. Allow the child to make choice. You have designed safe, respectful choices, so you can accept any choice.
3. Tell the child you accept her choice. Allow safe consequences to occur (e.g., if Janie continues to push Sue, "I see that you have chosen to sit next to Mrs. Doren for storytime"; if Janie stops pushing, "You chose to sit quietly next to Sue for storytime. I think she likes to have you next to her.").

14. RESOLVE CONFLICT THROUGH PROBLEM-SOLVING (CHAPTER 10)

Purpose of the strategy: Achieve a mutually agreeable solution to a problem without resorting to use of power. Support creative conflict resolution rather than punishing behavior accompanying conflict between children (e.g., teach children who are arguing how to resolve the conflict rather than punish them for fighting).

Steps in using the "no-lose" method of conflict resolution:

1. Identify and define conflict in nonaccusatory way (e.g., "Vinnie and Rachael, you have a problem. You both want the green paint").
2. Invite the children to participate in fixing the problem ("Let's think of how to solve the problem").
3. Generate possible solutions with the children. Accept a variety of solutions. Avoid evaluating them ("Yes, you could *both* use the same paint cup . . . you could take turns").
4. Examine each idea for merits and drawbacks. With the children, decide which to try. Thank the children for thinking of solutions ("You both want to use the green paint at the same time").
5. Put the plan into action ("You might have to take turns dipping your brushes into the paint . . . Try your idea").

6. Follow up. Evaluate how well the solution worked (teacher comes back in a few minutes, "Looks like your idea of how to solve your green paint problem really worked").

15. MANAGE STRONG EMOTIONS RESPONSIBLY (CHAPTER 7 FOR SPECIFIC STRATEGIES, CHAPTER 3 FOR BRIEF DESCRIPTION)

Purpose of the strategy: To support children in recognizing and learning responsible ways to manage strong emotions, such as anger. To avoid simply punishing children for behavior resulting from strong emotions.

Steps in teaching responsible anger management:

1. Model responsible anger management.
2. Create a safe emotional climate. Allow and encourage the children to acknowledge all their feelings while firmly not permitting them to hurt anybody because of those feelings.
3. Help the children understand the things to which they react with anger.
4. Help the children understand their body's reaction to anger.
5. Teach the children how to deal with the stress of anger.
6. State your expectations for responsible anger management.
7. Help some children learn to use words to describe angry feelings, and help other children expand their feelings vocabulary.
8. Use appropriate books and stories about anger management.

16. WITHDRAW FROM CERTAIN SITUATIONS (NOT TIME-OUT) (CHAPTER 3)

Goal: Solve a basic problem, not to punish.

Purpose of the strategy: To teach children how to take themselves out of situations when they lose control, are extremely angry, or endanger their own or someone else's safety; to teach children to avoid simply reacting to strong emotions; to get themselves under control so that they can deal with the cause of the strong emotion.

Steps in withdrawing from certain situations:

1. Identify and teach the child to recognize the behavior that is causing a problem.
2. Tell the child when you will request that she withdraw.
3. Demonstrate, explain, and make sure a child understands the process. Have the child help you pick a safe, calming, nonfrightening place for retreat when her anger heats up. This is not punishment or time-out.
4. Follow through. Help the child recognize target behavior.
5. Be respectful and unobtrusive as you help the child withdraw.
6. If appropriate, show the child how to do relaxation exercises to regain control.
7. Teach and encourage more appropriate behavior when the child returns to activity, or talk about the original problem that elicited such strong emotion.

Author Index

Subject Index